CORIOLIS GROUP BOOK

Practical Data Structures in C++

Bryan Flamig

John Wiley & Sons, Inc.

New York • Chichester • Brisbane • Toronto • Singapore

Library of Congress Cataloging-in-Publication Data

Flamig, Brayan.
 Practical data structures in C++ : with disk / Bryan Flamig.
  p. cm.
 "Coriolis Group book."
 Includes index.
 ISBN 0-471-55863-X (paper)
  1. C++ (Computer program language) 2. Computer algorithms.
 3. Data structures (Computer Science) I. Title.
 QA76.73.C153F52 1993
 005.7'3--dc20   91-47114
                  CIP

Printed in the United States of America

10 9 8 7 6 5 4 3 2

Contents

Preface

This book is about designing practical data structures. The practical orientation of this book is due, in no small part, to the fact that I was first trained as a mechanical engineer, and so my tendency is to design things from an engineering point of view, always balancing the ideals of theory with the reality of practice. The engineer in me has always been eager to understand the trade-offs involved in using one approach over another.

This book is the first part of a planned two-volume set. A subsequent volume, *Practical Algorithms in C++*, will pick up where this book leaves off, using the data structures designed in this book as tools to be used in many different algorithms. This second volume will be written from the same practical perspective.

In writing these two books, I hope to impart to you some of the interest and knowledge I have gained over the years on the subjects of data structures and algorithms, and to show you how elegantly and efficiently these constructs can be implemented in C++.

How This Book Is Different

A quick trip down to your local bookstore will show you that surprisingly few books cover the topic of data structures, let alone show you how to code them in C++. This is surprising because data structures are such a fundamental part of the programming process. In the books that do exist on data structures, the subject matter is covered more from a theoretical viewpoint, with sparse and incomplete coding examples. Many of these books leave a lot of the more interesting and complicated techniques as exercises for the reader.

This book, in contrast, was designed to cover data structures from a practical point of view, with as many complete examples as possible. *There are no exercises left for the reader.* You won't have to spend days trying to figure out how to accomplish something described in the book. If you're like me, you want to put the techniques to use immediately, to see if they are promising for your own applications. Only then do you want to dissect the code to see what makes it tick.

The data structures shown in this book are the most efficient, elegant, and robust designs that I know of. I didn't just code up the data structures using the first approach that came to mind. Instead, many different designs were implemented and studied to find those that seemed to work the best.

The data structures were crafted specifically for C++. This isn't just a rewrite of a C book with a few programs changed to use classes. With each data structure, I spent much time (literally months) trying to determine how C++ could best be put to use.

Since it's not feasible to show *all* of the code in the manuscript itself (due to space limitations), only the salient features of each technique are given. The disk included with this book has everything typed in, ready to run. Many of the programs on disk are designed to thoroughly test the data structures presented in this book.

WHO SHOULD READ THIS BOOK

This book is written primarily for intermediate-level C++ programmers. However, the book has been designed to be useful to both those programmers with little C++ experience as well as those at an advanced level. This is accomplished by approaching each subject at a basic level, providing simple techniques, and then progressing to more exotic and advanced techniques. Thus, if you are at the starting point of the C++ learning curve, you can work with the early parts of each chapter. As you become more proficient, you can tackle the more advanced sections. If you're a more experienced programmer, you can use the first parts of each chapter as refresher material, and then quickly move on to the advanced material.

I assume that you know the basics of C++. The focus is on learning how to code data structures, not on learning C++. One exception is the use of *templates*, a feature relatively new to C++ that allows you to define parameterized types. I devote the better part of a chapter to templates, since they are used quite heavily throughout the book. I use templates because they allow me to show data structures in a generic way, and they make it easy for you to "plug-in" the specific types of objects you wish to store in the data structures.

Why C++?

In my early years of programming, I was somewhat frustrated by the lack of a programming language that was both expressive and efficient enough for day-to-day use. The languages at hand were either high level but unfortunately too slow, or fast and regrettably too low level. Then came C++, the language I had been looking for. C++ is both expressive enough to code data structures in an elegant way, yet low level enough to allow efficient programs to be constructed.

Traditionally, most books covering data structures have used Pascal or some other Algol-like language. Pascal has been heavily favored, due to its reputation as a good language for teaching. The problem is that many professional programmers do not use Pascal, but rather C and C++. That's because standard Pascal lacks many features needed for writing real-world applications. Many dialects of Pascal have been invented to make up for these deficiencies, but these dialects are not standard, and you are tied to specific compiler vendors for their implementations.

C, on the other hand, is powerful enough to be used for a wide range of applications, without needing wildly divergent dialects. But because of C's relative terseness and low-level characteristics, many authors have rejected using C as a language for teaching data structures. However, C++ overcomes many of these difficulties, due to its superior type checking and encapsulation facilities. It does this without losing the efficiency of C. Thus, I feel C++ makes an excellent choice for showcasing the most practical data structures in current use.

How This Book Is Organized

This book includes fourteen chapters, progressing from the basics to more advanced material. The chapters are:

1. *Basic Concepts* looks at the design of data structures from a very general perspective, showing what all data structures have in common. Also, you learn the ways that you can judge the effectiveness and practicality of one data structure over another.

2. *Using C++ Effectively* provides a review of the features of C++ as they apply to the design of data structures. The emphasis is on creating safe, robust, and efficient classes.

3. *Data Structure Design in C++* discusses the four main approaches to data structures in C++. The difference between *concrete data types* and *abstract data types* is explained, along with a thorough discussion of *templates*, as well as the alternative approach of using *single-rooted hierarchies*.

4. *Basic Array Design* takes you step by step through the design of efficient, yet safe arrays. Covered are fixed-length, variable-length, resizable, stati-

cally allocated, and dynamically allocated arrays. Techniques for creating multidimensional arrays are also given.

5. *Heterogenous Arrays* discusses the issues involved in designing arrays to hold different types of data. Integral to this discussion is the use of "smart pointers" to reference-counted objects.

6. *Strings* combines the techniques explained in Chapters 4 and 5 in designing a safe and efficient string class.

7. *Vectors and Matrices* shows a relatively new way to design vector and matrix data structures using the notion of *vector strides* and shared representations of the underlying matrix data. You'll see objects invented by the author, called *vector pointers*, which allow unique and efficient implementations of *sub-matrices* and *matrix transpositions*.

8. *Linked Lists* takes you step by step through the design of linked lists as high-level objects in their own right. Contiguous (array-based) and non-contiguous (pointer-based) implementations are given for both singly-linked and doubly-linked lists. You'll see ways to improve the efficiency of allocating and de-allocating nodes used for linked lists.

9. *Stacks and Queues* takes a detailed look at the design of stacks and queues, two related data structures, with efficiency and flexibility in mind. Both array-based and list-based designs are given.

10. *Binary Trees* introduces another fundamental data structure, *trees*, often used in database searching applications. This chapter focuses on *binary trees* and, in particular, *binary search trees*. You'll learn how binary trees can be searched and how to efficiently traverse and print trees.

11. *Balanced Trees* is a continuation of Chapter 10 and describes how to balance search trees to improve their performance. Covered are *2-3-4 trees* and their binary analogues, *red-black trees*.

12. *Splay Trees* shows an intriguing type of self-organizing binary search tree. These trees have amortized costs that are equivalent to ordinary binary trees, yet splay trees can adapt to changing situations to provide very efficient searching. For instance, you'll see how splay trees can be used to implement *priority queues*.

13. *File-Based Objects* shows a unique and never before published technique of caching objects to disk. A new type of pointer, *cached-object pointers* (*Coptrs*), is implemented. With *Coptrs*, you can use cached objects almost like objects residing totally in memory. A file-based object heap allocator is also given, which works in conjunction with the caching.

14. *B-trees* is the culmination of the book and discusses perhaps the most widely used data structure for database applications, *B-trees*. An implementation is given for this important data structure that works from disk and uses the file-based caching techniques explained in Chapter 13.

WHAT YOU NEED

Every attempt was made to use generic C++ code in this book, with little that relies on any particular machine or compiler vendor. The code was written to be compliant with the AT&T C++ 3.0 specification. You'll need a compiler that's at least up to the AT&T C++ 2.1 specification and that also supports templates and the user-defined syntax of built-in types. If your compiler does not support templates, it's still possible to use the code in this book, though you'll have to make modifications to remove the template syntax. Chapter 3 discusses how to make such modifications.

The disk that's included with this book is formatted for MS-DOS, and project files are supplied so that you can easily compile the examples using Borland C++ 3.1, currently the only MS-DOS compiler that supports templates. (Many other compiler vendors will no doubt have templates implemented by the time you read this.) The code was extensively tested using Borland C++ 3.1, and was also tested (but not extensively) on Unix using the latest version of Cfront possible.

ACKNOWLEDGMENTS

I would like to thank Holly Mathews for her support and understanding in seeing me through the massive undertaking that was this book. Thanks go as well to my editor Paul Farrell at Wiley for the seemingly infinite amount of patience required to see this book come to fruition. I would also like to thank the production people at the Coriolis Group for doing a fine job on the layout. Special thanks go to technical reviewer Michael Mohle for providing a "sanity check" of the techniques presented, and for his efforts in ensuring that the code runs under Unix. Finally, my apologies to Dog Zilla, for all the walks he missed as I was writing this book.

CONTACTING THE AUTHOR

If you have questions about the contents of this book, you may contact me by mail at the address: Azarona Software, *Practical Data Structures in C++, P.O. Box 768, Conifer, CO 80433.* I can also be contacted on *CompuServe* [73057,3172], and on *Bix* [bflamig].

Bryan Flamig
Conifer, CO
February, 1993

Basic
Concepts

Techniques for storing and processing data are at the heart of all programs. The term *data structure* is used to describe the way data is stored, and the term *algorithm* is used to describe the way data is processed. As you might expect, data structures and algorithms are interrelated. Choosing a data structure affects the kind of algorithm you might use, and choosing an algorithm affects the data structures you use. In this chapter, we'll explore the basic, underlying concepts of data structures, and you'll learn how to judge the effectiveness and practicality of one data structure over another. For a similar discussion of algorithms, see the companion volume, *Practical Algorithms in C++* [Flamig 93].

DATA STRUCTURES: ORGANIZATIONS OF DATA

The collections of data you work with in a program have some kind of structure or organization. No matter how complex your data structures are, they can be broken down into two fundamental types: *contiguous* and *non-contiguous*.

In a *contiguous* structure, items of data are kept together in memory (either in RAM or in a file). An *array* is an example of a contiguous structure, since each element in the array is located next to one or two other elements. In contrast, items in a non-contiguous structure are scattered in memory, but are linked to each other in some way. A *linked list* is an example of a non-contiguous data structure. Here, the nodes of the list are linked together using pointers stored in each node. Figure 1.1 illustrates the difference between contiguous and non-contiguous structures.

Figure 1.1 Contiguous and non-contiguous structures compared.

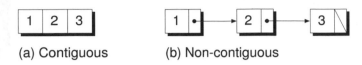

(a) Contiguous   (b) Non-contiguous

Contiguous Structures

Contiguous structures can be broken down further into two kinds: those that contain data items of all the same size, and those where the sizes may differ. Figure 1.2 shows examples of each kind. The first kind we'll call *arrays*. Figure 1.2(a) shows an example of an array of numbers. In an array, each element is of the same type, and thus has the same size.

The second kind of contiguous structure we'll call *structs*, because they can be defined using the C++ struct keyword. Figure 1.2(b) shows a simple struct consisting of a person's name and age. In a struct, elements may be of different types, and thus may have different sizes. For instance, a person's age can be represented with a simple integer that occupies perhaps two bytes of memory. But his or her name, represented as a string of characters, may require many bytes, and may even be of varying length.

C++ allows you to represent arrays and structs using built-in language features. For example, here's how the structures in Figure 1.2 could be coded in C++:

```
int array[3];

struct personnel_data {
  int age;
  char name[80];
};
```

Figure 1.2 Examples of contiguous structures.

```
int arr[3] = {1, 2, 3};     struct customer_data {
                                int age;
                                char name[80];
                            };

                            customer_data billy = {21, "Billy the Kid"};
```

```
┌───┬───┬───┐              ┌────┐
│ 1 │ 2 │ 3 │              │ 21 │
└───┴───┴───┘              └────┴─────────────────────┐
                                │  "Billy the Kid"     │
                                └──────────────────────┘
```

(a) Array   (b) Struct

Coupled with the atomic types (that is, the single data-item built-in types such as integers, floats, and pointers), arrays and structs provide all the "mortar" you need to build more exotic forms of data structures, including the non-contiguous forms you are about to see.

▼ **Note**   The contiguous structures we call structs can be defined with the C++ *class* and *union* keywords, as well as with the *struct* keyword.

Non-Contiguous Structures

Non-contiguous structures are implemented as a collection of data items, called *nodes*, where each node can point to one or more other nodes in the collection. The simplest kind of non-contiguous structure is a *linked list,* as shown in Figure 1.3(a). The nodes of a linked list might be defined in this way:

```
struct Node { // A node storing an integer
  int data;   // The node data
  Node *prev; // Pointer to previous node
  Node *next; // Pointer to next node
};
```

Since this node has two pointers, it's called a *doubly-linked list node*. If you had just one pointer per node serving as, for example, next pointers, the node would be a *singly-linked list node*.

A linked-list represents a linear, one-dimensional type of non-contiguous structure, where there is only the notion of backwards and forwards. A tree, such as the one shown in Figure 1.3(b), is an example of a two-dimensional non-contiguous structure. Here, there is the notion of up and down, and left and right. In a tree, each node has only one link that leads into the node, and links can only go down the tree. The most general type of non-contiguous structure, called a *graph*, has no such restrictions. Figure 1.3(c) is an example of a graph.

Hybrid Structures

It's not uncommon for the two basic types of structures to be mixed into a hybrid form—part contiguous and part non-contiguous. For example, Figure 1.4 shows how to implement a doubly-linked list using three parallel arrays, possibly stored apart from each other in memory. The array D contains the data for the list, whereas the arrays P and N hold the previous and next "pointers." The pointers are actually nothing more than indexes into the D array. For instance, $D[i]$ holds the data for node i, and $P[i]$ holds the index to the node previous to i, which may or may not reside at position $i - 1$. Likewise, $N[i]$ holds the index to the next node in the list.

Figure 1.3 Examples of non-contiguous structures.

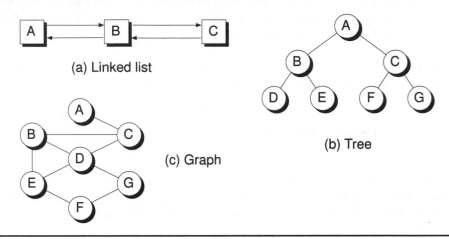

(a) Linked list

(b) Tree

(c) Graph

TREATING DATA STRUCTURES IN THE ABSTRACT

The design of a data structure involves more than just its organization. You also need to plan for the way the data will be accessed and processed—that is, how the data will be interpreted. The previous section showed how three parallel arrays can be interpreted as implementing a linked list. Actually, all of the non-contiguous structures that we introduced—including lists, trees, and graphs—can be implemented either contiguously or non-contiguously. Likewise, the structures that are normally treated as contiguous—arrays and structs—can also be implemented non-contiguously.

Figure 1.4 A doubly-linked list via a hybrid data structure.

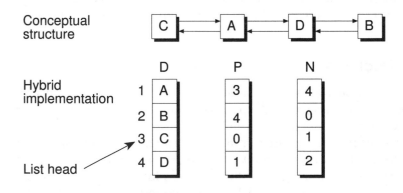

Why this seeming paradox? The problem is that the notion of a data structure in the abstract needs to be treated differently from whatever is used to implement the structure. The abstract notion of a data structure is defined in terms of the operations we plan to perform on the data.

For example, the tree structure we provided in Figure 1.3(b) is called a *binary tree*, since each node has two children. We could define a binary tree node as follows:

```
struct Node {  // A binary tree node holding integer data
  int data;    // Node data
  Node *left;  // Left child of node
  Node *right; // Right child of node
};
```

Compare this definition with the one we provided earlier for a doubly-linked list node. You'll notice that the two types of nodes have the same memory layout. However, we've given two completely different interpretations of this layout. The difference lies in how we expect to be processing the data. With doubly-linked list nodes, we expect to be doing list-type operations, such as *Next()* and *Prev()*. With binary tree nodes, we expect to use operations such as *Left()* and *Right()*.

Taken to its logical conclusion, considering both the organization of data and the expected operations on the data, leads to the notion of an *abstract data type*. An abstract data type is a theoretical construct that consists of data as well as the operations to be performed on the data.

A *stack* is a typical example of an abstract data type. Items stored in a stack can only be added and removed in a certain order—the last item added is the first item removed. We call these operations *pushing* and *popping*, which are illustrated in Figure 1.5. In this definition, we haven't specified how items are stored on the stack, or how the items are pushed and popped. We've only specified the valid operations that can be performed.

Figure 1.5 A push-down stack.

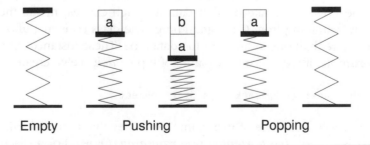

Empty   Pushing   Popping

Of course, to be useful, an abstract data type (such as a stack) has to be implemented, and this is where data structures come into play. For instance, we might choose the simple data structure of an array to represent the stack, and then define the appropriate indexing operations to perform pushing and popping. C++ allows you to create user-defined types to implement abstract data types, as you'll see next.

Classes: User-Defined Data Types

C++ provides an elegant way to both define and implement abstract data types (although the term *user-defined types* may be more appropriate), through the use of the *class, struct,* and *union* keywords. (The structs we declared earlier were simple forms of classes.) For example, here's how we might define a stack of integers in C++:

```
class Stack {
private:
  int data[10]; // Our stack can hold 10 items
  int top;      // Current "top" of stack
public:
  Stack()     { top = 0; }
  Push(int a) { data[top++] = a; }
  int Pop()   { return data[-top]; }
};
```

This code defines a *Stack* type and specifies a particular implementation for it. The function headers in the public portion of the class define the abstract operations that can be performed on the stack. The function headers provide the interface to the data and indicate what operations are expected to be performed on the data. The function bodies, along with the private data, provide the implementation. Of course, this implementation is only one of many possibilities. We could, for instance, use a linked-list to store the stack elements. The "guts" of the class would change accordingly, but the interface would remain the same.

The ability to merge the structure of a data type with the specifications that describe how to operate on that data, through classes, marks the departure of C++ programming from C programming. The class construct allows us to easily create more than one instance of the data type. These instances are called *objects.* For example, if we declare a variable of type *Stack,* we've created a *Stack* object:

```
Stack Mystack; // Mystack is a Stack object
```

A whole new style of programming has evolved around using objects, and in fact is called *object-oriented programming* (OOP). For a discussion of OOP principles, see the references. We'll be indirectly using OOP constructs throughout this book. But whether or not we use OOP to implement data structures is a side issue. The focus here is on the data structures themselves.

SELECTING A DATA STRUCTURE TO MATCH THE OPERATION

Probably the most important process in designing a program involves choosing which data structures to use. The choice depends greatly on the type of operations you wish to perform. We can explore the fundamental issues for this decision-making process at a high level by examining the tradeoffs between contiguous and non-contiguous structures.

Suppose you have an application that uses a sequence of objects, where one of the main operations is to delete an object from the middle of the sequence. Here's how code might be written to perform deletion for an array of integers:

```
void Delete(int *seq, int &n, int posn)
// Delete the item at posn from an array of n elements
{
  if (n) {
    int i = posn;
    n--;
    while(i<n) seq[i] = seq[i+1];
  }
  return;
}
```

This function shifts toward the front all elements that follow the element at position *posn*. This shifting involves data movement that, for integer elements, isn't too costly. However, suppose the array stores large objects, and lots of them. In this case, the overhead for moving data becomes high. The problem is that, in a contiguous structure, such as an array, the *logical ordering* (the ordering that we wish to interpret our elements to have) is the same as the *physical ordering* (the ordering that the elements actually have in memory).

If we choose a non-contiguous representation, however, we can separate the logical ordering from the physical ordering and thus change one without affecting the other. For example, if we store our collection of elements using a doubly-linked list (with previous and next pointers), we can do the deletion without moving the elements. Instead, we just modify the pointers in each node.

Using the doubly-linked list *Node* structure we gave earlier, here's how we can rewrite the *Delete()* function:

```
void Delete(Node *seq, int posn)
// Delete the item at posn from a list of elements
{
  int i = posn;
```

```
Node *q = seq;
while(i && q) {
  i--; q = q->next;
}
if (q) {
   // Not at end of list, so detach p by making previous
   // and next nodes point to each other
   Node *p = q->prev;
   Node *n = q->next;
   if (p) p->next = n;
   if (n) n->prev = p;
}
return;
}
```

The process of deleting a node from a list is independent of the type of data stored in the node, and can be accomplished with some simple "pointer surgery" as illustrated in Figure 1.6. Since very little data is moved during this process, the deletion using linked lists will often be faster than when arrays are used.

It may seem that linked lists are superior to arrays. But is that always true? There are tradeoffs. Our linked lists yield faster deletions, but they take up more room because they require space for two extra pointers per element.

Complexity Functions

One way to evaluate the effectiveness of one data structure over another is to consider their *space complexity functions*, which measure their respective space

Figure 1.6 Detaching a node from a list.

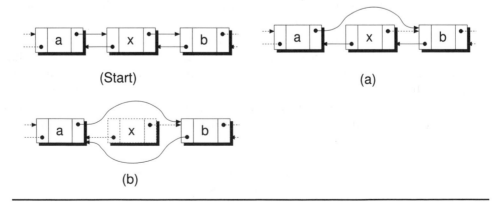

(Start)   (a)

(b)

overhead. The complexity function for many data structures is linear, and can be written as:

s(n)=an+b.

Here, *n* represents the number of objects being stored, *a* is the number of memory cells used per object, and *b* is the number of memory cells of overhead that's independent of how many objects are stored. For example, suppose you have an array of *n* elements, along with a number that indicates the length of the array. Suppose also that the memory cells are expressed in units of words, with each array element requiring two words and the array length requiring one word. The complexity function could then be written as:

s(n)=2n+1.

Compare this complexity with that of using a linked list. For a list of *n* objects, you not only have the space required by the objects themselves, but also space for the *prev* and *next* pointers. Assuming that each pointer requires one word, and that we again use a length indicator of one word, the following complexity function is obtained:

s(n)=4n+1.

These functions illustrate mathematically what we concluded in the previous section: that linked lists have more space overhead than arrays.

Complexity functions can also be used on algorithms as well. Here, the functions are usually expressed in time units, with *n* representing the number of items to process. Consider an array-printing algorithm, shown in the following code:

```
int i;
for(i = 0; i<n; i++) cout << a[i] << ' ';
cout << '\n';
```

For this algorithm, a step could be defined as the printing of one element. If *n* elements are in the array, there are *n* steps, and the *time complexity* of the algorithm can be written as the linear function:

t(n)=an+b.

Here, *a* is some constant multiplier that represents the time required to execute each step, perhaps in units of seconds, or in machine cycles. The constant *b* represents the setup time required to start the algorithm and to stop it.

While the time complexity function just given is linear, not all time complexities are linear. For example, the binary search trees of Chapter 10 can be searched with a logarithmic time complexity of:

$t(n) = a\log_2 n + b.$

For large n, log2n is much smaller than n. If n is one million, log2n is approximately 20. This result is significant. It means we can search through one million nodes in 20 steps, rather than the half-million steps needed for an array or linked list (assuming randomly ordered elements). This points out in a rather strong way how important it is to choose a data structure that matches the operations to be performed.

Since a linear function is so radically different from a logarithmic one, the constant terms and multipliers become less important when comparing the functions. In fact, time complexities are often expressed with the least significant terms dropped. For example, in a linear function, we say that the function is proportional to n. This proportionality is often denoted using what is called the *big-Oh* notation. For instance:

$t(n) = O(n).$

This statement is read "$t(n)$ is order n." If the time complexity were a logarithmic function, we would write:

$t(n) = O(\log n)$

and say that the function is order log$n$. If the time complexity were quadratic, as is the case in a simple nested for loop, we would write:

$t(n) = O(n^2)$

and say that the function $t(n)$ is order n^2.

Using the *big-Oh* notation for space complexities is less meaningful, because most data structures are order n in space complexity. Thus, the constant terms and multipliers become very important in comparisons.

▼ **Note**   For a complete discussion of the *big-Oh* notation, see the companion volume [Flamig 93].

PRACTICAL DESIGN ISSUES

Choosing an efficient algorithm or data structure is just one part of the design process. Next, we'll look at some design issues that are broader in scope. If you think that many of these issues are nothing more than common sense, you're right. However, it's easy to get caught up in the technical gadgetry of a sophisticated program, and sometimes our common-sense reasoning gets lost.

Three Design Goals

There are three basic design goals that you should strive for in a program:

1. Try to save time.
2. Try to save space.
3. Try to save face.

In almost all situations, a program that runs faster is a better program, so saving time is an obvious goal. Likewise, a program that saves space over a competing program is considered desirable. However, even the fastest, most memory efficient program is a bad one if it doesn't work. You want to "save face" by preventing your program from locking up or generating reams of garbled data.

These three design goals are often mutually exclusive. The classic tradeoff involves speed versus space. Implementing a faster algorithm generally involves using more memory. For example, consider the tradeoffs involved in maintaining a sorted collection using a linked list versus an array. You saw where a linked list approach can be generally faster, but requires more memory to store extra pointers in each element. The extra pointers are used to save time in rearranging the elements.

The time/space tradeoff works in reverse, as well. Consider a database program that uses a paging scheme to keep memory requirements fixed, even for large databases. Instead of loading all records into memory, a small cache of, let's say, 50 records is used, and records are paged in and out of this cache as the database is accessed. While this strategy does keep memory requirements at a minimum, it slows down access to the records, due to the page shuffling that takes place.

You can liken the time-space tradeoff to the situation of a wood sculptor forced to work in a small, crowded room. As the sculptor chips away at his or her masterpiece, the chips pile up and soon begin to interfere with the work in progress. The sculptor must frequently stop and clear the chips away. If the room were larger, less time would be spent clearing the chips away. Likewise, programs that have an adequate amount of memory to work with are likely to be faster; less time is spent rearranging the contents of memory in order to keep working. In our database example, a lot of time is spent shuffling records in and out of memory. This activity could be eliminated if enough memory were available to store all the records in memory.

Tradeoffs also exist between saving time or space and maintaining the resulting code. In many cases, the most efficient algorithms are also the most complicated, since smarter code is needed to make the algorithms perform at their peak. Unfortunately, the more complicated the code, the more difficult it is to fix, modify, and port to other environments. You might actually be better off taking a performance hit and using simpler code instead.

Although it doesn't happen often, you can sometimes get lucky, and make your code faster, tighter, and easier to maintain—all at the same time. An example of this is the use of inline functions in C++. Used properly, inline functions can save you time and space by eliminating function call overhead. And inline functions can make your code easier to maintain by encapsulating the details of the functions (even if those details are rather brief).

Balancing the three main design goals makes programming more of an engineering art than an exact science because a large number of factors—many difficult to quantify—come into play. The next section outlines some design principles to help you perform this balancing act.

Some Design Principles

Unless your job is to be theorist, you want to be practical in your designs. As a programmer, you are being paid to produce, a fact that you should never lose sight of. Here are some practical design principles to keep you on the right track. Many of these principles are related to each other, and some are simply paraphrases of others.

• **Design Principle 1.** *Maintain the viewpoint of a practitioner.* You have some programming task to accomplish. Your job is, first and foremost, to get the program working. Use whatever techniques are necessary to get the program working, no matter how inelegant those techniques may seem—that is, of course, unless an elegant solution is readily apparent and easily implemented, or if the alternatives are clearly inadequate. Try incorporating more elegant techniques only after the program is working, and only if it's warranted. For example, are you going to be using this program for years to come, or only once or twice?

• **Design Principle 2.** *"There is no such thing as a complex solution."* This quote from a colleague (see [Mohle 93]) sums up what is wrong with many programs today. A design that's too complex is no solution at all, since it may not be capable of being implemented (perhaps it takes too much memory), and may not be capable of being maintained, (and thus riddled with bugs). Chances are that a simpler, more elegant design is waiting out there in the ether for you to discover—if you just spend more time in the design phase.

- ***Design Principle 3.*** *Don't over-generalize.* Many books on object-oriented programming show how to build general-purpose collection classes. While there is nothing wrong with this per se, it's easy to overdo it. General-purpose code tends to be less efficient than code written specifically for the task at hand, since more cases must be handled. Ironically, the more flexible your code is, the more difficult it can be to maintain—the opposite of what you might expect!

  Use simple, direct designs whenever possible. For instance, if you need to store a small list of numbers, don't get carried away by using some massive set of general purpose collection classes. A simple array will do just fine.

  This doesn't mean you shouldn't strive to make your designs reusable and robust. But you should temper your eagerness to write, for example, the ultimate collection class, by asking yourself: "Is this really warranted? Will I (or someone else), be able to make changes to this code later on? What's the purpose of my activities? Is it my goal to write a general-purpose set of routines, or am I trying to solve just this one problem?"

- ***Design Principle 4.*** *General-purpose code is not always the most reusable.* This rule may seem at first like a paradox. But consider this: code that is very general purpose tends to be bloated and inefficient, due to the need to handle many cases. If the code is too bloated, you may not want to include it in your application. So it's not very reusable, is it? A surprising number of commercial toolkits suffer from this problem. One test that you can use on the objects you design is to ask yourself the following question: "Would I want to incorporate ten of these objects into another object?" This question will force you to think about how streamlined you've made your objects.

- ***Design Principle 5.*** *Follow the 80-20 rule.* This rule comes in many variations, including this one: in many programs, approximately 80 percent of the execution time is spent in 20 percent of the code. Few designs work well in all situations, so make your designs work well for the portion of code that's used most often. For the remaining code, the performance may suffer, but as long as your design doesn't totally stop working or produce the wrong results, don't worry about it too much. Of course, if you know a design that works well 100 percent of the time, and that design is cost-effective, by all means use it!

- ***Design Principle 6.*** *Design first, then optimize.* As programmers, we've all made the mistake of trying to write and optimize code before we've even considered the design choices. Before optimizing a data structure, for instance, ask yourself if there is perhaps a better choice. Choosing a good data structure can make much more difference than merely optimizing the one you already have. For instance, no matter how clever you are in optimizing a linked list for searching a large number of records, a balanced binary tree is likely to perform much better, even without any optimization.

• ***Design Principle 7.*** *Try to get the most leverage out of any overhead you must add.* Writing robust code often entails writing smarter code. And smarter code usually has more overhead associated with it. The issue is where this overhead is placed. For instance, consider the linear space complexity function $s(n) = a\,n + b$. The terms a and b represent overhead. The overhead represented by a is multiplied n times (where n is the number of objects stored), so you obviously want to avoid adding overhead there if you can. The overhead represented by b is much more benign since it's just a constant factor. Thus, strive to add type b overhead rather than type a overhead.

An example of this principle is discussed in Chapter 10. There, we discuss the possibility of using a threaded tree over an ordinary tree, where each node has an extra pointer back to its parent. This parent pointer represents overhead that's incurred in every node (so it's type a overhead). The reason for using parent pointers is to simplify the code. But it might be better to have slightly more complex code, eliminating the parent pointers, and thus be able to use type b overhead instead of type a overhead.

• ***Design Principle 8.*** *You shouldn't have to pay for something you aren't going to use.* Consider using a general-purpose collection class when all you really want is a simple array. Why should you pay for the extra overhead? Yet many poorly designed libraries want you to do just that.

It's interesting to note that Design Principle 8 permeates the design of the C++ language itself. While C++ adds object-oriented programming capabilities to C, you never pay for these capabilities when coding straight C without objects. Contrast this to the design of Smalltalk, where you are forced to pay for the overhead of using objects, regardless of whether you actually need to use objects to accomplish the task at hand.

SUMMARY

In this chapter, we've reviewed the basic concepts behind data structures, and have given a set of common-sense principles that apply to all designs. In Chapters 2 and 3 we'll begin to focus on more specific principles as they apply to designing code in C++, with data structures particularly in mind.

Using C++ Effectively

I n the previous chapter, we discussed general design principles without regard to any specific programming language. In this chapter, we will look at design principles that are specific to C++. We'll also discuss our general philosophy on how to use C++ effectively. To explain these general principles and their underlying philosophy, we'll provide examples showing the attributes that make up a well-designed class, and we'll show how to use those attributes in derived classes. This chapter is by no means a tutorial on C++, nor does it pretend to even remotely cover all aspects of the language. It's assumed you already know the basics, but might want a brief refresher course on creating well-designed classes.

C++: As High Level as Desired, but No Higher

One of the great attractions of C++ is the breadth and scope of programs that can be expressed in the language. Since C++ inherits virtually all the characteristics of C, you have the ability to code at a fairly low level, almost at the level of assembly language. At the same time, C++ allows you to express your designs at a fairly high level by using classes, constructors, destructors, and operator overloading. You can select the desired level of abstraction you would like to work with and, in fact, mix both high-level and low-level code together. Few other languages allow these combined capabilities.

C, Pascal, FORTRAN, and assembly are, for the most part, low-level languages because they can't be used to directly express high-level concepts. However, these languages have advantages, since they can produce code that's quite efficient. On the other hand, languages such as Lisp, Smalltalk, and Prolog are very high level, and it can be a joy working with the abstractions these languages allow. Unfortunately, these languages often produce very inefficient code. If you want to use their high-level constructs, you pay a high price. There needs to be some middle ground.

C++ provides that middle ground. When you want efficiency, you can have it. When you want high-level design, you can have that, too. Figure 2.1 illustrates this point. Of course, you can't always have both of these attributes at the same time. There is almost always a tradeoff between efficient code and high-level code. The important point is that C++ allows you to control this tradeoff.

Consider one of the main philosophies that went into creating C++: You should never have to pay for a feature you aren't using. This can be summed up another way:

> C++: As high level as desired, but no higher.

This means you can pick the level of abstraction you would like to use, but not pay for any higher abstractions. Great care went into the design of C++ to allow this. The designers were very concerned about efficiency issues, but also wanted the language to be much more expressive than C in specifying higher-level concepts. Inline functions are a good example. Used properly, inline functions aid in the encapsulation of the inner workings of a data type, without causing the overhead normally associated with functions.

Figure 2.1 C++: Low level and high level.

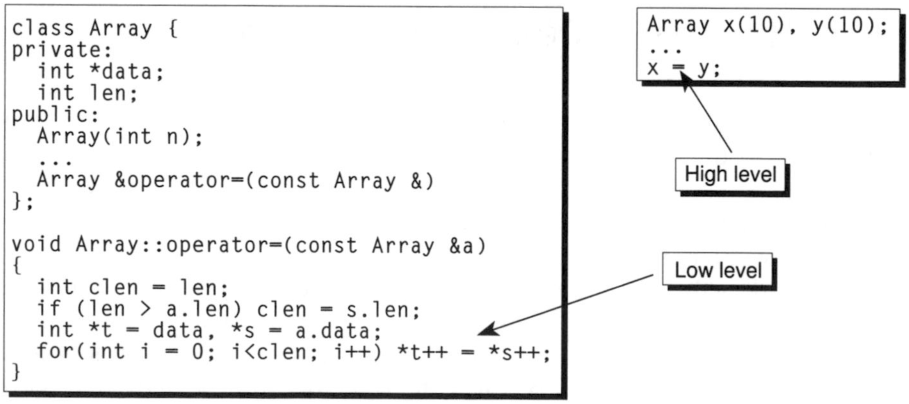

```
class Array {
private:
  int *data;
  int len;
public:
  Array(int n);
  ...
  Array &operator=(const Array &)
};

void Array::operator=(const Array &a)
{
  int clen = len;
  if (len > a.len) clen = s.len;
  int *t = data, *s = a.data;
  for(int i = 0; i<clen; i++) *t++ = *s++;
}
```

```
Array x(10), y(10);
...
x = y;
```

High level

Low level

It is highly recommended that you follow C++'s philosophy when designing your data structures and algorithms. Use as high a level of abstraction as you need, but don't get carried away and try to create the ultimate in general-purpose code. Don't try to create Smalltalk-like data structures unless that's your goal. As we pointed out in Chapter 1, simpler designs are often easier to debug and maintain than general designs, and will most likely be more efficient.

Well-Designed Classes

The most important feature of C++, especially in terms of data structure design, is the class construct. It's the class construct that allows you to encapsulate your data structures, hiding the inner workings. It's also the class construct that allows you to use inheritance, which is a powerful way of abstracting and reusing your code. Since classes are such a central feature, it's important to know what constitutes a good class design. Almost every non-trivial, well-designed class has the following attributes:

1. Encapsulated, or hidden, members

2. A default constructor

3. A copy constructor

4. An overloaded assignment operator

5. A virtual destructor

These attributes are illustrated in Figure 2.2. To demonstrate these five desired class attributes, let's take a look at a sample *Image* class. This class is used to create objects that store and display bitmaps. The bitmaps are allocated dynamically. The class definition is:

```
class Image {
protected:
  int w, h;     // Dimensions of image
  char *bitmap; // Bitmap of image
  int Copy(int iw, int ih, char *bm);
public:
  Image();                           // Default constructor
  Image(const Image &im);            // Copy constructor
  Image(int iw, int ih, char *bm);
  virtual ~Image();                  // Virtual destructor
  Image &operator=(const Image &im); // Overloaded assignment
  virtual void Show(int xs, int ys);
};
```

The code for this *Image* class can be found on disk in the file *ch2_1.cpp*.

Figure 2.2 Components of a well-designed class.

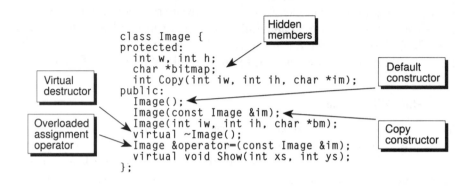

You can see that the *Image* class has all five of the attributes we've just mentioned. Please note that you are not required to use all of these attributes in your classes. In fact, don't include them if they don't make sense. Rather, when you see a class that *doesn't* have all of these attributes, it should signal a warning to you, and you should ask yourself *why* the class doesn't have them.

Encapsulation

There are two access sections in the sample *Image* class: a protected section and a public section. The protected section contains the inner workings of an *Image* object that are meant to be hidden from users of the *Image* class. The public section defines the interface to the class—that is, those members that are meant to be used directly. Quite often, the private and protected members of a class are predominately data members, whereas the public members are predominately functions.

Recall from your C++ studies that protected members are private to all outside users of a class, except for any classes derived from the class. We could have made the protected members of *Image* private, and disallowed even derived classes from accessing them. Some people argue that protected access should rarely be used, if at all. They even go so far as to say that the very way derived classes are implemented violates the principles of encapsulation. We won't get embroiled in such controversies here. Instead, we'll use the following convention:

Whenever a class is designed to be a base class, with inheritance in mind, the hidden members of the class will be made protected. If the class isn't to be a base class, the hidden members will be made private.

It is up to you to determine whether you wish to follow this convention for your own classes. Don't be afraid to use your own judgment.

We've chosen to place all the data members of the *Image* class in the protected section, along with the following function, which is used to copy one bitmap into another:

```
int Image::Copy(int iw, int ih, char *bm)
// Private helper function that allocates a bitmap
// of size iw*ih, and copies the bits stored in
// bm into it.
// ASSUMES bitmap isn't already allocated.
// Returns 1 if allocation successful; 0 otherwise.
{
  w = iw; h = ih;
  bitmap = new char[w*h];
  if (bitmap) { // Allocation worked
    memcpy(bitmap, bm, w*h);
    return 1;
  }
  else { // Allocation failed. Set image to null.
    w = 0; h = 0;
    return 0; // Allocation failed
  }
}
```

The *Copy()* function is used by several other functions in the class, and thus helps reuse some common functionality in the class. Functions like this are typical, and are sometimes called *helper functions*. Note that *Copy()* assumes that the bitmap isn't already allocated. Thus, it wouldn't be safe for this function to be used arbitrarily. For that reason, we've made it hidden. Only other member functions of the class have access to *Copy()*, and they presumably will call it in a safe manner.

Default Constructors

The *Image* class has the following *default constructor*:

```
Image::Image()
// Default constructor to create an empty image
{
  w = 0; h = 0; bitmap = 0;
}
```

Default constructors are so-named because they are used whenever a constructor must be called implicitly, such as when declaring an array of objects. A default constructor doesn't require any arguments when called, meaning that it either *has* no arguments or that all of its arguments have default values.

What should a default constructor do? Most people design their default constructors to create a "null" object, whatever that means. (It depends on what the object is.) Quite often, it means setting all data members to zero. Here, we've chosen to create an image that has an empty bitmap.

If you don't declare a default constructor, one will be generated automatically by the compiler, but the data members will not be initialized by this generated constructor. Thus, it behooves you to define your own default constructor.

Copy Constructors

Copy constructors are used whenever an object is to be created and initialized as a copy of some other existing object of the same type. For example, copy constructors are called whenever an object is a parameter passed by value to a function, or when an object is the return value of a function. This copy construction approach is illustrated in Figure 2.3.

In these cases, the constructor is called implicitly to make a copy of the parameter being passed in or the object being returned. Here is the copy constructor for the *Image* class. Note how the helper function *Copy()* is called:

```
Image::Image(const Image &im)
// Copy constructor. Allocates room for bitmap
// of same size and copies im's image into it.
{
  Copy(im.w, im.h, im.bitmap);
}
```

To be a copy constructor, a constructor must be callable by passing a single argument. That means it must either have only one argument or all arguments except the first must have default values. The first argument must be of the same class to which the constructor belongs, and must be passed by reference.

Figure 2.3 Copy constructing during function calling.

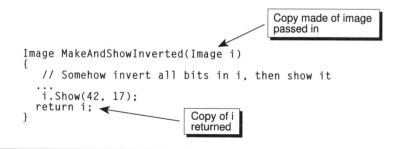

Note   If you don't pass the first argument of a copy constructor by reference, you'll end up with recursive calls to the constructor that will go on indefinitely, locking up your program.

The *Image()* copy constructor meets these criteria. Note that we pass not just a reference to an *Image* object to the constructor, but a reference to a *constant* object:

```
Image::Image(const Image &im);
```

We could have also used:

```
Image::Image(Image &im);
```

In a later section, we'll discuss why it's preferrable to use the *const* modifier in cases like this.

If you don't declare a copy constructor, the compiler will generate one automatically for you. This generated constructor will do a *member-wise copy*. That is, it will copy each data member, one by one. If a member is a pointer, then only the value of the pointer is copied, not what the pointer points to. This can lead to serious memory management problems, because two objects can end up with members pointing to the same dynamic storage locations, a situation called *aliasing*. This becomes a problem when it's time to free up the dynamic storage, since both objects will attempt to free the same memory locations, wreaking havoc on the heap.

Aliasing can be avoided at copy-construction time by defining your own copy constructor and having that constructor make copies of any dynamic data being pointed to, rather than just copying the pointers. Our *Image()* copy constructor does just that by calling the *Copy()* helper function.

Overloaded Assignments

We've overloaded the assignment operator for the *Image* class as follows:

```
Image &Image::operator=(const Image &im)
// Assignment operator. Deallocates existing
// bitmap; allocates a new one of same size.
// as im, and copies im's image into it.
{
  delete[] bitmap;
  Copy(im.w, im.h, im.bitmap);
  return *this;
}
```

The overloaded assignment operator, *operator=()*, performs much the same function as the copy constructor by allowing one object to be copied into another. One crucial difference is that, unlike the copy constructor, *operator=()* assumes that the target object is already built, and already has a bitmap allocated. Thus, *operator=()* must first delete the allocated bitmap, so that *Copy()* can allocate a new one of the proper size.

The previous paragraph points out the critical difference between *initializing* an object and *assigning* an object. Copy constructors are used whenever an object is created and initialized to be a copy, whereas assignment operators are used when assignment takes place. While it's usually fairly obvious which is occurring, it isn't always so. Consider the following code:

```
Image snapshot(3, 5, "some bitmap");
Image picture = snapshot; // Assignment or initialization?
picture = snapshot;       // Assignment or initialization?
```

The last two statements look almost identical, but they do very different things. The first creates and initializes *picture* to be a copy of *snapshot*; the second assigns a copy of the *snapshot* image to the existing *picture* object. The first statement uses the copy constructor; the second statement uses the overloaded assignment operator. The tipoff is that the first contains a type declaration, using the type *Image;* the second doesn't. Thus, we know that the first statement is actually a call to a constructor.

Like the copy constructor, the *operator=()* function takes a single argument that's a reference to a constant *Image* object. The *const* modifier is used for the same reason as it is in the copy constructor (discussed later). The object is passed by reference for efficiency's sake, and for notational convenience. Contrast the following two *operator=()* functions. One uses a reference parameter, while the other uses a pointer parameter:

```
X &X::operator=(const X &v);
Y &Y::operator=(const Y *v);

X a, b;
Y c, d;

a = b;  // Clean syntax
c = &d; // Awkward syntax
```

You are not required to use pass by reference for overloaded assignment operators like you are for copy constructors, but as you can see, it's a good idea.

We show the assignment operator as returning a reference to the object that was the target of the assignment. You are not required to do this, but it's often done to allow assignments to be chained together, as in the following:

```
Image ia, ib, ic;
ia = ib = ic;
```

This would actually result in the following calls:

```
ia.operator=(ib.operator=(ic));
```

If you don't overload the assignment operator for a class, the compiler will subsititute member-wise copying whenever assignments occur between two objects of that class. As is the case with copy constructing, this situation can result in aliasing. Thus, it's a good idea to include an overloaded assignment operator, especially when dynamic storage is being pointed to by the object.

Virtual Destructors

To properly de-allocate the bitmap data of an image, the *Image* destructor is used:

```
Image::~Image()
// Destructor that de-allocates bitmap. Note that bitmap
// might be null coming in, but delete() is supposed
// to handle that.
{
  delete[] bitmap;
}
```

Notice in the class definition that the destructor is virtual. This is done for safety reasons. For example, we'll be deriving a *HideableImage* class later on, which dynamically allocates some additional storage for a "backing store." This additional storage is to be used in saving what's underneath an image about to be drawn. When the destructor for *HideableImage* is called, we want the backing store to be freed as well as the bitmap data. It's critical that the correct destructor is called when the object is destroyed. By making the destructors virtual, code like the following will work just fine:

```
Image *p; // Can point to Image as well as HideableImage objects
Image *StaticPicture = new Image(3, 5, "Picture bits here");
HideableImage *NowYouSeeMe = new HideableImage(8, 10, "Bits go here");

p = StaticPicture;
delete p; // Image::~Image() called
p = NowYouSeeMe;
delete p; // HideableImage::~HideableImage() called
```

It's not always necessary or desirable to make a destructor virtual. For instance, if you don't plan on deriving from a class, there is no need to make any functions virtual. If you go ahead and make the destructor for the class virtual, you will cause an extra pointer to be stored in every object created from the class, thus wasting space. (This extra pointer points to a virtual function table.) The following rule of thumb will help you decide whether to use a virtual destructor:

> If your class uses virtual functions, you should always include a virtual destructor, even if that destructor doesn't do anything. (The derived class destructors might need to do something.) If your class needs no virtual functions, making the destructor virtual is optional. You might want to keep it non-virtual to save space.

Note Even though destructors can and most likely should be virtual, constructors can never be virtual.

Constants

One often overlooked feature of C++ is the use of constants. Constants in C++ are more robust than they are in C. In C++, constants have local scope. That is, a constant can be safely declared (defined *and* allocated) in a C++ header file, without worrying about having duplicate definitions when modules are linked. This allows C++ constants to be used where macros once were in C. For example, you might have a header file like the following:

```
// trigcons.h
const double pi = 3.141592654;
const double degtorad  = 0.017453292;
```

This header file can be included in more than one source file. Each source file gets its own private copies of the constants. Since these copies don't have global, external names, the linker won't complain when linking the source files.

Note For simple constants, such as integers and floating point numbers, a C++ compiler may not actually create any storage for the constants, but instead will use the values directly when needed.

In C, it would not be a good idea to include the complete declarations of constants in a header file like the one above. In C, constants have global scope, and the storage for the constants might be duplicated. You would probably use constants as in the following files:

```
/* trigcons.h: Declare constants in header */
const double pi;        /* extern by default */
const double degtorad;  /* extern by default */
```

```
/* trigcons.c: Allocate and define constants in source file */
const double pi = 3.141592654;
const double degtorad = 0.017453292;
```

Or, you might be tempted to use macros, saving yourself the bother of having another source file to link in:

```
#define pi 3.141592654
#define degtorad 0.017453292
```

However, the macro approach is less descriptive, since it doesn't tell you the intended type of the constants.

Constants are often used in conjunction with parameters passed by reference. When you use constants in this way, you can get safe, elegant, and efficient code. Contrast the following two functions. One passes a reference to an *X* object (which is presumed to be some large structure), while the other passes a pointer to an *X* object:

```
void DoSomething(const X &x);
void DoSomethingElse(X *x);

X myobj;
DoSomething(myobj);       // Elegant, efficient, and safe
DoSomethingElse(&myobj); // Efficient, but not as elegant or safe
```

Passing by reference argument is cleaner than passing by pointer, since you don't need to take the address of the object via the & operator. However, some people object to using references this way, since it isn't obvious that the object might be modified inside the function. With the pointer method, the & operator sends a clear warning flag. Using the *const* modifier solves that problem for the reference argument case, since the function won't be able to modify the object. (Actually, the function *can* modify the object by using some clever type casting, but the programmer must consciously choose to do that.)

You will see the *const X &x* syntax used quite often in this book. In particular, it's considered good style to use this syntax for overloaded assignment operators and copy constructors.

Another use of the *const* modifier is to declare *constant member functions*. Ordinarily, if you declare an object to be constant, then you can't call any of the object's functions.The functions might change the internal state of the object, violating the concept of a constant object. However, if a function truly doesn't change any part of the object, you can declare the function to be *constant*, and the compiler will let that function be called. Here's an example:

```
class TwoNum {
private:
  int a, b;
```

```
public:
  TwoNum(int aa, int bb);
  int First() { return a; }        // Not a constant function
  int Second() const { return b; } // A constant function
};

const TwoNum x(17, 42);
int y = x.First();  // Not legal
int z = x.Second(); // Legal
```

The *First()* function can't be called for the constant object *x*, since it's an ordinary member function. The *Second()* function can be called, since it was a declared constant. Note that the *const* keyword is placed after the parameter list but before the function body.

It's a good idea to declare member functions as being constant whenever possible. Here's why:

1. Someone might decide to declare an object of the class as being constant. By handling this possibility ahead of time, you've made the class more usable.

2. The *const* declaration allows the compiler to perform more optimizations.

Declaring an object constant happens more than you might think, especially if you are following good coding style. For instance, suppose we added a copy constructor for the *TwoNum* class, and chose to use the functions *First()* and *Second()* to aid in the copying:

```
TwoNum::TwoNum(const TwoNum &tn)
{
  a = tn.First();  // Not legal
  b = tn.Second(); // Legal
}
```

We could have avoided the problem here by using the members *tn.a* and *tn.b* directly. But you might not always be so fortunate in your classes.

Don't overlook using the *const* modifier as an aid to the compiler for optimization. Consider the following loop:

```
TwoNum tn(17, 42);
for (int i = 0; i<10; i++) {
    int y = tn.Second();
    ...
}
```

Since *Second()* is declared as a constant member function, the compiler knows that *tn* is not modified by the statement *y = tn.Second()*. Thus, if the data members of *tn* are for some reason already loaded in registers, they won't need to be reloaded after the statement, making the loop more efficient. Of course, the ability of your compiler to perform such optimizations is implementation-dependent.

USING INHERITANCE

Inheritance is a powerful part of C++ programming. Through inheritance, which is achieved by class derivation, you can express type-subtype relationships, as well as elegantly share and reuse code common to a system of classes. We'll now continue our *Image* class example to derive a new type of *Image* class, one that allows the image to be hidden and then later restored:

```
class HideableImage : public Image {
protected:
  int showing;         // Flag indicating that image is showing
  int x, y;            // Location where image is showing
  char *backing_store; // Bitmap of what's underneath
public:
  HideableImage();
  HideableImage(const HideableImage &hi);
  HideableImage(int iw, int ih, char *bm);
  virtual ~HideableImage();
  HideableImage &operator=(const Image &im);
  virtual void Show(int xs, int ys);
  void Hide();
};
```

The code for this class can be found on disk in the file *ch2_1.cpp*.

The *HideableImage* class adds data members to keep track of whether the image is currently showing and where. It also adds a "backing store" buffer, which keeps a copy of what was on the screen underneath the image before the image was shown. The *Show()* function is overidden to first copy to the backing store before displaying the image, and a *Hide()* function is added to allow the image to be temporarily hidden.

Like the *Image* class, the five attributes we've already listed are desirable for the *HideableImage* class. *HideableImage* maintains a protected section, which hides the additional variables, and it has a default constructor, copy constructor, overloaded assignment, and a virtual destructor. We'll now look at how each of these attributes is affected by the inheritance process.

Derived Class Constructors and Destructors

The *HideableImage* class has the following constructors defined:

```
HideableImage::HideableImage()
// Default constructor sets everything to zero.
// Note that base class constructor called implicitly
// before the body of this function executes.
{
  x = 0; y = 0; showing = 0; backing_store = 0;
}


HideableImage::HideableImage(const HideableImage &hi)
// Copy constructor. Note that the backing_store
// and associated flags are NOT copied. Thus, the
// base class constructor can do most of the work.
: Image(hi) // Call base class constructor explicitly
{
  // Initialize to "not showing," then allocate backing_store
  x = 0; y = 0; showing = 0;
  backing_store = new char[w*h];
}

HideableImage::HideableImage(int iw, int ih, char *bm)
// General constructor. Base class constructor does
// a lot of the work.
: Image(iw, ih, bm) // Call base class constructor explicitly
{
  // Initialize to "not showing," then allocate backing_store
  x = 0; y = 0; showing = 0;
  backing_store = new char[w*h];
}
```

These constructors all have one thing in common: they call the base class constructor. The derived class default constructor calls the default base class constructor implicitly. The other derived class constructors call the respective base class constructors explicitly. In each case, the base class constructor is called *before* the derived class constructor executes.

The way to remember the order of constructor calls is to look at how the base class constructors are called explicitly. Their calls are placed between the constructor parameter list and the constructor body, in the *member initialization list*:

```
HideableImage::HideableImage(const HideableImage &hi)
: Image(hi) // Call to base class constructor
{
  x = 0; y = 0; showing = 0;
  backing_store = new char[w*h];
}
```

The placement of the member initialization list correctly suggests when the base class constructors are called.

The member initialization list can also be used to initialize members of the class (hence its name). For instance, we could modify the constructor to initialize *x* and *y* to zero, as follows:

```
HideableImage::HideableImage(const HideableImage &hi)
: x(0), y(0), Image(hi)
{
    showing = 0;
    backing_store = new char[w*h];
}
```

Here, the syntax $x(0)$, $y(0)$, means to set $x = 0$, and $y = 0$. If *x* and *y* were objects of classes with constructors, the appropriate constructor calls would take place instead. Like the base class constructor calls, these initializations take place before the constructor body executes, so *x* and *y* get initialized before *backing_store* and *showing*. However, *x* and *y* get initialized *after* the call to the base class *Image()* constructor, even though they appear first in the list. That's because base class constructor calls always take place before the members of a derived class are initialized.

Except for the order in which the initializations take place, this modified constructor works the same as the original one. So why initialize members in the member initialization list? The most common reason is to initialize members that are constants, references, or objects that require constructors to be called explicitly in order to initialize them. (That is the only way these types of members *can* be initialized.) For instance:

```
class FunnyNums {
private:
    const int a;
    const int &b;
    CompoundNum c;
public:
    FunnyNums(int u, const CompoundNum &v);
};

FunnyNums::FunnyNums(int u, const CompoundNum &v)
// Initialize const a to have value u, and for reference
// b to point to a. Also, copy-construct c.
: a(u), b(a), c(v)
{
    // Nothing else to do
}
```

In the *FunnyNums* constructor, *a* gets initialized before *b* (and before *c*), not because *a* is first in the initialization list, but because it was declared first in the class definition. Actually, you shouldn't rely on the order in which members get initialized, as we've done here; it's not considered good style.

Because base class constructors must be called for derived class objects, it's very rare for a derived class not to have any constructors. This would happen only if the base class has only a default constructor or no constructor at all. In this case, you don't need to declare a derived class constructor. A default one will be generated, which will call the base class constructor.

Sometimes, the derived class constructors do nothing more than turn around and call the base class constructors. It can be tedious to declare derived class constructors for cases like these. But at least the constructors can be declared inline, to hopefully avoid function call overhead.

Derived class destructors work just the opposite of derived class constructors. First, the members of the derived class are destroyed (with their destructors being called if they have any); then, the derived class constructor body is executed; and finally, the base class destructor is called, implicitly. For example, here is the *HideableImage* destructor:

```
HideableImage::~HideableImage()
// Destructor de-allocates both the backing store
// and the shown bitmap. Note that the base class
// destructor, which de-allocates the shown bitmap,
// is called implicitly AFTER this body executes.
{
  Hide(); // Hide image first, if not already hidden
  delete[] backing_store;
}
```

Note that this destructor was declared virtual in the class definition, per our rules on well-designed classes.

Derived Class Overloaded Assignments

Derived classes can have overloaded assignment operators, just as base classes do. Assignments between two derived class objects work as follows: if the derived class has an overloaded assignment, it is called. Otherwise, a member-wise copy is performed on each additional member of the derived class (that is, on those members not in the base class). If the base class has an overloaded assignment operator, it is called for the base class members; otherwise, the base class members are copied in a member-wise fashion.

The consequences of these rules are twofold:

1. If the derived class object has members pointing to dynamic storage, you'll want to overload the assignment operator for the derived class to take care

of potential aliasing problems. Of course, if the dynamic data is pointed to by base class members, then presumably an overloaded base class assignment operator is already handling the problem.

2. If you do overload the assignment operator in the derived class, you must be sure that any base class overloaded assignment operator function is called, too. Or at least ensure that the actions that might have been performed by the base class assignment are performed in the derived class assignment operator function.

These two rules beg for an example. Here is the *HideableImage()* overloaded assignment operator, which embodies both rules:

```
HideableImage &HideableImage::operator=(const Image &im)
// Overloaded assignment operator. Copy just the
// image to be shown, and not the backing store.
// A new backing store will be created, though,
// with the same size.
{
  // We must re-allocate backing_store to new
  // size. But first we must hide the image
  // if it was showing.
  int ss = showing; // Keep track of show status
  Hide();
  delete[] backing_store;
  // Let base class assignment do its thing.
  Image::operator=(im);
  // Now, re-allocate the backing store to correct size
  backing_store = new char[w*h];
  if (ss) Show(x, y); // Redisplay image if necessary
  return *this;
}
```

Figure 2.4 illustrates the workings of the *HideableImage::operator=()* function, which must take care of two types of dynamic memory: the backing store and the bitmap stored in the base class. The storage for the backing store must be resized in case the source image has different dimensions. The bitmap storage is handled via an explicit call to the *Image::operator=()* function:

```
Image::operator=(im);
```

You might have noticed the parameter type used in the derived class assignment operator function:

```
HideableImage &HideableImage::operator=(const Image &im);
```

Figure 2.4 Assigning hideable images.

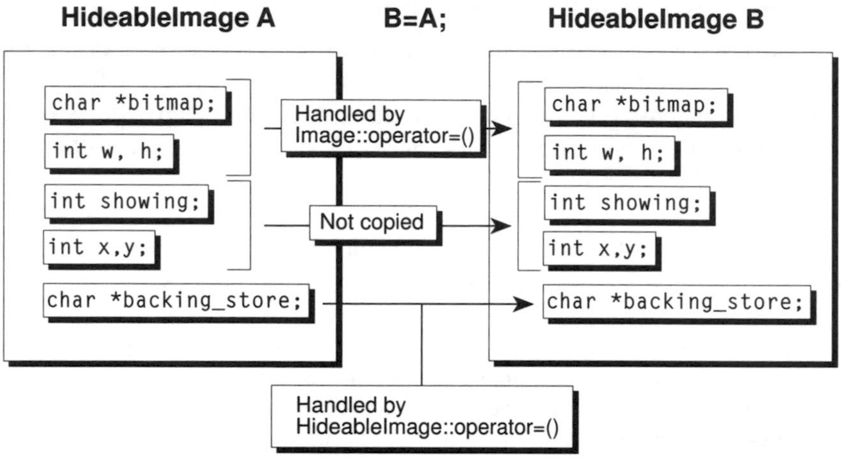

Instead of typing the parameter as a *HideableImage*, we've typed it as an *Image*. Why have we done this? We can assign an *Image* object to a *HideableImage* object just as easily as we can assign a *HideableImage* object to another *HideableImage* object. We could have provided two overloaded operators for this, but since the code would be the same, we chose to use just one function. Because a *HideableImage* object can be used anywhere an *Image* object is used, we chose to type the parameter as an *Image* object. Note that, had we done the reverse,

```
HideableImage &HideableImage::operator=(const HideableImage &im);
```

we would not be able to assign an *Image* object to a *HideableImage* object.

Although it's a little unusual, we'll use this technique in several places—particularly with the Array classes used in Chapter 4.

COOPERATING CLASSES

Class derivation, as you've seen in the previous sections, is just one example of two classes working together to create a data structure. It's also possible for two or more cooperating classes, not related by inheritance, to work in tandem. In this section, we'll show as an example a singly-linked list implementation, which has node and list classes. In this manner, not only will you learn about setting up cooperating classes, but you'll also be introduced to the inner workings of linked lists. We won't cover all aspects of linked lists here. See Chapter 8 for a more complete discussion of them.

Your First Singly-Linked List

A *singly-linked list* consists of nodes linked in one direction. Figure 2.5 shows an example of a singly-linked list. Each node contains two parts: the data held in the node and a pointer to the next node in the list (if any).

Here's how you might define a node structure holding a single character as its data:

```
struct ChNode { // Node holding a character
  char data;    // Data for the node
  ChNode *next; // Next node on the list
};
```

You'll notice we made this node a simple class, using the *struct* keyword instead of the *class* keyword. We've defined no constructors, destructors, or assignment operators. This isn't necessarily bad. For a simple structure such as this, there might not be a reason to hide any details, and the behaviors of the generated default constructor, copy constructor, and assignment functions may be satisfactory. You don't need to use all the C++ features just because they are there. We'll start with the simple *ChNode* definition and then dress it up later (after we've shown why you might want to do so).

The following code shows how we might construct the linked list in Figure 2.5 with *ChNode* objects:

```
main()
{
  ChNode a, b, c;
  a.data = 'a'; a.next = &b;
  b.data = 'b'; b.next = &c;
  c.data = 'c'; c.next = 0;
  return 0;
}
```

In this code, we set up the links between each node by hand, using the address of the next node. The last node gets a null pointer to end the list.

Constructing lists like this can be tedious and error prone. It's also easy to lose track of which node heads the list. (In our list, node *a* is the head.) To solve these problems, a new class, *ChList*, can be introduced to handle the overall management of a list. This new class holds a pointer to the head of the list and adds nodes to the list. In essence, the *ChNode* and *ChList* classes work

Figure 2.5 A singly-linked list.

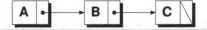

together to form the actual list structure. Such classes are called *cooperating classes.*

Here's a simple example of a list class that allows nodes to be added to the front of the list:

```
class ChList {
private:
  ChNode *head;
public:
  ChList();
  void Add(char c);
};

ChList::ChList()
// Default constructor creates an empty list
{
  head = 0;
}

void ChList::Add(char c)
// Add new node to the front, holding c as its data
{
  ChNode *p = new ChNode;
  p->data = c;
  p->next = head;
  head = p; // New node now head of list
}
```

Here's how we can rewrite our list construction example. Figure 2.6 illustrates the new way of representing the list.

```
main()
{
  ChList mylist;

  mylist.Add('c');
  mylist.Add('b');
  mylist.Add('a');
  return 0;
}
```

The file *ch2_2.cpp* on disk shows a complete running program of the simple node and list classes.

Note how we build the list backwards because we can only add nodes to the front of the list. However, we could certainly define a function for adding nodes to the tail of the list (although it's harder). In fact, our list class is quite

---

Figure 2.6 Alternate implementation of a singly-linked list.

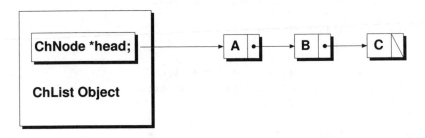

---

incomplete, because we have no way of deleting from the list, no way to walk through the contents of the list, and so forth. But before we fill out the list class, let's first see how we can improve the node class.

An Improved List Design

Here's a new *ChNode* class that embodies all five attributes of a well-designed class:

```
// More complete node class
class ChNode {
  friend ChList; // Let ChList access hidden parts
private:
  ChNode *next;  // Hide this "detail"
public:
  char data; // Keep this available to user
  ChNode();
  ChNode(const char &d, ChNode *n);
  ChNode(const ChNode &cn);
  ChNode &operator=(const ChNode &cn);
};

ChNode::ChNode()
// Default constructor
{
  data = 0; next = 0;
}

ChNode::ChNode(const char &d, ChNode *n)
// General constructor
{
  data = a; next = n;
}
```

```
ChNode::ChNode(const ChNode &cn)
// Copy constructor. Note that we don't copy the
// next pointer, but rather set it to zero.
{
  data = cn.data; next = 0;
}

ChNode &ChNode::operator=(const ChNode &cn)
// Assignment. Only data is copied; the next
// pointer is set to zero.
{
  data = cn.data; next = 0;
}
```

In our new *ChNode* class, we've hidden the next pointer, reasoning that the less we directly use pointers like this, the better. However, *something* must be able to access the *next* pointer, so we've made all of the *ChList* class a friend of *ChNode*, since *ChList* will be managing the nodes. This is a typical arrangement for cooperating classes. At least one of the classes is a friend of the other. Sometimes you may have a mutual friendship.

In contrast to the *next* pointer, we left *data* public, thinking that it might be useful for those who use *ChNode* to access the data directly. Using this variable directly is relatively harmless. We could, however, make it private and force it to be accessed through special access functions. Here's an example:

```
class ChNode {
private:
  char data;
  ...
public:
  void SetData(char c);
  char GetData();
  ...
};
```

Would this be worthwhile? Probably not. Whenever you start coding functions like *SetData()* and *GetData()*, you should stop and consider what you are doing. Using access functions in this manner isn't much different than using the data directly; and adding the functions just makes the class more complicated than it needs to be.

This isn't to say that all access functions are bad, but that perhaps you should think about how you want your design to be used at a high level. You need to ask yourself how the node objects are to be used. Here, since they are to be handled by the *ChList* class, it might be better for that class to handle the node data. For instance, we might design *ChList* to allow a user to add data to the list, without the user needing to know that list nodes even exist. Instead, we just pass *ChList* the data to be added, and let the list pass back any data that needs to be retrieved. This abstracts the workings of the data structure in a beneficial way. The best bet, then, is to make the data private, but leave out the access functions. Let *ChList*'s friendly access directly manipulate the data.

The copy constructor and overloaded assignment operator functions point out another interesting design issue. What does it mean to copy a list node? If we hadn't methodically included the copy and assignment functions in the node class, we might not have ever asked that question. This proves it's always a good idea to include these two functions in your classes, because you are then forced to think more about your design.

It seems likely that we would want the node data copied, but what about the *next* pointer? If we allow this pointer to be copied, aliasing problems could occur. It seems best to just set the *next* pointer to null in the node copy. That's what our copy constructor and overloaded assignment operator do.

Actually, we might want to go further than that. We might even want to disallow nodes from being copied. We can do this by placing both the copy constructor and overloaded assignment operator in the private section of the class, as we've done here:

```
class ChNode {
  friend ChList; // Let ChList access hidden parts
private:
  ChNode *next;  // Hide this "detail"
  char data;
  ChNode(const ChNode &cn); // Disallow copying
  ChNode &operator=(const ChNode &cn); // Disallow assignment
public:
  ChNode();
  ChNode(const char &d, ChNode *n);
};
```

Statements like the following would now be illegal:

```
ChNode a, b;
ChNode c(a); // Illegal
b = a; // Illegal
```

We've now put almost all of our members in the private section of the *ChNode* class. Why not go the full mile and make the entire class private? There are actually some valid reasons for doing so. Recall that the user of a list doesn't really need to know that list nodes exist. We can reinforce this by making the *ChNode* class completely private. That way, only the *ChList* class can use it.

The *ChNode* class is given on disk in the files *chlist.h* and *chlist.cpp*.

Passing Parameters Using Constant References

You'll see in the *ChNode()* general constructor that we pass in characters using a constant reference, as in

```
ChNode::ChNode(const char &d, ChNode *n);
```

This isn't the most efficient way to pass a character, since a character is generally smaller than a reference (the latter being implemented usually as a pointer). However, the use of constant reference syntax has benefits, because it keeps the code consistent with more general cases where we might be passing much larger structures than a character. Passing parameters using constant references is a good habit to develop, even when it may not be completely warranted from an efficiency standpoint. You'll notice that we use the syntax *const X &x* quite often.

It's also a good idea to use a constant reference rather than a plain reference. Besides preventing the object being passed in from being accidently changed, the use of a constant reference makes it easier to pass literals. For instance, we can call the *ChNode* constructor as follows:

```
ChNode mynode('x', 0);
```

Had we declared the constructor without the *const* modifier,

```
ChNode::ChNode(char &d, ChNode *n);
```

then the preceding constructor call would have caused a temporary copy of *'x'* to be made. That prevents the literal *'x'* from accidentally being changed to something else inside the function. Although making a copy of the character isn't really a problem, some compilers print warnings about it, which can be quite a nuisance. (It can also be a blessing in other cases.) Using *const char &d* solves the whole problem.

We're now ready to complete the design of *ChList*, making it more robust. Here is the new definition:

```
class ChList {
protected:
  int out_of_memory;
  ChNode *head;
  void Copy(const ChList &c);
public:
  ChList();
  ChList(const ChList &c);
```

```
  ~ChList();
  ChList &operator=(const ChList &c);
  int AddtoFront(const char &c);
  int RmvHead(char &c);
  void Clear();
  int IsEmpty();
  int IsFull();
};
```

We've added all the proper constructors, an overloaded assignment operator, and a destructor. We've also added a function to copy one list into another, as well as functions to clear the list by removing and freeing all nodes in the list. Also included are functions to determine whether the list is empty or whether it's full. For the latter, we say a list is full if the last *AddtoFront()* operation failed because we couldn't allocate enough memory for a list node. The *out_of_memory* flag keeps track of this. Here are some other functions of the *ChList* class:

```
void ChList::Copy(const ChList &s)
// Copies the list s into this list.
// Clears the contents of this list first.
// ASSUMES the default constructor sets the
// next pointer to zero. May set out_of_memory
// flag if couldn't allocate a node.
{
  Clear();
  ChNode *sn = s.head;
  if (sn) { // Anything to copy?
    ChNode *tn = new ChNode;
    head = tn;
    while(sn && tn) {
      tn->data = sn->data;
      sn = sn->next;
      if (sn) {
        tn->next = new ChNode;
        tn = tn->next;
      }
    }
    if (!tn) out_of_memory = 1;
  }
}

ChList::ChList(const ChList &c)
// Copy constructor
{
  head = 0; out_of_memory = 0;
  Copy(c);
}
```

```
ChList::~ChList()
// Destructor removes all nodes from the list
{
  Clear();
}

ChList &ChList::operator=(const ChList &c)
// Assignment operator. Clears contents of existing
// list, and makes a copy of list c.
{
  Copy(c);
  return *this;
}

int ChList::AddtoFront(const char &c)
// Adds a node to the front of the list,
// making a new head. Returns 1 if successful;
// otherwise, sets out_of_memory flag, and returns 0.
{
  ChNode *t = new ChNode(c, head);
  if (t) {
    head = t;
    return 1;
  }
  else {
    out_of_memory = 1;
    return 0;
  }
}

int ChList::RmvHead(char &c)
// Removes the head from the list, and set
// next node as the head. Returns 1 if there
// was a head to remove (i.e. list not empty),
// and clears memory full flag as well.
// Otherwise, a 0 is returned.
{
  if (head) {
    c = head->data;
    ChNode *p = head;
    head = head->next;
    delete p;
    out_of_memory = 0;
    return 1;
  }
  else return 0;
}
```

```
void ChList::Clear()
// Removes all nodes from the list
{
  char dmy;
  int r;
  do {
    r = RmvHead(dmy);
  } while(r);
}
```

 The *ChList* class is given on disk in the files *chlist.h* and *chlist.cpp*.

Nested Classes

Another way to "hide" the *ChNode* class, besides making all of its members private, is to simply include its class definition inside the *ChList* class. For example:

```
class ChList {
protected:
  class ChNode { // Hide the class by nesting it
  private:
    ChNode(const ChNode &cn);
    ChNode &operator=(const ChNode &cn);
  public:
    ChNode *next;
    char data;
    ChNode();
    ChNode(const char &d, ChNode *n);
  };
  int out_of_memory;
  ChNode *head;
  void Copy(const ChList &c);
public:
  ...
};
```

Nested classes work as follows: the nested class definition is hidden and the only way to access a nested class name is by qualifying it with the name of the enclosing class. For instance, here's how the default *ChNode* destructor is defined outside the class definitions:

```
ChList::ChNode::ChNode()
// Default constructor
{
  data = 0; next = 0;
}
```

The member function name *ChNode()* has two qualifications: *ChList* and *ChNode*, signifying that the function belongs to class *ChNode*, which belongs to class *ChList*. Here's another example using the overloaded assignment operator.

```
ChList::ChNode &ChList::ChNode::operator=(const ChNode &cn)
{
  data = cn.data; next = 0;
}
```

Note that the third use of *ChNode* (inside the parameter list) isn't qualified. We don't need to make this qualification because the context tells the compiler that we're referring to a *ChList::ChNode* object.

The nested class definition is affected by the *private, protected*, and *public* keywords in the enclosing class. We've made *ChNode* protected. That means only *ChList* member functions, or member functions of classes derived from *ChList*, have access to the name *ChNode*. Thus, only these functions can create *ChNode* objects. Had we placed the *ChNode* class definition in the *public* section of *ChList*, we could create *ChNode* objects on the outside, like this:

```
ChList::ChNode mynode; // Assumes ChNode has public access
```

Remember that this only works if *ChNode* is declared in a public section. If *ChNode* is declared in a protected or private section, you can't access the name *ChNode,* even using the *ChList* qualification.

Nested classes have no special access to the members of the enclosing class nor do members of the enclosing class have any special access to nested classes. It's as though the two classes were defined separately. The distinction is this: the *classes* are nested, but not *objects* of the classes. The member functions of *ChList* can only access the public members of *ChNode*, and only by way of a *ChNode* object. There is no direct access, as you might think. Likewise, members of *ChNode* can only access the public members of *ChList*, and only through *ChList* objects.

Note that we made most of the *ChNode* members public so that *ChList* could easily access them through an object. However, we kept the copy constructor and overloaded assignment operator private. This way, even *ChList* member functions cannot accidently copy *ChNode* objects.

While this alternative method for declaring cooperating classes has its merits, we'll be primarily using the first method (declaring the classes separately) because it is often less confusing.

The alternative design for the *ChNode* and *ChList* classes is given on disk in the files *chlist2.h* and *chlist2.cpp*.

Data Structure Design in C++

hapter 2 provided some overall principles for working with classes in C++. In this chapter, we'll get more specific by discussing some fundamental design issues involved in defining data structures. In particular, we'll discuss concrete data types, abstract data types, and then parameterized types (templates). Finally, we'll provide a discussion on using containers and single-rooted hierarchies.

This chapter should help explain why the data structures you'll see in later chapters are designed the way they are. We advocate a direct approach to data structure design, with concrete data types and templates playing a major role.

CONCRETE DATA TYPES

As you implement different data structures, you'll probably begin to build your own library containing the most effective and elegant designs. There are two fundamental ways you can go about this:

- Design the tools using concrete data types
- Design the tools using abstract data types

Concrete data types represent direct implementations of a concept, usually designed for specific purposes. For instance, the list and node classes used in Chapter 2 are concrete, since they give a specific implementation for linked lists and only work with character nodes. In contrast, *abstract data types* provide a general-purpose design; the idea is to allow the user to program at a fairly high level, with all the low-level details kept hidden. Abstract data types have concrete data types somewhere in their implementations. Typically, an abstract data type might provide two or more concrete data types as alternative imple-

43

mentations that can be interchanged freely, without disturbing too much of an existing application.

To see an example of a concrete data type, take a look at this very simple, and very hard-coded, character stack:

```
class ChStack {
private:
  char data[32]; // Room for 32 characters
  int top;        // Index to top of stack
public:
  ChStack()               { top = 0; }
  void Push(const char &c) { data[top++] = c; }
  void Pop(char &c)       { c = data[-top]; }
};
```

In many ways, classes like *ChStack* embody the best aspects of C++. The *ChStack* class is very efficient, almost and possibly as efficient as a more low-level design would be, yet encapsulation is used effectively. You can only access the contents of the stack through the conventional push and pop stack operations, and you can easily create multiple stacks without worrying about the stack variables interacting with each other. If you use this class in an application, and then later decide to use a more sophisticated implementation (perhaps one that does error checking), it would be simple to make the replacement. The code for the main part of the application might not even have to be changed.

Rational and Compound Numbers

The built-in types—such as *int*, *float*, and *double*—are concrete data types. It's also possible to make user-defined concrete data types that look like built-in types. This can be accomplished by judicious use of constructors, destructors, and overloaded operators. Many C++ implementations provide a complex number class along these lines. You can use the arithmetic and comparison operators on the complex numbers just as you would for any *int* or *float*. In this section, we'll take a similar approach and sketch out the implementation for rational and compound numbers.

A *rational number* is a representation for fractions. Each rational number has a numerator and a denominator. You can extend the notion of rational numbers to include a whole number part as well. A *compound number* contains both a whole number part and a fractional part (that is, a rational number). The following code highlights the main features of a *Rational* class and a *Compound* class used to implement rational and compound numbers:

```
class Rational{
private:
  long n, d; // Numerator and denominator
public:
  // Constructors and assignment
  Rational();
  Rational(long u);
  Rational(long u, long v);
  Rational(const Rational &r);
  Rational &operator=(const Rational &r);
  // Stream I/O operators
  friend istream &operator>>(istream &s, Rational &r);
  friend ostream &operator<<(ostream &s, const Rational &r);
  // Arithmetic operators that modify their operand
  Rational operator++(int);    // Postfix
  Rational operator-(int);     // Postfix
  Rational &operator++();      // Prefix
  Rational &operator-();       // Prefix
  Rational &operator+=(const Rational &r);
  Rational &operator-=(const Rational &r);
  Rational &operator*=(const Rational &r);
  Rational &operator/=(const Rational &r);
  // Arithmetic operators resulting in new object
  Rational operator-() const;
  Rational operator+() const;
  friend Rational operator*(const Rational &a, const Rational &b);
  friend Rational operator/(const Rational &a, const Rational &b);
  friend Rational operator+(const Rational &a, const Rational &b);
  friend Rational operator-(const Rational &a, const Rational &b);
  // Comparison operators
  friend int operator==(const Rational &a, const Rational &b);
  friend int operator!=(const Rational &a, const Rational &b);
  friend int operator<(const Rational &a, const Rational &b);
  friend int operator<=(const Rational &a, const Rational &b);
  friend int operator>(const Rational &a, const Rational &b);
  friend int operator>=(const Rational &a, const Rational &b);
  // Other helper functions
  ...
};

class Compound {
private:
  long w;      // Whole number part
  Rational f; // Fractional part
public:
  // Member functions, similar to those for the Rational class
  ...
};
```

Besides having the usual assortment of constructors, a destructor, and an overloaded assignment operator, the *Rational* and *Compound* classes implement most of the arithmetic operators, as well as the comparison operators. The idea is to make rational and compound numbers work just like ordinary integers or floats work for standard arithmetic and comparison operations.

The details of the *Rational* and *Compound* classes are beyond the scope of this book. See the code note below for more information. Our main goal here is to show that classes like *Rational* and *Compound* are good examples of concrete data types.

The code for the Rational class, along with a test program, can be found on disk in the files *rational.h*, *rational.cpp*, and *rattst.cpp*. The code for the Compound class, along with a test program, can be found in the files *cmpnd.h*, *cmpnd.cpp*, and *cmpndtst.cpp*.

ABSTRACT DATA TYPES

Abstract data types are the opposite of concrete data types, but are just as useful. The idea is to avoid being committed to a specific implementation. For instance, a stack can be implemented using an array or by using a linked list. At a high level, it doesn't matter which of these structures you use. What matters is that the operations *push* and *pop* are defined.

Abstract data types can be realized in C++ by using a class derivation hierarchy. The base class of the hierarchy spells out the operations to be performed on the abstract data type, providing as few details as possible. The derived classes then provide more concrete implementations. It's often advantageous to make the base class an *abstract class*, which has one or more *pure virtual functions*. A pure virtual function is a virtual function that does not have a body. Instead, the body is set to null. For example, here is an abstract character stack class:

```
class AbsChStk { // An abstract character stack class
private:
  // Prevent copy constructing and assignment
  AbsChStk(const AbsChStk &) { }
  void operator=(const AbsChStk &) { }
public:
  AbsChStk() { }
  virtual ~AbsChStk() { }
  virtual int Push(const char &c) = 0;
  virtual int Pop(char &c) = 0;
  virtual int IsEmpty() = 0;
  virtual int IsFull() = 0;
};
```

The functions *Push()*, *Pop()*, *IsEmpty()*, and *IsFull()* are all pure virtual functions. Since they have no bodies, it's not possible to actually call these functions (without getting runtime errors). Instead, the idea is to derive one or more classes that override these functions. The consequence is that you can't directly declare an object of an abstract class. You must only work with derived class objects. However, you can use abstract class pointers (or references), which point to derived class objects. For example:

```
class ChArrStk : public AbsChStk { }     // Derive array version
class ChListStk : public AbsChStk { }     // Derive list version

void Doit(AbsChStk *pstk)
{
  pstk->Push('x');                        // Calls virtual function
}

ChArrStk my_arr_stk;
ChListStk my_list_stk;
...
// Choose stack implementation at runtime:

Doit(&my_arr_stk);                        // Use array version
...
Doit(&my_list_stk);                       // Use list version
```

Code that uses abstract class pointers in this manner can be quite versatile.

Even though you can't directly declare abstract class objects, it's possible to cause their copy constructors or overloaded assignment operators to be invoked. Consider the following code:

```
AbsChStk *p, *q;
*p = *q; // AbsChStk::operator=() called
```

Normally you wouldn't do this, but it may happen by accident. The way to prevent accidental assignments like this is to define an overloaded assignment operator and make it private, as we did earlier for the *ChNode* class. We use this technique on the *AbsChStk* class for both the assignment operator and the copy constructor.

Once you have an abstract class defined, you can derive concrete implementations in two ways: using *single inheritance* or using *multiple inheritance*. With single inheritance, the derived class has only one direct parent. With multiple inheritance, the derived class may have two or more parents. Figure 3.1 illustrates these techniques within the context of creating stack classes.

Figure 3.1 Stack classes created with single versus multiple inheritance.

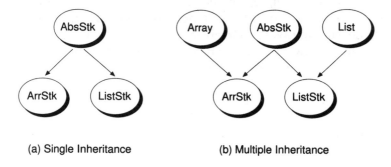

(a) Single Inheritance   (b) Multiple Inheritance

Using Single Inheritance

Let's look first at using the single inheritance technique for deriving classes. Here's how we might derive an array-based stack from the abstract stack class:

```
class ChArrStk : public AbsChStk {
private:
  int sz, top; // Dimensioned size and top of stack
  char *data;  // Stack data
  void Copy(const ChArrStk &s);
public:
  ChArrStk();
  ChArrStk(const ChArrStk &s);
  ChArrStk(int n);
  virtual ~ChArrStk();
  ChArrStk &operator=(const ChArrStk &s);
  virtual int Push(const char &c);
  virtual int Pop(char &c);
  virtual int IsEmpty();
  virtual int IsFull();
};
```

The storage for the stack is allocated dynamically to hold up to n elements using a constructor and de-allocated using the destructor:

```
ChArrStk::ChArrStk(int n)
{
  data = new char[sz = n];
  top = 0;
}
```

```
ChArrStk::~ChArrStk()
{
  delete[] data;
}
```

Again, we provide a full complement of constructors and an overloaded assignment, even though we may never need to use them. They provide us with an element of safety. Both the copy constructor and assignment operator (not shown), work by copying the stack data, rather than by copying just the pointer to the data.

The interesting part is how the pure virtual functions are overloaded in *ChArrStk* to implement array-based stack operations:

```
int ChArrStk::Push(const char &c)
// Pushes c onto the stack, if it can. Returns
// 1 if successful. Returns 0 if stack was
// full coming in.
{
  if (!IsFull()) {
     data[top++] = c;
     return 1;
  }
  else return 0;
}

int ChArrStk::Pop(char &c)
// Pops element from the stack, and returns
// its value in c. Returns 1 if stack wasn't
// empty before pop; otherwise, returns 0.
{
  if (!IsEmpty()) {
     c = data[-top];
     return 1;
  }
  else return 0;
}

int ChArrStk::IsEmpty() { return top == 0; }

int ChArrStk::IsFull()  { return top == sz; }
```

Both *Push()* and *Pop()* check for the stack being full and empty, respectively, before allowing the operations to occur. The *IsEmpty()* and *IsFull()* functions check the current top of the stack to see if it is in bounds, given the size of the array holding the stack data.

How efficient is the derived stack compared to the concrete stack we gave earlier? The derived stack class will be slower, due to the overhead caused by the indirect virtual function calls. In addition to this performance hit, the use of virtual functions also reduces the chances that the functions can be made inline. In our concrete stack class, *Push()* and *Pop()* could be inlined, resulting in significant performance gains. Whether this matters depends on how often *Push()* and *Pop()* are called and how tight a loop they might be in. For many applications, the virtual function overhead may not be noticeable.

Next, let's derive a list-based stack class:

```
class ChListStk : public AbsChStk {
protected:
  int out_of_memory;
  ChNode *head;
  void Copy(const ChListStk &s);
public:
  ChListStk();
  ChListStk(const ChListStk &s);
  virtual ~ChListStk();
  ChListStk &operator=(const ChListStk &s);
  void Clear();
  virtual int Push(const char &c);
  virtual int Pop(char &c);
  virtual int IsEmpty();
  virtual int IsFull();
};
```

This class is very similar to the *ChList* class we provided in Chapter 2. It even uses the same cooperating *ChNode* class to define the nodes of the stack. The main difference is that the list operations are defined in terms of stack operations. The *Push()* and *Pop()* routines are the same as the *AddToFront()* and *RmvFront()* *ChList* routines. For example, here's the *Push()* routine:

```
int ChListStk::Push(const char &c)
// Pushes c onto the stack, if it can. Returns
// 1 if successful; returns 0 if not.
{
  ChNode *t = new ChNode(c, head);
  if (t) {
    head = t;
    return 1;
  }
  else {
    out_of_memory = 1;
    return 0;
  }
}
```

The code for the array and list-based stacks, using single inheritance, is given on disk in the files *stk1.cpp* and *stk2.cpp*, respectively. The abstract stack class is given in the file *abschstk.h*.

Using Multiple Inheritance

In the previous section, we derived a list-based stack class from scratch. But you might have wondered why we didn't use the existing *ChList* class. In fact, we *can* do this by using multiple inheritance. This technique is one of the main uses of multiple inheritance. The basic idea is to merge one class with another, creating a new type of class. It's like doing genetic cross breeding. For instance, we can merge *AbsChStk* with *ChList* to create a new *ChListStk* class:

```
class ChListStk : public AbsChStk, private ChList {
private:
  void Copy(const ChListStk &s);
public:
  ChListStk();
  ChListStk(const ChListStk &s);
  virtual ~ChListStk();
  ChListStk &operator=(const ChListStk &s);
  virtual int Push(const char &c);
  virtual int Pop(char &c);
  virtual int IsEmpty();
  virtual int IsFull();
};
```

The trick is to override the virtual functions of the abstract base class and make calls to the list class to perform the operations. For example, here's how *Push()*, *Pop()*, *IsEmpty()*, and *IsFull()* are defined:

```
int ChListStk::Push(const char &c)
{
  return AddtoFront(c);    // Calls ChList::AddToFront()
}

int ChListStk::Pop(char &c)
{
  return RmvHead(c);       // Calls ChList::RmvHead()
}

int ChListStk::IsEmpty() { return ChList::IsEmpty(); }

int ChListStk::IsFull()  { return ChList::IsFull(); }
```

Notice how we had to qualify the *IsEmpty()* and *IsFull()* function calls to avoid ambiguities. That's because both *AbsChStk* and *ChList* have *IsEmpty()* and *IsFull()* functions. Resolving ambiguities like this is one reason why multiple inheritance can be tricky to use.

One subtle feature of our derived class is that we used private inheritance for the *ChList* base class. By doing so, we disallow the user of the stack class from directly calling the list-oriented functions (such as *AddToFront()*). We also disallow stack objects from being used as lists. We want to use the stack in terms of stack operations, not list operations.

How well does the multiple inheritance approach perform? Due to the multiple base classes, there is more overhead in virtual function calling. As a result, the runtime performance may be slightly slower than it would be for single inheritance. The class will probably also consume more space. However, these costs may be small prices to pay for the ability to elegantly piece together new classes from existing ones.

A complete running program using a list-based, multiply-derived stack class is given on disk in the file *stk4.cpp*. Also, a corresponding array-based version is given in *stk3.cpp*, and in the files *charr.h* and *charr.cpp*.

PARAMETERIZED TYPES (TEMPLATES)

The *AbsChStk* class that we created in the previous section is fairly general, but not as general as it could be. *AbsChStk* only works for stacks that store characters. But what if we want to store integers, or floats, or window objects? Ideally, we want the type of element that gets stored to be a parameter to the basic stack type itself. We can do this through the use of templates, which are C++'s way to implement *parameterized types*. Concrete data types and abstract data types can both be made into templates.

A Parameterized Stack Class

Let's return to our first concrete stack class and parameterize it so that we can define it for different types of elements. Here is the original definition:

```
class ChStack {
private:
  char data[32];
  int top;
public:
  ChStack()              { top = 0; }
  void Push(const char &c) { data[top++] = c; }
  void Pop(char &c)        { c = data[-top]; }
};
```

Note how we explicitly define the stack data to be of type *char*. We can make this definition more general by using a typedef to define the stack data type. While we're at it, we'll use a constant to define the size of the stack, and change the class name to *Stack*:

```
typedef char TYPE;
const int SIZE = 32;

class Stack {
private:
  TYPE data[SIZE];
  int top;
public:
  Stack()                 { top = 0; }
  void Push(const TYPE &c) { data[top++] = c; }
  void Pop(TYPE &c)        { c = data[-top]; }
};
```

Now, by changing the definition of *TYPE* and *SIZE,* we can easily define the stack to work with any type, and be any size we desire. Unfortunately, we can only define *TYPE* and *SIZE* once, which means we can't easily define more than one stack class. For example, we can't define a stack of windows as well as a stack of characters. Nor can we have a stack of 10 characters in conjunction with a stack of 100 characters.

The solution is to use C++ *templates*. Here is the stack class rewritten using templates:

```
template<class TYPE, int SIZE>
class Stack {
private:
  TYPE data[SIZE];
  int top;
public:
  Stack()                 { top = 0; }
  void Push(const TYPE &c) { data[top++] = c; }
  void Pop(TYPE &c)        { c = data[-top]; }
};
```

The *template<>* syntax is placed in front of the class definition. Between the <> brackets are the parameters that you want for the template. You can have two kinds of parameters: those that specify type names and those that specify constant expressions. Type names are identified by using the *class* keyword. (This use of the *class* keyword has nothing to do with its other use—to define classes.) You can use any valid type name as a parameter, such as *char, float,* or *ChNode.* You can even use another parameterized type!

For constant expression parameters, you must specify the type of the expression, otherwise it defaults to *int.*

With our stack template in hand, we can now define different types of stacks, then declare objects from them. For example:

```
Stack<char, 32> mystack;
Stack<int, 100> yourstack;
Stack<ChList, 42> exoticstack;
```

Each of these declarations defines a new stack type and then creates an object of that type. The third declaration defines a stack of linked lists (for some exotic purpose, presumably). Syntax such as *Stack<char, 32>* is known as a *template declaration.* You can use template declarations anywhere a type name can be used. For example, a template declaration can be used in a *typedef* statement:

```
typedef Stack<ChList, 42> StackOfLists;
StackOfLists exoticstack;
```

Template declarations actually cause classes to be generated internally by the compiler. Each generated class is called a *template instantiation.* For example, the compiler might internally generate the following class for the declaration *Stack<ChList, 42>.* (We've given the generated class an arbitrary but presumably unique name.)

```
class Stack_ChList_42 {
private:
  ChList data[42];
  int top;
public:
  Stack_ChList_42()          { top = 0; }
  void Push(const ChList &c) { data[top++] = c; }
  void Pop(ChList &c)        { c = data[-top]; }
};
```

For every template declaration with different parameters, the compiler creates a new instantiation of the template. With templates, we're reusing source code rather than compiled code. This is both the boon and the bane of templates. There is no runtime overhead associated with templates. A class instantiated from a template will be just as efficient as one defined directly. Unfortunately, a classic speed versus space tradeoff occurs, because each new template instantiation increases the program's code space. All of the methods of the class must be replicated (and then modified accordingly). Taken to the extreme, this is known as *source code explosion.*

With our stack template, the space requirements can become severe. Not only is a new class generated each time we use a new stack element type, but each time we declare a stack of a different size. For instance, the following declarations cause two stack classes to be generated:

```
typedef Stack<char, 4> QuadStack;
typedef Stack<char, 6> HexStack;
```

If, however, both parameters were to match in the declarations, only one stack class would be generated (as long as the compiler is smart enough not to generate the class twice). This is true even if we use parameters that appear different but are really the same. For instance, the following code creates two objects but only one stack class:

```
Stack<char, 4> mystack;
Stack<char, 2+2> yourstack;
```

One way to alleviate the code explosion in our stack template is to take the size parameter out of the template and place it in the stack constructor instead. This technique changes the allocation of the stack data from static to dynamic, as in the following code:

```
template<class TYPE>
class Stack {
private:
  TYPE *data;
  int top;
public:
  Stack(int sz) { top = 0; data = new TYPE[sz]; }
  ~Stack() { delete[] data; }
  void Push(const TYPE &c) { data[top++] = c; }
  void Pop(TYPE &c)        { c = data[-top]; }
};
```

The constructor takes care of the allocation, and the destructor de-allocates the data. Compare the way we create objects from this new stack template with the old way:

```
Stack<char, 42> mystk;       // Using static allocation
Stack<char> yourstk(42);     // Using dynamic allocation

void f(int sz)
{
  Stack<char, sz> mystk;     // Can't do; sz isn't constant!
  Stack<char> yourstk(sz);   // OK
}
```

Is it better to statically allocate or dynamically allocate the stack data? The dynamic method is certainly more flexible and leads to less source code explosion. However, it requires the use of a heap. With static allocation, we don't need a heap. This means we could more easily use a statically allocated stack in environments with scarce resources, such as ROM-based process control software.

 A sample program using a stack template similar to the one just shown is given on disk in the file *stktmpl.cpp*.

Function Templates

You can also define function templates. Actually, we've already done this with the stack class, since the stack methods are all templates. You may not have realized this because the methods were declared inline. To show the template syntax, we'll declare a few of the stack methods outside the class:

```
template<class TYPE>
Stack<TYPE>::Stack(int sz)
{
  top = 0; data = new TYPE[sz];
}

template<class TYPE>
void Stack<TYPE>::Push(const TYPE &c)
{
  data[top++] = c;
}
```

The *template<>* parameter list is placed in front of function templates, as is the case with class templates. Recall that class methods are qualified with the class type, using the *::* scoping operator. For class templates, the class type is parameterized. That's why we use the following syntax to qualify the functions:

```
Stack<TYPE>::Stack(int sz)
void Stack<TYPE>::Push(const TYPE &c)
```

Note that we don't use the syntax *Stack<TYPE>::Stack<TYPE>(int sz)* for the constructor. The function name *Stack* isn't parameterized, just as the function name *Push* isn't parameterized. Only the type name is parameterized.

Class methods aren't the only types of functions that can be made into templates. For example, we can parameterize a sort function, such as the following *InsertionSort()* routine. (See the companion volume for an explanation of insertion sorting [Flamig 93].)

```
template<class TYPE>
void InsertionSort(TYPE *a, int n)
{
  int i, j;
  TYPE item_to_sort;

  for(i = 1; i < n; i++) {
    item_to_sort = a[i];
    j = i;
    while(item_to_sort > a[j-1]) {
        a[j] = a[j-1];
        j -= 1;
        if (j == 0) break;
    }
    a[j] = item_to_sort;
  }
}
```

This sorting template will work for arrays of most types of data. For instance, we could sort an array of compound numbers as follows:

```
Compound arr[10];
...
InsertionSort(arr, 10);
```

When the compiler sees this function call, it looks at how the array is defined and determines that the *TYPE* parameter is *Compound*. It then generates a sort function specific to compound number arrays. Here's a sketch of what's generated:

```
void InsertionSort_Compound(Compound *a, int n)
{
  ...
  Compound item_to_sort;

  for(...) {
    ...
    while(item_to_sort < a[j-1]) {
    ...
    }
    ...
  }
}
```

Although the sort template will work for most array types, it does make one assumption. The operator < must be defined for *TYPE*. Thus, the template would work fine for integer arrays, float arrays, and so on, but you must be careful with arrays of user-defined objects. In our example, we defined < for compound numbers, so we're safe. If < isn't defined for *TYPE*, a compiler error will be generated.

In general, the types you use as parameters to templates should be fairly robust. At the very least, these types should have well-defined default constructors, copy constructors, and assignment operators. Also, if your function templates involve any arithmetic or comparison operations, you must ensure that the template parameter types have these operations defined as well. In fact, the closer the types are to looking like built-in types (as is the case with compound numbers), the more likely it is that you won't have problems.

Overriding Function Templates

A typical problem occurs when you try to sort character strings with a sort function template. For instance:

```
char names[10][80]; // An array of 10, 80 byte character strings
InsertionSort(names, 10);
```

Will this work as expected? No. The problem lies in the compare statement within the sort function:

```
while(item_to_sort < a[j-1]) {
```

Since the items being sorted are actually character pointers, we're sorting the values of the pointers instead of the text being pointed to. Thus, we would get back the array sorted by addresses. One solution is to define a class to handle the comparisons. For example:

```
class String {
private:
  char *text;
  ...
public:
  String(char *s);
  friend int operator<String &a, String &b);
  ...
};

String::String(char *s)
{
  text = strdup(s);
}
...
int operator<(String &a, String &b)
{
```

```
    return strcmp(a.text, b.text) < 0;
}
...
String strings[3] = { // Declare array of strings
  String("frosty"), String("morning"), String("cold")
};

InsertSort(strings, 3); // Sort the strings
```

Another method is to override the sort function template itself and provide a specific version just for character strings. You can override a function template for a specific set of template parameters by providing a function that takes the correct parameters. For example, here is a character string insertion sort function:

```
void InsertionSort(char **a, int n)
{
  int i, j;
  char *item_to_sort;

  for(i = 1; i < n; i++) {
    item_to_sort = a[i];
    j = i;
    while(strcmp(item_to_sort, a[j-1]) > 0) {
      a[j] = a[j-1];
      j -= 1;
      if (j == 0) break;
    }
    a[j] = item_to_sort;
  }
}
```

Here, we've replaced *TYPE* with *char **, and we've modified the while loop to call the *strcmp()* function. If the compiler sees this function when trying to instantiate the *InsertionSort()* template for *char **, it will use the function instead of the template. We can make the compiler use the overriding function by placing its function prototype in the same header file where the template occurs. The exact placement is implementation dependent. (We'll discuss the implementation-dependent details of templates later in this chapter.)

The *InsertionSort()* template is small enough to be easily overriden for different array element types. In general, though, the first method we described (defining the > operator properly through a *String* class) is probably a better solution. However, overriding template functions can be quite handy, as you'll see in later chapters. Also, there are other ways to handle the comparison operator problems for sort function templates. The book [Stroustrup 91] discusses some additional techniques that you can use.

Restrictions on Template Functions

Although most functions can be turned into templates, there is a restriction: Each parameter of the template must somehow be used in the parameters of the function. Why is this necessary? The compiler can only determine which template instantiation to use for a function call by looking at the function parameter types. For example, in the *InsertionSort()* function, the array parameter's type determines the template parameter *TYPE*. Here are some examples of illegal function templates:

```
template<class TYPE> void f(int v);        // Illegal: TYPE not used
template<class TYPE, int SZ> void g(TYPE *a);  // Illegal: SZ not used
```

This restriction isn't as noticeable for member functions. You don't need to explicitly use the template parameters here. Why? Each member function has a hidden *this* pointer passed as an argument, and this argument will have all of the template parameters as part of its type specification. For instance, the stack constructor is actually represented internally as something like:

```
Stack_TYPE(Stack<TYPE> *this, int sz);
```

Combining Templates and Inheritance

Since templates can cause source code explosion, you may wonder if they are really all that useful. If you were to use the *InsertionSort()* template for 20 different array types, then 20 different sort routines would be generated. A more general sort routine, built to use abstract class pointers and virtual functions, might be better in this case. But how often would you actually use a sort template for 20 different types, in any given application? Probably not as often as you might think. If the number of instantiations is small, and the templates in question are small, the total code space for the templates might actually be smaller than the space required for a general-purpose, inheritance-oriented version. In any case, the templates will most likely be faster.

You can sometimes get the best of both worlds by combining templates with inheritance. The idea is to create a base class that does most of the work, and then derive class templates that work for specific types. For example, consider the following *RecFile* class, which is designed to make it easy to do record-oriented I/O with file stream objects:

```
class RecFile {
protected:
  enum io_dir { f_read, f_write };
  fstream fs;    // Embedded fstream object
  int recsize;   // Record size in bytes
  long curr_rec; // Current record (count by zero)
```

```
  char name[80]; // Name of the file
  int IO(io_dir dir, void *data, int nrecs, long recno=-1);
public:
  RecFile(int rsize = 1); // Default to character I/O
  ~RecFile();
  virtual int Open(char *fname, int omode);
  virtual int Close(void);
  int IsOpen();
  int State();
  long Seek(long recno, io_dir which, ios::seek_dir mode=ios::beg);
};
```

With this class, the record size is stored in *recsize*, which is then used by the *Seek()* and *IO()* routines to compute the actual byte offset of a record. The trouble is that to read and write records, *IO()* uses a void pointer to pass the record data. Obviously, this isn't very type-safe, so we've made *IO()* a protected member. To actually use the *RecFile* class, you must derive classes that are type specific. The following *FileOf* derived class template shows how:

```
template<class TYPE>
class FileOf : public RecFile {
public:
  FileOf() : RecFile(sizeof(TYPE)) { }
  int Read(TYPE &data, long recno = -1) {
    return IO(f_read, &data, 1, recno);
  }
  int Write(TYPE &data, long recno = -1) {
    return IO(f_write, &data, 1, recno);
  }
};
```

Note how *sizeof(TYPE)* is passed to the base class *RecFile()* constructor to determine the record size, and how *Read()* and *Write()* cause the necessary type conversions to be performed when calling *IO()*. Here's a sketch of how you might use *FileOf*:

```
FileOf<Compound> myfile; // Declare file of compound number records

myfile.Open("test.fil", ios::in | ios::out | ios::trunc);

Compound x;
. . .
myfile.Write(x, 17); // Write x to record 17
myfile.Read(x, 1);   // Read record 1 into x
```

By using *FileOf*, we can implement an entire family of record-oriented file classes, one for each type of record, as shown in Figure 3.2. *FileOf* is especially

---

Figure 3.2 A template-based family of classes.

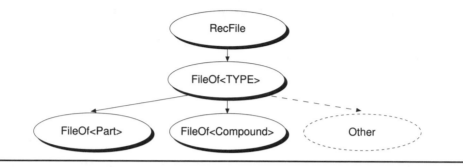

---

useful because it is type-safe, but because it uses inline functions exclusively it may not cause any extra code to be generated. Classes such as *FileOf* are often called *interface classes*, and they show once again that C++ can be both efficient and high level.

 A complete running program using the *RecFile* and *FileOf* classes can be found on disk in the files *recfile.h*, *recfile.cpp*, and *rftst.cpp*.

Compiler-Dependent Template Issues

As of this writing, the implementation of templates has not been completely standardized for the C++ language. The most significant problem lies in trying to keep all the template instantiations straight. There are three main difficulties:

- Like inline functions, the template definitions must be available when a template declaration is seen, so that the compiler can expand the template and generate the specific code.
- It's easy to produce multiple template instantiations, which can cause linker errors.
- Some compilers aren't able to automatically instantiate the correct templates in complex cases (such as when the templates are part of a class derivation hierarchy.)

To solve the first two problems, the ideal solution is to have the compiler automatically determine when a template is first being instantiated for a given set of parameters, and to prevent further instantiations. Currently, there is no standard way of doing this. However, two basic approaches have emerged:

1. *Include the complete template definition in a header file—methods and all.* That way, wherever the template is used, the compiler has all the information about the template at its disposal. Since header files are often included in more than one source file, this can lead to multiple definition errors.

Some compilers have smart linkers that detect these cases and throw out all but one of the instantiations.

2. *Include only the class template definitions (but not the non-inline functions) in the header files.* For non-inline function templates, include only the function prototypes. In one or more special source files, define the methods (and function bodies) for the templates, and then instantiate them for all sets of template parameters to be used by the application. Then link these source files into the application.

In this book, we will use the first approach (including all the template definitions in the header file). We do this not because it's better than the second approach, but because it's easier. Keep this in mind, and don't be afraid to change the code on the disk to suit your needs. To make it easier to switch between the two approaches, we will use the following strategy: only the class template definitions and function template prototypes will be given directly in the header files. The class template methods will be placed in special files with *.mth* extensions. (Here, *mth* stands for methods.) These *.mth* files will then be included in the header files via *#include* statements. Figure 3.3 illustrates this idea. You can easily take the *#include* statements out of the header files and rearrange the template code any way you wish.

The other problem we mentioned—(the inability of the compilers to automatically instantiate the correct template) may occur in some C++ compilers with early implementations of templates. (Borland C++ 3.0 and 3.1 are examples.) In some cases, you'll get linker errors saying that a function cannot be found, even though there is a template for it. In cases like this, the best strategy is to go ahead and declare a template function prototype with the correct parameters. Here is an example that uses the *Array* templates from Chapter 4:

```
void PrtArray(DVarray<int> &a); // Declare template function prototype
```

This is often enough to help out the compilers. See the code on disk for Chapter 4 for numerous examples of this.

Figure 3.3 File organization for templates used in this book.

stack.h:

```
template<class TYPE>
class Stack {
   ...
};
...
#include "stack.mth"
```

stack.mth:

```
template<class TYPE>
Stack<TYPE>::Stack(int sz)
{
   ...
}
...
```

Getting Along without Templates

In case your compiler doesn't support templates, we'll now show you how to turn the template code in this book into non-template code. The technique involves using a good editor that has search and replace capabilities. We'll use the constructor for the stack template as an example and turn it into a constructor that's specific for compound numbers. Similar techniques can be used for normal function templates, as well as complete template classes. Here is the original definition of the stack template constructor:

```
template<class TYPE>
Stack<TYPE>::Stack(int sz)
{
  top = 0; data = new TYPE[sz];
}
```

Follow these basic conversion steps:

1. Make a copy of the template to be modified. Then, remove all occurrences of the template prefix (for instance, *template<Parm1, Parm2, . . .>*) from this copy. The code provided in this book always keeps the prefix on a separate line, making this easy to do: Just delete the line that the prefix is on.

2. Remove all occurrences of *<Parm1, Parm2, . . .>* by using search and replace. (That is, replace the string with nothing.) For example:

```
Stack<TYPE>::Stack ===> Stack::Stack
```

3. Replace each occurrence of the template parameter names with the specific names you would like to use. For instance, we'll replace every occurrence of *TYPE* with *Compound.* Now our stack template looks like the following:

```
Stack::Stack(int sz)
{
  top = 0; data = new Compound[sz];
}
```

4. Replace all occurrences of the class name with a unique name. You can do this by using the template parameters in the name. For example, you could add the suffix _*Compound*:

```
Stack_Compound::Stack_Compound(int sz)
{
  top = 0; data = new Compound[sz];
}
```

Note that this search and replace process is fairly easy for simple templates, but when you start working with complicated template schemes (such as those that have multiple parameters or that mix in inheritance), it can get tricky.

It's possible to define templates using macros. In fact, many early C++ implementations had a *generic.h* header that provided a standard way to define templates with macros. However, this approach involves using multiple-line macros, a tedious and extremely error-prone technique. Your best bet is to find a compiler that directly supports templates.

CONTAINERS

Data structures such as arrays and linked lists are often called *containers,* because they are used to store, or contain, other objects. Stacks and trees are also examples of containers. Because containers are so widely used, it's worthwhile to look at some issues that are common to all containers. There are two fundamental issues:

- Can you have different types of data in the container?
- Who owns the data in the container?

Homogenous versus Heterogenous Containers

A container can hold objects that are all the same type, or it can hold objects of different types. The former is called a *homogenous container,* the latter is called a *heterogenous container.*

An array is an example of a homogenous container, since by definition it is a sequence of objects of the same type. Strictly speaking, *all* containers in C++—such as linked lists, trees, and so forth—are homogenous. That's because C++ is a statically typed language. For instance, list nodes can only store one type of data, as in the following character list node:

```
struct ChNode {
  char data; // Node data is a character
  ChNode *next;
};
```

If this is true, how can we get heterogenous containers? The answer for C++ is that we can't—at least not exactly. However, we *can* emulate heterogenous containers by storing pointers to objects in the containers, rather than the objects themselves. We could make our list node general purpose by changing the *char* type to a *void* pointer, as in:

```
struct GNode {
  void *data; // Points to data allocated elsewhere
  ChNode *next;
};
```

The same idea can be used with arrays:

```
void *general_array[42];
```

By using *void* pointers, we can use any type of data with our containers. While this is certainly the ultimate in flexibility, the downside is that we must be very careful that an object taken out of the container is given the same type it had when it went into the container. Safe type casting becomes a major concern. For example:

```
class Container { ... }; // Some type of container class

int i;
Compound c;
Container w;

w.PutAt(1, &i); // Store objects in container
w.PutAt(2, &c);

int j = *((int *)w.GetAt(2)); // Wrong type casts!
Compound d = *((Compound *)w.GetAt(1);
```

One way to tame unruly containers that store object pointers is to allow only certain types of pointers to be stored. For example, we can use base class pointers rather than *void* pointers. Because of the special relationship between base and derived classes, the base class pointers can point not only to base class objects but also to objects of any classes derived from the base. It can't, however, point to other types of objects (without unscrupulous typecasts, that is). It's actually quite useful and intuitive to restrict the type of object pointers being stored to those that belong to some hierarchy.

A perfect example of this approach is a stack of window objects. We might have different types of windows—such as dialog boxes, menus, and browsing windows—all derived from the same window root class. Figure 3.4 illustrates this setup, where we've used the class names *Window, Dialog, Menu,* and *Browser.* A window stack is used to define the overlapping order of the windows as they appear on screen. The stack might be defined and used as follows:

```
class WindowStack {
private:
  Window *contents[42]; // Allows 42 window object pointers
```

Figure 3.4 A window class hierarchy.

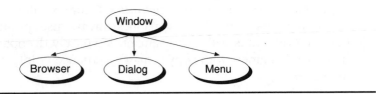

```
  ...
public:
  ...
  int Push(const Window *w);
  int Pop(const Window *&w);
};

WindowStack wstk;
Window *top;
Dialog d;
Browser b;

wstk.Push(&d);
wstk.Push(&b);

wstk.Pop(top);
top->Remove(); // Call virtual Remove() function

wstk.Pop(top);
((Browser *)top)->LoadFile(); // OOPS! Wrong cast
```

The last statement shows that, even with this setup, we don't eliminate type casting problems. Because generic *Windows* pointers are used, when we pop the current window off the stack, we won't know what type of window we just obtained. If we guess wrong, the results could be catastrophic. We'll have more to say about this later in the chapter.

A Question of Ownership

A problem immediately surfaces whenever we store an object in a container indirectly, through a pointer: Who owns the object? Who is responsible for making sure the object gets destroyed when it's no longer needed? Should it be the container, or the entity that initially created the object? Aliasing problems abound because we're using pointers to the object. It's safer to simply store a copy of the object. However, by storing a copy, we may lose the flexibility of storing different types of data. And if the objects are large, we may waste a lot of space. Here, the tradeoff is one of space versus flexibility.

Containers that share objects with other entities are said to have *share semantics*. Containers that store copies of objects (even if they're the only copies) are said to have *copy semantics*. Figure 3.5 illustrates this difference.

Containers with share semantics always use pointers or references to objects. Containers with copy semantics typically do not. But it's interesting to note that containers with copy semantics *can* use pointers. Consider the following code:

```
// An array of pointers with copy semantics
int *a[2];

a[0] = new int(42); // Only a[0] has access to new object
delete a[0];        // Only a[0] destroys the object

a[1] = new int(17); // Only a[1] has access to new object
delete a[1];        // Only a[1] destroys the object
```

As long as each element of the array is the only entity using the object being pointed to, no sharing occurs. Thus, the array *a* can certainly be said to have copy semantics. You won't normally see pointer arrays with copy semantics used directly like this, but it can occur quite often in classes. Consider the following *WindowManager* class, which handles the creation and deletion of the objects it stores.

```
class WindowMgr {
private:
  Stack<Window *> wstk;
public:
  ...
  CreateDialog(int w, int h) { wstk.Push(new Dialog(w, h)); }
  CreateBrowser(int w, int h) { wstk.Push(new Browser(w, h)); }
  RmvWindow(int id) { delete wstk[id]; FixupStack(); }
};
```

Figure 3.5 Copy and share semantics.

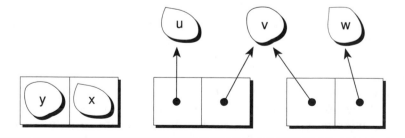

Sometimes, you'll want a container class to manage the objects for you. Sometimes you won't. To build in this flexibility, you might store a flag in the container. The flag indicates who is to own the objects: the container or something outside the container. This "ownership" flag can be set at runtime when the container is constructed.

To provide even more flexibility, you might let each object decide who owns it. For instance, an ownership flag could be stored in each object. When an object is passed to a container, the ownership flag can be set to indicate whether the object should be deleted when the container no longer needs it.

Generalizing further, you can store a counter in each object. The counter gets incremented and decremented when containers hold and let go of the objects. Counters such as this are called *reference counts*. When an object's reference count goes to zero, it can safely be destroyed, since no other object points to it. We'll be using reference count schemes throughout the book.

Collection Classes and Single-Rooted Hierarchies

It's possible to abstract the notion of container classes into what are called *collection classes*. While a container class directly uses a specific storage mechanism—such as an array, linked list, or tree—with a collection class, that underlying storage mechanism is kept hidden. Collection classes were made popular by the Smalltalk language, and many C++ libraries have attempted to emulate Smalltalk-like collection classes.

The following *Bag* class is an example of a collection class:

```
class Bag {
protected:
  // Some way of containing objects defined here
  ...
public:
  // Functions to add and remove objects from the bag
  int Add(Object *x);
  int Find(char *objkey, Object *x);
  int Remove(char *objkey);
  ...
};
```

A *Bag* is probably the ultimate collection class. You can "throw" objects into a bag and then retrieve them using a key. Ordering and sequencing are not concerns. Of course, you *can* have collections that are ordered or sequenced. For instance, you might have a *SortableCollection* class, derived from a *SequencedCollection* class.

Most collection classes are implemented so that they have share semantics and are by nature heterogenous. Indeed, that's where they get their power. To mitigate the aliasing and type casting problems caused by using share semantics, many collection classes only allow you to store objects derived from a single root class. In such a *single-rooted hierarchy*, the root class defines common features that all objects are to have. For example, each object might have the attributes shown in Table 3.1.

The following *Object* class represents a simple base class of a single-rooted hierarchy. It implements all of the features of Table 3.1, except reference counting:

```
class Object {
protected:
  virtual int IsEqualTo(const Object &fo) const = 0;
public:
  virtual ~Object() { }
  virtual const char *Name() const = 0;
  virtual int ClassId() const = 0;
  virtual ostream &Print(ostream &s) const = 0;
  int IsSameTypeAs(const Object &x) const;
  friend int operator==(const Object &a, const Object &b);
  friend int operator!=(const Object &a, const Object &b);
  friend ostream &operator<<(ostream &s, const Object &x);
};
```

Note that this class is abstract, since it uses pure virtual functions. Some of these functions perform important runtime type checking operations. For instance, the *ClassId()* function is supposed to return a unique integer code representing the actual type of the object. The *IsSameTypeAs()* function uses this:

```
int Object::IsSameTypeAs(const Object &x) const
// Same type of object?
{
  return ClassId() == x.ClassId();
}
```

Table 3.1 Typical attributes of an object from a single-rooted hierarchy.

Attribute	Purpose
Class name	Debugging aid
Class Id	Runtime type checking
Comparison functions	General sorting purposes
Reference count	Memory management
Printing function	Debugging aid, reporting

Note that the *Object* class does not specify where the Id is stored or how it is derived. That way, no space needs to be taken in the objects for the Id. However, you don't get something for nothing; to avoid storing the Id, we must use a virtual function, and that means each object must have a virtual function table pointer. (The objects probably will have virtual functions anyway.)

Each *Object* is required to provide a comparison function. For example, the *IsEqualTo()* virtual function is used by the overloaded *operator==()* function, as follows:

```
int operator==(const Object &a, const Object &b)
{
  return a.IsSameTypeAs(b) && a.IsEqualTo(b);
}
```

Note that, for two objects to compare equal, they must be of the same type, which is checked at runtime. This is one example of how a single-rooted hierarchy can alleviate type casting problems.

Let's look at the type casting issue further. Suppose we want to store a collection of bank accounts. For simplicity, we'll assume two possible types of accounts: checking and savings. Furthermore, we'll store these accounts using an array. The following code sketch shows how we might go about this:

```
//
// Checking account class
//

class CheckAcct : public Object {
protected:
  float balance;
  virtual int IsEqualTo(const Object &x) const;
public:
  CheckAcct();
  CheckAcct(float starting_balance);
  CheckAcct(const CheckAcct &ca);
  CheckAcct &operator=(const CheckAcct &ca);
  virtual float Deposit(float amt);
  virtual float Withdraw(float amt);
  float Balance() const;
  // Object management functions
  virtual const char *Name() const;
  virtual int ClassId() const;
  virtual ostream &Print(ostream &s) const;
};
```

```
//
// Savings account with interest
//

class SavingsAcct : public CheckAcct {
protected:
  float rate;              // Interest rate
  float accum_interest;   // Interest last paid out
  virtual int IsEqualTo(const Object &x) const;
public:
  SavingsAcct(float starting_balance=0.0, float r = 0.05);
  SavingsAcct(const SavingsAcct &ca);
  SavingsAcct &operator=(const SavingsAcct &ca);
  void PayInterest();
  float InterestPaid();
  // Object management functions
  virtual const char *Name() const;
  virtual int ClassId() const;
};
```

These classes are both derived from *Object* and, in particular, override the type management functions as follows:

```
int CheckAcct::IsEqualTo(const Object &x) const
// ASSUMES x is a checking account object. (That's why
// this function is protected.)
{
  return ((CheckAcct &)x).balance == balance;
}


const char *CheckAcct::Name() const
{
  return "Checking Account";
}


int CheckAcct::ClassId() const
{
  return CheckAcctType;
}



int SavingsAcct::IsEqualTo(const Object &x) const
// ASSUMES x is a savings account object. (That's
// why this function is protected.)
{
  return ((SavingsAcct &)x).balance == balance;
}
```

```
const char *SavingsAcct::Name() const
{
  return "Savings Account";
}

int SavingsAcct::ClassId() const
{
  return SavingsAcctType;
}
```

The *ClassId()* functions are the most interesting, since they return a constant storing a unique code for each class. These codes must be defined somewhere:

```
// Define class Id's for all types used

const int CheckAcctType = 1;
const int SavingsAcctType = 2;
```

Where should these constant definitions go? How do we ensure that two classes don't get the same Id? Unfortunately, C++, being a statically typed language, isn't really set up for runtime type checking. (Future versions may provide this feature, though.) We'll lay aside these problems for now, and show how the runtime type checking can come in handy. The following code sketch shows how an array of accounts can be built. Then, for each savings account, we pay the interest due on the account. We use runtime type checking to determine whether an account is a savings account.

```
const int num_accts = 2;
CheckAcct *MyAccts[num_accts];

MyAccts[0] = new SavingsAcct(1000.0);
MyAccts[1] = new CheckAcct(500.0);

// Pay interest on all accounts

for (i = 0; i<num_accts; i++) {
    if (MyAccts[i]->ClassId() == SavingsAcctType) {
        // Only now is type cast safe
        SavingsAcct *acct = ((SavingsAcct *)MyAccts[i]);
        acct->PayInterest();
    }
}
```

A complete running program for the checking account objects is given on disk in the files *object.h*, *object.cpp*, and *objtst.cpp*.

SUMMARY

In this chapter, you've seen some strikingly different ways to design data structures in C++. Which way is best? There really isn't one. Each technique can be very useful, given the right application. However, one approach will be used more frequently in this book than the others. Specifically, we'll use concrete data types, and we'll define these types using templates. The reason for doing this is threefold:

- Concrete data types are ideal for this book, since they allows us to show direct designs of a data structure

- Concrete data types are usually more efficient than the other approaches, and in many ways provide a "better match" for C++'s capabilities and philosophy

- By using templates, we can show direct designs that are still general enough to be used for many types of data

The second point is an important one. Concrete data types provide a good match for one of the main design philosophies behind C++, which is to allow code to be written in an encapsulated, object-oriented style—without sacrificing efficiency.

In contrast, the single-rooted hierachy, collection class approach isn't as well suited to C++. Many Smalltalk-like libraries have been built for C++, without considering whether these libraries make any sense in C++. Using these libraries often results in slow and bloated code. Also, the otherwise worthy notion of collection classes is sometimes abused by overzealous designers who don't stop to think about what they are creating. A case in point: some class libraries allow collections to be indexed as though the collection were an array, when in fact a linked-list or tree is being used! It's best not to use a data structure in unnatural ways such as this. Use a data structure for the purpose it was designed.

On the other hand, we don't want to imply that the single-rooted hierarchy approach is bad. Quite the contrary. Single-rooted hierarchies are ideal for applications like graphical user interfaces. Indeed, such interfaces were a major influence on the design of Smalltalk. But, aside from applications like these, you may want to consider whether a single-rooted hierarchy really makes sense.

Basic Array Design

In Chapters 4 through 7, we'll take an in-depth look at arrays. You might find it surprising that, even though an array is basically a simple data structure, there are many issues involved in it's design. C++ has built-in support for arrays, but this support is fairly rudimentary and is often more low-level than you might like. It can be advantageous to create user-defined arrays, so that's what we'll be doing in this set of chapters. Chapter 4 focuses on basic one-dimensional, homogenous arrays, with some discussion of multi-dimensional arrays. Other kinds of arrays will be covered in the next three chapters.

We begin by providing a brief review showing how arrays can be implemented using the built-in facilities of C++. Along the way, we'll explain some of the terminology associated wth arrays. Although some of this review may seem elementary, it provides an important foundation for the the design of the array classes that we'll show later in this and other chapters.

A REVIEW OF ONE-DIMENSIONAL ARRAYS

Conceptually, a one-dimensional array is a set of objects, called *elements*, that can be selected either in sequence or randomly through a subscripting operation. In the most common type of array, the elements are contiguous and the subscripting is accomplished by a numeric index. However, it's important to realize that nothing in the definition of arrays prevents them from being non-contiguous or from having non-numeric subscripts. For example, in an *associative array*, the subscript is a key, usually a string of characters, and the array elements may be stored in a search table implemented using linked lists or binary trees. Associative arrays are covered in the companion volume [Flamig 93]. In this chapter, we'll focus on the more common contiguous arrays that use numeric indexes.

Arrays may be *statically sized*, where the bounds of the array are determined at compile time, or *dynamically sized*, where the bounds are determined at runtime. We'll abbreviate the terminology and call such arrays *static* and *dynamic*, respectively. This example shows how to create both of these array types using the built-in C++ array facilities:

```
int sarr[10]; // Create static array of 10 characters

void f(int n)
{
  int *darr = new int[n]; // Create a dynamic array of n elements
  ...
  delete[] darr;          // Destroy it
}
```

As the function *f()* shows, you can reference arrays using pointers. In fact, arrays and pointers are very much intertwined in C++. The names of arrays, such as *sarr* and *darr*, are actually pointers to the first elements in the arrays. (But they're *not* pointers to arrays, as some people think!) In the case of static arrays, this pointer is constant—that is, the address stored in the pointer can't be modified. For example, the name *sarr* is typed as *const int ** and can't be redirected anywhere other than the array data created for it. In contrast, in a dynamic array, the pointer can be easily redirected elsewhere. So, *darr* is typed simply as *int **.

Lengths of Arrays

Arrays have two lengths associated with them, as shown in Figure 4.1. The *dimensioned length* of an array is the number of elements allocated or set aside

Figure 4.1 The two lengths of an array.

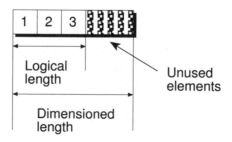

for the array. The *logical length* is the number of elements in actual use. An array that has the same dimensioned and logical length is called a *fixed-length array*. In a *variable-length array*, these lengths can be different. Determining whether an array is fixed- or variable-length does not depend on the way the array has been sized. For example, you can have statically sized variable-length arrays and dynamically sized fixed-length arrays.

You can also have *resizable arrays*, where the dimensioned length of the array can be varied. In theory, it's possible for a resizable array to be fixed or variable length, but usually the latter is true. By their very nature, resizable arrays are always dynamically sized.

Array Subscripting

Array elements are accessed by using subscripting operations that involve indexes. An index gives the numbers of the elements that come before the desired element. The index is thus an offset into the array. The subscripting can be expressed using the *[]* operator or by using pointer arithmetic. (Remember the relationship between pointers and arrays.) This can be seen easily by the following equivalent expressions:

```
a[i]   <===>   *(a + i)
```

In the pointer addition shown here, more is going on than meets the eye. At the machine level, pointers are nothing more than addresses to bytes of memory. Yet the compiler treats these pointers as though they are addresses to some type of object with a particular size. To access the *i*th element, then, the compiler must take into account the size of the elements. Assuming an array of elements of type *T*, the following equivalence with pointer arithmetic holds:

```
*(a + i)   <===>   *(T *)((char *)p + i*sizeof(T))
```

You can see that one-dimensional array subscripting involves an addition plus a multiplication. Ordinarily, you don't need to concern yourself with this, but the multiplication that takes place can significantly slow down your code, particularly for subscripting that occurs in tight loops. The problem becomes more acute when higher-dimensional arrays are involved. In Chapter 7, we'll take such problems into consideration.

Because subscripting is actually implemented as pointer arithmetic, one consequence is that the length of the array is not used! It's quite possible to have a subscript out of bounds, as you probably well know. Subscript checking isn't the norm, though, because it is *slow*. Code with range-checked arrays can easily be twice as slow as would otherwise be the case, and quite often can be much slower than that. Even so, it's useful to include subscript checking, especially during testing stages. The question is how to turn it on and off.

Arrays of Objects

When the elements of an array are user-defined objects, you must take into consideration how those objects are constructed and destructed. In the example we provided earlier, when array of type *T* is allocated, the default constructor for *T* is called for each element in the array, starting with the first. When the array is de-allocated, the destructor is called for each element, in reverse order.

These facts become important when we consider variable-length arrays. Should all of the allocated elements be constructed ahead of time, or only when they are used? In this chapter, we'll explore some ways to circumvent the normal construction and destruction of elements and to have these operations take place only when needed.

Designing User-Defined Arrays

Our review of arrays leads us naturally into some design issues for user-defined arrays:

- How do we create variable-length, resizable arrays?
- Can the arrays safely allow any type of element to be stored, including those elements that have constructors and destructors?
- How can subscript checking be accomplished?
- We support all kinds of arrays—fixed length, variable length, statically sized, dynamically sized, and so on. In turn, we want to make sure we can use these arrays interchangeably in our programs. How can we provide this support?
- Perhaps the most important design issue is one of performance. Even though you might succeed in creating a high-level interface for arrays, would you really want to use it in your programs? What do the arrays cost in terms of speed and space over their low-level counterparts?

The goal is to design array objects that are almost as efficient as built-in arrays. (They probably will never be *as* efficient; whenever you add power and sophistication, performance is bound to suffer.) You want to find the "sweet spot" between two opposing goals: wanting high-level abstraction and wanting efficiency. Your arrays should be designed so that, if you're not using a particular feature, you don't pay for it. We'll now show you a design for user-defined arrays that meets all these criteria. Many alternative approaches were tried before this design was chosen.

AN ARRAY CLASS HIERARCHY

The design for arrays given in this chapter centers around a hierarchy of classes, as shown in Figure 4.2. All of these classes are templates so that we can use them for any type of array element. The *Array* class is at he top of the hierarchy. This class serves as the common interface to all the array types, which are as follows:

- Fixed-length arrays, including those that are statically and dynamically sized.
- Variable-length arrays, where internal indexes keep track of current versus dimensioned lengths. Both statically and dynamically sized arrays are supported.
- Dynamic, resizable arrays, whose dimensions can grow and shrink on demand.

BASE ARRAY CLASS

The *Array* class has the following basic features:

- Storage for the array elements is allocated elsewhere.
- All copying is done via element-by-element assignment.
- The logical length and dimensioned length are differentiated, although only the logical length is actually stored.
- Subscript checking is controllable at compile time.

Figure 4.2 The Array Class Hierarchy.

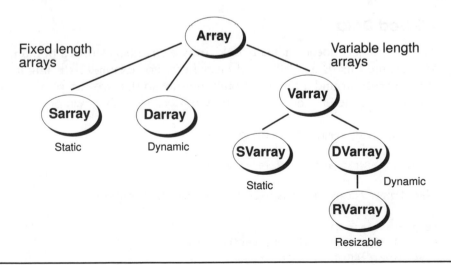

- To make functions that use arrays the most general, *Array*-typed pointers or references can be used for the parameters. This allows any type of array in the hierarchy to be passed to the functions.

Here is the *Array* class definition:

```
template<class TYPE>
class Array {
protected:
  TYPE *data;    // Pointer to actual data
  unsigned len; // Logical length
public:
  Array(TYPE *m, unsigned n);
  virtual ~Array();
  virtual void CopyN(const TYPE *s, unsigned n);
  void Copy(const Array<TYPE> &s);
  Array<TYPE> &operator=(const Array<TYPE> &s);
#ifndef NO_RANGE_CHECK
  unsigned CheckIndx(unsigned i) const;
#endif
  TYPE &operator[](unsigned i);
  const TYPE &operator[](unsigned i) const;
  unsigned Length() const;
  virtual unsigned DimLength() const;
  TYPE *Data();
  const TYPE *Data() const;
};
```

The code for the *Array* class is given on disk in the files *array.h* and *array.mth*.

Aliased Data

An *Array* object doesn't actually hold array elements; it stores a pointer to them. We assume this data is allocated elsewhere. For example, we might wrap an *Array* object around a low-level built-in array so that we can provide subscript checking for the elements. Here's how to declare such a "wrapper array":

```
int low_level_array[3] = {10, 2, 4};

Array<int> wrap_array(low_level_array, 3);
```

The *Array()* constructor is used to initialize the wrapper:

```
template<class TYPE>
Array<TYPE>::Array(TYPE *m, unsigned n)
: data(m), len(n)
{
```

```
  // Nothing more to do
}
```

Note that we don't provide a default constructor for *Array*. We chose not to because you shouldn't really declare *Array* objects directly (unless you are trying to create a wrapper array). Instead, you should be declaring objects from classes derived from *Array*. True to form, however, we do provide a virtual destructor, even though it doesn't do anything. Some of the derived array classes will use dynamic allocation for the array data, and we'll need to override the destructor to de-allocate this memory.

Copying Arrays

One important member function is *CopyN()*, which allows us to copy data from a low-level array into an *Array* object:

```
template<class TYPE>
void Array<TYPE>::CopyN(const TYPE *s, unsigned slen)
{
  unsigned clen = DimLength();
  if (clen > slen) clen = slen;
  for (unsigned i = 0; i<clen; i++) data[i] = s[i];
}
```

In *CopyN()*, we only copy as many elements as the source has, and never more than the target array is dimensioned to handle. The length of the array never changes, as illustrated in Figure 4.3. Also, the copying is carefully done, element-by-element (rather than by using something like *memcpy()*). This approach allows any overloaded assignment operator that *TYPE* might have to be called correctly. For example, the statement *data[i]=s[i]* is actually translated into:

```
data[i].operator=(s[i]);
```

Figure 4.3 Copying fixed-length arrays.

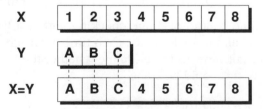

It is extremely important to strictly adhere to element-by-element assignment during copying, because it allows the appropriate assignment operator to be called, which may be necessary to avoid aliasing.

The *CopyN()* function is used by the *Copy()* function, which in turn is used by the overloaded assignment operator:

```
template<class TYPE>
void Array<TYPE>::Copy(const Array<TYPE> &s)
{
  CopyN(s.data, s.Length());
}

template<class TYPE>
Array<TYPE> &Array<TYPE>::operator=(const Array<TYPE> &s)
{
  if (this != &s) Copy(s);
  return *this;
}
```

Note that the assignment operator traps the case where we try to assign an array to itself; thus, we prevent redundant copying.

Subscript Checking

Array objects, unlike low-level arrays, allow us to provide range checking on subscripts. This can be accomplished by overloading the subscript operator. For performance reasons, it's also useful to allow range checking to be turned on and off at will. How can we accomplish this? Three methods are possible:

1. Allow range checking to be controlled at runtime, either for all arrays at once, or for individual arrays. The checking can be controlled by using internal flags inside the arrays or by using virtual functions.

2. Allow range checking to be controlled only at compile time by using conditional macros.

3. Provide direct access to the array data through an access function, allowing the overloaded subscript operator to be bypassed (and thus the range checking).

With runtime control of range checking, either a flag must be tested or a virtual function call must take place each time a subscript is used. The flag test or the function call allow us to determine whether the index should be checked. Here's one way this could be done:

```
TYPE &Array::operator[](unsigned i)
{
  if (range_check) i = CheckIndx(i);
```

```
    return data[i]; // Use low-level subscripting
}
```

This approach leads to runtime overhead—even when *range_check* is false—and the overhead can be significant for tight loops. By using a conditional macro at compile time instead, we can turn off range checking and thus have no overhead at runtime. In conjunction with the macro approach, we can also allow direct access to the array elements in order to bypass the overloaded subscript operator. This approach allows us to turn off range checking locally in code where speed is critical (and where the code has been thoroughly tested). The two *Data()* functions (one for non-*const* arrays, one for *const* arrays) are supplied for this purpose. Here are the *Data()* functions, followed by an example of their use:

```
template<class TYPE>
TYPE *Array<TYPE>::Data()
{
    return data;
}

template<class TYPE>
const TYPE *Array<TYPE>::Data() const
{
    return data;
}

void f(Array<int> &arr)
// Some function that's been thoroughly tested for
// proper bounds on array indexes
{
    int *a = arr.Data(); // Get to the low-level array
    ...
    a[17] = 42;
    ...
}

void g(const Array<int> &arr)
{
    int *a = arr.Data(); // Const form of Data() is used
    int x = a[17];       // Legal access
    a[0] = 1;            // Illegal access
    ...
}
```

In this chapter, we'll use the conditional macro approach combined with the raw data access functions. This combination allows us to use range checking if we need it, but there will be no residual overhead if we don't need range checking. Although this approach isn't as flexible as allowing runtime control of range checking, it meets one of our main design goals: we shouldn't have to pay for something that we're not going to use.

We'll now show how to implement the conditional macro approach. The overloaded subscript operator looks like the following:

```
template<class TYPE>
TYPE &Array<TYPE>::operator[](unsigned i)
{
  return data[CHECK(i)];
}
```

The operator function checks the incoming index by calling the macro *CHECK()*, which is conditionally defined as follows:

```
#ifdef NO_RANGE_CHECK
#define CHECK(i) i
#else
#define CHECK(i) CheckIndx(i)
#endif
```

The macro symbol *NO_RANGE_CHECK* is used to control range checking. If this symbol is defined, then *Check()* becomes a no-op. Otherwise, a call to the function *CheckIndx()* is made, which actually does the range checking:

```
template<class TYPE>
unsigned Array<TYPE>::CheckIndx(unsigned i) const
{
  if (i >= len) i = HandleRangeErr(i, len);
  return i;
}
```

HandleRangeErr is a pointer to a function that's designed to handle out-of-range subscripts. We've provided a default error handler that prints an error message and exits the program:

```
unsigned (*HandleRangeErr)(unsigned i, unsigned sz)
  = DefaultRangeErrHandler;

unsigned DefaultRangeErrHandler(unsigned i, unsigned sz)
{
  cout << "Subscript " << i << " out of range (0, "
       << (sz-1) << ")\n";
  exit(1);
  return 0; // Here to prevent compiler warnings
}
```

We could also define alternate handlers. All we would need to do is point to them via the *HandleRangeErr* function pointer.

Note Future versions of C++ promise more elegant error handling facilities that could be used in place of the function pointer technique.

There is also an alternate subscript operator function, which is used to provide read-only subscripting of *const* arrays:

```
template<class TYPE>
const TYPE &Array<TYPE>::operator[](unsigned i) const
// Subscripting operator for constant arrays.
{
  return data[CHECK(i)];
}
```

Note carefully the two uses of the *const* keyword. These keywords allow us to read the value of an element of a constant array, but they don't allow us to write to that element. For example:

```
int low_level_array[3] = {10, 2, 4};
const Array<int> myarray(low_level_array, 3);

int x = myarray[2]; // OK
myarray[2] = 17;    // Illegal
```

Without the *const* version of the subscript operator, even reading from a constant array element would be disallowed.

Logical versus Dimensioned Length

The functions *Length()* and *DimLength()*, respectively, return the logical and dimensioned length of an array:

```
template<class TYPE>
unsigned Array<TYPE>::Length() const
{
  return len;
}


template<class TYPE>
unsigned Array<TYPE>::DimLength() const
{
  return len;
}
```

Notice that the dimensioned length by default is the same as the logical length, but a derived class can override the virtual *DimLength()* function to change this. To save space, we avoid actually storing the dimensioned length in the *Array* object—in case both the logical and dimensioned length are the same (as it will be for fixed-length arrays). Again, our arrays have no more overhead than is absolutely necessary.

FIXED-LENGTH ARRAYS

With the base *Array* class defined, it's easy to derive fixed-length array classes. These are arrays that have the same logical length and dimensioned length. We'll define the two classes *Darray* and *Sarray*, which support dynamically and statically sized arrays, respectively. Here is the *Darray* class:

```
template<class TYPE>
class Darray : public Array<TYPE> {
public:
  Darray(unsigned n);
  Darray(const Darray<TYPE> &s);
  Darray(const Array<TYPE> &s);
  Darray(const TYPE *s, unsigned n);
  virtual ~Darray();
};
```

The constructors of *Darray* work by allocating the array elements using *new*, and by passing a pointer to these allocated elements to the base class constructor. Here are two constructors that illustrate this:

```
template<class TYPE>
Darray<TYPE>::Darray(unsigned n)
// Constructs an array of n dynamically allocated elements
: Array<TYPE>(new TYPE[n], n)
{
 // Nothing else to do
}

template<class TYPE>
Darray<TYPE>::Darray(const Darray<TYPE> &s)
// Copy constructor. Allocates enough room, and
// copies data from the source.
: Array<TYPE>(new TYPE[s.Length()], s.Length())
{
  Copy(s);
}
```

The destructor de-allocates the array elements:

```
template<class TYPE>
Darray<TYPE>::~Darray()
// De-allocates dynamically allocated array data
{
  delete[] data;
}
```

In contrast, the *Sarray* class uses a low-level array internally, which is sized and allocated at compile time:

```
template<class TYPE, unsigned N>
class Sarray : public Array<TYPE> {
protected:
  TYPE storage[N]; // Statically sized array data
public:
  Sarray();
  Sarray(const Sarray<TYPE, N> &s);
  Sarray(const Array<TYPE> &s);
  Sarray(const TYPE *s, unsigned n);
  Sarray<TYPE, N> &operator=(const Array<TYPE> &s);
};
```

In addition to the usual *TYPE* parameter, *Sarray* has the parameter *N*, which determines the size of the array. This parameter is used to declare an embedded low-level array of *N* elements that we've called *storage*. At construction time, the *data* pointer in the base *Array* class is linked to *storage*, as shown in the *Sarray* default constructor:

```
template<class TYPE, unsigned N>
Sarray<TYPE,N>::Sarray()
// Default constructor creates an array of length N
: Array<TYPE>(storage, N) // Link data to storage
{
  // Nothing more to do
}
```

The other *Sarray* constructors are defined similarly. Note that no destructor is defined for the *Sarray* class, since we don't need to delete the statically allocated elements. (A default destructor *is* created by the compiler, though, which calls the *TYPE::~TYPE()* destructor for each element in the array.)

The code for the *Darray* and *Sarray* classes is given on disk in the files *darray.h*, *darray.mth*, *sarray.h*, and *sarray.mth*. Two test programs are supplied: *tstarr.cpp* and *tstarr2.cpp*.

Fixed-Length Array Assignments

The *Sarray* class has an overloaded assignment operator function:

```
template<class TYPE>
Sarray<TYPE> &Sarray<TYPE>::operator=(const Array<TYPE> &s)
{
  if (this != &s) Copy(s);
  return *this;
}
```

We need to make two important points about this operator function. First, by passing a base class *Array* reference for the source of the assignment, we allow any object from the *Array* class hierarchy to be assigned to a *Sarray* object, such as a *Darray* object. Second, notice that the body of this function is identical to the *Array* class version. So why did we need to redefine it?

Recall how assignments in derived classes work: without an overloaded assignment function, the additional derived class members are copied member by member. Then, the base class members are copied either memberwise or with an overloaded assignment in the base class. Figure 4.4 illustrates this scenario. If we had no assignment function in *Sarray*, we would create a problem for the the *storage* member of *Sarray*. We want *storage* to be copied only once. Without the *Sarray* assignment function, *storage* would be copied as part of the default derived class assignment behavior, and then copied again via

---

Figure 4.4 A derived class assignment scenario.

```
class Base {                          class Derived : public Base {
protected:                            protected:
  char *p, *q;                          char *r;
public:                               public:
  Base();                               Derived();
  ~Base();                              ~Derived();
  Base &operator=(const Base &x);     };
};
```

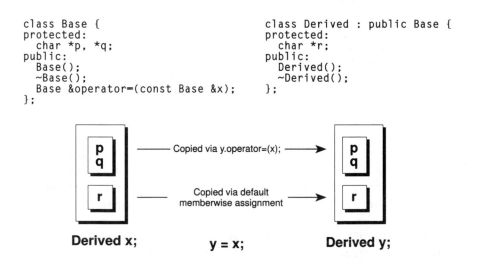

Derived x;   y = x;   Derived y;

the *Copy()* function inside the *Array* base class assignment function. Defining an assignment function in *Sarray* prevents this double copying.

You may have noticed that the *Darray* class doesn't have an assignment operator function. Why not? The *Darray* class has no additional data members defined, so the base *Array* class assignment function will handle everything properly. This is a subtle point. So, for consistency, you may want to define a *Darray* assignment function. (It would look identical to the *Sarray* version.) We haven't done so here because we want to minimize the amount of code generated by the *Darray* class. Also, to save space, *Darray* was not given a default constructor. It's not clear what the default constructor should do anyway. Should it make an array with no elements, or an array with a default length of, say, 10 elements?

Static versus Dynamic Arrays

Dynamic arrays are versatile because their dimensions can be determined at runtime. This same versatility makes dynamic arrays less efficient than those sized statically, since time is spent at runtime allocating and de-allocating the array data. This level of efficiency may be critical when arrays are used inside functions that are called frequently. For instance:

```
void f()
// Some function called frequently
{
  Darray<int> myarr(10); // Allocated on heap
  ...
  // Destructor called automatically to de-allocate array
}
```

Contrast this with the static allocation of the array:

```
void g()
// Some function called frequently
{
  Sarray<int, 10> myarr; // Allocated on stack
  ...
  // Array vanishes as stack is unwound
}
```

In the static array version, the array is allocated on the stack, which involves a simple manipulation of the stack pointer. The dynamic array version involves a much more involved heap management process. In addition, space overhead is needed for heap management. And don't forget the simple fact that a heap *is* required. If you want the fastest, most efficient arrays, and you aren't using a heap in your program for other purposes, you might want to use statically sized arrays.

Of course, a tradeoff is involved here. Since the size of the static array is a template parameter, a new class is generated every time you declare a static array of a different size. For instance, the following code causes three classes to be generated (one base class for character arrays in general, and two derived classes for different-sized arrays):

```
typedef Sarray<char, 10> tenchar;
typedef Sarray<char, 20> twentychar;
```

For this reason, you should limit the number of different-sized static arrays that you declare in your application (and limit the number of arrays of different element types). Note that dynamic arrays do not have this problem, since the array length is passed as a parameter to the constructor.

It's important to understand the difference between sizing an array and allocating it. For instance, statically sized arrays don't have to be statically allocated. You can allocate them dynamically, as in:

```
Sarray<int, 10> *p = new Sarray<int, 10>;
```

We might do this, for instance, to free up memory in the static data segments of our program, without having to implement both the static and dynamic array classes.

VARIABLE-LENGTH ARRAYS

A variable-length array is one where the logical length of the array is different from the dimensioned length. With a variable-length array, we can add elements to the array (thereby increasing the logical length) and remove elements (thereby decreasing the logical length).

As is true with fixed-length arrays, variable-length arrays can be either dynamic or static. Both of these types of arrays have much in common—in particular, the code that handles adding and removing elements. So it makes sense to make a general variable-length array class, and then derive specific dynamic and static versions. For instance, we've created the *Varray* class (which is derived from the *Array* class) and two classes derived from *Varray*— *DVarray* and *SVarray*. The *Varray* class is defined as follows:

```
template<class TYPE>
class Varray : public Array<TYPE> {
protected:
  unsigned dimlen;
public:
  Varray(TYPE *m, unsigned dim_sz);
  void CleanUpElements(unsigned s, unsigned f);
```

```
  virtual void CopyN(const TYPE *s, unsigned slen);
  Varray<TYPE> &operator=(const Array<TYPE> &s);
  virtual unsigned DimLength() const;
  virtual unsigned InsertNAt(unsigned p, const TYPE *s, unsigned n);
  unsigned InsertAt(unsigned p, const TYPE &s);
  unsigned InsertAt(unsigned p, const Array<TYPE> &a);
  unsigned Concatenate(const TYPE *s, unsigned n=1);
  unsigned Concatenate(const Array<TYPE> &a);
  unsigned Add(const TYPE &s);
  unsigned DeleteAt(unsigned p, unsigned n=1);
  unsigned Shrink(unsigned n);
};
```

The code for the *Varray* class is given on disk in the files *varray.h* and *varray.mth*. Two test programs are supplied: *tstvarr.cpp* and *tstvarr2.cpp*.

As is the case with the *Array* class, the *Varray* class doesn't dictate how the array elements are allocated. Instead, it aliases the elements through the following constructor:

```
template<class TYPE>
Varray<TYPE>::Varray(TYPE *m, unsigned dim_sz)
: Array<TYPE>(m, 0)
{
  dimlen = dim_sz;
}
```

The base *Array* constructor is called to do the aliasing and, surpisingly, a length of zero is passed. This represents the logical length of the newly constructed array. The dimensioned length is recorded in the additional data member *dimlen*. To differentiate between the logical length and dimensioned length, the *DimLength()* virtual function is overridden to return *dimlen*:

```
template<class TYPE>
unsigned Varray<TYPE>::DimLength() const
{
  return dimlen;
}
```

It may seem backwards to have the base class keep track of the logical length and the derived class keep track of the dimensioned length. But this arrangement gives the system of array classes its flexibility and economy.

With the *Varray* class, you can add single or multiple elements either to the end of the array (that is, after the current logical length) or somewhere in the middle. The *InsertNAt()*, *InsertAt()*, *Concatenate()*, and *Add()* functions handle these chores. The *DeleteAt()* and *Shrink()* functions allow you to delete one or more elements from the middle or end of the array, respectively. All of these functions manipulate the logical length of the array. We'll take a look at these functions later. First we need to discuss an important consideration: user-controlled allocation.

In-Place Construction

Some subtle issues are involved in adding and removing elements from a variable-length array. These issues revolve around two questions: when and where does an array element get constructed? When and where does it get destructed? To have safe, efficient, robust code, we must ensure that the constructors and destructors get called the proper number of times, in the right order, and only when necessary.

With fixed-length arrays, the construction and destruction of elements is quite simple: when the array elements are allocated—either by using *new* or through a static declaration—the default constructor of the element type is called for each element. When the array is to be destroyed, the destructor is called for each element. For example:

```
void f()
{
  MyType *darr = new MyType[17]; // Mytype constructor called 17 times
  MyType sarr[42]; // MyType constructor called 42 times
  ...
  delete[] darr; // MyType destructor called 17 times
  // At end of function, MyType destructor called 42
  // times for the elements of sarr
}
```

If you inspect the *Darray* and *Sarray* classes, you'll see that their array elements are constructed and destructed in this way.

For variable-length arrays, things get trickier. When a variable-length array is first constructed, it has a logical length of zero. Although the space for the array has been allocated, no constructed elements are stored there. That is, the array storage consists initially of unconstructed elements. As elements are added to the array, the constructor must be called for those elements. Figure 4.5 shows a variable-length array with four constructed elements. When elements are removed, the destructor must be called for each removed element. When it is time to destroy the array itself, if there are remaining elements in the array, the destructor should be called for each one.

Thus, the problem boils down to your ability to construct and destruct elements at will. You must be able to do the construction and destruction *at the place where the element occurs in the array.* This is the tricky part. Normally, when you construct an object, either the compiler and linker control the address

Figure 4.5 A variable-length array.

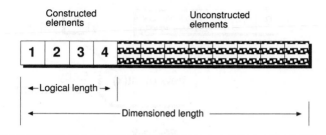

of the object (for statically allocated objects), or the heap manager controls the address (via the *new* operator). Fortunately, C++ provides the tools to let you control the address of the object yourself. For instance, you can override the *new* operator and pass in the address of the object to be constructed:

```
void *operator new(size_t, void *p)
{
  return p;
}
```

Actually, the *new* operator itself won't cause the constructor for the object to be called, but the compiler will insert the constructor call when it sees the new operator. The address of the object to be passed to the constructor (the *this* pointer) is returned by the *new* operator. Now you can see why the simple overloaded *new* operator works: it merely has to return the same address passed in. Note that the first parameter of *new* (the size of the object, which is required by the C++ syntax) isn't needed by the function. Normally, the size is used to tell the heap manager how many bytes to allocate. But, in this case, the space is assumed to be allocated already.

Note   An overloaded *new* operator function—such as the one we've just given—is sometimes called a *placement new* operator; it places a new object at a user-defined address. Using a *placement new* operator to construct an object at a specified address is called *in-place construction*.

Figure 4.6 illustrates how we could construct the fourth element of an array of *Compound* numbers (see Chapter 3), and initialize it to the value *<9 0/1>* using the *placement new* operator. The address of the second element is passed to *new,* and then the default constructor is called, as in the following code:

```
// Declare array of 6 compound numbers, initially unconstructed:
char myarr[6*sizeof(Compound)];
```

Figure 4.6 In-Place construction of an array element.

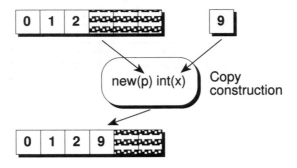

```
...
new(&myarr[3]) Compound(9); // Construct fourth element
```

Note how the array elements are initially allocated as characters, rather than *Compound* numbers. That's done to make the array have unconstructed bits initially. If we had used

```
Compound myarr[6];
```

then the *Compound* default constructor would have been called for all six elements, which isn't what we want.

You can also call the default constructor (or any other type of constructor, for that matter) with the *placement new* operator. For example:

```
new(&myarr[3]) Compound; // Default constructor called
```

With these ideas in mind, the following helper function templates are used by the *Varray* class to construct the elements of a variable-length array:

```
template<class TYPE>
void DefConstruct(TYPE *p)
// This function constructs an element at place p.
// Calls the default constructor.
{
  new(p) TYPE;
}

template<class TYPE>
void DefConstructElements(TYPE *t, unsigned len)
// Default constructs the elements of low-level array t,
// assumed to have been properly allocated
{
```

```
    for (unsigned i = 0; i<len; i++) DefConstruct(t++);
}

template<class TYPE>
void CopyConstruct(TYPE *p, const TYPE &x)
// Copy constructs object at address p, using
// object x for the copy
{
  new(p) TYPE(x);
}

template<class TYPE>
void CopyConstructElements(TYPE *t, const TYPE *s, unsigned len)
// Here, we assume raw space for t has been properly allocated,
// and we're ready to copy construct the elements of s into them
{
  for (unsigned i = 0; i<len; i++) CopyConstruct(t++, *s++);
}
```

The *CopyConstruct()* function template assumes *TYPE* has a copy constructor. If that's not the case, you can override the function template for a specific type. The overriding function can call the default constructor, and then do an assignment. For example:

```
void CopyConstruct(MyType *p, const MyType &x)
{
  new(p) MyType; // Call default constructor
  *p = x;        // Do assignment
}
```

In cases where *TYPE* doesn't have a constructor at all, such as for built-in types, you can simply do an assignment, as shown in the following overridden *CopyConstruct()* function for integers:

```
void CopyConstruct(int *p, const int &x)
{
  *p = x;        // Do assignment
}
```

Explicit Destructor Calls

Calls to destructors are normally handled automatically by the compiler. You can control when a destructor is called if you use the *delete* operator. However, this assumes that the object to be destroyed resides on the heap. But what do you do if the object resides as an element of an array? The solution is to make an explicit call to the destructor. Here's an example:

```
Compound *p = (Compound *)(&myarr[1]); // Point to element
...
p->Compound::~Compound(); // Explicit destructor call
```

The explicit destructor call requires that you know the address of the object being destructed, and you can only call the destructor through a pointer. You should never call the destructor for the same object twice, and never for an object that resides on the heap (since it won't be freed properly unless *delete* is called). The *Varray* class uses an explicit destructor call in the function *CleanUpElements()*:

```
template<class TYPE>
void Varray<TYPE>::CleanUpElements(unsigned s, unsigned f)
// Cleans up elements from start s to finish f-1, by calling
// destructors explicitly
{
  TYPE *p = data+s;
  for (unsigned i=s; i<f; i++, p++) p->TYPE::~TYPE();
}
```

This template function does have a problem, though. What if *TYPE* has no destructor? In theory, the compiler can simply ignore the explicit destructor call, since nothing needs to be done. In practice, if *TYPE* is a built-in type—such as *int* or *float*—rather than a user-defined class, many compilers will give you an error. For example:

```
int *p;
p->int::~int(); // Some earlier compilers can't handle this
```

The ability to use "user-defined class syntax" for built-in types—such as in explicit calls to destructors—was added to C++ 3.0. Many C++ 2.1 compilers will have troubles in this area. To solve this problem, a special *Destruct()* function template can be defined, as follows:

```
template<class TYPE>
void Destruct(TYPE *p)
// Calls the destructor for the object pointed to by p.
// ASSUMES the object was constructed using the placement
// new operator.
{
  p->TYPE::~TYPE();
}
```

Then, if the array you are using is for a built-in type, you can override the function template to do nothing. For example, here's how you can override *Destruct()* for *int*s:

```
void Destruct(int *p)
{
  // Do nothing
}
```

By using appropriate versions of *Destruct()*, we can rewrite *CleanUpElements()* to work for any type, as follows:

```
template<class TYPE>
void Varray<TYPE>::CleanUpElements(unsigned s, unsigned f)
{
  TYPE *p = data+s;
  for (unsigned i=s; i<f; i++) ::Destruct(p++);
}
```

Note The code for the placement *new* operator (and for associated special constructor and destructor helper functions) is given on the disk in the files *placenew.h* and *placenew.mth*.

Inserting Elements into an Array

Elements are inserted into a variable-length array by first shifting array elements down to make room for the new elements (unless the elements are added to the end), and then copy-constructing the new elements in place. Figure 4.7 illustrates the process. The workhorse function is *InsertNAt()*:

```
template<class TYPE>
unsigned Varray<TYPE>::InsertNAt(unsigned p, const TYPE *s, unsigned n)
// Inserts the data pointed to by s into the array. Up to n
// elements are inserted (truncating if necesary), starting at
// position p (counted by zero). If p >= len, then the data
// is concatenated to the end.
// Returns number of elements inserted.
```

Figure 4.7 Inserting elements into a variable-length array.

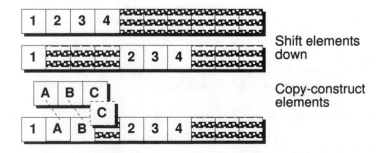

```
{
  unsigned i;

  if (n > dimlen - len) { // Keep things in range
    n = dimlen - len;
  }
  if (p >= len) { // We're concatenating
    p = len;
  }
  else {
    // Make room for inserted data somewhere in the middle
    memmove(data+p+n, data+p, (len-p)*sizeof(TYPE));
  }
  // Copy in source
  len += n;
  for(i = 0; i<n; i++) {
    // Copy-construct the elements in place (they're presumed
    // to be unconstructed at this time.)
    ::CopyConstruct(data+p+i, s[i]);
  }
  return n;
}
```

The important feature of this function is that the newly inserted elements are created element-by-element, using a copy-construction process. The other insert functions use *InsertNAt()* to do most of the work:

```
template<class TYPE>
unsigned Varray<TYPE>::Add(const TYPE &s)
// Add an element onto the end of the array
{
  return InsertNAt(len, &s, 1);
}


template<class TYPE>
unsigned Varray<TYPE>::InsertAt(unsigned p, const Array<TYPE> &a)
// Insert an array of elements into position p of the array
{
  return InsertNAt(p, a.Data(), a.Length());
}


template<class TYPE>
unsigned Varray<TYPE>::Concatenate(const Array<TYPE> &a)
// Add array a onto the end of this array
{
  return InsertAt(len, a);
}


template<class TYPE>
```

```
unsigned Varray<TYPE>::Concatenate(const TYPE *s, unsigned n)
// Concatenate an array of n elements, (from low-level memory),
// onto the end of the array.
{
  return InsertNAt(len, s, n);
}
```

Deleting Elements from an Array

Deleting elements from an array is the opposite of inserting elements, as illustrated in Figure 4.8. First, the destructor is called for each element to be deleted, and the remaining elements are then shifted up to take the place of the deleted elements. The *DeleteAt()* function does all the work:

```
template<class TYPE>
unsigned Varray<TYPE>::DeleteAt(unsigned p, unsigned n)
// Deletes up to n elements from array at position p.  If p
// is out of range nothing happens. If n == 0, nothing happens.
// Returns number of elements deleted.
{
  long pel; // long is used to prevent overflows during adds
  unsigned pe;

  if (p < len && n != 0) {
    // We may be chopping off the end, so keep in range
    pel = p + n;
    if (pel > len) pel = len;
    pe = unsigned(pel); // Guaranteed to be in range
    n = pe-p;
    // Now, clean up each element deleted
    CleanUpElements(p, pe);
    // Now, move elements up to take their place
    memmove(data+p, data+pe, (len-pe)*sizeof(TYPE));
    len -= n;
  } else n = 0;
  return n;
}
```

Figure 4.8 Deleting elements from a variable-length array.

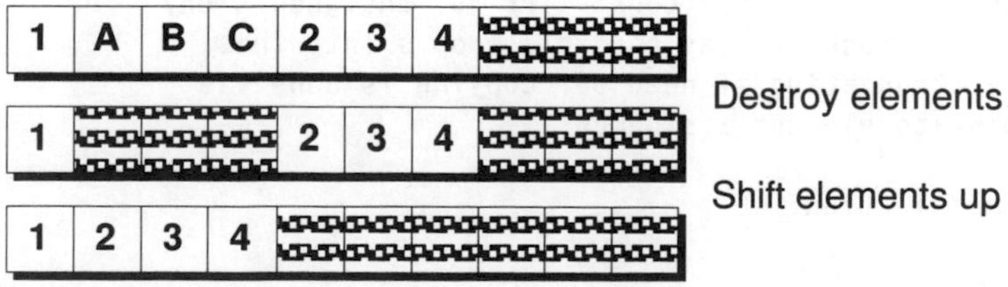

Destroy elements

Shift elements up

A special purpose function to delete elements from the end of the array, called *Shrink()*, uses *DeleteAt()*:

```
template<class TYPE>
unsigned Varray<TYPE>::Shrink(unsigned n)
// Shrink the array by n elements.
// Return number of elements we've shrunk.
{
  if (n > len) n = len;
  return DeleteAt(len-n, n);
}
```

Copying Variable-Length Arrays

As is true with all the array classes, an overloaded assignment operator is provided for the variable-length arrays. This assignment operator can use all the different types of arrays as the source:

```
Varray<TYPE> &Varray<TYPE>::operator=(const Array<TYPE> &s)
// Note that source of assignment can be any array type.
{
  if (this != &s) Copy(s);
  return *this;
}
```

The assignment operator calls the *Copy()* function, which in turn calls the virtual *CopyN()* function to do the actual copying. The details for copying into a variable-length array are different from those for copying into a fixed-length array. For this reason, the *Varray* class overrides *CopyN()*.

When you copy data into a variable-length array, you might not only be adding elements to the array, but you might also be overwriting existing elements. A copy-construction process is used for adding new elements, whereas an assignment operation takes place for existing elements. Also, if the source array is smaller than the target array, elements must be deleted from the target array. Figure 4.9 illustrates these cases. The following *CopyN()* function for *Varray* handles the details:

```
template<class TYPE>
void Varray<TYPE>::CopyN(const TYPE *s, unsigned slen)
// Copies as much data as possible from s into this
// array, truncating if need be. Copying is done via
// element-to-element assignment.
{
  unsigned i, tlen;
```

```
   // First, copy into the constructed portion
   tlen = len;
   if (tlen > slen) {
      Shrink(tlen-slen); // We might be getting smaller
      tlen = slen;
   }
   for (i = 0; i<tlen; i++) data[i] = s[i];
   len = tlen;
   // Now, copy into the unconstructed portion via concatenation
   if (tlen < slen) Concatenate(s+i, slen-tlen);
}
```

The *Concatenate()* function is cleverly called to handle the elements that must be copy constructed.

Dynamic Variable-Length Arrays

Now that we've created the *Varray* class, we can derive more specific dynamic and static versions. Here is the *DVarray* class for dynamic, variable-length arrays:

```
template<class TYPE>
class DVarray : public Varray<TYPE> {
public:
  DVarray(unsigned n);
  DVarray(const DVarray<TYPE> &s);
  DVarray(const Array<TYPE> &s);
  DVarray(const TYPE *s, unsigned n);
  virtual ~DVarray();
  DVarray<TYPE> &operator=(const Array<TYPE> &s);
};
```

Figure 4.9 Copying variable-length arrays.

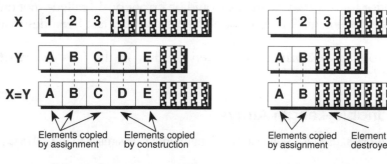

(a) Source longer than target   (b) Source shorter than target

---

The *DVarray* class allocates the array elements from the heap, but keeps those elements unconstructed until needed. This is done by creating an array of characters, which is then typecast into an array of *TYPE*. For the copy constructor, the array elements from the source array are constructed and copied, again by clever use of the concatenate function. (Remember that the array initially has a logical length of zero.)

```
template<class TYPE>
DVarray<TYPE>::DVarray(const DVarray<TYPE> &s)
// Copy constructor. Note that we first allocate an
// array of unconstructed bits. Using concatenate
// here effectively does the element-by-element copy
// construction for us.
: Varray<TYPE>((TYPE *)new char[s.DimLength()*sizeof(TYPE)],
               s.DimLength())
{
  Concatenate(s);
}
```

The other constructors work in a similar manner. The destructor performs the reverse process. First, any constructed elements remaining in the array are destroyed, and then the storage is freed from the heap:

```
template<class TYPE>
DVarray<TYPE>::~DVarray()
{
  // Clean up after all constructed members
  CleanUpElements(0, len);
  // Delete the storage
  delete[] (char *)data;
}
```

Note the typecast to *char* * in the *delete* call. Had we not used this typecast, the destructor for the array elements would be erroneously called—not only for unconstructed elements, but also for elements that had just been destroyed.

The code for the *DVarray* class is given on disk in the files *dvarray.h* and *dvarray.mth*.

Static Variable-Length Arrays

The *SVarray* class, used for static variable-length arrays, is similar to the *DVarray* class:

```
template<class TYPE, unsigned N>
class SVarray : public Varray<TYPE> {
```

```
protected:
  char storage[N*sizeof(TYPE)];
public:
  SVarray();
  SVarray(const SVarray<TYPE, N> &s);
  SVarray(const Array<TYPE> &s);
  SVarray(const TYPE *s, unsigned n);
  virtual ~SVarray();
  SVarray<TYPE, N> &operator=(const Array<TYPE> &s);
};
```

As was true with the *DVarray* class, the storage is allocated as an array of characters and then typecast to an array of *TYPE*, as the following copy constructor shows:

```
template<class TYPE, unsigned N>
SVarray<TYPE, N>::SVarray(const SVarray<TYPE, N> &s)
// Copy constructor. Note that storage is presumed
// to be unconstructed bits coming in. Using concatenate
// here effectively does the element-by-element copy
// construction for us.
: Varray<TYPE>((TYPE *)storage, N) // Link to storage
{
  Concatenate(s);
}
```

The destructor must clean up any remaining constructed elements, but of course no call to *delete* is needed:

```
template<class TYPE, unsigned N>
SVarray<TYPE, N>::~SVarray()
{
  // Clean up all constructed members
  CleanUpElements(0, len);
}
```

 The code for the *SVarray* class is given on disk in the files *svarray.h* and *svarray.mth*.

RESIZABLE ARRAYS

A resizable array is a more sophisticated type of array. Not only is a resizable array variable length (in terms of logical length), but its allocated, dimensioned length can also vary. By definition, resizable arrays are dynamically sized. In fact, we can derive a resizable array class, *RVarray*, from *DVarray*.

```
template<class TYPE>
class RVarray : public DVarray<TYPE> {
protected:
  int grow_by;
public:
  RVarray(unsigned n, int gb);
  RVarray(const RVarray<TYPE> &s);
  RVarray(const Array<TYPE> &s);
  RVarray(const TYPE *s, unsigned n);
  virtual void CopyN(const TYPE *s, unsigned n);
  RVarray<TYPE> &operator=(const Array<TYPE> &s);
  virtual unsigned InsertNAt(unsigned p, const TYPE *s, unsigned n=1);
  int Realloc(unsigned new_dimlen, int keep=1);
  int GrowBy(unsigned amt);
  int FreeExtra();
  void ChgGrowByInc(int gb);
};
```

Resizable arrays work as follows: if the array runs out of room while elements are being added, the array grows to a larger size. This is accomplished by allocating a new, larger space, for the array, copying all of the existing elements into the new space, and then deleting the old space. To avoid frequent resizing, the increment for the new size is always above a certain threshold, determined by the *grow_by* variable, which can be controlled by the user at construction time and through the *ChgGrowByInc()* function. If *grow_by* is zero, then the array can't be resized.

Realloc() is the workhorse function of the *RVarray* class:

```
template<class TYPE>
int RVarray<TYPE>::Realloc(unsigned new_dimlen, int keep)
// NOTE: If an error occurs, the data is left intact, and a
// 0 is returned. Otherwise it returns a 1 to indicate success.
{
  if (grow_by == 0) return 0;
  char *new_data = new char[new_dimlen * sizeof(TYPE)];
  if (new_data == 0) return 0;
  dimlen = new_dimlen;
  if (keep) {
    if (new_dimlen < len) {
        // Array is getting shorter. We must call the
        // destructor on all orphaned elements.
        CleanUpElements(new_dimlen, len);
        len = new_dimlen;
    }
    // Copy old data into new space
    memmove(new_data, data, len*sizeof(TYPE));
  }
```

```
  else {
    // We're not keeping any of the data, so clean it up
    CleanUpElements(0, len);
    len = 0;
  }
  delete[] (char *)data; // Delete old storage place
  data = (TYPE *)new_data;
  return 1;
}
```

Realloc() redimensions the array to the new length of *new_dimlen*. The *keep* option flag determines whether the existing elements are to be kept (when the array grows because we're adding elements) or whether the elements can be destroyed (when we're about to replace the contents of the array with data from another array). If the new size is to be smaller, the elements to be chopped off must be properly destroyed as well. Elements to be destroyed are handled through the *CleanUpElements()* function, which makes sure the appropriate destructor is called for each element.

The *RVarray* class overrides both the *CopyN()* and *InsertNAt()* functions of the *Varray* class, in order to allow resizing. Unlike all the other types of arrays, copying to a resizable array may change that array's dimensioned length if the source array is longer. Figure 4.10 illustrates the process. After the potential resizing has taken place, the *Varray* version of *CopyN()* is called, as shown in the following function:

```
template<class TYPE>
void RVarray<TYPE>::CopyN(const TYPE *s, unsigned n)
{
  if (n > dimlen) Realloc(n, 0);
  Varray<TYPE>::CopyN(s, n);
}
```

The new *InsertNAt()* function works in a similar fashion, first by handling any necessary resizing, and then calling the *Varray* version of *InsertNAt()*:

```
template<class TYPE>
unsigned RVarray<TYPE>::InsertNAt(unsigned p,const TYPE *s,unsigned n)
// Inserts the data pointed to by s into the array. Up to n
// elements are inserted (truncating if necesary), starting at
// position p (counted by 0). The array will grow in size
// if needed and if grow_by != 0. The size it will grow to
// will be the larger of grow_by and the room_needed.
// If p >= len, then the data is concatenated onto the end.
// Returns number of elements inserted, or 0 if error.
{
  unsigned room, needed;
```

Figure 4.10 Copying resizable arrays.

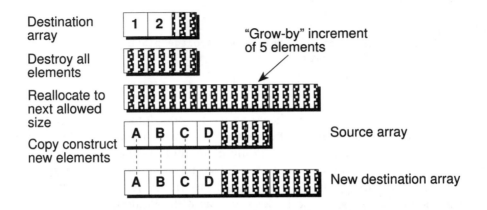

Destination array

Destroy all elements

Reallocate to next allowed size

Copy construct new elements

"Grow-by" increment of 5 elements

Source array

New destination array

```
room = dimlen - len;
if (n > room && grow_by != 0) {
   needed = n - room;
   if (needed < grow_by) needed = grow_by;
   // Grow the array by needed amount. Note that the
   // growth may fail, in which case the array stays
   // the same size, with data intact.
   GrowBy(needed);
}
return Varray<TYPE>::InsertNAt(p, s, n);
}
```

Although the resizing of *RVarrays* takes place automatically, you can manually resize the array through the *GrowBy()* and *FreeExtra()* functions.

```
template<class TYPE>
int RVarray<TYPE>::GrowBy(unsigned amt)
// Grows the dimensions of the array by the specifed amt.
{
  return Realloc(dimlen+amt);
}

template<class TYPE>
int RVarray<TYPE>::FreeExtra()
// Frees all unused space in the array.
{
  return Realloc(len);
}
```

The code for the *RVarray* class is given on disk in the files *rvarray.h* and *rvarray.mth*. Two test programs are supplied: *tstrva.cpp* and *tstrva2.cpp*.

MULTI-DIMENSIONAL ARRAYS

The *Array* classes allow you to use any type for the elements. So what will happen if you use an array itself as the element type? The result is an array of arrays, also called a two-dimensional array. Continuing the process further, you can use a two-dimensional array as the element type for a three-dimensional array, and so on. We'll now take a detailed look at the ways we can accomplish this. Note that the techniques shown in this chapter represent just one way to create user-defined, multi-dimensional arrays. In Chapter 7, we'll look at alternative methods—in the context of two-dimensional matrices.

Note In this book, we'll denote a multi-dimensional array of *n* dimensions as an *n-d* array.

Static Multi-Dimensional Arrays

It is particularly easy to declare user-defined *n-d* arrays if we fix the sizes statically. This approach involves the use of nested template instantiations of the *Sarray* class. (Realize that we are not nesting the template definitions themselves, only instantiations of them.) In this example, we define an array type that holds three rows by five columns of integers:

```
typedef Sarray<int, 5> IntArr5;
typedef Sarray<IntArr5, 3> IntArr3x5;
```

Note how the *IntArr5* type, used for each row of the array, is used as a parameter to the *IntArr3x5* type. The layout of the resulting *2-d* array is given in Figure 4.11. We've shown all of the memory used, including the virtual

Figure 4.11 A 2-d array implemented with sarray objects.

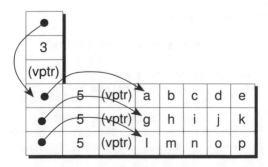

function table pointer for *Sarray* objects. Note that all of the memory cells shown are actually laid out in memory linearly, contrary to what's shown.

In this example, we'll declare and use such an array:

```
IntArr3x5 myarr;

myarr[2][4] = 17; // Set the lower-right corner element
```

Take a look at the double subscripting. The first subscript *a[2]* causes element 2 of the array *myarr* to be returned. This element happens to be an array itself, and the second subscript *[4]* causes element 4 of this secondary array to be returned. The double-subscripting results in the following code, where we call appropriate subscript operator functions from the *IntArr5* and *IntArr3x5* classes:

```
// First call IntArr3x5::operator[], then IntArr5::operator[]
(a.operator[](2)).operator[](4) = 17;
```

With this arrangement, we are able to use the same double-subscripting syntax that we would use with a built-in two-dimensional array. Here, though, we can have range checking done on the subscripts of our user-defined array—by virtue of the overloaded subscript operators.

We can take this approach one step further and define *3-d* arrays from *2-d* arrays. Here's a 2x3x5 integer array type and an example of using it:

```
typedef Sarray<IntArr3x5, 2> IntArr2x3x5;
IntArr2x3x5 b;
b[1][2][4] = 17; // Set lower-right corner element
```

Defining even higher-dimensional arrays works in a similar fashion.

You can get more sophisticated and create *2-d* static arrays whose logical dimensions vary at runtime by using *SVarray* instead of *Sarray*, as in the following code:

```
typedef SVarray<int, 5> IntArr5;
typedef SVarray<IntArr5, 3> IntArr3x5;

IntArr3x5 a; // Logical dimensions start out 0x0

a.Concatenate(IntArr5()); // Add a row
a[0].Concatenate(42);     // Add a column to row 0

a[0][0] = 17; // Change top-left corner element
a[0][1] = 25; // Error: second subscript out of bounds
a[1][0] = 17; // Error: first subscript out of bounds
```

This code illustrates the difference between the allocated dimensionality and the logical dimensionality of a *2-d* array. Each *IntArr3x5* array has *3x5* elements allocated, but starts out with a logical dimensionality of *0x0*. In effect, the array has no rows (and no columns for that matter). To use the array, we must add rows, and to each row we must add columns. The total number of rows that can be added is 3, and the total number of columns per row is 5. Each row can actually have a different number of logical columns (but only up to 5), as shown in Figure 4.12. (Again, the actual linearity of the data isn't shown.) In any case, each array actually has 3 rows of 5 columns allocated for its use.

Although there is a considerable amount of power here, the allocated dimensions of the array must be determined at compile time. But what if we want to determine the dimensions at runtime? For instance, suppose we sometimes need 5x100 arrays, but at other times only 3x5 arrays? In cases like this, we may want to defer the sizing until runtime, and only allocate space for 5x100 arrays when necessary.

Dynamic Multi-Dimensional Arrays

By using a technique similar to the one used in the previous section, we can define *n-d* arrays that have their allocated sizes determined in part at runtime. It's quite easy to size the first dimension at runtime, but unfortunately the other sizes must be set at compile time. For example, with a *2-d* array, we can determine the number of rows to be allocated at runtime, but we must fix the number of columns. This method involves using a *Darray* object instead of a *Sarray* object for the final dimension. For each row, we can use either *Sarray* or *SVarray* objects:

Figure 4.12 A jagged 2-d array implemented with SVarray objects.

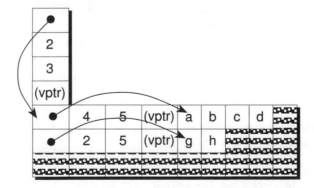

```
typedef SVarray<int, 5> IntArr5;
typedef Darray<IntArr5> IntArrNx5; // Note use of Darray

IntArrNx5 a(10); // Make a 10x5 array
IntArrNx5 b(3);  // Make a 3x5 array
```

We can get even more exotic by allowing the number of logical rows to vary after the array has been constructed. For example, we could use *DVarray* instead of *Darray*:

```
typedef SVarray<int, 5> IntArr5;
typedef DVarray<IntArr5> IntArrNx5; // Note use of DVarray

IntArrNx5 a(10); // Logical dimensions start out 0x0

a.Concatenate(IntArr5()); // Add a row
a[0].Concatenate(42);     // Add a column
a[1][4] = 17; // Subscript error!
```

Getting even fancier, we can use an *RVarray* instead of a *DVarray* so that we can change the allocated number of rows at runtime:

```
typedef Sarray<int, 5> IntArr5;
typedef RVarray<IntArr5> IntArrNx5; // Note use of RVarray

// Make an array that's initially allocated 3x5, but that
// can grow by 2 row increments.
IntArrNx5 a(3, 2);        // Logical size is 0x0
a.Concatenate(IntArr5()); // Add three rows
a.Concatenate(IntArr5());
a.Concatenate(IntArr5()); // Logical size is now 3x0
a.Grow(); // Allocate room for two more rows
```

Figure 4.13 shows what the memory layout of such an array might look like after adding some elements.

One thing we *can't* do, even using the *RVarray* class, is determine the number of columns to be allocated at runtime. That is, we can't implement the rows themselves with *RVarray*. (We could use *SVarray*, though.) Why not? Let's try it:

```
typedef RVarray<int> IntArrM;
typedef RVarray<IntArrM> IntArrNxM;

// Starting with 10 rows, but how many columns?
IntArrNxM a(10); // Compiler error!
```

Figure 4.13 A resizable 2-d array declared with the RVarray class.

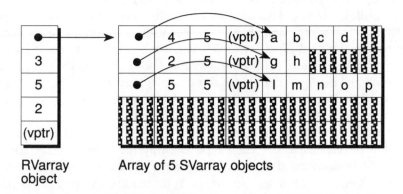

RVarray
object

Array of 5 SVarray objects

We could never declare objects of type *IntArrNxM*. *RVarray* doesn't have a default constructor, but one would be needed to set up each row. This default constructor would have to specify a default number of columns. But what should the default be? Even if we do supply a default, we're in essence fixing one dimension of the array, which puts us right back where we started.

It's interesting to note that built-in *2-d* arrays have a similar problem. For example, it's quite common to pass a *2-d* array to a function, where the number of rows is variable, but the number of columns is fixed:

```
void f(int (*a)[10], int nr)
// Pass in an array of nr rows and 10 columns
{
  for (int i = 0; i<nr; i++) a[i][0] = 1; // Set first col to 1's
}
```

Unfortunately, it's not possible to pass a 2-d array to a function where the columns dimension is also specified by a parameter. The reason involves the way built-in *2-d* arrays are implemented using pointers, a topic we'll discuss in Chapter 7.

Other Approaches to Multi-Dimensional Arrays

The inability to specify the number of columns dynamically is a major limitation to the nested template approach to declaring *2-d* arrays. And even when we allow the number of rows to vary, using the *RVarray* class, a lot of pointers and length variables are redundant and add overhead. Fortunately, there are ways around these problems. In Chapter 7, you'll see an alternative design to *2-d* arrays that uses a more compact representation, which also allows both dimensions to be determined at runtime.

USER-DEFINED ARRAYS VERSUS BUILT-IN ARRAYS

Let's step back and see how efficient the *Array* class hierarchy is compared to using built-in arrays. At a minimum, each array object requires space for a pointer to the array data, the array data itself, the length of the array, and a pointer to a virtual function table. Thus, the minimum space overhead, per array, is two pointers plus an integer. If you want variable-length arrays, an extra integer is required to store the dimensioned length. For resizable arrays, add another integer to store the *grow_by* increment. In any case, only when you need more sophistication do you pay for it.

Since each class in the *Array* hierarchy is actually a template, class methods will be replicated for each type of array element used. A specific *Array* class will be generated for any given array element type, plus one or more derived classes. With resizable arrays, four classes are generated per element type: *Array<TYPE>*, *Varray<TYPE>*, *DVarray<TYPE>*, and *RVarray<TYPE>*. The potential for code explosion does exist here, but it is mitigated by three facts:

- You may not have very many different types of objects being stored in arrays for a single application.

- Many of the class methods are short enough to be inlined, and often do nothing more than refer to other methods or return a data member value.

- You only pay for classes you need. For instance, no *RVarray<TYPE>* class will be generated if you're not using resizable arrays.

Subscripting will be slower with range checking, and in tight loops the reduction in speed may be significant. For instance, sorting an array with range checking turned on is typically twice as slow as it would be with range checking off. Even with range checking off, subscripting will be slightly slower than it would be if we used low-level arrays directly. The reason: we must access the array elements indirectly through the *this* pointer of the *Array* object. A clever compiler might preload a pointer to the elements into a register before a loop is performed. Thus, the subscripting in the loop would be as efficient as possible. Unfortunately, many compilers aren't that clever.

Even though subscripting with range checking is slower, we've made it as efficient as possible by carefully designing the arrays so that the overloaded subscript operator functions are not virtual. Also, the subscript operator functions need only be specified once, in the *Array* class. The result is minimum speed and space overhead.

ALTERNATIVE ARRAY DESIGNS

We chose to make the base *Array* class a template. That means whenever we instantiate a derived class array template, at least *two* classes will be generated: the base class and the derived class. We could eliminate generating a base class every time by using a non-template *Array* class. This can be done by using a *void* pointer to point to the array elements, rather than a *TYPE* pointer. For example:

```
class Array { // Note, not a template
protected:
  void *data;      // Point to any type of array data
  unsigned len; // Length of array
  int size;        // Size of an array element
  ...
};
```

The trouble with this approach lies in array subscripting. Because the type of data isn't known, we must store the size of the array element and use that size during subscripting operations. Worse, we must use a typecast to get the actual type of the array element. This leads both to performance and maintenance problems. We might decide not to define subscripting in the *Array* class, instead leaving that up to the derived classes (which are templates with specified element types). But then we couldn't pass generic *Array* pointers or references, rendering functions that use arrays less versatile.

5

Heterogenous Arrays

In Chapter 3, we introduced the use of heterogenous arrays to allow a container to store different types of objects. In that chapter, we mentioned ways that arrays could be used as heterogenous containers. This chapter will investigate some of these ways more thoroughly. In particular, we'll look at ways to implement reference counting, a technique used to handle the problems of pointer aliasing. But first, we'll review some of the ideas we presented in Chapter 3.

ARRAYS OF POINTERS

By definition, an array can only easily store one type of object, since each element must be the same size. So how do we create heterogenous arrays, where the elements are different object types—perhaps of different sizes? The answer is that we can't. We can, however, store *pointers* to the objects. That's because pointers are usually the same size, regardless of the type of object they point to. Figure 5.1 shows an example of a heterogenous array that points to shape objects.

Arrays Pointing to Any Type of Object

The *Array* classes discussed in Chapter 4 can be readily used to create heterogenous arrays. In the most general case, the element type should be *void **, which allows any type of object to be pointed to. However, this leads to all sorts of problems, since we can use the objects only if the pointers are typecast, an error-prone activity. For example:

Figure 5.1 A heterogenous array.

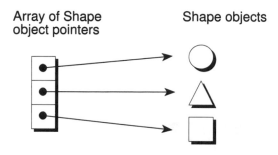

Array of Shape   Shape objects
object pointers

```
Darray<void *> vpa(2); // Create an array of void pointers

vpa[0] = new Toaster; // Store a Toaster object
vpa[1] = new Ufo;      // Store a Ufo object

((Ufo *)vpa[1])->Fly();          // Okay
((Ufo *)vpa[0])->Fly();          // Likely program crash!
```

Arrays Pointing to Objects from a Hierarchy

One way to reduce typecasting problems like those shown in the previous section is to restrict the objects to be only those from a particular class hierarchy. Then, good use of virtual functions will reduce (but not eliminate) the need for typecasting.

    For example, the following code shows a class hierarchy that consistis of a base *Shape* class and a derived *Circle* class. A virtual *Area()* function is defined in each class. For *Shape* objects, *Area()* returns 0. For *Circle* objects, the standard r² formula is used. We can store both types of objects in an array consisting of *Shape* pointers:

```
class Shape {
protected:
  float x, y;
public:
  Shape()                 { x = 0; y = 0; }
  Shape(float xx, float yy) { x = xx; y = yy; }
  virtual float Area()    { return 0; }
};

class Circle : public Shape {
protected:
  float r;
```

```
public:
  Circle() { r = 0; }
  Circle(float xx, float yy, float rr) : Shape(xx,yy) { r = rr; }
  virtual float Area() { return 3.14*r*r; }
};


Darray<Shape *> spa(2); // Create array of shape pointers

spa[0] = new Shape(1,2);
spa[1] = new Circle(3, 4, 5);

for(int i = 0; i<2; i++) cout << spa[i]->Area() << '\n';
```

Pointer Aliasing

On the surface, the use of arrays of pointers to implement heterogenous arrays seems quite easy. However, one major problem lurks beneath the surface: *pointer aliasing*. Both examples that we've shown neglected to do one important thing: delete the objects that were created on the heap. This isn't terribly difficult to do in simple cases. For instance, we could add the following two lines to our previous example:

```
delete spa[0]; // Delete object being pointed to
delete spa[1];
```

However, what happens if we were to have two arrays in our example, and we decide to copy one array into the other?

```
Darray<Shape *> spb(2);

spb = spa; // What happens here?
```

Due to the design of the *Array* classes, only the pointers to the *Shape* objects would be copied, not the objects themselves. The result is that both arrays would point to the same objects. Now the question is: which array should be responsible for deleting the actual objects? Or should we make copies of the objects instead?

We can use four basic methods—ranging from simple to complex—to handle this aliasing problem:

1. Use the convention that heterogenous arrays are never responsible for cleaning up the objects they point to. Instead, whatever created the objects is responsible. This is the default behavior when using one of the *Array* classes with pointer elements.

2. A flag could be stored in each array to indicate whether the array is responsible for cleaning up the objects or whether some other array is responsible. Only the first array that references a particular set of objects will have this flag set to one. For all other array copies, the flag is set to zero.

3. Store a flag in each object, indicating whether the object itself or the array it's associated with is responsible for cleanup of the object. In this scenario, a flag is still needed in each array, (as in method 2), in case the object's flag says it's some array's responsibility, and in case multiple array copies exist. We have to know *which* array is responsible for the objects.

4. Extend the idea of method 3 and, instead of using a boolean flag, use a counter to count how many references are made to the object. When this count goes to zero, the object should be destroyed. With this method, no flags are needed in the arrays themselves.

Method 4 is the *reference counting* scheme mentioned in Chapter 3. In that chapter, we didn't actually implement reference counting, so we'll do this next.

REFERENCE COUNTING

Reference counting works by storing a counter with each object. Each time the object is referenced by another entity (such as an array or perhaps some other object), the counter is incremented. When an entity is finished with the object, the counter is decremented. When the counter goes to zero, it means no entities are referencing the object, so it can be deleted. Thus, one way to safely implement heterogenous arrays is to point only to objects that are reference counted.

You can implement refererence counting in two basic ways:

1. *Embed a reference count directly into each object.* This works if you haven't defined your classes yet or don't mind modifying existing classes.

2. *Indirectly associate each object with a reference count.* This method is for those cases where you don't want to (or can't) modify your existing classes.

We'll investigate both of these methods next.

REFERENCE-COUNTED OBJECTS

The simplest and most efficient way to implement reference counting is to directly embed a reference count into each object. This suggests a single-rooted hierarchy, where every object type is derived from a base class that sets up the reference counting. For example, we can define a *CountedObj* class for this purpose:

```
class CountedObj {
protected:
  unsigned refcnt;
public:
  CountedObj()          { refcnt = 1; }
  virtual ~CountedObj() { }
  void IncRef()         { refcnt++; }
  void DecRef()         { refcnt-; }
  int UnReferenced()    { return refcnt == 0; }
};
```

From this class, we derive all the other types of objects we wish to have reference counted. In the case of the existing *Shape* and *Circle* classes given earlier, one simple modification will suffice—merely derive *Shape* from *CountedObj*:

```
class Shape : public CountedObj {
  ...
};
```

Now *Shape* and *Circle* objects have embedded reference counts. However, we have yet to show how these reference counts get manipulated. That's the responsibility of whatever uses the objects. In the case of heterogenous arrays, where pointers to objects are used, the responsibility falls on the pointers.

SMART POINTERS

To handle pointers to reference-counted objects, we'll define a new type of pointer called *smart pointers*. These work much like normal pointers, except they keep track of the number of references to the objects they point to. The following *SmartPtr* class implements smart pointers as a concrete data type.

```
template<class TYPE>
class SmartPtr {
protected:
  TYPE *objptr; // Actual pointer to object
  void Bind(const SmartPtr<TYPE> &p);
  void Unbind();
  void NewBinding(const SmartPtr<TYPE> &p);
public:
  static TYPE null_obj;
  SmartPtr(TYPE *p=0);
  SmartPtr<const SmartPtr<TYPE> &p);
  SmartPtr<TYPE> &operator=(const SmartPtr<TYPE> &p);
  ~SmartPtr();
```

```
  TYPE &operator*() const;
  TYPE *operator->() const;
};
```

Complete code for the *SmartPtr* class is given in the file *smartptr.h*. (The class is completely inlined.)

Each smart pointer has one data member, *objptr*, that points to the object being referenced. Any type of object can be used as long as it is reference-counted and has the member functions *IncRef()*, *DecRef()*, and *UnReferenced()*. The reference counter should be set to one by the type's constructor. As you might have suspected, any object type derived from the *CountedObj* class fits these requirements.

Constructing Smart Pointers

To set up a smart pointer to an object, you must first allocate and initialize the object on the heap (with the reference count set to one), and then pass a pointer to the object in a call to the *SmartPtr* constructor. For example:

```
SmartPtr<Shape> ps(new Shape(1,1));
SmartPtr<Shape> pc(new Circle(2,3,4));
```

In the second constructor call above, *pc* can point to a *Circle* object—even though *pc* is typed to point to a *Shape* object—since *Circle* was derived from *Shape*. This important feature lends itself quite nicely to the creation of heterogenous arrays. For example, we can define a heterogenous array of *SmartPtr<Shape>* objects that point to both *Shape* and *Circle* objects. For simplicity, we use a built-in array:

```
SmartPtr<Shape> arr[2] = { new Shape(1, 2), new Circle(3, 4, 5) };
```

Figure 5.2 shows the memory layout of the array we've just constructed. Note that, when building the array, two implicit calls are made to the *SmartPtr* constructor. We'll look at that constructor now:

```
template<class TYPE>
SmartPtr<TYPE>::SmartPtr(TYPE *p)
{
  if (p) {        // Do we have an object to point to?
    objptr = p; // Point to the object
  }
  else {          // No. Then point to the null object.
    objptr = &null_obj;
```

```
    objptr->IncRef(); // Must account for reference
  }
}
```

The constructor works as follows: if the parameter *p* isn't a null pointer, we initialize *objptr* to reference the object pointed to by *p*. However, if the allocation of the object fails, *p* will be null. Rather than have *objptr* also be null, we point to the special static object *null_obj*, set aside for just this purpose. By using *null_obj*, we can guarantee that *objptr* will never be null. This greatly simplifies the rest of the *SmartPtr* code. If we do reference *null_obj*, we must increment its reference count, as shown in the constructor. If *p* isn't null, it's assumed that the reference count for the object pointed to by *p* is already set, and that this *SmartPtr* is currently the only reference to it.

The constructor can be used as a default constructor because *p* defaults to zero. By using the default constructor, you can have a smart pointer automatically set up to point to *null_obj*. This is useful in declaring an array without explicitly constructing each element. For example:

```
// Default SmartPtr constructor called 10 times below
Darray< SmartPtr<Shape> > myarr(10);
```

Notice how we're using a nested template declaration here, declaring a *Darray* object of *SmartPtr<Shape>* elements. In this example, each element of *myarr* will initially point to *null_obj*.

The static *null_obj* object must be allocated once somewhere in our program. Also note that we must have one of these objects for each type of smart pointer. For example, if we're going to use smart pointers to point to *Shape* objects and, let's say, *Toaster* objects, we would write:

```
// Allocate null objects for each type of smart pointer
Shape SmartPtr<Shape>::null_obj;
Toaster SmartPtr<Toaster>::null_obj;
```

Figure 5.2 A heterogenous array of smart Shape pointers.

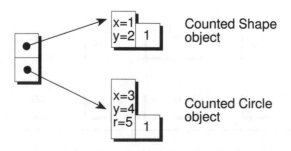

Binding Smart Pointers

A smart pointer can be *bound* to an object by pointing *objptr* to it and then adjusting the reference count for the object. As you've seen, the constructors do this for us initially. But afterwards, we can bind to another object by using the following three routines:

```
template<class TYPE>
void SmartPtr<TYPE>::Bind(const SmartPtr<TYPE> &s)
// Assumes the object is not already bound
{
  objptr = s.objptr;
  objptr->IncRef();
}

template<class TYPE>
void SmartPtr<TYPE>::Unbind()
{
  objptr->DecRef();
  if (objptr->UnReferenced()) delete obj;
}

template<class TYPE>
void SmartPtr<TYPE>::NewBinding(const SmartPtr<TYPE> &s)
{
  if (objptr != s.objptr) { // Prevents accidental deletion
      Unbind();
      Bind(s);
  }
}
```

The *Bind()* routine sets *objptr* to point to the same object that some other smart pointer is using. Aliasing occurs at this point, which is recorded by incrementing the reference count for the object. The *Unbind()* routine does the reverse by decrementing the reference count. If the reference count goes to zero,

---

Figure 5.3 Binding to a new object.

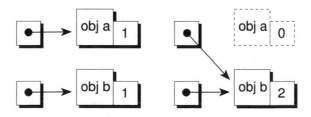

the object is de-allocated by calling *delete*. The *NewBinding()* routine combines the actions of *Bind()* and *Unbind()* by first unbinding from the current object and then binding to a new one. Figure 5.3 shows an example of this process.

The copy constructor, overloaded assignment, and destructor use the binding routines:

```
template<class TYPE>
SmartPtr<TYPE>::SmartPtr(const SmartPtr<TYPE> &p)
{
  Bind(p);
}

template<class TYPE>
SmartPtr<TYPE> &SmartPtr<TYPE>::operator=(const SmartPtr<TYPE> &p)
{
  NewBinding(p);
  return *this;
}

template<class TYPE>
SmartPtr<TYPE>::~SmartPtr()
{
  Unbind();
}
```

As is true with any normal pointer, copying one smart pointer into another causes only the pointer *objptr* to be copied, not the object being pointed to. However, smart pointers, unlike normal pointers, also keep track of the number of references made to the object. In the case of the copy constructor, a single call to *Bind()* does the trick. But for assignments, we must first unbind from the object currently being pointed to, and then bind to the new one. The *NewBinding()* routine does the work here.

When a smart pointer is destroyed, a call to *Unbind()* is made to decrement the reference count for the object being referenced. The object itself won't be deleted unless the reference count goes to zero.

Using Smart Pointers Like Ordinary Pointers

In Chapter 3, we espoused the virtues of using concrete data types. The idea is to be able to use a user-defined type as though it were built into the language. It would be convenient if we could use smart pointers like any other pointer. For example, we should be able to de-reference them as though they were ordinary pointers. We can do this by overloading the two operators '*' and '->':

```
template<class TYPE>
const TYPE &SmartPtr<TYPE>::operator*() const
{
  return *objptr;
}

template<class TYPE>
TYPE *SmartPtr<TYPE>::operator->() const
{
  return objptr;
}
```

When combined, these operators make a *SmartPtr<TYPE>* object appear to be a *TYPE* * object. For example, we can make a smart *Shape* pointer look like a *Shape* pointer, as in:

```
SmartPtr<Shape> sp = new Shape(1, 2);

// Two calls to operator'->'
sp->x = 42;
cout << "Area: " << sp->Area() << '\n';

Shape s = *sp; // Call to operator'*'

*sp = s;       // Illegal!
```

The last statement tries to do a wholesale assignment to a de-referenced *Shape* object via the *operator*()* function. This shouldn't be allowed because the embedded reference count will get set as well—greatly messing up the scheme of things. To disallow such dangerous statements, *operator*()* returns a reference to a constant TYPE, not just a TYPE. This means the object can only be read, not written to.

We didn't use the same *const* modifier on the *operator->()* function, however. There ought to be *some* way to change the underlying object's data! Unfortunately, this creates a loophole because, even though *refcnt* is protected, the functions *IncRef()* and *DecRef()* aren't. This means we can write corrupting code like:

```
sp->DecRef(); // Not cool!
```

Surprisingly, it can be difficult to fix this loophole. We would like to make the functions *DecRef()* and *IncRef()* private to only the classes that need access to them, such as the appropriate *SmartPtr* class. We could do this by declaring *refcnt* protected or private in the *CountedObj* class, and then declare *SmartPtr* as a friend. The problem is that *SmartPtr* is a template, and we can't specify all instantiations of a template as friends of a particular class. We must spell out the instantiations one at a time. For example:

```
class Shape;      // Forward class declarations
class Widget;

template<class TYPE> class SmartPtr; // Forward template declaration
class CountedObj {
private:
  friend class SmartPtr<Shape>;
  friend class SmartPtr<Widget>;
  ... // All other friends go here
  unsigned refcnt;
public:
  ...
};
```

We've left the loophole in so that we don't have to go to all this trouble. So be careful!

To make smart pointers look even more like ordinary pointers, you might also want to overload the comparison operators '==' and '!='. We didn't do that in the *SmartPtr* class, but here's how *operator==()* and *operator!=()* might be defined as friend functions:

```
template<class TYPE>
int operator==(const SmartPtr<TYPE> &a, const SmartPtr<TYPE> &b)
{
  return a.objptr == b.objptr;
}


template<class TYPE>
int operator!=(const SmartPtr<TYPE> &a, const SmartPtr<TYPE> &b)
{
  return a.objptr != b.objptr;
}
```

Finally, you might also want to conveniently test whether a *SmartPtr* is "null" by overloading the '!' operator and providing an *int* type conversion operator. Here's how:

```
template<class TYPE>
int SmartPtr<TYPE>::operator!()
// Returns 1 if pointer references null_obj; otherwise, returns 0
{
  return objptr == &null_obj;
}
```

```
template<class TYPE>
SmartPtr<TYPE>::operator int()
// Returns 1 if pointer doesn't reference null_obj; otherwise, returns 0
{
  return rep != &null_obj;
}


...


SmartPtr<Shape> p(new Shape(1, 2));

if (!p) cout << "Allocation failed\n";
if (p) cout << "Allocation succeeded\n";
```

Arrays of Smart Pointers

We'll now take a closer look at smart pointers by using them with the user-defined *Array* classes created in Chapter 4. Here is a dynamic array of smart shape pointers:

```
typedef SmartPtr<Shape> SmartShapePtr;

// Declare a dynamic array of smart shape pointers
Darray<SmartShapePtr> arr(2);
```

With such a declaration, the two smart shape pointers stored in the array will reference the null shape object. We could assign them to new objects, as follows:

```
arr[0] = new Shape(42, 25);
arr[1] = new Circle(55, 17, 3);
```

Note that, when the assignments take place, the array elements are unbound from the null shape object, and then bound to the new objects just created.

The array elements can be used just as though they were pointers to *Shape* objects, as in:

```
for (int i = 0; i<2; i++) cout << arr[0]->Area() << '\n';
```

Since *Area()* is virtual, and we are using base class *Shape* pointers, the appropriate area of each shape is printed.

When you use an array of smart pointers, rest assured that the constructors and destructors for all referenced objects are called the correct number of times, even if the array is a variable-length, resizable array. This is true because both the *Array* and *SmartPtr* classes are designed to carefully handle construction and destruction of array element objects.

For example, suppose we define a static variable-length array of *Shape* pointers, and then add some elements. As a twist, we'll make the second and third elements point to the same *Shape* object. To understand what's going on, remember that all elements of a variable-length array start out unconstructed.

```
SVarray<SmartShapePtr, 5> shapes; // 5 unconstructed elements

// Construct the first two elements
shapes.Add(new Shape(1,1));
shapes.Add(new Circle(0, 0, 4));

// Create a third element bound to null shape object
shapes.Add(0);
// Now, bind it to same shape that the second element references
shapes[2] = shapes[1];
```

Figure 5.4 shows the memory layout of the resulting array. As you can see from the figure, when one element is assigned to another, only the pointers are assigned—not the objects being pointed to. Since the overloaded *SmartPtr<Shape>* assignment operator is in use, the proper binding and un-binding takes place. For the same reason, copying between smart pointer arrays also works properly. This copying is very efficient, especially when the referenced objects are large.

Figure 5.4 Memory layout of a smart pointer array.

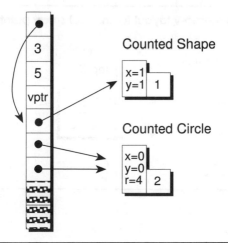

What is the cost of using smart pointers rather than ordinary pointers in an array? In both cases, heap space will be allocated for the target object of each array element. When smart pointers are used, each target object will also have one extra integer to store the reference count. Hence, that is the net overhead for using smart pointers over ordinary pointers. Normally, this overhead won't be noticeable, but it *is* there.

At this point, you might be concerned about the amount of code space required for the smart pointer class templates themselves. Note that the member functions are all very simple and can easily be inlined. The amount of code added by using smart pointers, while not zero, won't be too great for most applications.

Two test programs *tstsp.cpp* and *tstsp2.cpp* are provided on the disk to illustrate how smart pointers are used in both fixed-length and resizable heterogenous arrays of shapes.

INDIRECT SMART POINTERS

The smart pointer technique that we've just shown works great—as long as you can directly embed a reference count into each object. But suppose you have an existing class that you want reference counted, and don't want to modify the class? One way to add the reference counting is by using *indirect smart pointers.*

Indirect smart pointers are like ordinary smart pointers except that one extra level of indirection is required to get to the object. Between the pointer and the target object is another object, which stores a reference count and a pointer to the target object. This intermediate object serves to make the target object look like a reference-counted object. Figure 5.5 illustrates the proposed setup.

Figure 5.5 Sample memory layout for indirect smart pointers.

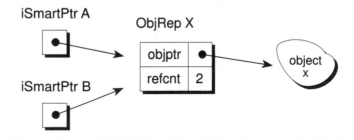

Here is a class that can serve as the intermediate object type:

```
template<class TYPE> class iSmartPtr; // Forward template declaration

template<class TYPE>
class ObjRep {
// Assumes the object pointed to is stored on heap,
// except for null_obj
private:
  friend class iSmartPtr<TYPE>;
  unsigned refcnt;
  TYPE *objptr;
  ObjRep();
  void IncRef();
  void DecRef();
  ObjRep(TYPE *p);
  static TYPE null_obj;
};

template<class TYPE>
ObjRep<TYPE>::ObjRep()
// To be used only once to create a null ObjRep object
{
  objptr = &null_obj;
  refcnt = 1;
}

template<class TYPE>
ObjRep<TYPE>::ObjRep(TYPE *p)
{
  objptr = p;
  refcnt = 1;
}

template<class TYPE>
void ObjRep<TYPE>::IncRef()
{
  refcnt++;
}

template<class TYPE>
void ObjRep<TYPE>::DecRef()
{
  refcnt--;
  if (refcnt == 0) delete objptr;
}
```

The name *ObjRep* stands for *object representation*. The class represents an ordinary object as though it were a counted object. You'll notice that *ObjRep* is very similar to the *CountedObj* class. The main difference is that the target object is not stored in the *ObjRep* object, but rather is pointed to by *objptr*. The parameterized constructor sets up *objptr* and also initializes the reference count. The *DecRef()* function is responsible for deleting the target object when the reference count goes to zero. Note that the *CountedObj* class does not delete the object, since it *is* the object! In this case, the deletion is left as a task for the *iSmartPtr* class.

Notice that we've declared a static member, *null_obj*. This is the target object to point to when we want a null *ObjRep* object. We do this for the same reason it was done in the *SmartPtr* class—to guarantee that we never have a real null pointer.

Having defined the *ObjRep* class, we can now show the *iSmartPtr* class, which is used to implement indirect smart pointers. Note the lowercase *i* in the prefix:

```
template<class TYPE>
class iSmartPtr {  // Indirect smart pointers
protected:
  static ObjRep<TYPE> null_rep;
  ObjRep<TYPE> *rep;
  void Bind(const iSmartPtr<TYPE> &p);
  void Unbind();
  void NewBinding(const iSmartPtr<TYPE> &p);
public:
  iSmartPtr(TYPE *p=0);
  iSmartPtr<TYPE> &operator=(const iSmartPtr<TYPE> &p);
  ~iSmartPtr();
  TYPE &operator*() const;
  // Will only compile if TYPE is a structure
  TYPE *operator->() const;
};
```

Complete code for the *ObjRep* and *iSmartPtr* classes is given in the file *ismartptr.h*. (The classes are completely inlined.)

The two classes *ObjRep* and *iSmartPtr* provide an example of cooperating classes. The *ObjRep* class gives the low-level data representation for reference-counted objects, while the *iSmartPtr* class provides the high-level interface. This technique of arranging two classes, one being a high-level wrapper around a low-level representation, is sometimes referred to as the *letter-envelope idiom*. See [Coplien 92]. Here, the *iSmartPtr* class is the "envelope" that wraps around the "letter" class *ObjRep*.

The *iSmartPtr* class is very similar to the *SmartPtr* class. The main difference is that it points to an *ObjRep<TYPE>* object rather than directly to a *TYPE* object. A static *ObjRep* object, *null_rep*, is declared (to be used in lieu of a null pointer). This is in addition to the null static *TYPE* object declared in the *ObjRep* class, which is in fact referenced by *null_rep*. Both of these objects must be allocated once somewhere in your program—one pair per type of indirect smart pointer. The following statements show how to do this for indirect smart *Shape* pointers:

```
// Allocate a null Shape object to be referenced by
// a null ObjRep object, also allocated
Shape ObjRep<Shape>::null_obj;
ObjRep<Shape> iSmartPtr<Shape>::null_rep;
```

The *iSmartPtr* functions are virtually the same as their *SmartPtr* counterparts, and, as such, many will not be shown here. The functions not shown can be defined by taking the corresponding *SmartPtr* functions and replacing *objptr* with *rep*. Here are the functions that require changes other than this:

```
template<class TYPE>
void iSmartPtr<TYPE>::Unbind()
{
  rep->DecRef(); // ObjRep handles any object deletions
}

template<class TYPE>
iSmartPtr<TYPE>::iSmartPtr(TYPE *p)
{
  rep = (p) ? new ObjRep<TYPE>(p) : 0;
  if (rep == 0) {
     rep = &null_rep;
     rep->IncRef();
  }
}

template<class TYPE>
TYPE &iSmartPtr<TYPE>::operator*() const
{
  return *(rep->objptr);
}

template<class TYPE>
TYPE *iSmartPtr<TYPE>::operator->() const
// Will only compile if TYPE is a structure
{
  return rep->objptr;
}
```

Note how the functions *operator*()* and *operator->()* return a pointer not to the object representation, but rather directly to the target object. Since the target object does not store the reference count, we don't have any unsafe loopholes with these functions. For that reason, *operator*()* returns a *TYPE* reference, instead of a *const TYPE* reference as was the case in the *SmartPtr* class. This allows assignments like the following to take place:

```
iSmartPtr<Shape> sp(new Shape(1,1));
Shape s(42, 17);

*sp = s; // Update the referenced shape object with a new shape
```

One potential problem with the *operator->()* function: it will only compile if *TYPE* is a structure. If TYPE isn't a structure, you'll have to comment the function out. (Too bad there's no way to tell at compile time whether a type is a structure!) Note that the *operator->()* function for *SmartPtr* doesn't have this problem, since in this case *TYPE* will always be a structure.

Arrays of Indirect Smart Pointers

We'll now show what an array of indirect smart pointers looks like. The following array is the same as one we gave earlier for direct smart pointers, except now we use indirect smart pointers:

```
typedef iSmartPtr<Shape> SmartShapePtr;

SVarray<SmartShapePtr, 5> shapes; // 5 unconstructed elements

// Construct the first two elements
shapes.Add(new Shape(1,1));
shapes.Add(new Circle(0, 0, 4));

// Create a third element bound to the null ObjRep<Shape> object
shapes.Add(0);
// Now, bind it to same shape that the second element references
shapes[2] = shapes[1];
```

Figure 5.6 shows the resulting memory layout of the indirect smart pointer array. Compared to the use of ordinary pointers (or even to the use of direct smart pointers), indirect smart pointers cost more overhead. An extra heap allocation is needed for the intermediate *ObjRep* object, which stores the reference count and target object pointer. Note that, like the *SmartPtr* class, the *iSmartPtr* class and its associated *ObjRep* class can be completely inlined, so very little overhead occurs in creating the class itself.

Figure 5.6 Memory layout of a variable-length indirect smart pointer array.

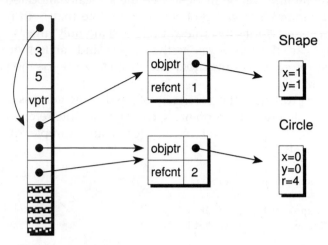

Whether the overhead that results from using indirect pointers becomes a problem depends on how big the target objects are initially, and how many of them you try to store. In the case of large arrays of reference-counted integers, the overhead would be significant. If you need aliasing protection, try to use direct smart pointers if you can, since their overhead is much smaller.

Test programs for indirect smart pointers are given on disk in the files *tstisp.cpp* and *tstisp2.cpp*. These programs test both fixed-length and resizable arrays of indirect smart pointers.

SMART POINTER SAFETY ISSUES

The *SmartPtr* class has a loophole where the reference count can be manipulated directly by using the *operator->()* function. Unfortunately, there is also another loophole, (which exists in the *iSmartPtr* class as well). When either a direct or indirect smart pointer object is constructed, a pointer to the target object to be referenced is passed. Although the target object is supposed to be allocated on the heap, nothing prevents you from passing the address of an object allocated statically. For instance, you might accidentally try:

```
Shape s(1, 1);

Shape> sp(&s); // Not a good idea!
```

Things will go haywire when the reference count for *sp* goes to zero because an attempt will be made to free the statically allocated object from the heap. A program crash will probably result. Note that both the *SmartPtr* and *iSmartPtr* classes violate this rule with their static null target objects. However, these objects are defined private to the classes, and can't otherwise be manipulated. Their reference counts should never go to zero—as long as everything is working correctly.

Another problem is the possibility of passing the address of the same target object to two different smart pointers, creating multiple reference counts for the object. Again, confusion will result. Here's an example of something you should never do:

```
Shape *p = new Shape(1, 1);

SmartPtr<Shape> sp1(p); // Okay
SmartPtr<Shape> sp2(p); // Not!
```

Keep in mind that the *iSmartPtr* class has these same problems.

DERIVED SMART POINTERS

You can help prevent duplicate reference counts from being accidentally created for an object. The idea is to define a smart pointer class that handles the construction of the referenced object itself. For example, we could create a *SmartShapePtr* class, derived from *SmartPtr*, to work directly with *Shape* objects, as follows:

```
class SmartShapePtr : public SmartPtr<Shape> {
public:
  SmartShapePtr(int x, int y);
};

SmartShapePtr::SmartShapePtr(int x, int y)
: SmartPtr<Shape>(new Shape(x, y))
{
  // Nothing else to do
}


...
SmartShapePtr(0, 1); // Much higher level than before
```

Now there's no possibility for accidental duplicate reference counts. A *SmartCirclePtr* class could be coded similarly:

```
class SmartCirclePtr : public SmartPtr<Shape> {
public:
  SmartCirclePtr(int x, int y);
};

SmartCirclePtr::SmartCirclePtr(int x, int y, int r)
// Note that we use the SmartPtr<Shape> class below, rather
// than SmartPtr<Circle> to save some template generation
: SmartPtr<Shape>(new Circle(x, y, r))
{
  // Nothing else to do
}
```

Note that this same technique can also be used for the indirect smart pointer class *iSmartPtr*.

With this technique, we must construct, by hand, a smart pointer class for every type of object we wish to point to. This can quickly get tedious. We need constructors with different parameters for each object that we want to point to, but templates are not flexible enough to allow us to specify the various types of constructors. So, unless we restrict the types being used to always have constructors with similar arguments, we're stuck.

The result is this: if you want absolute safety, you must code separate smart pointer classes by hand. If you don't need absolute safety, or don't want to pay for it, you can use the *SmartPtr* and *iSmartPtr* classes by themselves.

6

Strings

trings are perhaps one of the more useful type of arrays. Strings are variable-length sequences of characters that normally have defined operations such as concatenation (adding one string to the end of another), pattern matching, and the ability to form substrings from larger strings. They are useful mainly for representing data in human-readable form, and for this reason it's hard to imagine a language without strings. In this chapter, we'll look at a robust, efficient design for strings that's user-definable.

C++ does not have a string type *per se*, but instead provides library support for null-terminated character arrays, where the last character is a '\0' to signal the end of the array. Compared to strings in languages such as BASIC, null-terminated strings in C++ are quite primitive:

- You must deal with arrays that hopefully have enough memory allocated for them, and you must ensure the last character has the value '\0'. This is, to say the least, quite error prone.

- It's not possible to store arbitrary binary data in a null-terminated string, since '\0', a valid binary number, would end the string prematurely. A better way would be to store the length of the string in a string header. Figure 6.1 contrasts these two approaches.

- There's no high-level way to assign one string to another, nor to do efficient substring and concatenation operations. For example, to add one string to another, you must scan completely down the first string to find the point of concatenation.

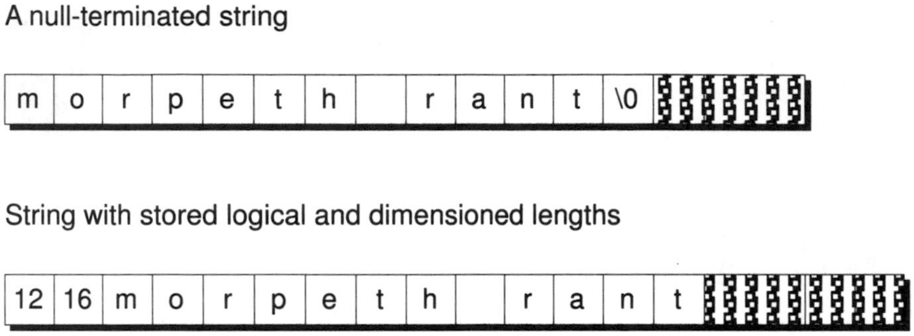

Figure 6.1 Two methods for representing strings.

A null-terminated string

| m | o | r | p | e | t | h | | r | a | n | t | \0 | ▨▨▨▨ |

String with stored logical and dimensioned lengths

| 12 | 16 | m | o | r | p | e | t | h | | r | a | n | t | ▨▨▨▨▨ |

A User-Defined String Design

As you might expect, you can get around the problems of null-terminated strings by defining your own strings. As always, you want a design that's efficient enough to be practical, yet at the same time high-level enough to be easily used. Toward this end, the *String* class given in this chapter has the following features:

- Strings are implemented as a concrete data type, with the appropriate constructors, destructors, and overloaded operators defined.
- Resizable, variable-length strings of arbitrary binary data are supported.
- Concatenation, substring, pattern matching and filling operations are supported.
- The strings use *lazy copying*. When doing string assignments or creating substrings, string text is shared. No copying takes place until one of the strings is modified.

The last feature is perhaps the most critical in the design of the *String* class. With lazy copying, it's possible to define substring and concatenation operations, safely and efficiently.

Reference Counting Revisited

Lazy copying implies that aliasing is occurring, which of course is something to be handled carefully. As we did with the smart pointers in Chapter 5, we can handle this aliasing by using reference counting. But instead of reference counting each array element, the elements of a string will be reference counted *as a unit*.

Strings can be defined with the same letter-envelope technique that we used for smart pointers, with two classes involved. The first class, *StrRep,* holds the string text and its associated reference count. The second class, *String,* provides the high-level interface and keeps track of which portion of the string text is used by a particular string. This layout of reference-counted strings is shown in Figure 6.2.

The StrRep Class

The *StrRep* class is defined as follows:

```
class StrRep {
private:
  friend class String;
  unsigned refcnt; // Reference count for the text of the string
  char data[1];    // Start of the string text
  StrRep();
  void *operator new(size_t n, unsigned d);
  void operator delete(void *p);
  static StrRep null_rep; // For null strings
};
```

The peculiar thing about this class is that *data,* which is the start of the string text, appears to have room for only one character! However, the *StrRep* structure is actually meant to be allocated dynamically and, during that time, enough additional memory will be reserved to handle the desired maximum string length. This additional memory follows immediately after *data.* Figure 6.3 illustrates this layout.

We achieve this kind of dynamic allocation by overloading the *new* and *delete* operators for the *StrRep* class. Here is the *new* operator:

```
void *StrRep::operator new(size_t n, unsigned d)
// Here, n is sizeof(StrRep) and d is the desired
```

Figure 6.2 The layout of reference-counted strings.

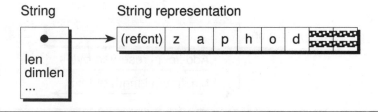

```
// number of allocated characters in the string.
// If allocation fails, we reference null_rep.
{
  // Note: n already accounts for one of the characters
  void *p = new char[n+d-1];
  if (p == 0) {
     p = &null_rep;
     ((StrRep *)p)->refcnt++;
  }
  return p;
}
```

Normally, *new* takes just one argument: the size of the object to be allocated, in this case *sizeof(StrRep)*. We've added a second argument, *d*, that indicates how long the text should be. The overloaded *new* operator then uses *d* to determine how much memory to actually allocate. The memory is allocated as though it were a simple array of characters. Keep in mind that the first portion of this memory will be occupied by the reference count. Here's how a call to *new* is made for *StrRep* objects:

```
// Allocate enough room for 10 characters
StrRep *p = new(10) StrRep;
```

Note the call to the constructor for *StrRep* after the *new* operator. The lexical ordering in this statement suggests what actually happens: first, *new* is called to allocate space for the object, then the object is constructed. The *StrRep* constructor is quite simple—it initializes the reference count to one. The text is left uninitialized, however:

```
StrRep::StrRep()
{
  refcnt = 1;
}
```

Figure 6.3 Dynamic allocation of a StrRep object.

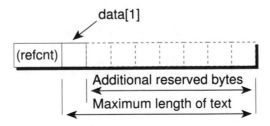

Because of their special memory allocation scheme, *StrRep* objects must always be allocated dynamically. Otherwise, how would you allocate a text size greater than one? The exception to this rule is for the unique *StrRep* object, *null_rep,* that we've incorporated into our design. This object is a static member of the *StrRep* class and is thus statically allocated. As such, *null_rep* can hold only one byte of text. The purpose of *null_rep* is the same as used for the smart pointers in Chapter 5: to guarantee that a string will have somewhere to point to. Null strings always point to *null_rep.* You'll see later that this allows the *String* functions to quite elegantly handle null strings without doing any explicit testing.

The *delete* operator is responsible for deleting a *StrRep* object, which is pointed to by argument *p* in the *delete()* function.

```
void StrRep::operator delete(void *p)
{
  delete[] (char *)p;
}
```

Note that we delete the object as though it were a character array, which is exactly how it was allocated in the first place by *new.* Also, note that *delete()* won't ever be called for *null_rep* because, supposedly, its reference count will never go to zero. Because all *StrRep* objects besides *null_rep* are dynamically allocated, we don't need to explicitly declare a destructor for *StrRep.* The overloaded *delete* operator handles everything.

The *StrRep* class doesn't actually handle many of the reference counting chores. As was true with smart pointers, the envelope class (in this case *String*) handles the binding and unbinding.

THE STRING CLASS

With the *StrRep* class defined, we can show the definition for the *String* class:

```
class String {
private:
  StrRep *rep;
  char *text;       // Pointer to start of string text
  unsigned dimlen;  // Maximum length of text without reallocation
  unsigned len;     // Logical length of text
  int grow_by;      // Minimum resizing increment
  enum { defsize = 16, definc = 16 };
  int Alloc(unsigned n, int gb);
  void Bind(const String &s);
  void Unbind();
  void NewBinding(const String &s);
public:
```

```
    String(unsigned n = String::defsize, int gb = String::definc);
    String(const String &s);
    String(const String &s,
           unsigned ofs, unsigned n, int gb = String::definc);
    String(const char *s, int gb = String::definc);
    String(const char *s, unsigned n, int gb = String::definc);
    ~String();
    int IsNull() const;
    int IsUnique() const;
    String Clone() const;
    int EnsureUnique();
    String &operator=(const String &s);
    void Copy(const char *s);
    void Copy(const String &s);
    String &operator=(const char *s);
#ifndef NO_RANGE_CHECK
    unsigned CheckIndx(unsigned i) const;
#endif
    char &operator[](unsigned i);
    const char &operator[](unsigned i) const;
    unsigned DimLength() const;
    unsigned Length() const;
    int GrowBy(unsigned amt);
    int Grow();
    int FreeExtra();
    void ChgGrowByInc(int gb);
    void SetLength(unsigned n);
    int Realloc(unsigned new_dimlen, int keep=1);
    void CopyN(const char *s, unsigned n);
    unsigned InsReplAt
      (unsigned p, const char *s, unsigned n, int ins=1);
    unsigned DeleteAt(unsigned p, unsigned n);
    char *Text();
    const char *Text() const;
    unsigned InsertAt(unsigned p, const char *s, unsigned n);
    unsigned InsertAt(unsigned p, const char *s);
    unsigned InsertAt(unsigned p, const String &s);
    unsigned ReplaceAt(unsigned p, const char *s, unsigned n);
    unsigned ReplaceAt(unsigned p, const char *s);
    unsigned ReplaceAt(unsigned p, const String &s);
    void Fill(const char c, unsigned ofs = 0, unsigned m = 0);
    void Fill(const char *p, unsigned n, unsigned ofs=0, unsigned m=0);
    void Fill(const char *s, unsigned ofs = 0, unsigned m = 0);
    void Fill(const String &s, unsigned ofs = 0, unsigned m = 0);
    const char *String::NullTermStr();
    String Mid(unsigned p, unsigned n) const;
    String Left(unsigned n) const;
    String Right(unsigned n) const;
    unsigned Find(char *s, unsigned ofs=0) const;
```

```
  unsigned Find(unsigned n, char *s, unsigned ofs=0) const;
  unsigned Find(const String &s, unsigned ofs=0) const;
  void Concatenate(const char *s, unsigned n);
  void operator+=(const String &s);
  void operator+=(const char *s);
  void operator+=(const char c);
  friend String operator+(const String &a, const String &b);
  friend int Compare(const String &a, const String &b);
  friend int operator==(const String &a, const String &b);
  friend int operator!=(const String &a, const String &b);
  friend int operator>(const String &a, const String &b);
  friend int operator>=(const String &a, const String &b);
  friend int operator<(const String &a, const String &b);
  friend int operator<=(const String &a, const String &b);
  friend ostream &operator<<(ostream &strm, const String &s);
  friend istream &operator>>(istream &strm, String &s);
};
```

The complete code for the *String* class—and it's associated *StrRep* class—is given on disk in the files *strobj.h* and *strobj.cpp*. A test program is given in the file *strtst.cpp*.

The *String* class is quite large, having more than 60 members. This is typical for a concrete data type. Ordinarily, you should try to avoid large classes, but many of the member functions here are used to make strings appear built-in to the language. Not all of the functions are strictly necessary, being mainly "convenience functions" that make it easier to work with strings. As a saving grace, many of these functions are simple enough to be inlined.

The *String* class has five data members: *rep, text, len, dimlen,* and *grow_by*. The most important is *rep*, which points to the associated *StrRep* object. Note that *StrRep* only keeps track of the actual text and the reference count for that text. It doesn't store the logical and dimensioned lengths, which is the reponsibility of the *String* class. Since the strings are to be resizable, we have members such as *len, dimlen,* and *grow_by*, which are used exactly as they were in the *RVarray* class of Chapter 4.

This brings up an important point. Since strings are to be resizable, why not implement them using an *RVarray<char>* class? In fact, we could. For instance, *StrRep* could be defined as:

```
class StrRep { // Alternative representation
private:
  unsigned refcnt;
  RVarray<char> data;
  ...
};
```

We chose to use a more direct representation for several reasons: First, if we were to use an *RVarray* object, the memory layout for strings would be more complicated than necessary. It would be composed of the *String* object, the *StrRep* object, and the *RVarray* object inside of the *StrRep* object, which has a pointer to the actual text. That's three separate pieces to be allocated on the heap, rather than just two with the more direct implementation. Also, the *RVarray* class is more general than we need, since it calls constructors and destructors for array elements, which in this case are characters that don't have constructors or destructors. (We can circumvent the latter problem by overriding the appropriate placement constructor and destructor templates to do nothing.)

Thus, even though the *RVarray* class *could* be used, it's probably better to implement a more direct design for strings. The code will be smaller and easier to understand, and the resulting *String* objects will be more compact. Having made these points, we should also tell you that the *String* class was implemented originally using an *RVarray<char>* class, and then this code was optimized specifically for character arrays. You'll notice that some of the member functions of *String* are similar, if not identical, to their *RVarray* counterparts. These functions include *Realloc()*, *InsReplAt()*, *DeleteAt()*, *Grow()*, *GrowBy()*, *FreeExtra()*, *Length()*, and *DimLength()*. Most of these functions will not be repeated here.

The last data member of the *String* class, *text*, is a character pointer to the start of the actual data for the string. Normally, *text* is set to point to the beginning of the *data* member of the corresponding *StrRep* object. However, for substrings, *text* will actually point to some offset from *data*. It wouldn't be strictly necessary to store a pointer here. We could use an integer representing the offset. However, pointing directly using *text* makes operations such as subscripting simpler and faster. Contrast these two logically equivalent functions:

```
const char &operator[](unsigned i) const
// One way to do subscripting
{
  return rep->data[i+ofs]; // Ofs = where substring starts
}

const char &operator[](unsigned i) const
// Another, simpler way using a pre-initialized text
// pointer to the start of the substring
{
  return text[i];
}
```

The idea is to initialize *text* once when the string is built, with a statement such as:

```
text = rep->data[i+ofs];
```

Then, subsequent string operations don't have to keep adding the offset to find the start of the text. Figure 6.4 shows how to use the *text* pointer for a substring.

The *String* class has functions such as *Bind()*, *Unbind()*, and *NewBinding()* to handle the reference counting needed when binding and unbinding text to a string. These functions are similar to those used with the smart pointers of Chapter 5, and are called by the higher-level constructor, destructor, and assignment functions.

CONSTRUCTING STRINGS

A full complement of constructors is defined for the *String* class. You can create strings with a specified starting size and growth increment, create strings that copy data from null-terminated strings, and create strings from raw memory bytes. Here are a few of the constructors:

```
String::String(unsigned n, int gb)
// Constructor to create a string of allocated
// length n, and a grow_by increment of gb.
{
  Alloc(n, gb);
}

String::String(const char *s, int gb)
// Creates a string by copying bytes from a null-
// terminated array, with a grow_by increment of gb.
{
  unsigned slen = strlen(s);
  unsigned dlen = slen;
  if (gb) { // Compute next highest multiple of gb
     unsigned addval = (dlen % gb) ? gb : 0;
     dlen = (dlen / gb) * gb + addval;
  }
```

Figure 6.4 The string text pointer.

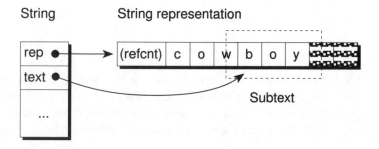

```
   if (Alloc(dlen, gb)) CopyN(s, slen);
}

String::String(const char *s, unsigned n, int gb)
// Create a string of allocated length n, grow_by
// increment of gb, copying bytes from s
{
  if (Alloc(n, gb)) CopyN(s, n);
}
```

The first constructor can actually be used as a default constructor, since both its arguments have defaults. An enumerated type, defined in *String*, holds a default initial size and growth increment:

```
enum { defsize = 16, definc = 16 };
```

You'll notice that this enumerated type has no name (that is, it's an anonymous enumerated type). You can use anonymous enumerated types like this to conveniently define and initialize integer-based constants in a class.

All three of the constructors shown call an auxiliary function, *Alloc()*, which handles the initial allocation of the string object. Note the call to the overloaded *StrRep new* operator:

```
int String::Alloc(unsigned n, int gb)
// Allocate a new string of allocated size n, and
// a grow by increment of gb
{
  rep = new(n) StrRep; // Allocate string rep
  text = rep->data;    // Point to starting text element
  len = 0;
  if (IsNull()) { // Wasn't able to allocate space
    dimlen = 1;   // null_rep has one byte of text
    grow_by = 0;
    return 0; // Indicate failure
  }
  else {
    dimlen = n;
    grow_by = gb;
    return 1; // Indicate success
  }
}
```

If *Alloc()* isn't able to allocate space for the string, a null string is constructed by first referencing the *null_rep* object (handled by the call to the overloaded *new* operator), and then setting the grow-by increment to zero. This prevents the null string from growing, and also allows other string operations (such as concatenation and subscripting) to behave properly without any explicit checks for a null string.

Note the logical length is always set to zero—regardless of whether the memory was allocated or not. Thus, to use a string, you must explicitly add text to it. Two of the constructors do this by calling the *CopyN()* function, (given later).

The destructor is responsible for unbinding the string from its possibly shared text, and deleting the text if necessary. The *Unbind()* function does all the work:

```
String::~String()
// Destructor unbinds from the shared text
{
  Unbind();
}
```

Here are some examples of constructing strings:

```
// Empty string with initial dimensioned length of 10,
// and a default growth increment
String a(10);

// Empty string with intial dimensioned length of 10
// that can't grow
String b(10,0);

// String containing a copy of a null-terminated string,
// with default growth increment
String s("This is a test");

// String containing a copy of some raw bytes, with a
// default growth increment
char bytes[7] = {34, 56, 7, 42, 17, 25, 55];
String t(bytes, 7);

// String that's a copy of another string
String u(t);
```

STRING COPYING

Unlike the other constructors, the following copy constructor doesn't actually do any copying of string data. Instead, the new string is bound to the same data as the old string by calling *Bind()*. In other words, the copy constructor uses *share semantics*:

```
String::String(const String &s)
// Copy constructor, which uses share semantics
{
  Bind(s);
  len = s.len;
  dimlen = s.dimlen;
  grow_by = s.grow_by;
  text = s.text;
}
```

What *isn't* shared between two strings are the bookkeeping variables *len*, *dimlen*, *grow_by*, and *text*. Separate copies are maintained for them. This keeps the strings independent in terms of the way they interpret the length of the text, the text's starting location, and how the strings may be resized. This independence is useful in creating substrings, as you are about to see.

The assignment operator is defined with the same share semantics as the copy constructor:

```
String &String::operator=(const String &s)
// Assigns one string to another. Checks for assignment
// to self. Uses share semantics.
{
  if (this != &s) {
      NewBinding(s);
      len = s.len;
      dimlen = s.dimlen;
      grow_by = s.grow_by;
      text = s.text;
  }
  return *this;
}
```

CREATING SUBSTRINGS

To illustrate how two or more strings can have different interpretations of the same shared text, we'll look at how substrings are defined. The following constructor is at the heart of substring creation. Like the copy constructor, it uses share semantics. However, the substring's variables *len*, *dimlen*, *grow_by*, and *text* all have different values than the source string:

```
String::String(const String &s, unsigned ofs, unsigned n, int gb)
// A constructor to create a substring of string s.
// The substring shares its data with s, starting at
// offset ofs, and of length n. It has an allocated
// length of n, and a grow_by increment of gb.
```

```
{
  Bind(s);
  // Keep ofs and length in range
  if (ofs > s.len-1) ofs = s.len-1;
  if (n + ofs > s.len) n = s.len-ofs;
  // Set max and logical bounds of the substring
  dimlen = n;
  len = n;
  grow_by = gb;
  text = s.text + ofs; // Compute starting text element
}
```

The only differences between a string and a substring is that the *text* pointer may start at some offset from *data*, and that *dimlen* doesn't have quite the same meaning for substrings as it does for normal strings. In normal strings, *dimlen* is the actual number of characters allocated in the corresponding *StrRep* object. For substrings, *dimlen* gives the maximum extent that the substring is allowed to cover over the underlying shared text.

Rather than call the substring constructor directly, the following convenience functions are defined to return left, mid, and right substrings of another string:

```
String String::Left(unsigned n) const
// Returns the left substring of length n
{
  return String(*this, 0, n);
}

String String::Mid(unsigned p, unsigned n) const
// Returns a substring of length n, starting at
// index p
{
  return String(*this, p, n);
}

String String::Right(unsigned n) const
// Returns a right substring of length n
{
  if (n > len) n = len; // Trap possible overflow
  return String(*this, len-n, n);
}
```

The substring functions call the substring constructor to do most of the work. Note that the *gb* parameter, which defines the *grow_by* increment, has a default value of *String::definc* for the substring constructor. The default is used because the substring functions don't specify this parameter.

In each substring function, the newly created substring is returned by value, which causes the object's copy constructor to be called. In the case here, this means *two* identical substrings are created, the second to be the one actually returned by the function. However, since the *String* copy constructor uses share semantics, very little is actually copied. The initially constructed substring is destroyed upon the function return, but because of the reference counting, the shared text lives on. Both the original source string and the returned substring have references to it.

These examples illustrate how to use the substring functions:

```
String s("Supercalifragilisticexpialadocius");

String Super = s.Left(5);
String fragil = s.Mid(9,6);
String docius = s.Right(6);
```

You might wonder what happens if you modify a substring. Do both the substring and original string get modified? Also, what happens if you make substrings overlap, as shown in Figure 6.5? Won't things get confused? The answer to all of these questions is "No," as we'll explain in the next section.

IMPLEMENTING LAZY COPYING

Lazy copying allows strings that have been copied to share their text, until one of the strings gets modified. Only then does the text actually get copied. We'll use the term *unique string* for a string that has data with a reference count of one. Thus, we want to ensure a string is unique before modifying it. If it's not unique, a copy of its data is made. Figure 6.6 illustrates this process.

Figure 6.5 Overlapping substrings.

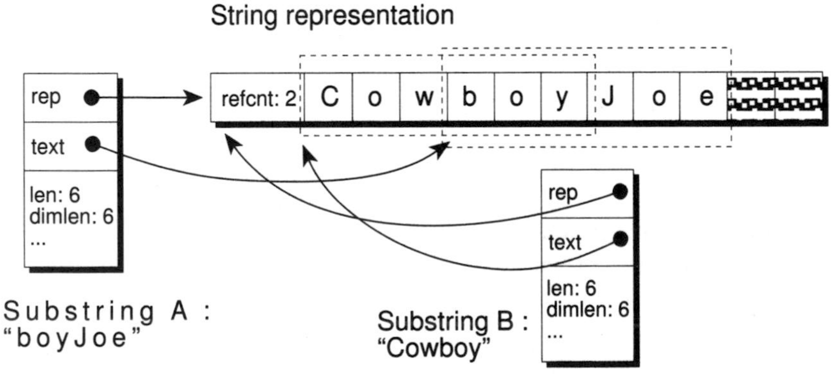

String representation

Substring A : "boyJoe"

Substring B : "Cowboy"

Figure 6.6 Updating shared string text.

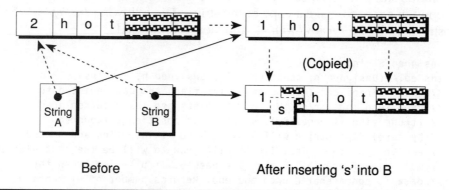

| Before | After inserting 's' into B |

The following functions allow us to take a string and make it unique:

```
int String::IsUnique() const
// Returns 1 if the string's text has refcnt == 1
{
  return rep->refcnt == 1;
}


String String::Clone() const
// Return a copy of this string. The copy will
// be unique (with refcnt = 1).
// Note: If allocation of copy fails, a null
// string is returned.
{
  String temp(dimlen, grow_by);
  temp.CopyN(text, len);
  return temp;
}


int String::EnsureUnique()
// Ensures that this string uniquely owns its string
// rep (ie. the reference count is 1).
// Might have to copy the string text to ensure this.
// Returns 1 if it can make the string unique, 0 if it can't (allocation
// for copy failed).
{
  if (!IsUnique()) {          // Need to copy to make unique
    String &c = Clone();      // Attempt to copy
    if (c.IsNull()) return 0; // Couldn't copy
    NewBinding(c); // Bind to copy
    text = c.text; // Reset starting text pointer
  }
  return 1;
}
```

The *EnsureUnique()* function returns one if it was able to guarantee a unique string. Otherwise, it returns zero, which means it was unable to allocate enough space to make a copy of the string. The following *InsReplAt()* function shows how the *EnsureUnique()* function can be used:

```
unsigned String::
InsReplAt(unsigned p, const char *s, unsigned n, int ins)
// Inserts/replaces (depending on ins flag) the data pointed to
// by s into the string. Up to n elements are inserted/replaced
// (truncating if necesary), starting at position p (counted
// by zero). The string will grow in size if inserting and needed
// and grow_by != 0. The size it will grow to will be the next highest
// multiple of grow_by >= the size needed. If p >= len, then the
// data is concatenated onto the end. Returns number of elements
// inserted/replaced, or 0 if error occurs.
{
  unsigned room, needed, addval;

  if (ins) {
     room = dimlen - len;
     if (n > room && grow_by != 0) {
        needed = (n - room);
        addval = (needed % grow_by) ? grow_by : 0;
        needed = (needed / grow_by) * grow_by + addval;
        // Grow the string by needed amount. Note that the
        // growth may fail, in which case the string stays
        // the same size, with data intact.
        GrowBy(needed);
    }
  }

  // Note: At this point, GrowBy() may have already made
  // our string unique

  if (!EnsureUnique()) return 0; // Can't update

  // Don't allow gaps
  if (p >= len) p = len; // We'll be concatenating

  if (ins) {
     // Keep things in range. May have to truncate.
     if (n > dimlen - len) n = dimlen - len;
     if (p < len) {
        // Make room for inserted data somewhere in the middle
        memmove(text+p+n, text+p, len-p);
     }
  }
  else {
```

```
      // Keep things in range. May have to truncate.
      if (n > dimlen - p) n = dimlen - p;
   }

   // Copy in source; compute final length
   memmove(text+p, s, n);
   if (ins) {
      len += n;
   }
   else {
      if ((p+n) > len) len = p+n;
   }
   return n;
}
```

The *InsReplAt()* function is essentially the same as the *InsertNAt()* function used in the *RVarray* class, except this one also allows text replacement as well as insertions. Note how a check is made to ensure that the string is unique before modifying it. If the string can't be made unique, the function exits and returns a failure code of zero. The *DeleteAt()* function (not shown) uses a similar technique.

By placing calls to *EnsureUnique()* judiciously, it's possible to make the check for uniqueness in only a few places. For instance, *InsReplAt()* is a workhorse function called by many of the other string functions. To illustrate, the following *CopyN()* function copies raw bytes of data into a string. The *CopyN()* function in turn is called by two *Copy()* functions, and another form of overloaded assignment:

```
void String::CopyN(const char *s, unsigned n)
// Copies the data from s, resizing the string if n is
// larger than the dimensioned length, and grow_by != 0.
// The string is guaranteed unique as well.
// If the string can't be resized, it keeps its old size,
// and not all of the data will be copied.
{
   len = 0;            // Cleverly set length to zero
   InsReplAt(0, s, n); // and let InsReplAt() do all the work
}

void String::Copy(const char *s)
// Copies data from a null-terminated string into
// this object. The string might be resized if
// necessary and allowable.
{
   CopyN(s, strlen(s));
}
```

```
void String::Copy(const String &s)
// Copies data from String s into this string.
// The string might be resized if necessary
// and allowable.
{
  CopyN(s.text, s.len);
}

String &String::operator=(const char *s)
// Copy a null-terminated string into this object. The
// string might be resized if necessary and allowable.
{
  Copy(s);
  return *this;
}
```

Unlike the standard assignment operator (which assigns one *String* to another), this operator assigns a null-terminated string to a *String* object, and uses copy semantics rather than share semantics. (The latter would make no sense in this case). Here is an example:

```
String s(80);
s = "The answer is 42"; // Copied into s
```

SUBTLE SUBSCRIPTING ISSUES

When using subscripts, we must be careful when we modify a string. We've defined an overloaded subscripting operator that allows us to treat a *String* like any other subscripted array. Since the returned element may be an *lvalue* (on the left-side of an assignment), the subscripting operation may modify the string. Thus, we must be careful to make the *String* unique before returning the element:

```
char &String::operator[](unsigned i)
// Subscripting that may update a character in the string,
// so we must make the string unique
{
  if (EnsureUnique())
    return text[CHECK(i)];
    else return StrRep::null_rep.data[0];
}
```

What do we do if we can't make the string unique? The way *operator[]* is defined, we must return a reference to *something*. That something might be modified, so we reference the lone data byte in *null_rep* and allow it to be modified. This may not be the best approach. Instead, we might want to print an error message and exit the program. Note the call to the *CHECK()* macro. This is the same macro used by the *Array* class to invoke range checking on subscripts.

Here's an example showing the use of the subscript operator:

```
String s("I can't speel");
s[11] = 'l'; // Correct the spelling
```

When the last statement is executed, *EnsureUnique()* is called to ensure that the string data is unique before we modify the eleventh element. Note that *EnsureUnique()* is called even when the content of the string element is only being read, as in:

```
char c = s[11]; // s still is made unique
```

This situation is unfortunate, because it means an unnecessary copy of the string is made. Unfortunately, there's no way to detect it. About the only thing we can do is declare the string as a constant, and then provide a second *operator[]()* function meant for constant strings. This operator doesn't have to ensure that the string is unique. For instance:

```
const char &String::operator[](unsigned i) const
// Read only version of subscript operator.
// Note the two uses of the const keyword!
{
  return text[CHECK(i)];
}

const String s("I can't speel"); // A constant string

// Invoke constant subscript operator
char c = s[11]; // Fine, just reading
s[11] = 'l';    // Can't do. Compiler error.
```

The critical part of this design is that the *operator[]()* function passes back a constant reference to the element, not just a reference. This is what disallows the updating.

STRING CONCATENATION

String concatenation is another form of string updating, where you add a copy of one string to the end of another. The '+=' operator is overloaded to implement string concatenation. Three versions are supplied to allow you to add one *String* object to another, add a null-terminated string, or add a single character. The string grows in size if necessary:

```
void String::operator+=(const String &s)
// Adds String s to the end of this string
{
  Concatenate(s.text, s.len);
}

void String::operator+=(const char *s)
// Adds a null-terminated string s onto the end of
// this string. The null byte isn't added.
{
  Concatenate(s, strlen(s));
}

void String::operator+=(const char c)
// Adds a single character to the end of the string
{
  Concatenate(&c, 1);
}
```

All of these functions call the following *Concatenate()* function, which in turn calls the *InsReplAt()* function to do all the work (including ensuring uniqueness):

```
void String::Concatenate(const char *s, unsigned n)
// Adds n bytes from s onto the end of this string
{
  InsReplAt(len, s, n);
}
```

The '+' operator is also overloaded to add two strings together, resulting in a third string. The following overloaded '+' operator cleverly lets the '+=' operator do most of the work:

```
String operator+(const String &a, const String &b)
// Adds two strings together and returns the result
{
  String r(a.text->Length() + b.text->Length());
  r += a;
  r += b;
  return r;
}
```

Note how a string is constructed to be big enough to hold the result, and how this result is returned from the function by value. (That's the only way we *can* do it.) Again, because of lazy copying, only a minimum amount of data is actually moved during the function return process.

Here are some examples of string concatenation and string addition:

```
String a("This is "), b("a test);
String c(80);

c = a + b;
c += " of the emergency broadcast system";
```

STRING COMPARISONS

To make strings look as much as possible like built-in types, all of the comparison operators are overloaded. Here's how two of them are defined:

```
int operator==(const String &a, const String &b)
{
  return Compare(a, b) == 0;
}

int operator>=(const String &a, const String &b)
{
  return Compare(a, b) >= 0;
}
```

The other comparison operators are defined similarly. They all call the following *Compare()* function, which does the actual work:

```
int Compare(const String &a, const String &b)
// Uses unsigned decimal value of characters for collating order.
// Returns -1 if a < b, 0 if a == b, and 1 if a > b.
{
  unsigned an = a.text->Length();
  unsigned bn = b.text->Length();
  unsigned sn = (an < bn) ? an : bn;
  unsigned char *ap = (unsigned char *)a.text->Data();
  unsigned char *bp = (unsigned char *)b.text->Data();
  for (unsigned i = 0; i<sn; i++) {
      if (*ap < *bp) return -1;     // a < b
      if (*ap++ > *bp++) return 1;  // a > b
  }
  // Equal unless lengths are different
  if (an == bn) return 0;
  if (an < bn) return -1;
  return 1;
}
```

These examples show the use of string comparisons:

```
String a("abc"), x("xyz"), s("ab");

if (a < x) cout << "Yes"; else cout << "No";  // Returns "Yes"
if (a == s) cout << "Yes"; else cout << "No"; // Returns "No"
```

PATTERN MATCHING AND FILLING

Three *Find( )* functions are defined to search for the starting index of a pattern in a string. The pattern can be another *String* object, a null-terminated string, or a sequence of raw bytes of a specified length. Here's how *Find( )* is defined for null-terminated pattern strings. The others are defined similarly:

```
unsigned String::Find(char *s, unsigned ofs) const
// Returns index of first occurrence of pattern s
// (assumed to be null-terminated) beginning at
// offset ofs. Returns 0xffff if not found, or
// offset not in bounds.
{
  char *q = text + ofs; // Start of string data
  char *p = q;          // Next string element ptr
  char *t = s;          // Next pattern element ptr
  unsigned i = ofs;     // Next string element index

  while(i<len && *t) {
    if (*p == *t) {
      t++;
      if (*t == 0) return i; // We found it!
      p++;
    }
    else {
      i++;
      q++;
      p = q;
      t = s;
    }
  }
  return 0xffff;
}
```

Note that a value of 0xffff is returned if no match is found. (We can't use a flag such as -1 since the indexes are unsigned.)

An optional *ofs* parameter (which defaults to zero) can be defined to specify where to start the search in the string. The algorithm used to search for a pattern in a string is implemented in a brute force way. Other, more sophisticated methods are available to search for patterns in a string, as given in the companion volume [Flamig 93]. You could incorporate those algorithms into the *Find()* functions.

Here's an example that shows how to use *Find()* to locate all occurrences of the pattern *"the"* in a string:

```
String test("The cow jumped over the moon");
char pat[] = "the";

unsigned ofs = 0;
while((ofs = test.Find(pat, ofs)) != 0xffff) {
  cout << "Pattern found at offset " << ofs << '\n';
  ofs += strlen(pat); // Start at next possible spot in string
}
```

Also defined are four *Fill()* functions, which can fill a string—up to the dimensioned length—with a pattern that can be either another string, a null-terminated string, a single characer, or a pattern of raw bytes of a specified length. The latter function is used as the workhorse function for the others:

```
void String::
  Fill(const char *p, unsigned n, unsigned ofs, unsigned m)
// Fills the string with pattern p of length n, up to length m
// or the dimensioned length of the string, whichever is smaller,
// starting at offset ofs. If m is 0, it means use the dimensioned
// length of the string. Pattern repeats if necessary. Does not
// cause the string to grow, but it may have to make a copy to
// ensure the string is unique.
{
  if (dimlen == 0 || n == 0) return; // Nothing to do
  if (!EnsureUnique()) return;       // Can't fill
  // Keep parms in range
  if (m == 0) m = dimlen;
  if (ofs >= dimlen) ofs = dimlen-1; // dimlen must be > 0!
  if (m+ofs > dimlen) m = dimlen - ofs;
  len = m+ofs;
  char *t = text+ofs;
  if (n == 1) {
    // Use fast method for single character fills
    memset(t, *p, m);
  }
  else {
    // Multi-character pattern fills
    unsigned np = n;
    const char *s = p;
    while(m) {
      *t++ = *s++;
```

```
        if (np == 1) {
            np = n;
            s = p;
        } else np--;
        m--;
    }
  }
}
```

As is true for all functions that modify a string, we must ensure the uniqueness of the string before filling it. Here's an example where we fill a string with a pattern up to the maximum length of the string:

```
String s(15);
s.Fill("1234567890"); // s = "123456789012345"
```

Design Critique

It's difficult to imagine how the *String* class could be implemented more robustly or efficiently. It successfuly defines strings as concrete data types and provides a lot more versatility and flexibility than null-terminated strings. At the same time, *String* objects are quite safe, due to the use of reference counting and the incorporation of a special *null_rep* object. (Although, as with anything in C++, it's possible to compromise that safety through typecasting trickery.)

At what cost does this versatility come? Analyzing the data structures, we see that each string has one *StrRep* pointer, a character pointer, and three integers to keep track of string lengths and resizability. In addition, each string has an associated *StrRep* object, which contains one integer and then the data itself.

In contrast, a null-terminated string has just the text and an extra null byte at the end. We see a net difference, then, of two pointers—and three integers minus a character. Don't forget that a *StrRep* object consumes heap space whether we want it to or not, while a null-terminated string does not require heap space. Partially offsetting this disadvantage is the fact that multiple *String* objects can share the same *StrRep* heap space. This makes heap usage less of a factor when a lot of substring operations take place.

The extra space requirement is the price paid for speed: *String* objects can be copied, concatenated, and made into substrings much more efficiently than null-terminated strings. In addition, finding the length of a *String* object involves a simple member reference, not a scan down the array as is the case for null-terminated strings. Once again, we see the almost inevitable speed versus space tradeoff. Here, the tradeoff is more than worth it. The *String* class is certainly efficient and robust enough for routine use.

7

Vectors
and Matrices

ectors and *matrices* are important components in mathematical computations. These are fixed-length *1-d* and *2-d* arrays, respectively, usually composed of numbers, with defined operations such as matrix multiplication, transposition, determinants, and so on. Vectors and matrices figure prominently in applications like coordinate transformations and in solving simultaneous equations. In this chapter, we'll look at how to create user-defined versions of these useful data structures.

Vectors and matrices have a special relationship. It's common to take *1-d* slices of a matrix and call them vectors. For example, a row of a matrix is called a *row vector*. A column is known as a *column vector*. If the matrix is square (with the number of rows equal to the number of columns), you can think in terms of *diagonal vectors*, which span the diagonal of a matrix. Figure 7.1 shows a matrix with an example of each type of vector.

Figure 7.1 Vector types.

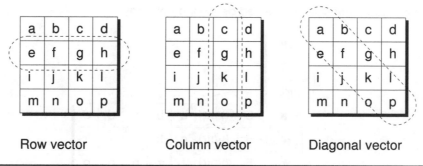

Row vector   Column vector   Diagonal vector

Since matrices are arrays, you might be tempted to implement them using the array-of-arrays technique described in Chapter 4. If you do, however, the result will be less than satisfactory—for several reasons. First, it's not possible to allow both dimensions to be determined at runtime. Second, even if you use the most compact statically-sized form, you will still have some unnecessary overhead. For example, each row of a *2-d* array implemented with *Sarray* objects has its own length variable, virtual function table pointer, and pointer to its array elements, as illustrated in Figure 7.2. Most of these variables are redundant. You could keep just one of each for the entire matrix.

A worse problem lies in figuring out how to represent vectors associated with a matrix. Row vectors are easy, since each row is already an array. But what about column vectors, or diagonal vectors? There is no easy way to treat the elements of a column or diagonal as an array in its own right, since each element is stored in a separate row array. To further explore this fundamental problem, we'll step back and take a look at how two-dimensional arrays are organized using the built-in C++ array types.

ROW-MAJOR AND COLUMN-MAJOR MATRICES

Consider the following two-dimensional 3x5 matrix:

```
float m[3][5];
```

In C++, this matrix is stored, row by row, as a *1-d* array. Matrices stored in this way are called *row-major* matrices. Scanning down the *1-d* representation, the column index varies the fastest, while the row index varies the slowest. Some languages, such as Fortran, use *column-major* matrices, where the matrices are laid out column by column. Here, the row index varies fastest, while the column index varies the slowest. Figure 7.3 shows the difference between these two types of organization.

Figure 7.2 A matrix implemented as an array of arrays.

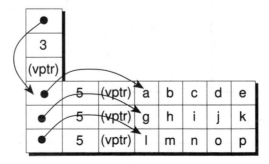

The way a matrix is stored affects the way subscripting works. To find the *i*th row and *j*th column of a row-major matrix, the following subscript calculation is used:

```
m[i][j]  <==> *(m + i*ncols + j); // For row-major matrices
```

For a column-major matrix, the calculation is:

```
m[i][j]  <==> *(m + i + j*nrows); // For column-major matrices
```

In both cases, we need the size of only one dimension to compute the subscript. For row-major matrices, we need the number of columns, and for column-major matrices, we must know the number of rows.

The memory layout of a matrix directly affects what type of vectors can be easily obtained from the matrix. For a row-major matrix, it's easy to define row vectors, since the elements of each row are contiguous. Column vectors are more difficult to define, since the elements are non-contiguous. For column-major matrices, the opposite is true, with row-vectors being difficult to define and column vectors easy to define.

Actually, it's not all that difficult to define non-contiguous vectors. The secret lies in usng *vector strides*, our next topic.

VECTOR STRIDES

The *stride* of a vector is the distance, in elements, between successive elements in the vector. Consider a row-major matrix. The stride of a row vector in such a matrix is one. This is known as the matrix's *row stride*. The *column stride*—that

Figure 7.3 Memory layouts of row- and column-major matrices.

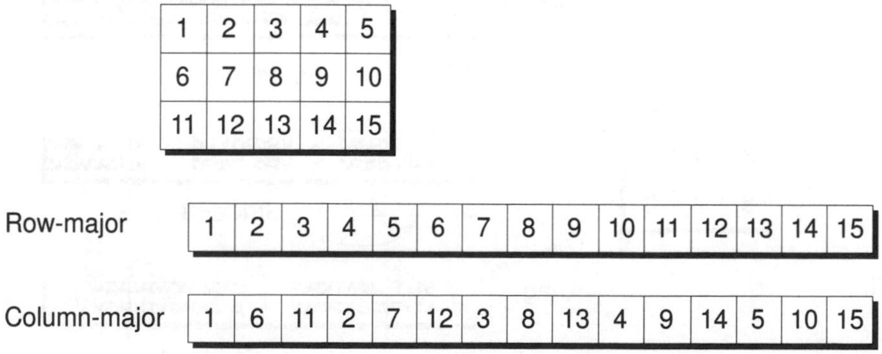

is, the stride of a column vector—is equal to the number of columns in the matrix. The *diagonal stride* is equal to the number of columns (or rows, since they're supposed to be equal), plus one. Figure 7.4 illustrates the different strides of a row-major matrix.

The situation is reversed for column-major matrices. The row stride is equal to the number of rows in the matrix, and the column stride is equal to one. The diagonal stride remains the same.

Strides come in handy when you need to compute the subscripts of a vector. As is true with arrays, you can implement vectors by using pointers. In general, the pointer arithmetic corresponding to a vector subscript calculation is:

```
v[i] <==> *(v + i*stride)
```

This equation is significant because it works no matter what kind of vector you have—be it row, column, or diagonal. All you need to do is supply the correct stride!

One frequently used optimization technique is to convert subscripting, which entails a multiplication, into pointer incrementing. You can do this if you are scanning through an ordinary array in sequence. For example:

```
float a[5];

float *p = a;
for(int i = 0, i<5; i++) *p++ = 0; // Set elements to zero
```

You can use this same technique with pointers to vector elements, except instead of simply incrementing the pointers, their strides must be added. For example, given some *float* vector *v,* of length *n*, having stride *s*:

Figure 7.4 Vector strides of a row-major matrix.

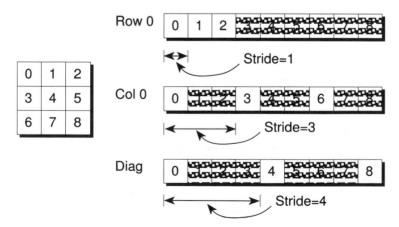

```
float *vp = v;    // Point to vector elements of v
for(int i = 0; i<n; i++) {
  *vp = 0;
  vp += s;   // Next element in the vector
}
```

VECTOR POINTERS

It's possible to incorporate the ideas in the previous section into a new type of pointer, which we'll call *vector pointers*. These pointers are generalizations of ordinary pointers. An ordinary pointer always has a stride of one. That is, it's assumed the array elements are contiguous. Vectors may be non-contiguous (with evenly spaced elements, though), so a vector pointer can have a stride different than one. The following *VecPtr* class encapsulates these notions:

```
template<class TYPE>
class VecPtr {
private:
  TYPE *p;                 // Ordinary pointer
  const unsigned stride;   // Pointer stride
public:
  VecPtr(TYPE *t, unsigned s=1)       : p(t), stride(s) { }
  VecPtr(const VecPtr<TYPE> &s)       : p(s.p), stride(s.stride) { }
  void operator=(const VecPtr<TYPE> &s) { p = s.p; }
  void operator=(TYPE *t)             { p = t; }
  void operator++()                   { p += stride; }
  void operator++(int)                { p += stride; }
  void operator+=(unsigned n)         { p += stride * n; }
  TYPE &operator[](unsigned i) const  { return p[stride*i]; }
  operator TYPE *() const             { return p; }
  TYPE &operator *() const            { return *p; }
#ifdef TYPE_IS_STRUCTURE
  TYPE *operator->() const            { return p; }
#endif
};
```

This class exemplifies everything that's right about C++. It turns vector pointers into concrete data types that look virtually like ordinary pointers. The class is flexible in that, being a template, it can be used for any vector element type. Yet because the class is completely inlined, there is very little overhead (if any). This class can be as efficient as any hand-coded, low-level pointer implementation.

The basic purpose of the *VecPtr* class is to hide the stride calculations. For example, the overloaded '++' operator turns vector pointer incrementing into stride additions. This allows us to write code like:

```
for(int i = 0; i<n; i++) { *v = 0; v++; }
```

rather than

```
for(int i = 0; i<n; i++) { *v = 0; v += stride; }
```

The pointer de-referencing operators '*' and '->' are overloaded to make vector pointers look even more like ordinary pointers. For instance, the expression *v returns the vector element that is currently being referenced. Likewise, v->m returns the member m of the element being referenced. For this to work, *TYPE* must be a structure; otherwise, the class won't compile. We've commented out the *operator->()* function using *ifdef* statements in the class declaration.

The subscript operator is overloaded to allow vector pointers to be used like the name of an array. For example:

```
for(int i = 0; i<n; i++) v[i] = 0;
```

Of course, a loop like this won't be as efficient as one that uses pointer incrementing, since it takes an extra multiplication for the subscript operation.

Optimizing Vector Pointers

Vector pointers can be further optimized. Note that, when a value is added to a pointer, more is going on than just the addition. In fact, a multiplication takes place! This is because the compiler must turn pointers into machine addresses, which work in byte units. Thus, given some pointer *p*, which points to an object of type *T*, we have the following equivalence:

```
p + i  <==>  ((char *)p) + i * sizeof(T)
```

Vector pointers can be optimized by pre-multiplying the vector stride by *sizeof(T)*. The stride then becomes a *byte stride*. In pointer arithmetic, the pointer can be cast as a *char *, which saves the extra multiplication. For example, the following functions of the *VecPtr* class can be optimized this way:

```
template<class TYPE>
class VecPtr {
  ...
  VecPtr(TYPE *t, unsigned s=1) : p(t), stride(s*sizeof(TYPE)) { }
  void operator++()                { (char *)p += stride; }
  void operator++(int)             { (char *)p += stride; }
  void operator+=(unsigned n)      { (char *)p += stride * n; }
  TYPE &operator[](unsigned i) const {
```

```
    return *((TYPE *)((char *)p + stride*i));
  }
  ...
};
```

This change may speed up vector pointers by as much as 20 percent. Note that the optimization is completely encapsulated in the *VecPtr* class. Outside the class, you continue to work with pointer strides in their normal vector element units.

The following example shows how to use vector pointers with matrices. A matrix is created using built-in arrays and is then initialized to be a unit matrix (with all elements zero except on the diagonal, where ones are stored.)

```
float m[3][3]; // Declare a 3x3 row-major matrix

// Set all values to zero by pointing to matrix with
// a vector that can access all elements. A stride of
// 1 will do the trick.
VecPtr<float> va(m, 1);
for (int i = 0; i<9; i++) va[i] = 0;

// Set diagonal elements to 1 with another vector pointer
VecPtr<float> vd(m, 4); // Stride is ncols + 1
for (int j = 0; j<3; j++) vd[j] = 1;
```

The resulting matrix would be:

```
100
010
001
```

Pointer Increment Problems

One unfortunate limitation with vector pointers is the inability to use expressions like *p++. Why can't you use this? Consider what the expression translates into in terms of operation function calls:

```
*p++  <==>  (v.operator++()).operator*()
```

First, the post-increment operator is called, and the pointer—as it existed before the increment—is returned. This pointer is then de-referenced to return the element. However, there is no way to return the original pointer *before* it has been incremented. Only a copy can be returned. On the surface, the following *operator++()* function seems to work:

```
VecPtr<TYPE> operator++(int)
{
  VecPtr before(*this); // Make copy of object
  p += stride;          // Do increment
  return before;        // Return copy
}
```

However, what happens in the following (admittedly concocted) expression?

```
(v++)++; // Undefined result
```

Such constructs are actually undefined. That's because the result of a post-increment operation is not an l-Value (it can't be assigned to). So it's really illegal to try and increment the result again. Note that pre-increment operators are l-Values and don't have this problem.

We've forced both forms of *operator++()* to return *void.* That way, expressions like *(v++)++* and **p++* won't compile, so there's no danger of receiving erroneous results. Due to the *void* returns, both the prefix and suffix forms of *operator++()* can be implemented using the same prefix semantics. There's no way to use the operators in illegal ways.

DYNAMIC MATRICES

When you use the built-in array types, it's not possible to directly define matrices that have both their dimensions determined at runtime. Now that you know about pointers and strides, we can show you why this is true. In Chapter 4, we mentioned that, although the number of columns must be fixed, there *is* a way to make the number of rows variable. Here is one way to do it:

```
typedef float ArrNx5[5]; // Declare array-of-5-columns type

void f(unsigned n)
{
  // Dynamically allocate nx5 matrix, referenced by p
  ArrNx5 *p = new ArrNx5[n];

  // Set lower-right element to 99
  p[n-1][4] = 99;
}
```

The variable *p* represents a pointer to the first element in the first row of the respective matrix. Even though this variable points to a floating point element, its type isn't *float* * or even *float* ** as you first might think. Instead, *p is a pointer to floating point array of five columns.* This can easily be seen by *p's* declaration.

A stride is implicit with a pointer to an array. In this case, p has the constant 5 as its stride. With this in mind, we have the following equivalence:

```
p[i]  <==> *(p + i*5)
```

An ordinary pointer gets returned by subscript of a pointer to array. This pointer points to the first element of the *i*th row. The pointer can then be used in a subscript calculation to find the *j*th column of the row. Hence, double subscripts such as *p[i][j]* can be used.

Interestingly enough, the subscripting equation just shown is the same one used for vector pointer strides! The crucial difference is that, here, the stride is constant. Because of this, the compiler is able to easily plug in the constant stride in subscript and pointer increment calculations.

Contrast this with variable strides (such as in a dynamic matrix with the number of columns determined at runtime). Here, the compiler could not simply plug in values for the stride, because it doesn't know what the stride should be! The compiler would be forced to create a special data structure that carries the stride around with the pointer. This approach ought to sound familiar to you, since that's exactly what vector pointers do!

The conclusion is this: if you want to have dynamic matrices with both dimensions determined at runtime, you need to have vector pointers. Since C++ doesn't have vector pointers built in, it isn't able to handle dynamic matrices directly. However, nothing prevents you from creating your own dynamic matrices, as you'll now see.

A Simple Dynamic Matrix Class

From the preceding discussions, two basic techniques emerge for defining dynamically sized matrices:

1. Represent the matrix as a one-dimensional array, using row-major or column-major order (row-major ordering is easiest). Allocate this array dynamically.

2. Use vector pointers to conveniently access rows, columns, and diagonals.

The following *SimpleMatrix* class uses these techniques:

```
template<class TYPE>
class SimpleMatrix {
private:
  TYPE *data;
  unsigned nrows, ncols;
public:
  SimpleMatrix(unsigned nr, unsigned nc);
  SimpleMatrix(const SimpleMatrix<TYPE> &m);
```

```
~SimpleMatrix();
void Copy(const SimpleMatrix<TYPE> &m);
SimpleMatrix<TYPE> &operator=(const SimpleMatrix<TYPE> &m);
TYPE *operator[](unsigned r);
VecPtr<TYPE> RowPtr(unsigned r=0);
VecPtr<TYPE> ColPtr(unsigned c=0);
VecPtr<TYPE> DiagPtr();
VecPtr<TYPE> PtrToAll();
const TYPE *operator[](unsigned r) const;
VecPtr<const TYPE> RowPtr(unsigned r=0) const;
VecPtr<const TYPE> ColPtr(unsigned c=0) const;
VecPtr<const TYPE> DiagPtr() const;
VecPtr<const TYPE> PtrToAll() const;
unsigned NRows() const;
unsigned NCols() const;
unsigned NElems() const;
};
```

Note   The complete code for the *SimpleMatrix* class is given on disk in the files *simpmat.h* and *simpmat.mth*. Test programs for this class are given in the files *tstsmat.cpp* and *tstsmat2.cpp*.

This class isn't a complete implementation of matrices. Its purpose is to show you the basic design and to point out some performance and safety problems. Later in this chapter, we'll create complete *Vector* and *Matrix* classes that are more robust.

The *SimpleMatrix* class stores the matrix data in a row-major *1-d* array, pointed to by the member *data*, as shown in the following constructor:

```
template<class TYPE>
SimpleMatrix<TYPE>::SimpleMatrix(unsigned nr, unsigned nc)
// General constructor
{
  nrows = nr; ncols = nc;
  data = new TYPE[nrows*ncols];
}
```

The size of the matrix is stored in the variables *nrows* and *ncols*, which are also used in calculating vector strides. The functions *RowPtr()*, *ColPtr()*, and *DiagPtr()* all return vector pointers of their respective types:

```
template<class TYPE>
VecPtr<TYPE> SimpleMatrix<TYPE>::RowPtr(unsigned r)
// Return a row vector pointer to row r
{
```

```
    return VecPtr<TYPE>(data + r*ncols, 1);
}

template<class TYPE>
VecPtr<TYPE> SimpleMatrix<TYPE>::ColPtr(unsigned c)
// Return a column vector pointer to column c
{
  return VecPtr<TYPE>(data+c, nrows);
}

template<class TYPE>
VecPtr<TYPE> SimpleMatrix<TYPE>::DiagPtr()
// Return a diagonal vector pointer. In case matrix
// isn't square, the smallest dimension is used to
// determine the diagonal stride.
{
  unsigned dstride = ((nrows > ncols) ? ncols : nrows) + 1;
  return VecPtr<TYPE>(data, dstride);
}
```

Also, the *PtrToAll()* function returns a vector pointer, with a stride of one, which allows you to access the matrix as though it were a one-dimensional array. This is useful for operations that apply to all elements, such as zeroing the matrix, scaling the matrix, and so on.

```
template<class TYPE>
VecPtr<TYPE> SimpleMatrix<TYPE>::PtrToAll()
// Return pointer to all elements of the matrix
{
  return VecPtr<TYPE>(data, 1);
}
```

Here is an example that uses these functions:

```
SimpleMatrix<int> m(3, 3);
int i;

// Set all elements to '4'
VecPtr<int> va = m.PtrToAll();
for(i = 0; i<m.NElems(); i++) va[i] = 4;

// Set row 1 elements to '2'
VecPtr<int> vr = m.RowPtr(1);
for(i = 0; i<m.NCols(); i++) vr[i] = 2;

// Set col 1 elements to '3'
VecPtr<int> vc = m.ColPtr(1);
```

```
for(i = 0; i<m.NRows(); i++) vc[i] = 3;

// Set diagonal elements to '1'
VecPtr<int> vd = m.DiagPtr();
for(i = 0; i<m.NRows(); i++) vd[i] = 1;
```

The resulting matrix would be:

```
134
212
431
```

Two-Dimensional Subscripting

The *SimpleMatrix* class overloads the subscript operator *[]* to return an ordinary pointer to the first element in row *r*:

```
template<class TYPE>
TYPE *SimpleMatrix<TYPE>::operator[](unsigned r)
{
  return data + r*ncols;
}
```

By using a subscript on the returned pointer as well, two-dimensional subscripting can be achieved using a double subscript, as illustrated in Figure 7.5, and in the following code:

```
SimpleMatrix<float> m(3,4); // Declare 3x4 matrix

m[1][2] = 99;
```

Figure 7.5 Two-dimensional subscripting.

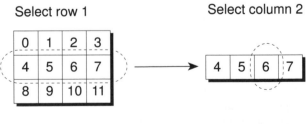

$$m[1][2] \iff *(m+1*ncols + 2) = *(m+6)$$

You might wonder why the *operator[]()* function doesn't return a row vector pointer. For instance, we could have written:

```
// Alternative definition for []

template<class TYPE>
VecPtr<TYPE> SimpleMatrix<TYPE>::operator[](unsigned r)
{
   return VecPtr(data + r*ncols, 1);
}
```

This function is identical to *RowPtr()* (except for its name). Since row vectors themselves have subscripting defined, we can use the same double subscripting as we used earlier:

```
m[2][4] = 99; // Set lower-right element to 99
```

However, the result won't be as efficient as using the original form of the subscript function. The statement translates into:

```
// First call SimpleMatrix::operator[], then VecPtr::operator[]
(m.operator[](2)).operator[](4) = 99;
```

By substituting the bodies of the two different operator functions, we can transform the statement into the following equivalent pointer arithmetic:

```
*((data + 2*ncols) + 1*4) = 99;
```

Two multiplications take place: one to compute the start of row 2 and one to find column 4 of that row. Note that the multiplication 1*4 has to take place, even though just using the number 4 would suffice. That's because the number 1 represents the value stored in the stride variable for the row vector. Because a general vector pointer type is being used, we can't optimize for some vectors having a stride of 1. In the case where an ordinary pointer is returned, this optimization automatically takes place. A more efficient calculation results:

```
*((data + 2*ncols) + 4) = 99; // Optimized version
```

Tests show that returning an ordinary pointer from the matrix subscript function, rather than returning a vector pointer, yields speeds almost twice as fast for operations like matrix multiplication. Next, we'll show you how to define matrix multiplication.

Matrix Multiplication

Matrix multiplication is perhaps the most common operation done on matrices, and can be defined as follows: given two matrices *a* and *b*, one of size *mxn* and the other of size *nxp*, the result of multiplying the two matrices is a new matrix, *c*, of size *mxp*, where the elements of *c* are computed by the equation:

$$c(i, j) = \sum_{k=1}^{n} a(i, k)^* \, b(k, j), \ \forall i \in 1..m, j \in 1..p$$

In other words, each row of *a* is paired with each column of *b*, and the corresponding elements of these vectors are multiplied and then summed. The sum becomes one element of the result matrix. Figure 7.6 illustrates this process.

The following function implements matrix multiplication:

```
void MatMult(SimpleMatrix<Number> &c,
   const SimpleMatrix<Number> &a, const SimpleMatrix<Number> &b)
{
  unsigned i, j, k;

  for (i = 0; i < a.NRows(); i++) {
      for (j = 0; j < b.NCols(); j++) {
          Number sum = 0;
          for (k = 0; k < b.NRows(); k++) sum += a[i][k] * b[k][j];
          c[i][j] = sum;
      }
  }
}
```

We can also overload the '*' operator for matrix multiplication, as follows:

```
template<class TYPE>
SimpleMatrix<TYPE>
operator*(const SimpleMatrix<TYPE> &a, const SimpleMatrix<TYPE> &b)
{
  SimpleMatrix<TYPE> r(a.NRows(), b.NCols());
  MatMult(r, a, b);
```

Figure 7.6 Matrix multiplication.

a	b		e	f	g		ae+bh	af+bi	ag+bj
c	d	X	h	i	j	=	ce+dh	cf+di	cg+dj

```
    return r; // Copy constructor called
}
```

This example multiplies two matrices:

```
SimpleMatrix<float> a(3,2), b(2,4), c(3,4);
...
c = a * b;
```

Unfortunately, the operator *"*"* function leads to a lot of copying. First, the result matrix is created, the matrix multiply is performed by *MatMult()*, and a copy of the result is returned. (We can't safely return a reference to the result.) Then, the assignment to *c* takes place, where yet another copy takes place. The *Matrix* class given later in this chapter avoids this problem.

As shown in *MatMult()*, double subscripting is the obvious way to implement matrix multiplication. However, this implies a multiplication for each subscripting operation. Since we are accessing array elements in sequence, it might be faster to use pointer incrementing. Here's an alternative matrix multiplication function that uses vector pointers—and is roughly 25 percent faster than the double-subscripting method—for double-precision floating-point matrices:

```
template<class TYPE>
void MatMult1(SimpleMatrix<TYPE> &c,
  const SimpleMatrix<TYPE> &a, const SimpleMatrix<TYPE> &b)
{
  unsigned i, j, k;

  VecPtr<const TYPE> ar = a.RowPtr();
  VecPtr<const TYPE> ac = a.ColPtr();
  VecPtr<const TYPE> br = b.RowPtr();
  VecPtr<const TYPE> bc = b.ColPtr();
  VecPtr<TYPE> cr = c.RowPtr();
  VecPtr<TYPE> cc = c.ColPtr();

  TYPE const *bstart = br;

  for (i = 0; i < a.NRows(); i++) {
      cr = cc; // Point to row i. Note: stride not copied
      br = bstart;
      for (j = 0; j < b.NCols(); j++) {
          TYPE sum = 0;
          ar = ac; // Point row i. Note: stride not copied.
          bc = br; // Point column j. Note: stride not copied.
          for (k = 0; k < b.NRows(); k++) {
              sum += *ar * *bc;
```

```
                ar++; // Next column
                bc++; // Next row
        }
        br++; // Next column
        *cr = sum;
        cr++; // Next column
    }
      ac++; // Next row
      cc++; // Next row
  }
}
```

This function uses six vector pointers, two for each matrix. By incrementing a column vector pointer, we can advance to the next row of a matrix. Incrementing a row vector pointer advances us to the next column of the row. To understand *MatMult1()*, it's important to realize that when vector pointer assignments take place only the underyling ordinary pointers are copied—*not* the strides. (You can verify this by looking at the definition for *VecPtr* given earlier.) Thus, we can safely assign a column vector pointer to a row vector pointer without confusing the strides.

There's a way to be even more efficient. Note that the row vectors always have a stride of one, so we can replace them by ordinary pointers. You may see speed improvements of 5 to 10 percent by doing this. The changes involved are:

```
Original Statement                   New Statement

VecPtr<const TYPE> ar = a.RowPtr();  const TYPE *ar = a.RowPtr();
VecPtr<const TYPE> br = b.RowPtr();  const TYPE *br = b.RowPtr();
VecPtr<TYPE> cr = c.RowPtr();        TYPE *cr = c.RowPtr();
```

You may wonder about the use of the *const* keywords in these statements. We'll look at these keywords next.

Constant Vectors and Matrices

True to the design principles explained in Chapters 2 and 3, we've made the *VecPtr* and *SimpleMatrix* classes work for constant objects. You'll notice that we supply two versions of the *[]* operator for *SimpleMatrix*:

```
template<class TYPE>
TYPE *SimpleMatrix<TYPE>::operator[](unsigned r)
// Called for non-const matrices
{
  return data + r*ncols;
```

```
template<class TYPE>
const TYPE *SimpleMatrix<TYPE>::operator[](unsigned i) const
// Called for const matrices
{
  return data + r*ncols;
}
```

The latter is a constant function, and is the one that's called for matrices declared to be constant. In this case, we shouldn't be able to modify any elements in the row that's returned, so a *const TYPE ** is returned (meaning a pointer to a constant), instead of just a *TYPE **. We also use this strategy when returning vector pointers. For example, two *ColPtr()* functions are defined:

```
template<class TYPE>
VecPtr<TYPE> SimpleMatrix<TYPE>::ColPtr(unsigned c)
// Called for non-const matrices
{
  return VecPtr<TYPE>(data+c, nrows);
}

template<class TYPE>
VecPtr<const TYPE> SimpleMatrix<TYPE>::ColPtr(unsigned c) const
// Called for const matrices
{
  return VecPtr<const TYPE>(data+c, nrows);
}
```

When returning a column vector from a constant matrix, we must somehow prevent the elements of the vector from being modified. To do this, we type the vector pointer to reference *const TYPE* elements, rather than *TYPE* elements. Note this is not the same as making the vector pointer itself constant. For instance, had we written *const VecPtr<TYPE>* instead of *VecPtr<const TYPE>*, we would have created a pointer that couldn't be modified. Thus, we couldn't do things like pointer incrementing, so the pointer would be somewhat useless.

Matrix Transposition

Another common matrix operation is to take the *transpose* of a matrix. The transposition is accomplished by interchanging the rows and the columns. Figure 7.7 shows an example.

The following *Transpose()* function shows the obvious implementation of a matrix transposition.

```
template<class TYPE>
SimpleMatrix<TYPE> Transpose(const SimpleMatrix<TYPE> &m)
```

Figure 7.7 Transpose of a matrix.

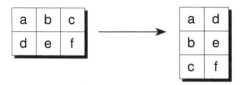

```
{
  SimpleMatrix<TYPE> t(m.NCols(), m.NRows());

  for (unsigned i = 0; i<m.NRows(); i++)
      for (unsigned j = 0; j<m.NCols(); j++) t[j][i] = m[i][j];

  return t; // Copy constructor called.
}
```

With this implementation, though, an extra copy takes place when the transposed version is returned. We could circumvent this problem by modifying *Transpose()* to assume that the result matrix has already been built, and to pass it as a parameter:

```
template<class TYPE>
void SimpleMatrix<TYPE>
Transpose(SimpleMatrix<TYPE> &t, const SimpleMatrix<TYPE> &m)
{
  for (unsigned i = 0; i<m.NRows(); i++)
      for (unsigned j = 0; j<m.NCols(); j++) t[j][i] = m[i][j];
}
```

Of course, this design assumes that you have created the result matrix with the proper size, an error-prone activity.

When it's acceptable to modify the matrix in place, there is another way to accomplish matrix transposition. Transposing a matrix is like changing it from row-major to column-major ordering. Instead of actually moving elements around, you can simply view the matrix as though it were column major. Here are the steps needed to make this work:

1. Generalize the vector operations—such as *RowPtr()*, *ColPtr()*, and *operator[]()*—to use row and column strides, rather than the number of rows and columns directly. Maintain the row and column strides in separate variables.

2. Interchange the number of rows and columns, and interchange the row and column strides.

The basic idea here is to change what used to be row vectors into column vectors, and vice versa. In a row-major matrix, the row stride is one and the column stride is the number of columns in the matrix. If the matrix is transposed in place, the row stride becomes equal to the number of rows in the new matrix (which is the same as the number of columns in the original matrix), and the column stride becomes one. Assuming the variables *rowstride* and *colstride* were added to the *SimpleMatrix* class, here is a new in-place *Transpose()* function, along with modified *RowPtr()*, *ColPtr()*, and *operator[]()* functions:

```
template<class TYPE>
void SimpleMatrix<TYPE>::Transpose()
// Transpose a matrix in place
{
  // Interchange nrows and ncols
  unsigned temp = nrows;
  nrows = ncols;
  ncols = temp;
  // Interchange row stride and column stride
  temp = rowstride;
  rowstride = colstride;
  colstride = temp;
}

template<class TYPE>
VecPtr<TYPE> SimpleMatrix<TYPE>::RowPtr(unsigned r)
{
   return VecPtr<TYPE>(data + r*colstride, rowstride);
}

template<class TYPE>
VecPtr<TYPE> SimpleMatrix<TYPE>::ColPtr(unsigned r)
{
   return VecPtr<TYPE>(data + c*rowstride, colstride);
}

template<class TYPE>
VecPtr<TYPE> SimpleMatrix<TYPE>::operator[](unsigned r)
{
   return VecPtr<TYPE>(data + r*colstride, rowstride);
}
```

Notice the generalized calculations used to determine the row and column vectors. Remember that, in these functions, either *rowstride* or *colstride* is equal to one. The other variable is equal to the number of columns in the original, non-transposed matrix. Another important point is that the *operator[]()* function can no longer return an ordinary pointer because there's no guarantee that a row vector will have a stride of one. The matrix might be transposed.

This technique eliminates the need to actually move the matrix elements around. Of course, this only works if you want to transpose a matrix in place. If you need to leave the original matrix alone, you must make a copy. In this case, doing the actual interchange between rows and columns is just as efficient. However, as we'll discuss next, a more sophisticated matrix class can be defined that eliminates the data movement, even when the original matrix is to be left untouched.

More Robust Vectors and Matrices

The *SimpleMatrix* class introduced you to techniques for defining dynamic matrices. However, some aspects of *SimpleMatrix* are not entirely safe, and can lead to a lot of redundant copying.

The *SimpleMatrix* class uses vector pointers as a fundamental part of its design. While vector pointers are fast and efficient, there is no way to do range checking on subscripts, since vector pointers do not keep track of the bounds of the vectors. This isn't necessarily a problem. Since range checking can easily reduce the performance of your code by 50 percent, you don't always want to use it. However, the capability should still be provided.

A more insidious problem is that, by their very nature, vector pointers induce aliasing. In the *SmartPtr* and *String* classes, aliasing was made safe by using reference counting. The same can be done for vectors and matrices. By allowing safe sharing, we can also eliminate a lot of the redundant copying that takes place.

Along these lines, we'll next present two classes, *Vector* and *Matrix*, that are extensions of the *VecPtr* and *SimpleMatrix* classes and that incorporate the techniques of range checking and reference counting. Fundamental to the design of these two classes is that, strangely enough, each matrix object is actually composed of a *1-d* vector object! The purpose of the *Matrix* class is to interpret the vector data as though it were two-dimensional.

Because vector objects will use a shared representation, it follows that matrices will, as well. This shared representation allows us to easily support efficient submatrix and matrix transpose operations. As you study the following design, note how much overhead is caused by the shared representation, and how much that overhead is compensated for by more efficient matrix operations.

The Vector Class

The *Vector* class is similar in many ways to the *String* class described in Chapter 6. (You should review that chapter now if you haven't already read it.) The *Vector* class uses the same letter-envelope reference counting scheme, having an underlying vector representation class *VecRep*:

```
template<class TYPE> class Vector; // Forward declaration

template<class TYPE>
class VecRep {
private:
  friend class Vector<TYPE>;
  unsigned alloclen;
  unsigned refcnt;
  TYPE data[1];
  VecRep(unsigned d);
  void *operator new(size_t n, unsigned d);
  void operator delete(void *p);
public: // So we can set up null_rep
  static VecRep<TYPE> null_rep;
  VecRep();
  ~VecRep();
};
```

The complete code for the *VecRep* class is given on disk in the files *vector.h* and *vector.mth*.

The *VecRep* class dynamically allocates the elements of the vector in the same way that the *StrRep* class allocates the text for strings: by overloading the *new* and *delete* operators (not shown here). The difference is that vector elements can be of any type, not just characters, and these types might have constructors and destructors. As is true in *StrRep*, the vector elements are initially allocated as characters so that we can easily keep the reference count next to the elements in memory. Thus, we must construct each vector element by hand from this array of characters. This task is handled by the *VecRep* constructor, using the same in-place construction technique covered in Chapter 4:

```
template<class TYPE>
VecRep<TYPE>::VecRep(unsigned d)
// Constructor to initialize a shared vector rep
{
  if (this != &null_rep) {
    // We only want to do the following if we're
    // not referencing null_rep
    alloclen = d;
    refcnt = 1;
    // We must call the default constructor for
    // all but the first element
    TYPE *q = data + 1;
    for(unsigned i = 1; i<d; i++, q++) new(q) TYPE;
  }
}
```

Note that the first element of the vector already has its constructor called implicitly by the *VecRep* constructor, because *VecRep* is defined with one element allocated. The *VecRep* destructor works exactly in reverse of the constructor:

```
template<class TYPE>
void VecRep<TYPE>::~VecRep()
// Destructor to explicitly destroy all elements
// of the vector, except the first
{
  TYPE *q = data + 1;
  for(unsigned i = 1; i<alloclen; i++, q++) q->TYPE::~TYPE();
}
```

With *VecRep* objects, we must track the number of elements in the vector so that we know how many times to call the constructor and destructor. To do this, the *alloclen* member is stored with each *VecRep* object.

As is true with strings, we use a null-vector representation called *null_rep*, which allows us to elegantly handle empty vectors—particularly those caused by memory allocation problems. Unlike all other *VecRep* objects that must be allocated dynamically, *null_rep* must be allocated statically. You must allocate one *null_rep* object per vector element type somewhere in your program. A macro is supplied to make this easier:

```
#define INITNULLVEC(TYPE) VecRep<TYPE> VecRep<TYPE>::null_rep;
```

With the *VecRep* class in hand, the *Vector* class can be defined:

```
template<class TYPE> class Matrix; // Forward declaration

template<class TYPE>
class Vector {
protected:
  friend class Matrix<TYPE>;
  VecRep<TYPE> *rep; // Pointer to shared vector data
  TYPE *start;       // Pointer to logical start of data
  unsigned len;      // Number of logical elements
  unsigned stride;   // Stride (offset to next logical element)
  int Alloc(unsigned n);
  void Bind(const Vector<TYPE> &v);
  void Unbind();
  void NewBinding(const Vector<TYPE> &v);
public:
  Vector(unsigned n = 0, const TYPE *s = 0);
  Vector(const Vector<TYPE> &v);
  Vector(const Vector<TYPE> &v, SliceType styp,
```

```
        unsigned n=0, unsigned str=1, unsigned ofs=0);
  ~Vector();
#ifndef NO_RANGE_CHECK
  unsigned CheckIndx(unsigned i) const;
#endif
  TYPE &operator[](unsigned i);
  const TYPE &operator[](unsigned i) const;
  void CopyN(const TYPE *src, unsigned n);
  void Copy(const Vector<TYPE> &v);
  void Share(const Vector<TYPE> &v);
  void SetElements(const TYPE &x);
  Vector<TYPE> &operator=(const Vector<TYPE> &v);
  Vector<TYPE> &operator=(const TYPE &x);
  int IsNull() const;
  int IsUnique() const;
  Vector<TYPE> Clone() const;
  int EnsureUnique();
  unsigned Length() const;
  unsigned Stride() const;
  // Low-level hooks
  VecPtr<TYPE> All();
  VecPtr<const TYPE> All() const;
};
```

The complete code for the *Vector* class is given on disk in the files *vector.h* and *vector.mth*. Test programs for vectors are supplied in *tstvec.cpp*, *tstvec2.cpp*, and *tstvec3.cpp*.

The *Vector* class has four data members: *rep*, a pointer to the vector representation object; *start*, a pointer to the logical start of the vector elements; *len*, the logical length of the vector; and *stride*, the vector's logical stride. The *start* member is analogous to the *text* member of the *String* class. Normally, *start* points to *rep->data*, but in case the vector is a subvector, it may point at some offset from *rep->data*.

The *Vector* class has functions virtually identical to those in the *String* class to support lazy copying—such as *Bind()*, *Unbind()*, *NewBinding()*, *Share()*, *EnsureUnique()*, *Clone()*, and *IsUnique()*. The main difference is that lazy copying isn't automatically performed in the *Vector* class. With the *String* class, we want to ensure that, when modifications are made to a string, the string is unique in order not to affect any other strings sharing the same text. With vectors, the design is just the opposite. Because vectors are going to be used to access shared slices of matrices, we *want* vector modifications to affect the underlying shared matrix data. Functions like *EnsureUnique()* are not used automatically, but are provided in case you do want to ensure a unique copy before modifying data.

The *Vector* class has three constructors. The first allocates a new vector representation of a specified length, and can optionally copy data from a low-level array into it:

```
template<class TYPE>
Vector<TYPE>::Vector(unsigned n, const TYPE *s)
// Constructor to allocate space for an n element vector,
// and, if s != 0, to copy low-level array into it.
// If n == 0 or allocation fails, we bind to null rep,
// and do no copying.
{
  if (Alloc(n) && s) CopyN(s, n);
}
```

This constructor is also used as the default, with *n* and *s* defaulting to 0. In this mode, the vector created will reference the null vector representation *null_rep*, as shown in the following *Alloc()* function called by the constructor:

```
template<class TYPE>
int Vector<TYPE>::Alloc(unsigned n)
// Allocates a block of n elements for this vector.
// If n == 0 or allocation fails, we bind to the null rep.
// ASSUMES TYPE has a default constructor.
// Returns 0 if we've bound to null_rep otherwise, returns 1.
{
  if (n) {
     rep = new(n) VecRep<TYPE>(n);
  }
  else {
    rep = &VecRep<TYPE>::null_rep;
    rep->refcnt++;
  }
  start = rep->data;
  if (rep != &VecRep<TYPE>::null_rep) {
    len = n;
    stride = 1;
    return 1;
  }
  else {
    len = 0;
    stride = 1;
    return 0;
  }
}
```

The *Alloc()* function is similar to the one used in the *String* class, with the overloaded *new* operator for *VecRep* handling the dynamic allocation chores.

Also, to handle any allocation problems, we use a zero-length vector that references *null_rep*. Note that new vectors initially have a stride of one, and that the vectors are fixed length (with the logical length set to the allocated dimensioned length). Here are some ways to create vectors:

```
Vector<float> v(10);  // Create a new vector of 10 elements
Vector<int> w;        // Create a null vector
```

Like the *String* copy constructor, the *Vector* copy constructor actually uses share semantics:

```
template<class TYPE>
Vector<TYPE>::Vector(const Vector<TYPE> &v)
// Copy constructor that shares all of the vector v
{
  Bind(v);
  len = v.len;
  stride = v.stride;
  start = v.start;
}
```

The copy constructor's use of share semantics is all-important, since this allows us to return vectors from functions by value, without having to copy all of the vector elements.

The assignment operator also uses share semantics:

```
template<class TYPE>
Vector<TYPE> &Vector<TYPE>::operator=(const Vector<TYPE> &v)
// Share semantics used for assignment
{
  if (this != &v) Share(v); // Note trap for assignment to self
  return *this;
}
```

The *Share()* function is very similar to the copy constructor, except it calls *NewBinding()* instead of *Bind()* because the vector is presumably already bound to a vector representation:

```
template<class TYPE>
void Vector<TYPE>::Share(const Vector<TYPE> &v)
// Used to shares data with vector v
{
  NewBinding(v);
  len = v.len;
  stride = v.stride;
  start = v.start;
}
```

Subvectors

One of the constructors lets us create *subvectors*, analogous to substrings:

```
template<class TYPE>
Vector<TYPE>::Vector(const Vector<TYPE> &v, SliceType styp,
                     unsigned n, unsigned str, unsigned ofs)
// Constructor used to create a subvector, either shared or
// copied. If styp = SHARED, then the new vector of
// length n shares its data with the old vector with the
// desired stride and offset. Otherwise, a copy is made
// with a length of n, stride of 1, and offset of 0.
// If n == 0, it means use v.len for the length.
// If copying and allocation fail, no copy takes place.
{
  len = (n) ? n : v.len;
  if (styp == SHARED) {
    // Share existing data in v, accumulating offset
    // and stride as needed
    Bind(v);
    start = v.start + ofs * v.stride;
    stride = str * v.stride;
  }
  else {
    // Allocate data, then copy the desired slice of the
    // source vector into the destination vector.
    // Note clever recursive call to constructor.
    if (Alloc(len)) Copy(Vector<TYPE>(v, SHARED, len, str, ofs));
  }
}
```

Subvectors are more complex than substrings. Not only do they have a starting offset and length, but subvectors can also have a different stride from the original vector. For example, by using a stride of two, it's possible for a subvector to incorporate every other element of a base vector, as shown in the following code and illustrated in Figure 7.8:

```
int low_level_arr[8] = {0, 1, 2, 3, 4, 5, 6, 7};

Vector<int> v(8, low_level_arr);   // v = {0,1,2,3,4,5,6,7}
Vector<int> w(v, SHARED, 4, 2, 1); // w = {1, 3, 5, 7};
```

The enumerated type *SliceType* is used to specify whether the subvector is to be its own copy, or whether it shares its data with the base vector:

```
enum SliceType { SHARED, COPIED };
```

Figure 7.8 A subvector of every other element.

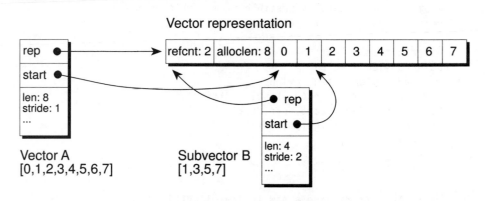

If the subvector is a copy, the stride will be one for the copy, regardless of the stride of the original vector. However, if the vector is shared, the strides and offsets are accumulated. For example, if the stride of the first subvector is two, and a shared sub-subvector also has a stride of two, the overall stride for the shared sub-subvector will be four. We can show this by creating a sub-subvector from the subvector w given earlier:

```
Vector<int> z(w, SHARED, 2, 2, 0); // z = {1, 5}
```

When we create a subvector copy, the subvector constructor is ingeniously designed to recursively call itself. To create a subvector copy, we allocate room for the new vector, and then create a shared subvector with the appropriate stride, offset, and length. This shared subvector is passed to the *Copy()* function as the source vector. (It may take you awhile to understand what's going on here.) This trick reduces the amount of code needed for the constructor, without affecting performance.

At first glance, the ability to create shared subvectors may seem a little bizarre. But this feature allows us to easily return row, column, and diagonal vectors from a matrix. That's because the data for a matrix is actually stored in a vector with a stride of one. If the matrix has a width of five columns, then to return a column vector we merely create a shared subvector, with a stride of five!

Copying Vectors

Because vectors can have different strides, we must be careful to account for the strides when copying one vector's data into another. The *Copy()* function illustrates this:

```
template<class TYPE>
void Vector<TYPE>::Copy(const Vector<TYPE> &v)
// Copies as much data as possible from v into this
// vector, truncating if need be
{
  unsigned tlen = len;
  unsigned vlen = v.len;
  if (tlen > vlen) tlen = vlen;
  VecPtr<const TYPE> src(v.start, v.stride);
  VecPtr<TYPE> dest(start, stride);
  for (unsigned i=0; i<tlen; i++) {
      *dest = *src;
      src++;
      dest++;
  }
  len = tlen; // We have a new logical length!
}
```

The secret to the *Copy()* function lies in the way it creates vector pointers to the source and target vectors with the correct strides. The copy loop is then fairly simple to implement. Because vectors aren't ever resized, the *Copy()* function may have to truncate data if the source vector is larger than the destination vector. If the source vector is smaller, then the destination vector is given a new, smaller length. Unlike true variable-length arrays, however, we don't destroy the elements now outside the length of the vector. Those will get destroyed along with all the others when the vector data itself is destroyed. Thus, vectors aren't really fixed length, nor are they variable length, either.

Accessing Vector Elements

As is true with all the array classes that we've shown in this book, the subscript operator is overloaded for the *Vector* class and allows for the subscripts to be range checked. As usual, two forms are given: one for non-*const* vectors and one for *const* vectors (the latter isn't shown):

```
template<class TYPE>
TYPE &Vector<TYPE>::operator[](unsigned i)
// For non-const vectors
{
  return start[CHECK(i)*stride];
}
```

In case you want more direct access to vector elements, two *PtrToAll()* functions are provided (the one for constant vectors isn't shown), which return vector pointers to all the elements:

```
template<class TYPE>
VecPtr<TYPE> Vector<TYPE>::PtrToAll()
// Returns a pointer to the beginning of
// this vector's elements
{
  return VecPtr<TYPE>(start, stride);
}
```

Because the *PtrToAll()* function creates an additional reference to the vector data that isn't accounted for, you must be careful to treat this function as a low-level "hook," and use it only for performance reasons.

SetElements() allows you to set all elements of a vector to a specified value:

```
template<class TYPE>
void Vector<TYPE>::SetElements(const TYPE &x)
// Sets every element of this vector to x
{
  VecPtr<TYPE> cursor(start, stride);
  for (unsigned i = 0; i<len; i++) {
     *cursor = x;
     cursor++;
  }
}
```

Note the careful use of the vector pointer, *cursor*, in the loop, which ensures that the vector stride is accounted for. Another form of overloaded assignment uses the *SetElements()* function:

```
template<class TYPE>
Vector<TYPE> &Vector<TYPE>::operator=(const TYPE &x)
// Sets each element of the vector to the value x
{
  SetElements(x);
  return *this;
}
```

Here's an example of these functions:

```
Vector<int> v(10);      // Create a vector a 10 elements
Vector<int> w(v, 5, 2); // Create vector of even elements of v
Vector<int> z(v, 5, 1); // Create vector of odd elements of v

w.SetElements(0); // Set all even elements to 0
z = 1;            // Set all odd elements to 1
```

The value of these types of vector operations is more evident when they are used in conjunction with matrices. For instance, given a vector *d* that's the diagonal of a matrix, you can easily set the diagonal elements to one:

```
d = 1; // Set diagonal elements to 1
```

THE MATRIX CLASS

The extended *Matrix* class adds safe, efficient, matrix transposition and submatrices to the basic *SimpleMatrix* design, and is defined as follows:

```
template<class TYPE>
class Matrix {
protected:
  Vector<TYPE> data;
  unsigned nrows, ncols, rowstride, colstride;
public:
  Matrix(unsigned nr=0, unsigned nc=0, const TYPE *s = 0);
  Matrix(const Matrix<TYPE> &m);
  Matrix(const Matrix<TYPE> &m, SliceType styp,
          unsigned sr=0, unsigned sc=0,
          unsigned nr=0, unsigned nc=0);
  void Copy(const Matrix<TYPE> &m);
  void Share(const Matrix<TYPE> &m);
  Matrix<TYPE> Transpose();
  Matrix<TYPE> &operator=(const Matrix<TYPE> &m);
  Matrix<TYPE> &operator=(const TYPE &x);
#ifndef NO_RANGE_CHECK
  unsigned CheckRow(unsigned i) const;
  unsigned CheckCol(unsigned i) const;
#endif
  Vector<TYPE> operator[](unsigned r);
  const Vector<TYPE> operator[](unsigned r) const;
  TYPE &operator()(unsigned r, unsigned c);
  const TYPE &operator()(unsigned r, unsigned c) const;
  Vector<TYPE> Row(unsigned r, SliceType styp=SHARED);
  Vector<TYPE> Col(unsigned c, SliceType styp=SHARED);
  Vector<TYPE> Diag(SliceType styp=SHARED);
  Vector<TYPE> All(SliceType styp=SHARED);
  const Vector<TYPE> Row(unsigned r, SliceType styp=SHARED) const;
  const Vector<TYPE> Col(unsigned c, SliceType styp=SHARED) const;
  const Vector<TYPE> Diag(SliceType styp=SHARED) const;
  const Vector<TYPE> All(SliceType styp=SHARED) const;
  // Mid-level hooks. Use these at your own risk:
  VecPtr<TYPE> RowPtr(unsigned r=0);
  VecPtr<TYPE> ColPtr(unsigned c=0);
  VecPtr<TYPE> DiagPtr();
```

```
VecPtr<TYPE> PtrToAll();
VecPtr<const TYPE> RowPtr(unsigned r=0) const;
VecPtr<const TYPE> ColPtr(unsigned c=0) const;
VecPtr<const TYPE> DiagPtr() const;
VecPtr<const TYPE> PtrToAll() const;
int IsNull() const;
int IsUnique() const;
Matrix<TYPE> Clone() const;
int EnsureUnique();
unsigned NCols() const;
unsigned NRows() const;
unsigned RowStride() const;
unsigned ColStride() const;
int IsRowMajor() const;
int IsColMajor() const;
int IsSquare() const;
};
```

The complete code for the *Matrix* class is given on disk in the files *matrix.h* and *matrix.mth*. Test programs are provided in the files *tstmat.cpp*, *tstmat2.cpp*, *tstmat3.cpp*, and *tstmat4.cpp*.

The *Matrix* class has five data members. The elements of a matrix are stored in the *1-d Vector* object *data*, which of course means the matrix data can be shared. This data is interpreted as a *2-d* array, with *nrows* number of rows and *ncols* number of columns. The two other members, *rowstride* and *colstride*, keep track of the current row and column stride of the matrix. These members are useful when the matrix is transposed and also for submatrices, as you'll see. Figure 7.9 shows the layout of a typical matrix.

Figure 7.9 Layout of a typical matrix.

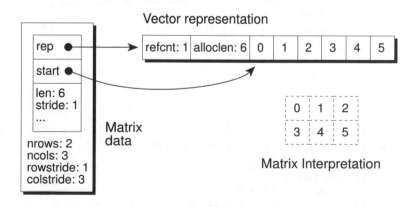

Constructing and Assigning Matrices

The first *Matrix* constructor allocates and constructs a brand new matrix by calling the *Vector* constructor for *data* and then setting up the matrix size and strides:

```
template<class TYPE>
Matrix<TYPE>::Matrix(unsigned nr, unsigned nc, const TYPE *s)
: data(nr * nc, s)
{
  if (data.IsNull()) {
     nrows = 0; ncols = 0; colstride = 1; rowstride = 1;
  }
  else {
     nrows = nr; ncols = nc; colstride = nc; rowstride = 1;
  }
}
```

Note how the possibility of null matrices (due either to passing zero sizes or memory allocation problems) is handled properly.

The copy constructor and overloaded assignment operators use share semantics:

```
template<class TYPE>
Matrix<TYPE>::Matrix(const Matrix<TYPE> &m)
: data(m.data)
{
  if (data.IsNull()) {
     nrows = 0; ncols = 0; colstride = 1; rowstride = 1;
  }
  else {
     nrows = m.nrows; ncols = m.ncols;
     colstride = m.colstride; rowstride = m.rowstride;
  }
}

template<class TYPE>
Matrix<TYPE> &Matrix<TYPE>::operator=(const Matrix<TYPE> &m)
// Share semantics used for assignment.
{
  if (this != &m) Share(m); // Note trap for assignment to self
  return *this;
}

template<class TYPE>
void Matrix<TYPE>::Share(const Matrix<TYPE> &m)
{
  data.Share(m.data);
  nrows = m.nrows; ncols = m.ncols;
  colstride = m.colstride; rowstride = m.rowstride;
}
```

Here's an example of these functions:

```
float one_d_arr[4] = {0, 1, 2, 3};

Matrix<float> m(3,5);            // Elements left uninitialized
Matrix<float> w(2,2,one_d_arr); // Elements set to {{0,1},{2,3}}
Matrix<float> z(w);             // Copy constructor called

m = z;                          // m now reassigned to z's data
```

Creating Submatrices

The *Matrix* class can support submatrices, which *SimpleMatrix* couldn't do. These submatrices can either overlay an existing matrix (with the data being shared) or be separate copies. Figure 7.10 shows an example of overlaying a 3x5 submatrix onto a 6x7 matrix.

One of the *Matrix* constructors is used to construct submatrices. This constructor is in a sense the two-dimensional analog of the subvector constructor of the *Vector* class. The submatrix can either be shared or copied, depending on the value of *styp*:

```
template<class TYPE>
Matrix<TYPE>::Matrix(const Matrix<TYPE> &m, SliceType styp,
                     unsigned sr, unsigned sc,
                     unsigned nr, unsigned nc)
// Constructor that constructs a submatrix of matrix m
// If styp==SHARED, it means to share the data with m
// NOTE: If sharing, we initially create a null vector, and
// then we immediately rebind to shared vector. If copying,
// a row-major submatrix is created, and if nr == 0,
// then m.nrows is used. If nc == 0, then m.ncols is used.
```

Figure 7.10 A submatrix of a matrix.

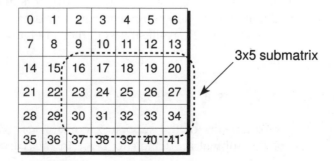

3x5 submatrix

```
    : data((styp == SHARED) ?
          0 : ((nr ? nr : m.nrows) * (nc ? nc : m.ncols)))
{
  unsigned start_ofs, n;
  if (nr) nrows = nr; else { nrows = m.nrows; sr = 0; }
  if (nc) ncols = nc; else { ncols = m.ncols; sc = 0; }
  if (styp == SHARED) { // Sharing
     // When sharing, strides are always the same as parent strides
     colstride = m.colstride;
     rowstride = m.rowstride;
     // Calculate length of underlying vector and offset.
     // Remember: either colstride or rowstride == 1.
     if (rowstride == 1) {
        n = colstride * (nrows-1) + ncols;
     }
     else {
        n = rowstride * (ncols-1) + nrows;
     }
     start_ofs = sr * colstride + rowstride * sc;
     data.Share(Vector<TYPE>(m.data, SHARED, n, 1, start_ofs));
  }
  else {
    if (data.IsNull()) {
       nrows = 0; ncols = 0; colstride = 1; rowstride = 1;
    }
    else {
       // Set up as a row-major matrix
       colstride = ncols; rowstride = 1;
       // Copy data from shared submatrix into allocated space.
       // Note that the constructor is called recursively here
       // to create a shared submatrix used for the copy.
       Copy(Matrix<TYPE>(m, SHARED, sr, sc, nrows, ncols));
    }
  }
}
```

When making a submatrix copy, we use the same type of recursive call to the constructor that we used in the constructor for subvectors in the *Vector* class.

Here's an example of a 3x5 submatrix that shares its data with a 6x7 matrix, starting at row and column (2,2), as illustrated earlier in Figure 7.10:

```
Matrix<float> m(6,7);
...
Matrix<float> subm(m, SHARED, 2, 2, 3, 5);
```

The last four parameters of the submatrix constructor, which define the origin and size of the submatrix, default to zero. In this case, the submatrix encompasses all of the original matrix. This approach can be used to create an actual copy of the matrix—which the copy constructor can't do—since it uses share semantics exclusively. For example:

```
Matrix<float> copy_of_m(m, COPIED);
```

The two variables *rowstride* and *colstride* provide the key to allowing a submatrix to share data with its parent. For normal row-major matrices, the column stride is always equal to the number of columns in the matrix. However, that isn't necessarily true for submatrices. Consider, for instance, the 3x5 submatrix shown earlier in Figure 7.10. You can see that its column stride should be the number of columns of the parent 6x7 matrix, and thus should be 7 instead of 5.

If one of the matrices is transposed or yet another submatrix is taken of a submatrix, the matter is further complicated. However, by judicious use of *rowstride* and *colstride*, the strides are never confused. Here's the basic rule: the row and column strides of a submatrix are always the same as their parents' strides and must always reflect the physical layout of the data. The real data lies somewhere up the chain of parents and is organized in row-major order. Of course, if one parent is transposed, the row and column strides will be interchanged.

Transposing Matrix Objects

Data sharing allows us to define an efficient matrix transposition function for *Matrix* objects by merely interchanging *nrows* and *ncols* and interchanging *rowstride* and *colstride*:

```
template<class TYPE>
Matrix<TYPE> Matrix<TYPE>::Transpose()
// Returns a transposition of this matrix. Does not have to move
// the elements of the matrix around, just merely changes
// interpretation between row-major and column-major ordering.
{
  Matrix<TYPE> t(*this); // Remember, copy constructor shares

  // Interchange number of rows and cols
  unsigned temp = t.nrows;
  t.nrows = t.ncols;
  t.ncols = temp;

  // Interchange row stride and column stride
  temp = t.colstride;
  t.colstride = t.rowstride;
  t.rowstride = temp;
```

```
    return t;
}
```

Unlike the similar optimized *Transpose()* we showed for the *SimpleMatrix* class, this function does not need to assume that the matrix is to be transposed in place. Thus, the original matrix is untouched. Here's an example of this function:

```
Matrix<float> m(3,5); // Create a 3x5 matrix
...
Matrix<float> t;       // Create a null matrix

t = m.Transpose();
```

Because both assignment and copy construction use share semantics, we can write statements like the last one without worrying about undue copying taking place. If the matrix being transposed is large, we can indeed avoid a lot of data movement.

Of course, you don't get something for nothing. Clever use of *rowstride* and *colstride* for matrix transposition does have its price. The *vector extraction functions*, to be given next, aren't as efficient as they could be; they can't assume anything about the vector strides. For instance, a row vector may or may not have a stride of one, so we can't use an ordinary pointer to it.

Extracting Vectors from a Matrix

As is true with the *SimpleMatrix* class, the functions *RowPtr()*, *ColPtr()*, *DiagPtr()*, and *PtrToAll()* all are defined for the *Matrix* class. We'll refer to these as *vector extraction functions*. These functions use the modifications we suggested earlier—to handle the potential transposition of the matrix—by using *rowstride* and *colstride* rather than *nrows* and *ncols* directly. By using *rowstride* and *colstride*, the extraction functions also work for submatrices.

Here are the *RowPtr()* and *ColPtr()* functions for the *Matrix* class. The other extraction functions are defined similarly. Also note that *const* versions can be defined for constant matrices (not shown):

```
template<class TYPE>
VecPtr<TYPE> Matrix<TYPE>::RowPtr(unsigned r)
// Returns vector pointer to row r
{
   return VecPtr<TYPE>(data.start+CHECKROW(r)*colstride, rowstride);
}

template<class TYPE>
VecPtr<TYPE> Matrix<TYPE>::ColPtr(unsigned c)
```

```
// Returns vector pointer to column c
{
  return VecPtr<TYPE>(data.start+CHECKCOL(c)*rowstride, colstride);
}
```

In these functions, range checking is handled by calls to the macros *CHECKROW()* and *CHECKCOL()*. These macros are the two-dimensional counterparts to the *CHECK()* macro used in the *Array* classes (described in Chapter 4), and are defined in the *range.h* header file. The macros do nothing if *NO_RANGE_CHECK* is undefined.

The range checking is done when the vector pointers are created. But remember that, when you use the vector pointers, nothing prevents you from going out of bounds. For this reason, another set of vector extraction functions are defined. These functions, which return fully range-checked *Vector* objects, are *Row()*, *Col()*, *Diag()*, and *All()*. Here are examples of *Row()* and *Col()*:

```
template<class TYPE>
Vector<TYPE> Matrix<TYPE>::Row(unsigned r, SliceType styp)
// Return a row slice of a matrix
{
  return Vector<TYPE>(data, styp,
                      ncols, rowstride, CHECKROW(r)*colstride);
}

template<class TYPE>
Vector<TYPE> Matrix<TYPE>::Col(unsigned c, SliceType styp)
// Return a column slice of a matrix
{
  return Vector<TYPE>(data, styp,
                      nrows, colstride, CHECKCOL(c)*rowstride);
}
```

Notice that, by using the *styp* parameter, the vectors returned can either share their data with the original matrix or can be separate copies. The default action is to share the data.

Subscripting with the Matrix Class

To return a row vector, the subscript operator is overloaded for the *Matrix* class. As such, *operator[]()* is the same as *Row()*, except the returned vector always shares its data with the matrix:

```
template<class TYPE>
Vector<TYPE> Matrix<TYPE>::operator[](unsigned r)
// Row subscripting operator for non-const matrices.
```

```
// This routine does the same thing as Row(r,SHARED).
{
  return Vector<TYPE>(data, SHARED,
                      ncols, rowstride, CHECKROW(r)*colstride);
}
```

Since vectors have their own subscript operator function defined, you can write code like the following:

```
Matrix<float> m(3,5);

m[2][4] = 99; // Set lower-right element to 99
```

Thus, you can use the same double-subscripting syntax that's used for built-in arrays. There's only one problem. The *SimpleMatrix* class returned an ordinary pointer from the first subscript. Here, though, a full vector object is returned, and this object must be constructed. The construction process, while fairly efficient due to share semantics, still takes time. In fact, a matrix multiply routine that uses *Matrix* objects with double-subscripting is more than *six times slower* than its *SimpleMatrix* counterpart! And you'll only get this performance level when range checking is turned off. If you turn on range checking, the performance could be more than *ten times* slower.

You can circumvent this problem by defining *operator[]()* to return a vector pointer rather than a full vector. This will yield a more efficient subscript operation (perhaps only twice as slow as the fastest version), but you lose the ability to do range checking on the row vector. Of course, you can eliminate the subscripting altogether and instead use vector pointer incrementing. Doing so will yield speeds as fast as those for the *SimpleMatrix* class. This is an important benefit because you can obtain improved the performance even though you now have generalized matrices (such as transposed submatrices).

Another alternative is to define a different style of subscript operator. For example, you can overload the *()* operator (normally used for function call syntax) to do two-dimensional subscripting:

```
template<class TYPE>
TYPE &Matrix<TYPE>::operator()(unsigned r, unsigned c)
{
  return data.start[CHECKROW(r)*colstride + CHECKCOL(c)*rowstride];
}
...
Matrix<float> m(3,5); // Construct matrix
...
m(2,4) = 99;              // Set lower-right element to 99
```

The equation used in the *operator()()* function is a generalization of the two-dimensional subscript equation used for row-major matrices. Normally, you multiply the row index by the number of columns and then add the column index, as in:

```
m(r,c)  =   *(m + r*ncols + c)
```

However, in the general case, the matrix might be transposed and might be a submatrix. Thus, we have to multiply both the row index and the column index by the appropriate row and column *strides*. Note that one of the strides will be one, so in effect we'll have either

```
m(r,c) = *(m + r*colstride + c) // If row major
```

or

```
m(r,c) = *(m + r + c*rowstride) // If column major
```

Thus, one of the multiplications in *operator()()* is redundant. That's the price we pay for generality. Even so, expressions like $m(i,j)$ have been timed to be two to three times faster than their *m[i][j]* counterparts.

The expression $m(i,j)$ is actually the conventional notation used in mathematics for subscripting. Because of this, some people prefer to use the two-dimensional operator over its double-subscripting *m[i][j]* counterpart. Others prefer the more conventional C++ syntax for subscripting. Regardless of your personal preference, the mathematical notation will be significantly faster unless you define the *[]* operator for matrices to return a vector pointer rather than a full vector. In that case, the results are fairly even.

Non-Contiguous Submatrices

A matrix is said to be *contiguous* if you can access all of the elements using a single *1-d* vector. Normal matrices created by the *Matrix* class will always be contiguous, regardless of whether they are transposed. However, its possible for submatrices that are shared with a parent to be non-contiguous. Figure 7.11 shows some examples of contiguous and non-contiguous submatrices, assuming a row-major organization.

From Figure 7.11, the following rule emerges for determining whether a submatrix is contiguous: either the number of columns must equal the column stride or the number of rows must be one. For column-major matrices (not shown in Figure 7.11), the number of rows must equal the row stride or the

---

Figure 7.11 Some non-contiguous submatrices.

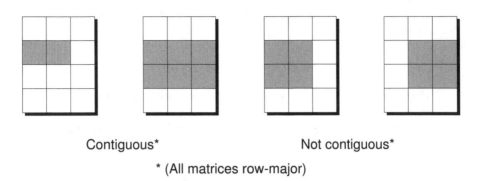

Contiguous*   Not contiguous*

* (All matrices row-major)

---

number of columns must be one. The function *All()*, which attempts to return a *1-d* vector to all the elements in a matrix, makes these tests for contiguousness. If the matrix isn't contiguous, *All()* returns a null vector because it isn't possible to access all the elements with a single vector:

```
template<class TYPE>
Vector<TYPE> Matrix<TYPE>::All(SliceType styp)
// Returns a 1-d vector with all of the data for the matrix.
// If it isn't possible for the 1-d data to be contiguous
// (as will be the case for some submatrices), then a
// null vector is returned.
// ASSUMES either colstride or rowstride == 1.
{
  if ((rowstride == 1 && nrows > 1 && ncols != colstride) ||
      (colstride == 1 && ncols > 1 && nrows != rowstride))
      return Vector<TYPE>(); // Return a null vector
  return Vector<TYPE>(data, styp, nrows * ncols, 1, 0);
}
```

As an example of handling non-contiguous submatrics, here is an overloaded assignment operator that sets all the elements of the matrix to a specified value. This is done by doing the assignments row by row, using vector pointers:

```
template<class TYPE>
Matrix<TYPE> &Matrix<TYPE>::operator=(const TYPE &x)
// Set all elements in the matrix to the value x.
// Assumes a worst case non-contiguous submatrix.
{
  // tc = column vector pointer to rows of t
  // tr = row vector pointer to columns of t
```

```
VecPtr<TYPE> tc(data.start, colstride);
VecPtr<TYPE> tr(data.start, rowstride);
for (unsigned i = 0; i<nrows; i++) {
    tr = tc; // Remember, strides aren't assigned!
    for (unsigned j = 0; j<ncols; j++) {
        *tr = x;
        tr++;   // Next column
    }
    tc++;       // Next row
}
return *this;
}
```

DESIGN CRITIQUE

In this chapter, you've seen in detail how to define generalized dynamic vectors and matrices. In our design, we were careful to remove all potential inefficiencies, without sacrificing generality. However, any time you make something general, performance is bound to suffer. This is manifested in basically one form: vector pointers must be used rather than ordinary pointers. Because of their generality, vector pointers with strides of one may be less efficient than ordinary pointers (depending on how well your compiler optimizes), even though the two are logically equivalent.

However, by using such tricks as vector pointers and reference counting, we can define certain operations to be much more efficient than the obvious ways would suggest. Consider, for instance, matrix transposition, which can be done by merely swapping some variables. Returning matrices from functions also becomes very efficient, making the code less clumsy. Never does an unnecessary copy of matrix elements take place.

There are some overriding questions: What is the cost of generality? Do the potential speed improvements offset the potential slowdowns? The answers, of course, depend on the particular application (and your compiler). However, in most non-trivial applications, the *Vector* and *Matrix* classes will probably be just as as efficient as simple, static built-in matrices.

An interesting test is to compare matrix multiply times for built-in statically sized matrices, *SimpleMatrix* objects, and *Matrix* objects. Table 7.1 shows the fastest times possible for all three types (using all the tricks described in this chapter). The results were obtained by multiplying two 30x30 double precision floating-point matrices together, 100 times, and taking the average. The tests were performed using 32-bit pointers on a 486 33-MHz machine.

As you might expect, statically sized matrices yielded the fastest results. Using a generalized matrix resulted in a 32 percent drop in speed, which isn't bad considering the flexibility that we gain. Interestingly enough, the general *Matrix* class performed slightly better than the *SimpleMatrix* class (probably due to some compiler optimization quirk). Their performance is close enough to suggest that the main performance penalty is due mostly to the use of dynamically sized matrices and not the fact that, in the case of the *Matrix* class, submatrices and efficient transposition are supported.

What is the space cost of generalized matrices? Figure 7.9 given earlier shows the memory layout of a *Matrix* object. Note that, in addition to the matrix elements themselves, a *Matrix* object has four data members plus a *Vector* object with four data members—one of which points to a *VecRep* object using two data members. Thus, an independent, unique matrix has an overhead of 10 data members (probably in the range of 20 to 40 bytes, depending on the implementation). This may be significant if you have a lot of small 3x3 or 4x4 matrices. However, for larger matrices, the overhead becomes less important, especially in light of the flexibility gained. And, of course, if the matrix data is shared, the overhead is reduced by two members plus the elements shared.

Table 7.1 Relative performance of different matrix types.

Type of Matrix	Time in Seconds	Performance Relative to Fastest (Smaller Is Better)
Statically sized built-in 2-d arrays	0.0470	1.0
SimpleMatrix objects	0.0660	1.40
Matrix objects	0.0621	1.32

Linked
Lists

L inked lists are the (usually) non-contiguous counterparts to arrays. Like arrays, linked lists are a fundamental type of data structure used to represent sequences of objects. In the first three chapters, you were given various examples of linked-lists. Here, we will take a detailed look at linked-lists, from basic design to some of the possible variations. The chapter culminates with a contiguous array-based linked list hybrid design.

WHY USE LINKED LISTS?

Before you begin studying the design of linked lists, you might be wondering what they are good for. Like arrays, linked lists are good for representing sequences of objects, but they have a different set of advantages, as shown in Table 8.1. Linked lists excel in allowing you to rearrange the sequences, and in allowing those sequences to grow and shrink. The tradeoff is that linked lists take more space per element than arrays.

Table 8.1 Tradeoffs between linked lists and arrays.

Feature	Arrays	Linked Lists
Sequential access	Efficient	Efficient
Random access	Efficient	Inefficient
Resizing	Inefficient	Efficient
Element rearranging	Inefficient	Efficient
Overhead per element	None	1 or 2 links

LINKED LIST BASICS

A linked list is composed of *nodes,* or elements, linked together. Conceptually, each node holds data, plus one or two links to other nodes. A list containing nodes with only one link is called a *singly-linked list.* Figure 8.1(a) shows an example. In a singly-linked list, each node points to the next node in the sequence. Because only a single pointer is used, singly-linked lists can only be efficiently processed in one direction.

A *doubly-linked list* node contains two links: one pointing to the next node and one to the previous node. Figure 8.1(b) shows an example. Doubly-linked lists can be efficiently processed both forwards and backwards. However, they require an extra link in each node.

A linked-list node can be represented as a simple structure holding the node's data and pointers for links to other nodes. Within this structure, it makes sense to also incorporate functions that aid in building lists. Examples are functions to insert and remove nodes. Next, we'll show you how to define both singly-linked and doubly-linked node classes, and how to construct lists from them.

Singly-Linked List Nodes

Here is a typical definition of a singly-linked node class, written as a template holding information of type *TYPE*:

```
template<class TYPE>
struct Snode {
  TYPE info;           // Holds the data for the node
  Snode<TYPE> *next;   // Pointer to next node in the list
  Snode(const TYPE &x);
  void InsertAfter(Snode<TYPE> *n);
  Snode<TYPE> *RmvNext();
};
```

The constructor initializes the *info* field by copying the parameter *x* and then sets the *next* pointer to zero. It's assumed that *TYPE* has a copy constructor or is a built-in type:

Figure 8.1 Singly-linked versus doubly-linked lists.

(a) Singly-linked list   (b) Doubly-linked list

```
template<class TYPE>
Snode<TYPE>::Snode(const TYPE &x)
: info(x)
{
  next = 0;
}
```

Setting *next* to zero is optional, but it aids in constructing *null-terminated lists*—that is, lists whose last nodes have null *next* pointers.

Inserting a node into a linked list is illustrated in Figure 8.2, and is implemented with the following *InsertAfter()* function:

```
template<class TYPE>
void Snode<TYPE>::InsertAfter(Snode<TYPE> *n)
// Insert node n after this node
{
  n->next = next; // See Fig 8.2a
  next = n;       // See Fig 8.2b
}
```

Insertion works by copying the current node's *next* pointer into the *next* pointer of the new node, and then having the current node point to the new node. Here is an example that creates the list shown previously in Figure 8.1(a):

```
Snode<char> mylist('a');

mylist.InsertAfter(new Snode<char>('c'));
mylist.InsertAfter(new Snode<char>('b'));
```

This code takes advantage of the fact that the constructor for *Snode* sets the *next* pointer to zero. Thus, the linked list is guaranteed to be null terminated. You'll notice that we built part of the list backwards because it's more efficient to add to the front of the list than to the back. (Later, we'll show you some ways

Figure 8.2 Inserting a node into a singly-linked list.

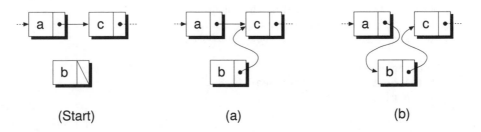

(Start)　　　　　　　　(a)　　　　　　　　(b)

to get around this.) Also, the first node was allocated statically, but the other nodes were allocated dynamically. It doesn't really matter how linked-list nodes are allocated. Later, we'll exploit that fact, implementing linked-lists through various memory allocation schemes.

Suppose you want to insert a node *before* another node. With singly-linked lists, this is awkward because you must scan the list from the beginning to get to the previous node. Assume that *p* starts out pointing to the front of a null-terminated list, and *n* is the node you wish to insert before the node *q*. Here are the necessary steps:

```
Snode<char> *p = &mylist;
while(p && p->next != q) p = p->next; // Scan down the list
if (p) p->InsertAfter(n); // Equivalent to inserting before q
```

You may have noticed that it isn't possible to insert before the first node in the list. (Think about the case where *q* equals the intial value of *p*.) To solve this problem, you can incorporate a dummy header node at the front of the list. This node's only purpose is to provide a "handle" for the list. The *info* field is ignored. Here, we show another way to build the list shown previously in Figure 8.1a—this time, using a dummy header node (the header node isn't shown in Figure 8.1a):

```
Snode<char> mylist(0); // Header node, with an arbitrary info field
mylist.InsertAfter(new Snode<char>('c')); // List built backwards
mylist.InsertAfter(new Snode<char>('b'));
mylist.InsertAfter(new Snode<char>('a'));
```

Each *InsertAfter()* operation inserts before the previous first node of the list, starting with no first node.

The complement to the *InsertAfter()* function is the following *RmvNext()* function, which, given a node, allows you to remove the node that follows it. Figure 8.3 illustrates the steps involved in removing a node from a singly-linked list.

```
template<class TYPE>
Snode<TYPE> *Snode<TYPE>::RmvNext()
// Removes the node following this node.
// Tests for next being null.
// Returns a pointer to the node removed.
{
  Snode *p = next;
  if (p) next = p->next; // See Fig 8.3
  return p;
}
```

Figure 8.3 Removing a node from a singly-linked list.

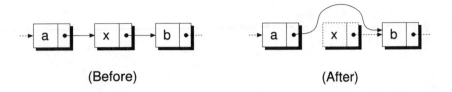

(Before)   (After)

Here's an example that shows how to remove and delete the first node of the list given previously:

```
Snode<char> *p;
p = mylist.RmvNext(); // Detach the node from the list
delete p;              // Then, de-allocate the node
```

Note that *RmvNext()* does not de-allocate the node, but rather just detaches the node from the list. The de-allocation is handled separately. Removing a node from a singly-linked list has the same awkwardness as inserting a node. Suppose you have a node *q*, and you wish to remove that node rather than the one that follows it. Here's how this can be done (assuming a null-terminated list with a header):

```
Snode<char> *p = &mylist; // Point to head of list
while(p && p->next != q) p = p->next;
if (p) p->RmvNext();
```

The removal involves *m* steps, where *m* is the position of *q* in the list. The awkwardness of singly-linked lists can be alleviated by adding another link to each node, pointing to the previous node. We'll examine such doubly-linked nodes next.

Sample code for implementing a singly-linked list is given on disk in the file *ch8_1.cpp.*

Doubly-Linked List Nodes

Here is a typical definition of a doubly-linked list node, written as a template holding information of type *TYPE*:

```
template<class TYPE>
struct Dnode {
  TYPE info;
```

```
    Dnode<TYPE> *prev;
    Dnode<TYPE> *next;
    Dnode(const TYPE &x);
    void InsertBefore(Dnode<TYPE> *n);
    void InsertAfter(Dnode<TYPE> *n);
    Dnode<TYPE> *Rmv();
};

template<class TYPE>
Dnode<TYPE>::Dnode(const TYPE &x)
: info(x)
{
  prev = 0; next = 0;
}

template<class TYPE>
void Dnode<TYPE>::InsertBefore(Dnode<TYPE> *n)
// Inserts node n before this node.
// Tests for prev being null.
{
  n->prev = prev;
  n->next = this;
  if (prev) prev->next = n;
  prev = n;
}

template<class TYPE>
void Dnode<TYPE>::InsertAfter(Dnode<TYPE> *n)
// Attaches node n after this node.
// Tests for next being null.
{
  n->next = next;           // See Fig 8.4a
  n->prev = this;           // See Fig 8.4b
  if (next) next->prev = n; // See Fig 8.4c
  next = n;                 // See Fig 8.4d
}

template<class TYPE>
Dnode<TYPE> *Dnode<TYPE>::Rmv()
// Removes this node from the list it is on.
// Tests for prev and next being null.
{
  if (prev) prev->next = next; // See Fig 8.5a
  if (next) next->prev = prev; // See Fig 8.5b
  return this;
}
```

Each *Dnode* has both a *prev* and *next* pointer. With the *prev* pointer, it's easy to write the *InsertBefore()* function. Also the *RmvNext()* function can be replaced with a *Rmv()* function that directly removes a node—without having to find the node that precedes it.

The steps for inserting a node into a doubly-linked list are given in Figure 8.4; the steps for removing a node are shown in Figure 8.5. Note that the only difference between *InsertBefore()* and *InsertAfter()* is the interchanging of *prev* and *next*.

This next example creates the list shown previously in Figure 8.1(b)—this time using both the *InsertBefore()* and *InsertAfter()* functions. Again, a null-terminated list is built (in both directions) due to the constructor setting the *prev* and *next* pointers to null. We've created a dummy header node as we did before:

```
Dnode<char> mylist(0); // Header with arbitrary info field
mylist.InsertAfter(new Dnode<char>('c'));
Dnode<char> *p = new Dnode<char>('b');
mylist.InsertAfter(p);
p->InsertBefore(new Dnode<char>('a'));
```

Sample code for implementing a doubly-linked list is given on disk in the file *ch8_2.cpp*.

Figure 8.4 Inserting a node into a doubly-linked list.

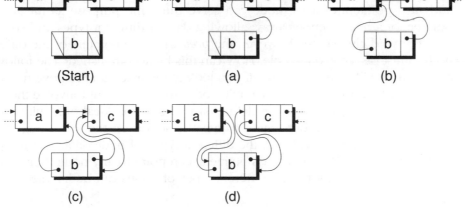

Figure 8.5 Removing a node from a doubly-linked list.

(Start)

(a)

(b)

HETEROGENOUS LISTS

The lists constructed in the previous sections are *homogenous.* That is, their nodes hold only one kind of data. In contrast, the nodes in a *heterogenous list* have different kinds of data. As is true with heterogenous arrays, two issues are involved with heterogenous lists: we have to deal with different sized data and typecasting problems.

With linked lists, handling different sized data is easy, since the nodes don't have to be the same size (as do array elements). This fact is due to the non-contiguous nature of linked lists. A heterogenous list node can store its data directly instead of using an indirect pointer scheme. In a sense, the *prev* and *next* pointers of a list node can serve the same purpose as the indirect pointers of a heterogenous array: allowing data of different types and sizes.

To avoid clumsiness, however, the *prev* and *next* pointers of the different nodes must be type compatible. How can this be accomplished? The following observation will give you a clue: if you look at the insert and remove functions of the *Snode* and *Dnode* classes, you'll notice that they do not involve the node data! This fact suggests you can define base classes that deal only with the list aspects of a node, without regard to what is stored on the list. Then, classes could be derived that deal with the different types of node data. The *prev* and *next* pointers, typed as base class pointers, can point to any node derived from the base class. Thus, lists with different types of nodes can be handled.

Abstract List Nodes

Here is an abstract class, *Snodeb,* designed for singly-linked list nodes, that uses the concepts of the previous section:

```
struct Snodeb { // An abstract singly-linked list node base class
  Snodeb *next; // Pointer to next node in the list
  Snodeb();
  void InsertAfter(Snodeb *n);
  Snodeb *RmvNext();
};
```

The functions of *Snodeb* are just like those of *Snode*, except the links are typed as *Snodeb* pointers. Also, keep in mind that a *Dnodeb* class can be similarly defined for doubly-linked nodes.

To show how to create a heterogenous list using *Snodeb*, we'll use the *Shape* and *Circle* class hierarchy defined in Chapter 5 (where heterogenous arrays were discussed). Given those two classes, we can derive node classes specifically for storing *Shape* and *Circle* objects:

```
struct ShapeNode : public Snodeb {
  Shape info;
  ShapeNode(float x=0, float y=0);
};

ShapeNode::ShapeNode(float x, float y)
: info(x, y)
{
  // Nothing else to do
}

struct CircleNode : public Snodeb {
  Circle info;
  CircleNode(float x = 0, float y = 0, float r = 0);
};

CircleNode::CircleNode(float x, float y, float r)
: info(x, y, r)
{
  // Nothing else to do
}
```

The following example creates and uses a list with two nodes (plus a dummy header) that stores a shape and circle object:

```
Snodeb mylist; // Create the header
mylist.InsertAfter(new ShapeNode(1, 2));
mylist.InsertAfter(new CircleNode(3, 4, 5));
```

Figure 8.6 illustrates the list that is created. Note in particular that the header, typed as an *Snodeb* node, doesn't contain any data. We've conveniently

Figure 8.6 A heterogenous list.

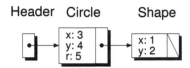

eliminated the problem of wasting space in the header for data that isn't used. You'll see this technique used again later in this chapter.

Polymorphic List Nodes

While it's easy to create a heterogenous list, it's another matter to actually use the list. Take a look at what happens if we walk the list created in the previous section and print the areas of the shapes in each node:

```
Snodeb *p = &mylist.next;
cout << "Area is: " << ((CircleNode *)p)->info.Area() << '\n';
p = p->next;
cout << "Area is: " << ((ShapeNode *)p)->info.Area() << '\n';
```

A nasty typecasting problem surfaces. We must remember what the node types really are so that the proper *Area()* function is called. This is the same typecasting problem that occurs with all heterogenous containers.

One way to tame the typecasting is to use the same technique we did for arrays: store pointers to the data in the nodes, rather than storing the data directly. Again, it's especially beneficial to use base class pointers. For example, we could define the *ShapeNode* class as follows, which will work for both *Shapes* and *Circle* objects:

```
struct ShapeNode : public Snodeb {
  Shape *info; // Point to shape object
  ShapeNode(const Shape *p);
};

ShapeNode::Shape(const Shape *p)
{
  info = p;
}
```

Now we can create a heterogenous list, as follows:

```
Snodeb mylist; // Create the header.
mylist.InsertAfter(new ShapeNode(new Shape(1, 2)));
mylist.InsertAfter(new ShapeNode(new Circle(3, 4, 5)));
```

The list created is shown in Figure 8.7. Now take a look at what happens when we walk the list:

```
Snodeb *p = &mylist.next;
cout << "Area is: " << ((ShapeNode *)p)->info->Area() << '\n';
p = p->next;
cout << "Area is: " << ((ShapeNode *)p)->info->Area() << '\n';
```

Because *p* is defined as an *Snodeb* pointer, we haven't eliminated the typecasting, but we've at least eliminated the problem of knowing whether a node points to a *Shape* or *Circle* object. That is handled by the fact that *Area()* is a virtual function.

We can reduce the typecasting further by providing another function, *Next()*, whose sole purpose is to typecast the *next* pointer as a pointer to a *ShapeNode* object:

```
ShapeNode *ShapeNode::Next()
{
  return (ShapeNode *)next;
}
...
ShapeNode *p = ((ShapeNode *)(&mylist))->Next();
cout << "Area is: " << p->info->Area() << '\n';
p = p->Next();
cout << "Area is: " << p->info->Area() << '\n';
```

We still must do a typecast for the header node, but at least when walking the list no other typecasts are necessary—as long as we use *Next()* instead of

---

Figure 8.7 A heterogenous list using indirect pointers.

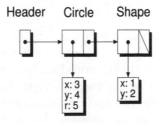

next. We could eliminate the typecast on the header node by defining it as a *ShapeNode*, rather than an *Snodeb* object. However, the *info* field of the header would then be wasted.

List Nodes as Roots of Class Hierarchies

We can also create polymorphic list nodes using a method that allows us to store data directly in the nodes. The idea is to define the types of data to be stored on lists as *bona fide* nodes themselves. We can do this in two basic ways:

1. Derive the data types to be stored on lists from abstract node classes. For example, we could derive *Shape* from *Snodeb*:

```
class Shape : public Snodeb {
  // ... Shape class as in Chapter 5
  Shape *Next();
};


...
Shape *Shape::Next()
{
  return (Shape *)next;
}
```

2. Define the data type to directly have list pointers. For example, you could define *Shape* to have a *next* pointer and the corresponding *InsertAfter()* and *RmvNext()* functions:

```
class Shape {
  // ... Shape class code as in Chapter 5
  Shape *next;
  void InsertAfter(Shape *n);
  Shape *RmvNext();
};
```

With both of these techniques, every class derived from *Shape* (such as *Circle*) will inherit list pointers and thus will be list nodes themselves. This is better than using indirect data pointers. The resulting list structures will be less complicated and take up less room. However, both techniques require list pointers for all data types to be stored on lists, which may be undesirable. For example, you may want to use the data types for applications other than lists.

Here is an example of the first technique. Note that, instead of writing *p->info->Area()*, we write *p->Area()*. That is, the *info* field no longer exists. The node data is a direct part of the node itself:

```
Snodeb mylist; // Create the header
mylist.InsertAfter(new Shape(1, 2)));
mylist.InsertAfter(new Circle(3, 4, 5)));

Shape *p = ((Shape *)(&mylist))->Next();
cout << "Area is: " << p->Area() << '\n';
p = p->Next();
cout << "Area is: " << p->Area() << '\n';
```

Contrast this with the second technique:

```
Shape mylist; // Create a header with shape data not used
mylist.InsertAfter(new Shape(1, 2)));
mylist.InsertAfter(new Circle(3, 4, 5)));

Shape *p = mylist.next;
cout << "Area is: " << p->Area() << '\n';
p = p->next;
cout << "Area is: " << p->Area() << '\n';
```

The second technique is cleaner because we don't need a *Next()* function. The *next* pointer is already typed as a *Shape* pointer. Unfortunately, as the code shows, header nodes must store shape data that isn't used. If we make the header an *Snodeb* node, then typecasting difficulties are created.

The second technique also forces every type of list (such as a shape list, a window list, a bank account list, and so on) to be from a different hierarchy. There is no common *Snodeb* class. As a result, functions like *InsertAfter()* and *RmvNext()* have to be duplicated for each type of list. Even with these problems, the second technique is often used because of its directness. In fact, you'll see us use it in Chapter 13 when we develop a caching data structure that implements a doubly-linked list of "buckets."

Linked Lists as Concrete Data Types

Classes like *Snodeb* and *Snode* define the nuts and bolts of a linked list, but they don't allow us to treat linked lists at a high level. For example, it would be convenient to use linked lists the way we use arrays (without the subscripting, of course). Toward this end, it would be helpful to have functions to support such operations as copying, assignment, and concatenation. In this section, we'll show you how to define linked lists as concrete data types. Ten classes are implemented—*Snodeb, Slistb, Snode, Slist, TempSlist, Dnodeb, Dlistb, Dnode, Dlist,* and *TempDlist*—to provide all the necessary tools for implementing singly-linked and doubly-linked lists. (Don't worry, many of these classes are nothing but typecasting interfaces—with many functions that can be inlined.)

Before we explain the design details, we should note that, traditionally, many programmers never use linked-lists as separate entities and are prone to directly embedding list pointers (and associated functions) into their objects. It's not clear whether this is due to the historical lack of good development tools (for example, defining and using generic lists in C is somewhat clumsy) or whether the directness outweighs the advantages of reusable linked-list code. It is possible to define reasonably reusable, safe, and efficient linked-list classes using C++, as you are about to see. Only time will tell whether using linked lists as objects in their own right becomes a widespread technique.

Linked List Design Features

The linked lists that we'll present have the following design features:

- Header nodes are used to allow convenient insertion into the front of a list. Also, extra *back* pointers are added to allow convenient insertions to the back of lists.

- Circular lists are used rather than null-terminated lists (you'll see this arrangement shortly) because they lead to more elegant insertion and removal operations.

- The linked list code is abstracted so that it can be reused for lists storing different types of data.

- The list classes are designed with robustness and efficiency in mind—with a full complement of constructors, destructors, and overloaded operators.

- The lists are homogenous by nature, although heterogenous lists can be created by using pointers as the node data types.

- The allocation of nodes for a linked list is made flexible so that many different memory allocation schemes can be supported.

- We implement a clever way to efficiently return linked lists by value. This technique, in combination with overloading the '+' operator, allows us to use expressions like $a = b + c$ without redundant copying.

We'll now explain the second feature (circular lists) in detail. Rather than terminate a list by giving the last node a null *next* pointer, you can instead have the last node point to the first node. Such a list is called a *circular list*. Figure 8.8 shows an example of a singly-linked circular list with a header node. The figure

Figure 8.8 A circular singly-linked ist.

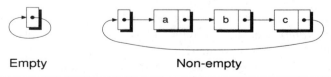

Empty   Non-empty

also shows an empty circular list consisting of a header node that points to itself. With circular lists, node insertion and removal can be done more elegantly. You never have to worry about a *prev* or *next* pointer being null, eliminating many special cases, as you'll see later.

Singly-Linked List Abstract Classes

We'll now focus on the two classes *Snodeb* and *Slistb,* which support singly-linked lists in an abstract sense. (The node data isn't part of their definitions.) The *Snodeb* class is almost identical to the one given earlier, except that it uses encapsulation to the fullest (all members are protected). It is also set up to support circular lists, through the addition of a *SelfRef()* function:

```
class Snodeb {
protected:
  Snodeb *next;
  void InsertAfter(Snodeb *n);
  Snodeb *RmvNext();
  void SelfRef();        // New function
  friend class Slistb;   // For convenient access
};

void Snodeb::SelfRef()
// Make this node point to itself
{
  next = this;
}
```

Because we'll use circular lists, the functions *InsertAfter()* and *RmvNext()* can be coded quite elegantly—with no special cases needed when the list is empty (or about to become empty).

```
void Snodeb::InsertAfter(Snodeb *n)
{
  n->next = next;
  next = n;
}

Snodeb *Snodeb::RmvNext()
{
  Snodeb *p = next;
  next = p->next;
  return p;
}
```

You might try these functions on paper—using various situations that involve circular lists—to convince yourself that they will always work properly (as long as you don't try to remove a list header node).

Complete code for the *Snodeb* class, as well as the *Slistb* class (presented next), is given on disk in the files *slistb.h* and *slistb.cpp*.

With the *Snodeb* class available, we can define the *Slistb* class:

```
class Slistb : private Snodeb {
protected:
  virtual void MakeEmpty();
public:
  Snodeb *back;
  Slistb();
  virtual ~Slistb();
  Snodeb *Front() const;
  Snodeb *Back() const;
  virtual Snodeb *DupNode(const Snodeb *n) = 0;
  virtual void FreeNode(Snodeb *n) = 0;
  virtual void Clear();
  int Copy(const Slistb &sl);
  int Concatenate(const Slistb &sl);
  void InsertAfter(Snodeb *a, Snodeb *b);
  Snodeb *RmvNext(Snodeb *n);
  Snodeb *RmvFront();
  void AttachToFront(Snodeb *n);
  void AttachToBack(Snodeb *n);
  void Absorb(Slistb &sl);
  void SplitAfter(Snodeb *n, Slistb &sl);
  int IsEmpty() const;
  int IsHeader(const Snodeb *n) const;
};
```

This class is truly abstract, having the pure virtual functions *DupNode()* and *FreeNode()*. These are made virtual to support different types of memory allocation. Also, because *Slistb* doesn't know the type of data to be stored in the nodes, it can't be responsible for constructing them. Note that the code for *Slistb* will be shared for many types of singly-linked lists.

One of the most unusual features of *Slistb* is that it is derived from *Snodeb*. An *Slistb* object represents the header of a list. Since the list is circular, the last node will point to this header. By making *Slistb* type-compatible with *Snodeb*, we alleviate some typecasting difficulties otherwise encountered.

Since *Slistb* is derived from *Snodeb*, it inherits a *next* pointer, which is used to point to the first node of the list or back to itself if the list is empty. Another pointer, *back*, is defined to point to the last node in the list. This allows the efficient addition of nodes at the end of the list. (Otherwise, you would have to scan the list from start to end.) Interestingly, the presence of the *back* pointer doesn't mean you can efficiently *remove* nodes from the end of the list. There's no efficient way to do this with singly-linked lists.

Many design alternatives are possible for circular lists. Figure 8.9 shows some of these alternatives. You can choose whether to have a header, and whether to include the header in the cycle—with or without a *back* pointer. Figure 8.9(d) shows the alternative we've chosen for the *Slistb* class. By making the header node part of the cycle, it can serve as a flag to test when the end of the list is reached during a list walk. The *IsHeader()* function is provided for this purpose:

```
int Slistb::IsHeader(const Snodeb *n) const
// Sees if node n is the list head
{
  return n == this;
}
```

This example uses *IsHeader()* to walk a list:

```
Snodeb *p = &mylist;
while(1) {
  p = p->next;
  if (mylist.IsHeader(p)) break;
  // Process node p
}
```

When deriving the *Slistb* class, *Snodeb* was declared as a private base class. This disallows direct access to the *next* pointer and to the functions *InsertAfter()*

Figure 8.9 Some alternative circular list designs.

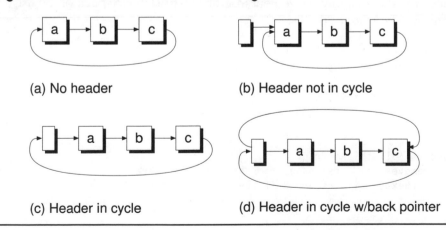

(a) No header

(b) Header not in cycle

(c) Header in cycle

(d) Header in cycle w/back pointer

---

and *RmvNext().* Instead, we must use access functions, such as the following *Front()* function:

```
Snodeb *Slistb::Front() const
{
  return next; // Header is returned if list is empty
}
```

The *Slistb* class defines its own *InsertAfter()* and *RmvNext()* functions, which is done to support the *back* pointer. Whenever a node is added to the end of the list, or if the last node of the list is removed, the back pointer must be updated. The *RmvNext()* function includes a test to ensure that we don't try to remove the list header itself. Both functions assume that the appropriate node actually resides on the list.

```
void Slistb::InsertAfter(Snodeb *a, Snodeb *b)
{
  a->InsertAfter(b);
  if (a == back) back = b; // Assumes a resides on this list
}

Snodeb *Slistb::RmvNext(Snodeb *n)
// ASSUMES n resides on this list.
{
  if (n->next == this) return 0; // Can't detach list header!
  Snodeb *p = n->RmvNext();
  if (p == back) back = n;
  return p;
}
```

Three more higher-level functions that use *InsertAfter()* and *RmvNext()* are provided to allow convenient insertion to the front or back of the list, and to remove the front of the list:

```
void Slistb::AttachToFront(Snodeb *n)
// Inserts node n after the header
{
  InsertAfter(this, n);
}


Snodeb *Slistb::RmvFront()
// Removes the first node from the list. Note that
// RmvNext() will return 0 if the list is empty.
{
```

```
  return RmvNext(this);
}

void Slistb::AttachToBack(Snodeb *n)
// Inserts the node n after the back node.
{
  InsertAfter(back, n);
}
```

A default constructor is provided to create an empty list:

```
Slistb::Slistb()
{
  MakeEmpty();
}
```

The constructor calls the *MakeEmpty()* function, which makes the list point to itself and also sets the *back* pointer to point to the list header:

```
void Slistb::MakeEmpty()
{
  SelfRef();
  back = this;
}
```

A companion function can be used to test if a list is empty:

```
int Slistb::IsEmpty() const
{
  // Typecast needed because of const keyword
  return next == (Snodeb *)this;
}
```

You can clear a list by calling the *Clear()* function:

```
void Slistb::Clear()
{
  Snodeb *n = next;
  while(!IsHeader(n)) {
    Snodeb *nn = n->next;
    FreeNode(n);
    n = nn;
  }
  MakeEmpty();
}
```

The *Clear()* function works by freeing each node in the list and then setting the list empty. Note that *FreeNode()* is a pure virtual function. Since *Slistb* doesn't know what kind of data is stored in a node, it can't properly free the node. Classes derived from *Slistb* (such as *Slist,* to be presented later in this chaper) are responsible for providing the appropriate definition of *FreeNode()*.

The *Slistb* class has a virtual destructor. Contrary to what you might think, this destructor doesn't do anything, not even call *Clear()* to empty the list! The reason is that *Clear()* calls *FreeNode()* and, since that function is virtual, it isn't safe to call it from the base class destructor. Classes derived from *Slistb* should override their destructors to call *Clear()*.

Two functions are provided to help in concatenating one list to the end of another, and in doing list copying. There's only one difference between list concatenation and copying. When a copy is made, the target list is cleared first:

```
int Slistb::Concatenate(const Slistb &sl)
{
  if (this == &sl) return 0;   // Can't concatenate to self
  const Snodeb *p = sl.next;
  while(!sl.IsHeader(p)) {      // For all nodes in sl
    Snodeb *q = DupNode(p);     // Make duplicate of the node
    if (q == 0) return 0;       // Incomplete copy made
    AttachToBack(q);
    p = p->next;
  }
  return 1; // Successful concatenation
}

int Slistb::Copy(const Slistb &sl)
{
  if (this == &sl) return 1; // Nothing to do
  Clear();
  return Concatenate(sl);
}
```

Note that *Concatenate()* calls the virtual function *DupNode()*, which is supposed to allocate a new node and duplicate the data from the source node into it. Again, derived classes must provide their own versions of *DupNode()* to handle the type of data they are going to use.

An *Absorb()* function is provided, similar to *Concatenate()*, which can be used to "smash" two lists together. The nodes of the list to be appended are not copied, but rather are absorbed through pointer manipulation. The source list then becomes empty. The steps in the absorption process are illustrated in Figure 8.10.

```
void Slistb::Absorb(Slistb &sl)
{
```

```
    if (sl.IsEmpty() || this == &sl) return; // Already absorbed
    back->next = sl.next; // See Figure 8.10a
    sl.back->next = this; // See Figure 8.10b
    back = sl.back;       // See Figure 8.10c
    sl.MakeEmpty();       // See Figure 8.10d
}
```

The counterpart to *Absorb()* is the *SplitAfter()* function, which splits a source list after some specified node *n*. The tail of the split list is absorbed onto the end of a target list. If the target list comes in empty, the effect is to split the source list into two parts. The steps involved are similar to *Absorb()* in that most of the work concentrates on adjusting the *back* pointers. Figure 8.11 shows the result of splitting a list after the first node.

Figure 8.10 Absorbing one list into another.

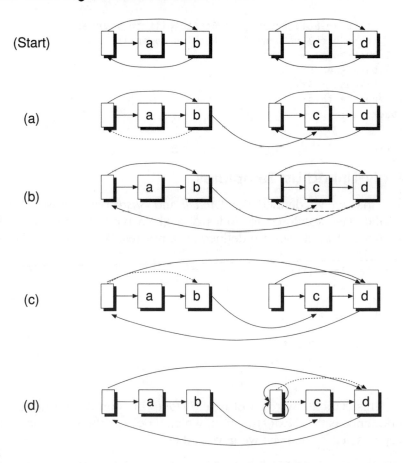

Figure 8.11 Splitting a list.

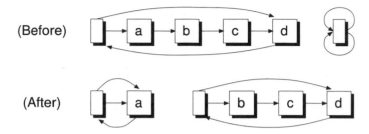

```
void Slistb::SplitAfter(Snodeb *n, Slistb &tl)
// Assumes n is actually on this list. It's allowed to be
// the header (in which case, the list will go empty).
{
  if (this == &tl) return; // Can't split to yourself
  if (n == back) return;   // Nothing to split
  tl.back->next = n->next;
  tl.back = back;
  back->next = &tl;
  n->next = this;
  back = n;
}
```

Singly-Linked List Templates

Now that we've defined the *Snodeb* and *Slistb* base classes, we can derive specific classes tailored to nodes of a given type. To provide generality, the *Snode* and *Slist* classes are defined as templates. We start with the *Snode* class:

```
template<class TYPE>
class Snode : public Snodeb {
public:
  TYPE info;
  Snode();
  Snode(const TYPE &x);
  Snode<TYPE> *Next();
};
```

This class allows data of type *TYPE* to be stored on a node. Of particular importance is the *Next()* function, which typecasts the next pointer to be of the proper type, for reasons we gave earlier.

```
template<class TYPE>
Snode<TYPE> *Snode<TYPE>::Next()
// This function is for typecasting convenience
{
  return (Snode<TYPE> *)next;
}
```

The *Slist* class, used to create lists storing *TYPE* data, is defined as follows:

```
template<class TYPE>
class Slist : private Slistb {
protected:
  virtual Snode<TYPE> *AllocNode(const TYPE &x);
  virtual Snodeb *DupNode(const Snodeb *sn);
  virtual void FreeNode(Snodeb *dn);
  Slistb::MakeEmpty; // Keep this protected
public:
  friend class TempSlist<TYPE>;
  friend class ArraySlist<TYPE>;
  Slist();
  Slist(const Slist<TYPE> &s);
  Slist(TempSlist<TYPE> &s);
  virtual ~Slist();
  void operator=(const Slist<TYPE> &s);
  void operator=(TempSlist<TYPE> &s);
  Snode<TYPE> *Header() const;
  Snode<TYPE> *Front() const;
  Snode<TYPE> *Back() const;
  Slistb::Clear;    // Make this base function public
  Slistb::IsEmpty;  // Make this base function public
  int Copy(const Slist<TYPE> &sl);
  void InsertAfter(Snode<TYPE> *a, Snode<TYPE> *b);
  void AttachToFront(Snode<TYPE> *n);
  void AttachToBack(Snode<TYPE> *n);
  Snode<TYPE> *RmvNext(Snode<TYPE> *n);
  Snode<TYPE> *RmvFront();
  int DelNext(Snode<TYPE> *n);
  int DelFront();
  void Absorb(Slist<TYPE> &sl);
  void SplitAfter(Snode<TYPE> *n, Slist<TYPE> &sl);
  int IsHeader(const Snode<TYPE> *n) const;
  int Concatenate(const Slist<TYPE> &sl);
  int operator+=(const Slist<TYPE> &sl);
  Snode<TYPE> *operator+=(const TYPE &x);
  friend TempSlist<TYPE>
          operator+(const Slist<TYPE> &a, const Slist<TYPE> &b);
  Snode<TYPE> *
          NodeBeforeMatch(const TYPE &x, Snode<TYPE> *p=0) const;
```

```
   Snode<TYPE> *AddToFront(const TYPE &x);
   Snode<TYPE> *AddToBack(const TYPE &x);
   Snode<TYPE> *AddAfter(const TYPE &x, Snode<TYPE> *n);
};
```

Complete code for the *Snode* and *Slist* classes is given on disk in the files *slist.h* and *slist.mth*. A test program is given in the file *sltst.cpp*.

The main purpose of *Slist* is to serve as a type-specific interface to the *Slistb* class. Many of the functions of *Slist* are nothing more than typecasting interfaces that can be easily inlined, such as the following *Front()* and *Back()* functions:

```
template<class TYPE>
Snode<TYPE> *Slist<TYPE>::Front() const
{
  return (Snode<TYPE> *)Slistb::Front();
}

template<class TYPE>
Snode<TYPE> *Slist<TYPE>::Back() const
{
  return (Snode<TYPE> *)Slistb::Back();
}
```

The typecasts in these functions are somewhat unsafe. In the case of an empty list, both *Front()* and *Back()* will return a pointer to the header node, which isn't an *Snode<TYPE>* node even though it's returned as one. Before you try to redesign this, remember that the design we've given is really no more unsafe than returning a null pointer in case of an empty list. In either case, you must check for a valid pointer. The *IsHeader()* function can be used for that purpose (not shown here). The *Header()* function, which returns a pointer to the header node, is the counterpart to *IsHeader()*. The *Header()* function has a similar problem to *Front()* and *Back()* in that it returns a pointer to the header node as though it were an *Snode<TYPE>* node:

```
template<class TYPE>
Snode<TYPE> *Slist<TYPE>::Header() const
{
  return (Snode<TYPE> *)this;
}
```

The *Header()* function was designed for typecasting convenience when iterating through a list, and should be used only for that purpose. The following *NodeBeforeMatch()* function shows an example of using *Header()*:

```
template<class TYPE>
Snode<TYPE> *Slist<TYPE>::
NodeBeforeMatch(const TYPE &x, Snode<TYPE> *p) const
{
  // Note that Next() is used, rather than 'next'
  // directly. This is for typecasting convenience.

  if (p == 0) p = Header(); // p == 0 is the default

  while(!IsHeader(p->Next())) { // Scan until end of list
    if (p->Next()->info == x) return p; // Match found
    p = p->Next();
  }

  return 0; // No match
}
```

Given some data of type *TYPE*, this function scans the list looking for the node that contains matching data. Note that the node *before* the matching node is returned, in case you want to remove the matching node using *RmvNext()*. Both *Header()* and *Next()* return *Snode<TYPE>* pointers, which alleviate the need to use direct typecasts between *Snodeb* pointers and *Snode<TYPE>* pointers. The typecasting problem isn't eliminated; it's just encapsulated as much as possible.

The following *InsertAfter()* and *RmvNext()* functions also serve as type-casting interfaces:

```
template<class TYPE>
void Slist<TYPE>::InsertAfter(Snode<TYPE> *a, Snode<TYPE> *b)
{
  Slistb::InsertAfter(a, b);
}

template<class TYPE>
Snode<TYPE> *Slist<TYPE>::RmvNext(Snode<TYPE> *n)
{
  return (Snode<TYPE> *)(Slistb::RmvNext(n));
}
```

Other functions are defined similarly, such as *AttachToFront()*, *RmvFront()*, and *AttachToBack()*. As is true with the *Slistb* class, these functions are only responsible for attaching or detaching nodes to a list; they don't allocate or de-allocate the nodes. Since *Slist* knows the type of node data to be used, functions can be added to automatically allocate and de-allocate the nodes, such as the following *AddAfter()* and *DelNext()* functions:

```
template<class TYPE>
Snode<TYPE> *Slist<TYPE>::AddAfter(const TYPE &x, Snode<TYPE> *n)
{
  Snode<TYPE> *p = AllocNode(x);
  if (p) InsertAfter(n, p);
  return p;
}

template<class TYPE>
int Slist<TYPE>::DelNext(Snode<TYPE> *n)
{
  Snode<TYPE> *p = RmvNext(n);
  if (p) {
    FreeNode(p);
    return 1;
  }
  return 0;
}
```

The *AllocNode()* and *FreeNode()* functions are virtual. Here are the specific versions for the *Slist* class:

```
template<class TYPE>
Snode<TYPE> *Slist<TYPE>::AllocNode(const TYPE &x)
// A function that allocates a new Snode<TYPE> node,
// holding a copy of x as its data
{
  return new Snode<TYPE>(x);
}

template<class TYPE>
void Slist<TYPE>::FreeNode(Snodeb *n)
// Deletes node n. Assumed to be a Snode<TYPE> node.
{

  delete((Snode<TYPE> *)n);
}
```

The typecast used in *FreeNode()* seems rather unsafe, since it assumes that *n* is actually an *Snode<TYPE>* node. Consequently, you'll notice this function (as well as *AllocNode()*) is protected. Note that *n* is guaranteed to be an *Snode<TYPE>* node for all uses of *FreeNode()* in the *Slist* class.

You may wonder why the unsafe typecast is used at all. Why not instead make the destructor for *Snodeb* virtual? Then, the *delete* operator would work properly without the typecast. However, adding a virtual function to *Snodeb* would add overhead in the form of one extra pointer (to the virtual function table) in *every* node. The typecast, then, can save a lot of space in the lists.

Here, we're trading elegance for space efficiency. As always, you should pay attention to details like this, particularly if your designs are to become part of a general-purpose library.

The following *DupNode()* function, used to create a copy (except for the *next* pointer) of a node, is related to *AllocNode()*:

```
template<class TYPE>
Snodeb *Slist<TYPE>::DupNode(const Snodeb *n)
{
   return AllocNode(((Snode<TYPE> *)n)->info);
}
```

Recall that *Slistb::Copy()* uses *DupNode()* when making copies of each node in a list. The *Slistb::Copy()* function is used by *Slist::Copy()*, which in turn is used by the *operator=()* function:

```
template<class TYPE>
int Slist<TYPE>::Copy(const Slist<TYPE> &sl)
{
   return Slistb::Copy(sl);
}

template<class TYPE>
void Slist<TYPE>::operator=(const Slist<TYPE> &sl)
{
   Copy(sl); // Traps copies to self
}
```

In addition to overloading the '=' operator, we've overloaded the '+=' operator to provide a convenient notation for concatenating both single nodes and lists onto other lists:

```
template<class TYPE>
int Slist<TYPE>::operator+=(const Slist<TYPE> &sl)
{
   return Concatenate(sl);
}

template<class TYPE>
Snode<TYPE> *Slist<TYPE>::operator+=(const TYPE &x)
{
   return AddToBack(x);
}
```

The *Slist* class provides another way to add one list to another by using the '+' operator:

```
template<class TYPE>
TempSlist<TYPE> operator+(const Slist<TYPE> &a, const Slist<TYPE> &b)
{
  Slist<TYPE> copy_of_a(a);
  copy_of_a.Concatenate(b);
  return copy_of_a; // copy_of_a absorbed into temp result
}
```

The *operator+()* function makes a copy of both source operands and returns the result as a new list. This allows statements like the following to be used, where *a*, *b*, and *c* are lists:

```
a = b + c; // Add lists a and b together; store in c
```

You might think a lot of copying is taking place in such statements: one copy made in returning the result and another in assigning the result to the destination list. Instead, a clever trick is used to avoid the copying. The temporary list that's constructed to hold the result can be absorbed (using *Absorb()*) into the list that's returned. The returned list can then be absorbed into the destination list, which is cleared beforehand. (Recall the *Absorb()* function smashes two lists together, rather than copying the nodes.)

In effect, we must find a way for the copy constructor (used in the function return) and the overloaded assignment operator (used in the assignment) to use absorption rather than copying. How can we do this? One way is to provide special versions of the copy constructor and assignment operator that work only for temporary lists. You'll notice that *operator+()* returns a *TempSlist* object, instead of an *Slist* object. The *TempSlist* class is defined as follows:

```
template<class TYPE>
class TempSlist : private Slistb {
private:
  friend class Slist<TYPE>;
  virtual Snodeb *DupNode(const Snodeb *);
  virtual void FreeNode(Snodeb *);
public:
  TempSlist(Slist<TYPE> &sl);
};
```

Complete code for the *TempSlist* class is given on disk in the file *Slist.h*.

The sole purpose of *TempList* is to provide a way to trap cases when the list is meant to be temporary. A *TempSlist* object is just like an *Slist* object: all that's changed is the type name (and the implicit restriction of its use only for temporary lists). The class has a single copy constructor that takes a normal list and uses absorption to turn it into a temporary list:

```
template<class TYPE>
TempSlist<TYPE>::TempSlist(Slist<TYPE> &sl)
{
  Slistb::Absorb(sl); // Note: sl goes empty
}
```

The *TempSlist* copy constructor is used in returning the result of a list addition. Then, if the temporary list is to be used in an assignment (such as $c = a + b$), the following overloaded assignment operator for *Slist* objects is used:

```
template<class TYPE>
void Slist<TYPE>::operator=(TempSlist<TYPE> &sl)
{
  Clear();
  Slistb::Absorb(sl); // sl goes empty in the process
}
```

You should walk through the steps involved in statements like $c = a + b$ to assure yourself that indeed no redundant copying takes place. The trick of defining a new type, such as *TempSlist*, for the sole purpose of trapping special cases in overloaded function calls is useful to remember.

There's one last function to consider for *Slist*—the destructor:

```
template<class TYPE>
Slist<TYPE>::~Slist()
{
  Clear();
}
```

This destructor causes any remaining nodes in the list to be freed at list-destruction time. As we mentioned earlier, it's very important that the call to *Clear()* be placed here, not in the base *Slistb* class destructor, due to the virtual function calls to *FreeNode()* inside *Clear()*.

In the following example, we've used the *Slist* class to construct and manipulate singly-linked lists:

```
void f()
{
  Slist<char> x, y, z; // Construct empty lists

  x.AddToBack('a');
  x += 'b';             // Same as x = AddToBack('b');
  y += 'c';
  y += 'd';

  x += y;               // x now holds [a b c d], y holds [c d]
```

```
    y.Clear();              // Remove all nodes from y

    y.AddToFront('f');
    y.AddToFront('e');

    z = x + y;              // z now holds [a b c d e f], x [a b c d], y [e f]

    Snode<char> *p = z.NodeBeforeMatch('c'); // Look for 'c'
    if (p) z.RmvNext(p); // Remove node holding 'c'

    // All lists destroyed implicitly here
}
```

Doubly-Linked List Classes

The five classes that support doubly-linked lists—*Dnodeb, Dlistb, Dnode, Dlist,* and *TempDlist*—are very similar to their singly-linked counterparts and will not be shown here. (They are given on disk, however.) Figure 8.12 shows examples of circular doubly-linked lists that can be created using the five classes.

 Complete code for the *Dnodeb, Dlistb, Dnode, Dlist,* and *TempDlist* classes is given on disk in the files *dlistb.h, dlistb.cpp, dlist.h,* and *dlist.mth.* A test program is given in the file *dltst.cpp.*

VARIATIONS ON A THEME

With *AllocNode()* and *FreeNode()* available as virtual functions, we can create many variations in allocating the nodes of linked lists. In this section, we'll look at some of the possibilities. We'll culminate with a hybrid array-based linked-list design.

Cached List Nodes

The nodes for a linked list are typically allocated and de-allocated using the heap. With some heap implementation techniques, this can be a relatively slow

---

Figure 8.12 Circular doubly-linked lists.

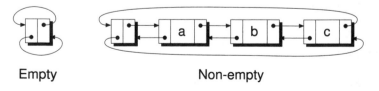

Empty   Non-empty

process. If your list application frequently adds and removes nodes, particularly in a tight loop, this reduction in performance can be noticeable. One way to alleviate this problem hit is to cache freed nodes on an auxillary list (often called the *free list* or *node pool*). Figure 8.13 illustrates the use of a free list. When new nodes are to be created, they are obtained first from the free list if it isn't empty; otherwise, the normal heap is used.

We'll now look at two classes—*SnodePool* and *Cslist*—that work together to provide lists with cached free nodes. The *Cslist* class (which stands for *cached singly-linked list*) declares a static *SnodePool* object that's shared between all *Cslists* of the same type. Here is the *Cslist* definition:

```
template<class TYPE>
class Cslist : public Slist<TYPE> {
protected:
  virtual Snode<TYPE> *AllocNode(const TYPE &x);
  virtual void FreeNode(Snodeb *n);
public:
  static SnodePool<TYPE> node_pool;
  Cslist();
  Cslist(const Cslist<TYPE> &sl);
  Cslist(TempSlist<TYPE> &sl);
  virtual ~Cslist();
  void operator=(const Cslist<TYPE> &sl);
  void operator=(TempSlist<TYPE> &sl);
};
```

Complete code for both the *Cslist* and *SnodePool* classes are given on disk in the files *cslist.h* and *cslist.mth*. A test program is given in the file *csltst.cpp*. Also, doubly-linked versions of these classes—*Cdlist* and *DnodePool*—are given in the files *cdlist.h*, *cdlist.mth*, and *cdltst.cpp*.

Figure 8.13 Using a free list.

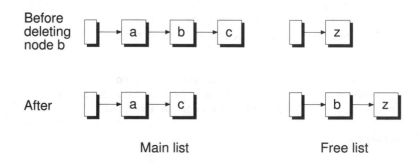

The *Cslist* class is inherited from the *Slist* class. The critical feature is that *AllocNode()* and *FreeNode()* are overridden to utilize the static node pool:

```
template<class TYPE>
Snode<TYPE> *Cslist<TYPE>::AllocNode(const TYPE &x)
// Allocates a node for the list by using node_pool
{
  return node_pool.Alloc(x);
}

template<class TYPE>
void Cslist<TYPE>::FreeNode(Snodeb *n)
// Frees a node by using the node pool.
// Assumes n is a Snode<TYPE> node.
{
  node_pool.Free((Snode<TYPE> *)n);
}
```

Here is the *SnodePool* class definition, followed by the *Alloc()* and *Free()* functions that are called by the *AllocNode()* and *FreeNode()* functions of *Cslist*:

```
template<class TYPE>
class SnodePool : private Slist<TYPE> {
protected:
  int num_nodes, max_nodes;
public:
  SnodePool(int mn);
  virtual Snode<TYPE> *Alloc(const TYPE &x);
  virtual void Free(Snode<TYPE> *n);
  Slist<TYPE>::Clear; // Keep this function public
};

template<class TYPE>
Snode<TYPE> *SnodePool<TYPE>::Alloc(const TYPE &x)
{
  Snode<TYPE> *p;
  if (IsEmpty()) {     // No free nodes cached
    p = AllocNode(x); // Allocate node from heap
  }
  else {
    p = RmvFront();   // Grab node from this pool
    p->info = x;      // Overwrite previous info contents
    num_nodes-;       // One less node in the pool
  }
  return p;
}

template<class TYPE>
```

```
void SnodePool<TYPE>::Free(Snode<TYPE> *n)
{
  if (num_nodes < max_nodes) { // Room to cache node
    AttachToFront(n);
    num_nodes++;
  }
  else {
    FreeNode(n); // Pool full, so actually free the node
  }
}
```

The *SnodePool* class keeps track of the number of nodes in the pool, *num_nodes*, as shown in *Alloc()* and *Free()*. A maximum number of nodes, *max_nodes*, is specified when the node pool is constructed. This allows you to control the amount of memory you are willing to reserve for cached free nodes. If the node pool is full when a node is to be added (because the node is to be freed from the main list), the node is deleted instead. Here is the chain of events that occurs when a node is freed: First, *Cslist::FreeNode()* is called, which in turn calls *SnodePool::Free()*, which, if the node pool is full, calls *Slist::FreeNode()*, which actually deletes the node from the list.

When a node is to be allocated and the node pool is empty, then *AllocNode()*, inherited from *Slist*, is called to allocate a new node from the heap. If the node pool isn't empty, the first node in the pool is detached, the information in *x* is copied into it, and a pointer to the node is returned.

Note that *SnodePool* doesn't define a destructor. As such, the *Slist* destructor will be used to clear all of the cached nodes—actually deleting them from the heap. At any time, you can clear the node pool by calling the function *Clear()*, which is the only function from *Slist* that has been declared public. Due to the private derivation from *Slist*, all other *Slist* functions are disallowed. This means an *SnodePool* list can only be used in restricted ways—as a node pool.

In contrast to *SnodePool*, *Cslist* has a destructor, which calls *Clear()*:

```
template<class TYPE>
Cslist<TYPE>::~Cslist()
{
  Clear();
}
```

You might have wondered whether the base class *Slist* destructor could do the clearing for us. After all, it calls *Clear()* as well. The answer is that *Clear()* calls *FreeNode()*, which is virtual, so we *must* call *Clear()* in the derived class for it to work properly. By the time the *Slist* destructor is called, the list will be empty, so the call to *Clear()* there will have no effect. This arrangement is tricky, but is typical of hierarchies where the allocation of objects is modified in the derived classes. You should keep a watchful eye for situations like this.

Array-Based Linked Lists

While the *Cslist* class caches freed nodes, it still uses the heap to allocate nodes initially. Also, each node is allocated separately, which can lead to heap fragmentation. Another alternative is to allocate the nodes in blocks. In fact, if you know the maximum size of a list ahead of time, you can pre-allocate the nodes in a single array. The result is a hybrid structure—an *array-based linked list*. Figure 8.14 shows an example of a null-terminated singly-linked list where all the nodes are allocated contiguously in an array.

It's actually quite easy to derive array-based linked lists from the *Slist* and *Dlist* classes and, in the process, reuse a lot of existing code. The secret is to include a constructor that allocates an array of nodes, and then to override *AllocNode()* to grab nodes from this array. Also, a free list can be maintained simultaneously with the main list, threading together all the nodes in the array that are not in use. Unlike the *Cslists* used in the previous section, though, each array-based list will have its own free list, rather than sharing a global one. The *ArraySlist* class, sketched below, illustrates how an array-based singly-linked list can be defined:

```
template<class TYPE>
class ArraySlist : private Slist<TYPE> {
protected:
  virtual Snode<TYPE> *AllocNode(const TYPE &d);
  virtual void FreeNode(Snodeb *n);
  int nodes_used, max_nodes;
  Slist<TYPE> free_list;
  Snode<TYPE> *nodes;
  virtual void MakeEmpty();
  void Setup(int mn);
  ... // Other private functions
public:
  ArraySlist(int mn);
```

Figure 8.14 An array-based linked list.

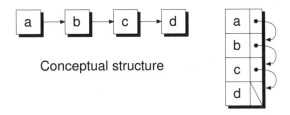

Conceptual structure

Implementation

```
    virtual ~ArraySlist();
    virtual void Clear();
    ...// Other public functions
};
```

Complete code for the *ArraySlist* class is given on disk in the files *aslist.h* and *aslist.mth*. A test program is provided in the file *asltst.cpp*. Also, a doubly-linked version, *ArrayDlist*, is provided in the files *adlist.h, adlist.mth,* and *adltst.cpp*.

The *ArraySlist* constructor sets up the array-based linked list by calling a *Setup()* function, which allocates an array of nodes of size *mn*.

```
template<class TYPE>
ArraySlist<TYPE>::ArraySlist(int mn)
{
  Setup(mn);
}

template<class TYPE>
void ArraySlist<TYPE>::Setup(int mn)
{
  nodes_used = 0;
  nodes = (Snode<TYPE> *)(new char[mn * sizeof(Snode<TYPE>)]);
  max_nodes = (nodes == 0) ? 0 : mn;
}
```

The node array that gets created is actually a variable-length array, where *num_nodes* represents the logical length and *max_nodes* represents the dimensioned length. Initially, no nodes are in use. Note that the array's logical length can only grow, not shrink. When a node is to be freed, it is placed on the free list. Eventually, all the nodes will either be on the main list or the free list. As we did for the variable-length arrays defined in Chapter 4, the node array is actually constructed as an array of characters. This prevents the nodes from being constructed until they are actually used.

When a node is to be used, the placement *new* operator is called to handle the construction of the nodes. This can be seen in the following *AllocNode()* function (which overrides *Slist*'s version):

```
template<class TYPE>
Snode<TYPE> *ArraySlist<TYPE>::AllocNode(const TYPE &x)
{
  Snode<TYPE> *p = 0; // Default to failure
  if (!free_list.IsEmpty()) {
    p = free_list.RmvFront();
  }
```

```
  else if (nodes_used < max_nodes) {
     p = nodes + nodes_used++;
  }
  if_(p)_new(p) Snode<TYPE>(x); // Use in-place construction
  return p;
}
```

The *AllocNode()* function works as follows: if the free list is empty (which it will be at the start), then a node is grabbed from the array and constructed in place. It's possible for all the nodes in the array to be in use, in which case the list is full, so a null pointer is returned. If the free list isn't empty, one of its nodes is used. It's important to realize that the nodes themselves are never moved physically. All that changes is their placement either on the main list or the free list.

The *FreeNode()* function works by attaching a node onto the free list. A critical part of this process is the call to the node's destructor—using an explicit destructor call. This must be done because *AllocNode()* assumes that the nodes it grabs aren't constructed.

```
template<class TYPE>
void ArraySlist<TYPE>::FreeNode(Snodeb *n)
{
  typedef Snode<TYPE> typenode; // This typing helps some compilers
  typenode *p = (typenode *)n;
  p->typenode::~typenode();     // Explicitly destroy node
  free_list.AttachToFront(p);   // Attach to the free list
}
```

Figure 8.15 A sample ArraySlist object.

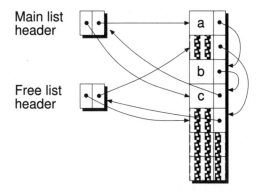

We explicitly destroy the node to ensure that the destructor for the *info* field is called. Note, however, that the *next* pointer will be set to point to the next node in the free list. Thus, nodes in the free list are actually partially constructed. Figure 8.15 shows a sample list created with the *ArraySlist* class, with some nodes on the main list (fully constructed), some on the free list (partially constructed), and some nodes not yet constructed. Note that the main list and free list headers are stored separately from the node array.

Even though a node might be destroyed, it isn't actually freed until the list itself is destroyed, as the following *ArraySlist* destructor shows.

```
template<class TYPE>
ArraySlist<TYPE>::~ArraySlist()
{
  Clear();
  delete[] (char *)nodes;
}
```

The *ArraySlist* destructor is somewhat tricky because the destructors for the nodes must be handled properly. It's quite possible for some of the nodes to be in use (and thus constructed) but others to be unused (and thus be unconstructed). Somehow, the *ArraySlist* destructor must cause the node destructor to be called only for those nodes currently in use. This is accomplished by calling the following virtual *Clear()* function:

```
template<class TYPE>
void ArraySlist<TYPE>::Clear()
{
  typedef Snode<TYPE> typenode;
  typenode *q, *p;
  p = Front();
  while(!IsHeader(p)) {          // For each node in use
    q = p->Next();
    p->typenode::~typenode(); // Explicitly destroy node
    p = q;
  }
  // The list is now made to appear empty, so that when the
  // base class destructor calls Clear(), it works properly.
  // Note that both the main and free lists are made empty.
  MakeEmpty();
}
```

Once the nodes in use are destroyed, the memory for the nodes is de-allocated by calling *delete* in the *ArraySlist* destructor. The nodes are de-allocated as though they were an array of characters, which is how they were allocated initially. The typecast to *char ** is important; otherwise, the node destructors would be erroneously called again.

Array-based linked lists provide compactness and speed. Because they are contiguous, array-based linked lists don't waste space that might result from heap fragmentation. Also, adding and removing nodes from the list is very fast since no heap manipulation is used. Of course, these improvements come at a price: you must allocate the maximum size of the linked list ahead of time, negating one of the advantages of linked lists. However, all other advantages remain, the most important being the ability to rearrange the elements of the list with minimal data movement.

Cursor-Based Singly-Linked Lists

If you wish to use array-based linked lists, you should be aware that yet another variation is possible. Rather than use pointers for the node links, you can use array indexes. For example, a singly-linked node might be defined as follows:

```
template<class TYPE>
class Snode {
  TYPE info;
  unsigned next; // Index, or cursor, to next node
};
```

The *next* variable is now an index that provides the offset in the array to the next node in the list. This index is sometimes called a *cursor*. In fact, array-based linked lists that use indexes rather than pointers are often called *cursor-based linked lists*. Figure 8.16 shows an example of a null-terminated, cursor-based singly-linked list. In the figure, it's assumed that the elements are indexed starting at 1, and that 0 represents the end of the list.

Figure 8.16 A sample cursor-based singly-linked list.

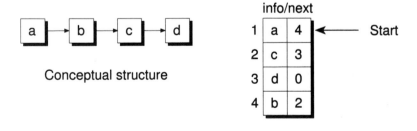

Conceptual structure

Implementation

You gain the following advantages by using cursors instead of pointers for links:

- *Smaller.* Depending on the implementation, a cursor may occupy less room than a pointer. For instance, a cursor might be an 8- or 16-bit integer, whereas a pointer will probably be either 16 or 32 bits. Thus, cursor-based linked lists can be more compact than those using pointers.
- *Relocatable.* Since cursors are indexes relative to the beginning of the array, the array can be relocated elsewhere in memory—without having to update the cursors. If pointers are used instead for links, they would all have to be modified to reflect the new locations of the nodes.

There is one drawback, however, to the use of cursors rather than pointers: cursors are slower. To find the next node using a cursor, subscript arithmetic must be used (involving an addition and multiplication). In contrast, to find the next node using a pointer, a simple pointer de-reference is all that's required.

There's another variation sometimes used with cursors. Represent the linked list as two separate parallel arrays—one holding the node data and one holding the cursors—rather than implementing a single node array that holds both. In Figure 8.17, the singly-linked list portrayed in Figure 8.16 is implemented using parallel arrays.

The following *CursorSlist* class uses this parallel array approach to implement a singly-linked list as a concrete data type:

```
template<class TYPE>
class CursorSlist {
protected:
  TYPE *info;         // The node data array
  unsigned *next;     // Next cursors (next[0] == front)
```

Figure 8.17 Using parallel arrays to represent a singly-linked list.

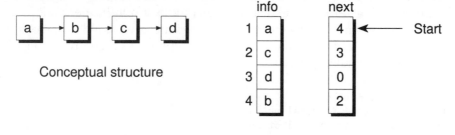

Conceptual structure

Implementation

```
   unsigned num_nodes; // Number of nodes allocated
   unsigned back;      // Cursor to back of list
   unsigned avail;     // Cursor to front of avail list
   void InsertAfter(unsigned p, unsigned x);
   unsigned RmvNext(unsigned p);
   int Alloc(int n);
   void MakeEmpty();
public:
   CursorSlist(int n);
   unsigned Next(unsigned p) const;
   unsigned AddAfter(const TYPE &x, unsigned p);
   int DelNext(unsigned p);
   TYPE &operator[](unsigned p);
   // ... Other functions
};
```

Complete code for the *CursorSlist* class is given on disk in the files *curslist.h* and *curslist.mth*. A test program is given in the file *cursltst.cpp*.

The first element of the *next* array is reserved for the list header, and the list is circular. Thus, an empty list has *next[0]* = *0*. Note that the reserved header element forces all non-header list elements to have cursors > 0. To avoid wasting node data for the header, the *info* array has one less element than *next*. Given a positive cursor *p*, the elements *info[p-1]* and *next[p]* make up, conceptually, one full list node.

In addition to the two arrays, we need to provide some other variables. The *back* variable is a cursor to the last node on the list. If the list is empty, *back* = *0*. The *num_node* variable keeps track of the dimensioned size of the arrays. As is the case with the *ArraySlist* class, *CursorSlist* incorporates a built-in free list. The *avail* cursor points to the front of the free list. Initially, all nodes except for the header are placed on the free list. (In contrast, the *ArraySlist* class started the free list as an empty list). Thus, *avail* is initialized to one. Note that the free list does not use a *next* element for its header and is null-terminated, with the cursor of the last node being zero. (Recall that zero can't index a non-header node.)

The following *Alloc()* and *MakeEmpty()* functions, called by the constructor, show how a *CursorSlist* object is set up to represent an empty list. Figure 8.18 illustrates the resulting layout.

```
template<class TYPE>
int CursorSlist<TYPE>::Alloc(int n)
// Allocates room for n list nodes
{
   // Create unconstructed array for the node data

   info = (TYPE *) new char[n * sizeof(TYPE)];
   if (!info) return 0; // Out of memory
```

Figure 8.18 An empty CursorSlist object.

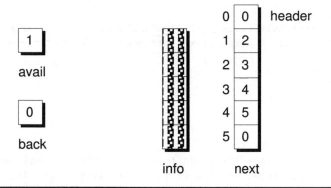

```
               // Create the next cursor array. Leave room for the
               // header element.

               next = new unsigned[n+1];
               if (!next) {
                  delete[] (char *)info;
                  return 0; // Out of memory
               }

               // Set up all nodes on the free list
               // Boundaries handled after loop
               for(unsigned i = 1; i<n+1; i++) next[i] = i+1;
               avail = 1;   // Starting cursor of the free list
               next[n] = 0; // Null-terminate the free list
               MakeEmpty(); // Start the main list to be empty
               num_nodes = n;
               return 1;    // Successful
               }

template<class TYPE>
void CursorSlist<TYPE>::MakeEmpty()
// Makes the list empty by pointing header to
// itself and pointing back to the header, too
{
  next[0] = 0;
  back = 0;
}
```

The *Alloc()* function allocates the *info* array as unconstructed bits. The corresponding *info* element will be constructed (using an in-place construction process) only when a node is placed on the main list. The following *InsertAfter()*

and *AddAfter()* functions show how nodes are obtained from the free list and added to the main list.

```
template<class TYPE>
void CursorSlist<TYPE>::InsertAfter(unsigned p, unsigned x)
// Inserts a node indexed by x after node indexed by p.
{
  next[x] = next[p];
  next[p] = x;
  if (p == back) back = x;
}

template<class TYPE>
unsigned CursorSlist<TYPE>::AddAfter(const TYPE &x, unsigned p)
// Grabs a node from the free list, copies data x into it,
// and adds the node after node indexed by p
{
  unsigned n = avail;         // Get cursor to next avail node
  if (n == 0) return 0;       // No room
  avail = next[avail];        // One less node available
  InsertAfter(p, n);          // Insert node into main list
  new(info + n - 1) TYPE(x);  // In-place copy construction
  return n;                   // Return cursor the node
}
```

It's interesting to compare node insertions using cursors with those using pointers, as shown in Table 8.2.

Removing a node from a list works in the opposite fashion. The node is detached from the list and placed at the front of the free list. The node data is then explicitly destructed. The following *RmvNext()* and *DelNext()* functions show the details:

```
template<class TYPE>
unsigned CursorSlist<TYPE>::RmvNext(unsigned p)
// Removes from the main list the node
// following the node indexed by p
{
```

Table 8.2 Different techniques for node insertions.

Cursor-Based	**Pointer-Based**
next[x] = p;	x->next = p;
next[p] = x;	p->next = x;

```
  unsigned n = next[p]; // Like n = p->next
  next[p] = next[n];    // Like p->next = n->next
  if (n == back) back = p;
  return n;
}


template<class TYPE>
int CursorSlist<TYPE>::DelNext(unsigned p)
// Removes the node following the node indexed by p, placing
// the node on the free list. The node data is destroyed.
{
  if (next[p] == 0) return 0;     // Can't remove header
  unsigned n = RmvNext(p);        // Detach from list
  (info + n - 1)->TYPE::~TYPE();  // Destroy node data
  next[n] = avail;                // Add to front of free list
  avail = n;                      // New free list header
  return 1;                       // Indicate success
}
```

Figure 8.19 illustrates the layout of a cursor-based list with nodes both on the main list and free list.

The *CursorSlist* class has functions similar to the *ArraySlist* class, such as *Front()*, *Back()*, *IsHeader()*, *AddToFront()*, *AddToBack()*, and so on. One unusual function is the following overloaded *[]* operator function (a *const* version is also supplied in the class):

Figure 8.19 A non-empty CursorSlist object.

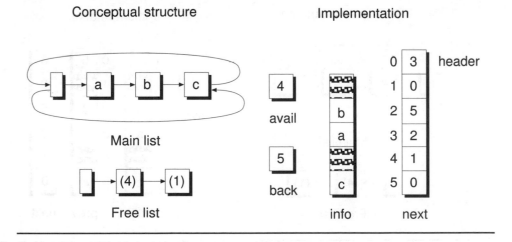

```
template<class TYPE>
TYPE &CursorSlist<TYPE>::operator[](unsigned p)
{
  return info[p-1];
}
```

This allows you to obtain the information stored at a node by using a normal array-subscripting operation. The index *p* must point to a valid non-header node, but that isn't checked. (Doing so would be very difficult.) Here's an example, of walking through a list and printing out the node information:

```
unsigned p = mylist.Front();
while(!mylist.IsHeader(p)) {
  cout << mylist[p] << ' - ';
  p = mylist.Next(p);
}
```

The last statement calls the *Next()* function, which allows you to conveniently get the next node in sequence:

```
template<class TYPE>
unsigned CursorSlist<TYPE>::Next(unsigned p) const
{
  return next[p];
}
```

Figure 8.20 A non-empty CursorDlist object.

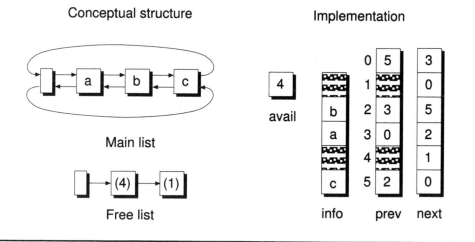

Cursor-Based Doubly-Linked Lists

A doubly-linked cursor-based list can be defined by adding a third array, representing *prev* cursors, as illustrated in Figure 8.20. Note that the free list is implemented as a singly-linked null-terminated list, even though the main list is a circular doubly-linked list. The *CursorDlist* class, a doubly-linked analog to *CursorSlist*, can be defined as:

```
template<class TYPE>
class CursorDlist {
protected:
  TYPE *info;          // The node data array
  unsigned *prev;      // Prev cursors
  unsigned *next;      // Next cursors
  unsigned avail;      // Cursor to front of avail list
  unsigned num_nodes;  // Number of nodes allocated
  void InsertAfter(unsigned p, unsigned x);
  void InsertBefore(unsigned p, unsigned x);
  unsigned Rmv(unsigned p);
  ...
};
```

Complete code for the *CursorDlist* class is given on disk in the files *curdlist.h* and *curdlist.mth*. A test program is given in the file *curdltst.cpp*.

The *CursorDlist* class is very similar to the other list classes we've defined, so we won't show it in detail here. However, it's interesting to note the symmetry of the *InsertAfter()*, *InsertBefore()*, and *Rmv()* functions. (The comments illustrate equivalent pointer-based manipulations.)

```
template<class TYPE>
void CursorDlist<TYPE>::InsertBefore(unsigned p, unsigned x)
// Inserts a node indexed by x, assumed to be already
// detached from the free list, before node indexed by p
{
  prev[x] = prev[p]; // Like x->prev = p->prev
  next[prev[p]] = x; // Like p->prev->next = x
  next[x] = p;       // Like x->next = p
  prev[p] = x;       // Like p->prev = x
}

template<class TYPE>
void CursorDlist<TYPE>::InsertAfter(unsigned p, unsigned x)
// Inserts a node indexed by x, assumed to be already
// detached from the free list, after node indexed by p
{
```

```
   next[x] = next[p]; // Like x->next = p->next
   prev[next[p]] = x; // Like p->next->prev = x
   prev[x] = p;       // Like x->prev = p
   next[p] = x;       // Like p->next = x
}

template<class TYPE>
unsigned CursorDlist<TYPE>::Rmv(unsigned p)
// Removes the node indexed by p from the main list
{
   next[prev[p]] = next[p]; // Like p->prev->next = p->next
   prev[next[p]] = prev[p]; // Like p->next->prev = p->prev
   return p;
}
```

SUMMARY

In this chapter, you've seen some of the variations possible for linked lists. These data structures are quite versatile and, along with arrays, form the basis for many of the more complicated data structures. We've attempted to turn linked lists into concrete data types with classes like *Slist, ArraySlist, CursorSlist,* and so on. However, keep in mind that list-type links are sometimes directly embedded into other objects, as you will see in later chapters. As such, the most important functions to keep in mind are ones like *InsertAfter(), InsertBefore(), Rmv(),* and *RmvNext(),* which work on a node-by-node basis.

The linked lists presented here are designed to work in memory. However, it's quite possible, and useful, to have linked lists that are stored on files. This can be done by using file offsets for links (equivalent to cursors), rather than pointers. In later chapters, we'll show you how to do this.

One final comment: as is true with any data structure, linked lists are designed for certain types of applications and may work very poorly for others. Linked lists excel in cases where you need only sequential access and where the objects to be stored are rearranged frequently. Linked lists aren't as useful with random access or when the objects being stored need to be searched. Other data structures—such as arrays or search trees—work better in this regard.

9

Stacks
and Queues

I n this chapter, we take a look at two data structures, *stacks* and *queues*, that can be created from the fundamental array and linked-list structures. In Chapters 1 and 3, you saw some examples of stacks. Here we will design stacks as concrete data types, with an eye on efficiency. Queues will be implemented with the same design philosophy. The idea is to define stack and queue classes that are readily usable in your own applications—with minimum overhead.

Stacks and queues are related data structures. Both are sequences of elements with restricted access. A *stack* is known as a last-in, first-out (LIFO) structure, where access to the elements takes place at one end of the sequence (called the *top*), using the operations *push* and *pop*. Figure 9.1 shows an example of a stack. A *queue* is a sequence where elements are inserted at one end (the *tail*), and extracted from the other end (the *head*). Queues work in a first-in, first out (FIFO) manner, as illustrated in Figure 9.2. Lines of cars at a

---

Figure 9.1 A sample stack.

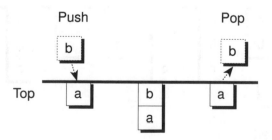

Figure 9.2 A sample queue.

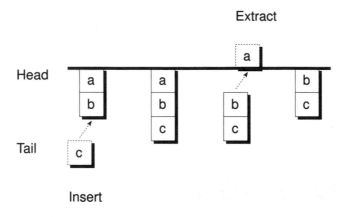

traffic light, lines at the post office, and computer jobs waiting to be printed are all conceptual examples of queues.

It's possible to combine a stack and queue to arrive at another data structure, which we'll call a *staque.* (This terminology was invented by the author.) In a staque, the stack operations push and pop are defined, as well as the queue operations *insert* (into the tail) and *extract* (from the front.) Of course, the extract operation is identical to the pop operation.

By taking this approach one step further, we could also allow extraction from the tail. The result is known as a *double-ended queue,* or *deque.* Figure 9.3 shows an example of a deque.

Figure 9.3 A Double-ended queue.

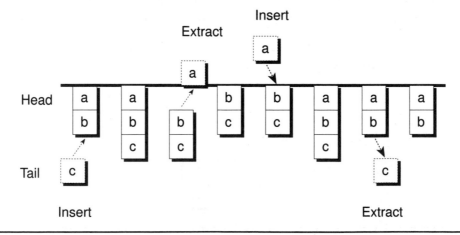

A *priority queue* is another variation of a queue. Here, the elements are ordered by priorities that have been assigned to them, rather than by the order in which the elements are inserted. Figure 9.4 shows an example of a prioriity queue, with numbers representing the priority order. Notice that the sequence of elements are in descending order. You'll see priority queues implemented in Chapters 12. See also the companion volume [Flamig 93].

We'll now take a detailed look at stacks and queues, starting with fixed-size stacks.

Fixed-Size Stacks

The most common type of stack is a fixed-size stack, implemented as an array of elements. When you define array-based stacks, you need to consider these three main design issues:

• Should the stack be statically or dynamically allocated?

• How should you keep track of the top of the stack and the bounds of the stack?

• When should the stack elements be constructed and destructed?

The first issue can be handled quite easily. As we did for the arrays defined in Chapter 4, a base class can be defined that purposely avoids specifying how the stack elements are allocated. Then, we can derive specific classes for both statically and dynamically allocated stacks.

You can take two basic approaches to resolve the second issue (keeping track of the top and bounds of the stack). One approach is to use an index to indicate which element is at the top of the stack. When doing pushing and popping, this index can be checked with the bounds of the stack. This is the approach used in most books to implement array-based stacks. (Indeed, we used this approach in Chapters 3.) However, an index is not the best way to

Figure 9.4 A priority queue.

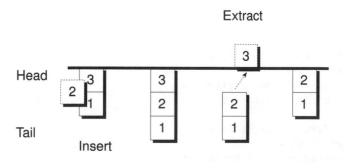

push and pop stack elements because subscripting involves multiplication and addition. A more efficient approach is to use pointers, both to reference the top of the stack and to mark the bounds of the stack.

You can also take two approaches to resolve the third issue (determining when to construct and deconstruct stack elements). The easiest approach is to construct the elements using default constructor calls when the stack is first built, and to destroy all the elements when the stack itself is destroyed. Indeed, that's the conventional way that C++ handles arrays. The second approach is to construct the stack elements individually during push operations, and to destroy elements one at a time during pop operations. This can be done using in-place copy constructor calls and explicit destructor calls—the same techniques we used for the variable-length arrays in Chapter 4.

Why bother with the in-place construction method? It's intuitively appealing and, in some cases, more correct to construct elements only when they are used. For example, constructed elements might use other resources (such as open file handles), allocate memory buffers, and so on. By deferring construction until the element is actually used, and destroying the element after it's no longer needed, you can ensure that the resources used by the element are acquired and freed in a timely fashion.

The types of constructors available can help you determine whether to use in-place construction. It may not make sense for the element type to have a default constructor (perhaps there is no sensible notion of a "null" object of that type). In this case, in-place construction is the best choice. Of course, for in-place construction to be used, the type must have a copy constructor, something that may not always be desirable either.

A Base Class for Array-Based Stacks

Using the preceding design principles, we'll now define a base class, *ArrStk*, which handles the basic operations of a fixed-sized array-based stack. The class assumes the stack elements are allocated elsewhere:

```
template<class TYPE>
class ArrStk {
protected:
  TYPE *start, *finish, *nxt;
  unsigned dimlen;
  void Setup(TYPE *m, unsigned n);
  ArrStk(const ArrStk<TYPE> &);
public:
  ArrStk(TYPE *m, unsigned n);
  virtual ~ArrStk();
  void operator=(const ArrStk<TYPE> &s);
  void Copy(const ArrStk<TYPE> &s);
```

```
  int Push(const TYPE &x);
  int Pop(TYPE &x);
  int Pop();
  void FastPush(const TYPE &x);
  void FastPop(TYPE &x);
  TYPE *Top();
  const TYPE *Top() const;
  TYPE *History(unsigned n);
  const TYPE *History(unsigned n) const;
  void Rewind(unsigned n=0);
  int IsFull() const;
  int IsEmpty() const;
  unsigned Size() const;
};
```

Complete code for the *ArrStk* class is given on disk in the files *arrstk.h,* *arrstk.mth,* and *placenew.h*. Through the use of defined macros, the code on disk can handle both the in-place copy-construction method and the conventional default-construction method. In this book, we show only the in-place construction method.

The *ArrStk* constructor takes a pointer to the stack elements (assumed to be already allocated, but not constructed) and the number of elements allocated. The *Setup()* function does all the work:

```
template<class TYPE>
ArrStk<TYPE>::ArrStk(TYPE *m, unsigned n)
// Sets up a stack with n already-allocated elements
// pointed to by m
{
  Setup(m, n);
}

template<class TYPE>
void ArrStk<TYPE>::Setup(TYPE *m, unsigned n)
{
  start = m;
  nxt = start;
  if (start) { // Was memory actually allocated?
    finish = start + n;
    dimlen = n;
  }
  else {
    finish = start;
    dimlen = 0;
  }
}
```

The *Setup()* function initializes the three pointers *start*, *nxt*, and *finish*, and the maximum stack size *dimlen*. The *start* and *finish* pointers mark the beginning and end of the stack, where *finish* actually points one element past the end. The *nxt* pointer references the next available stack element. The top of the stack—that is, the previous element pushed—can be found at *nxt-1*. When *nxt* equals *start*, the stack is empty. When *nxt* equals *finish*, the stack is full. Figure 9.5 shows the arrangement of an *ArrStk* object at various stages.

An element is pushed onto the stack by copy-constructing the data in place, at the location referenced by *nxt*, and then incrementing the *nxt* pointer, as given in the following *Push()* function. Figure 9.(6)a illustrates the pushing process.

```
template<class TYPE>
int ArrStk<TYPE>::Push(const TYPE &x)
// Pushes a copy of x onto the stack unless
// stack is full. Returns 1 if not full;returns 0 otherwise.
{
  if (!IsFull()) {
    new(nxt++) TYPE(x); // In-place copy construction
    return 1;
  }
  else return 0;
}
```

The *Pop()* function works in reverse, first decrementing the *nxt* pointer and then invoking an explicit destructor call. Figure 9.6(b) illustrates the popping process.

```
template<class TYPE>
int ArrStk<TYPE>::Pop(TYPE &x)
// Pops the top element from the stack, returning
```

Figure 9.5 An ArrStk object at various stages.

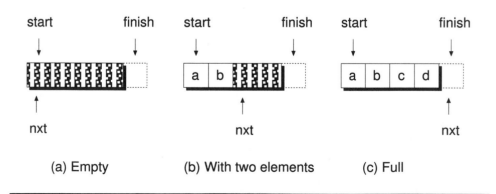

(a) Empty   (b) With two elements   (c) Full

Figure 9.6 Using an ArrStk object.

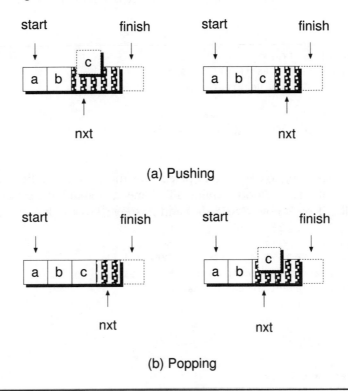

(a) Pushing

(b) Popping

```
// a copy of it in x, unless stack is empty. Returns 1
// if stack wasn't empty before the pop; otherwise, returns 0.
{
  if (!IsEmpty()) {
    x = *(--nxt);        // Make a copy
    nxt->TYPE::~TYPE(); // Explicit destruction
    return 1;
  }
  else return 0;
}
```

Both *Push()* and *Pop()* check to make sure the bounds of the stack aren't violated. To optimize speed, you may want to forgo these checks—but only if this is warranted! The following *FastPush()* and *FastPop()* functions are provided to bypass the stack checks. These functions can be easily inlined:

```
template<class TYPE>
void ArrStk<TYPE>::FastPush(const TYPE &x)
// For fastest, but unsafest pushes.
```

```
{
  new(nxt++) TYPE(x);  // In-place copy construction
}


template<class TYPE>
void ArrStk<TYPE>::FastPop(TYPE &x)
// For fastest, but unsafest pops.
{
  x = *(--nxt);          // Make a copy
  nxt->TYPE::~TYPE();    // Explicit destruction
}
```

It's interesting to compare in-place construction and explicit destruction with the conventional method, where all elements remain constructed during the stack's life. Here's how *FastPush()* and *FastPop()* would be coded for the latter:

```
template<class TYPE>
void ArrStk<TYPE>::FastPush(const TYPE &x)
// If in-place construction isn't being used
// (assumes element already constructed)
{
  x = *nxt++;
}


template<class TYPE>
void ArrStk<TYPE>::FastPop(TYPE &x)
// If in-place construction isn't being used
// (assumes element to remain constructed)

{
  x = *(--nxt);
}
```

You can see that the in-place construction used during a push is replaced by an assignment and that the code for a pop is the same as before, except no destructor call is made. For many element types, an assignment and a copy construction involve roughly the same amount of work. Thus, the push operation will take basically the same amount of time regardless of the method used. For pop operations, more work is being done in the extra destructor call for the in-place construction method. The data type being stored determines whether this is a problem or whether the reverse situation (not doing a destructor call) is a problem.

The in-place construction method provides the most rigorous design and is probably worth using, even if there is a slight performance penalty. Of course, for built-in types, this is a moot point since copy construction reduces to an assignment, and the destructor becomes a no-op.

The *Rewind()* function is related to *Pop()*, and lets you unpop *n* elements off the stack:

```
template<class TYPE>
void ArrStk<TYPE>::Rewind(unsigned n)
{
  if (n == 0) n = dimlen; // Ensures all elements popped
  // Explicit destructor called for each element popped
  while(n-- && nxt != start) (--nxt)->TYPE::~TYPE();
}
```

Unlike *Pop()*, the *Rewind()* function doesn't copy and pass back the data being popped from the stack. The data is simply discarded and destroyed. The *Rewind()* function can be used to clear the stack by unpopping all the elements. By convention, passing a number 0 to *Rewind()* (the default) results in the stack being cleared.

History() is another related function, and lets you inspect the element *n* positions back into the stack:

```
template<class TYPE>
TYPE *ArrStk<TYPE>::History(unsigned n)
{
  if (IsEmpty()) return 0;
  TYPE *p = nxt-1;
  while(1) {
    if (n-- == 0) return p;     // Found the element
    if (p-- == start) return 0; // Out of range
  }
}
```

In the strictest sense, *History()* violates the rules of a stack. However, this function can be quite useful, when stacks are used in conjunction with tree-traversal algorithms. In the case of *n = 0*, the top element of the stack is inspected. The *Top()* function provides an efficient form for this special case:

```
template<class TYPE>
TYPE *ArrStk<TYPE>::Top()
{
  return IsEmpty() ? 0 : (nxt-1);
}
```

To make *ArrStk* a concrete data type, we also provide an overloaded assignment operator to allow stacks to be copied. This operator function calls *Copy()* to do most of the work:

```
template<class TYPE>
void ArrStk<TYPE>::operator=(const ArrStk<TYPE> &s)
// Traps assignment to self
{
  if (this != &s) Copy(s);
}

template<class TYPE>
void ArrStk<TYPE>::Copy(const ArrStk<TYPE> &s)
// Clears the stack, and then copies the elements
// of s onto the stack. Note that if s.dimlen >
// dimlen, not all elements will be copied.
{
  Rewind();
  TYPE *t = s.start;
  unsigned n = dimlen;
  // Elements copied via in-place copy construction
  while (n- && t != s.nxt) new(nxt++) TYPE(*t++);
}
```

The *Copy()* function doesn't change the dimensioned length of the stack and, for that reason, a truncation may result during the copy.

You'll notice that a copy constructor is defined for *ArrStk*, but it is placed in the private section of the class. The constructor body (not shown) is actually empty. This approach prevents the user from trying to create a stack via copy construction. As defined, the *ArrStk* class is not responsible for allocating the stack elements, so it can't allocate a new stack to hold a copy of another stack. Likewise, a virtual destructor is defined in *ArrStk*, but it does nothing. It's up to the derived classes to handle the de-allocation of the stack elements.

The remaining *ArrStk* functions are those that determine the maximum size of the stack and whether the stack is empty or full:

```
template<class TYPE>
unsigned ArrStk<TYPE>::Size() const
{
  return dimlen;
}

template<class TYPE>
int ArrStk<TYPE>::IsEmpty() const
{
  return nxt == start;
}

template<class TYPE>
```

```
int ArrStk<TYPE>::IsFull() const
{
  return nxt == finish;
}
```

Statically Allocated Stacks

With the *ArrStk* class now defined, it's easy to derive a new class, *SarrStk*, that allocates the stack elements statically:

```
template<class TYPE, unsigned SIZE>
class SarrStk : public ArrStk<TYPE> {
protected:
  char elem[sizeof(TYPE)*SIZE]; // Notice the char type!
public:
  SarrStk();
  SarrStk(const ArrStk<TYPE> &s);
  SarrStk(const SarrStk<TYPE, SIZE> &s);
  virtual ~SarrStk();
  void operator=(const ArrStk<TYPE> &s);
};
```

The *SarrStk* class uses the same strategy that was used for the statically allocated, variable-length arrays in Chapter 4. The stack elements are allocated and de-allocated as an array of characters. This approach defers the construction of the elements until they are actually used, and prevents them from being destroyed twice when the stack itself is destroyed. Here is one of the constructors, and the destructor, to illustrate this technique. In the destructor, the stack must be rewound so that we can call the destructors for all elements in use:

```
template<class TYPE, unsigned SIZE>
SarrStk<TYPE, SIZE>::SarrStk()
: ArrStk<TYPE>((TYPE *)elem, SIZE)
{
  // Nothing else to do
}

template<class TYPE, unsigned SIZE>
SarrStk<TYPE, SIZE>::~SarrStk()
{
  Rewind();
}
```

Complete code for the *SarrStk* class is given on disk in the file *sarrstk.h*. A test program *tstsastk.cpp* is also provided.

Dynamically Allocated Stacks

The *DarrStk* class defines stacks that are dynamically allocated. As was done with the *SarrStk* class, we use a typecasting trick so that the stack elements can be allocated without being constructed at the same time. This next class definition, followed by one of the constructors and the destructor, illustrates the technique. This time, the destructor must not only rewind the stack, but also must delete the elements:

```
template<class TYPE>
class DarrStk : public ArrStk<TYPE> {
public:
  DarrStk(unsigned n);
  DarrStk(const ArrStk<TYPE> &s);
  DarrStk(const DarrStk<TYPE> &s);
  virtual ~DarrStk();
  void operator=(const ArrStk<TYPE> &s);
};

template<class TYPE>
DarrStk<TYPE>::DarrStk(unsigned n)
// Elements are allocated as an array of characters
// to defer their construction until needed
: ArrStk<TYPE>((TYPE *)new char[sizeof(TYPE)*n], n)
{
  // Nothing else to do
}

template<class TYPE>
DarrStk<TYPE>::~DarrStk()
{
  Rewind();
  // Elements are deleted as an array of characters,
  // since that's how they were allocated
  delete[] (char *)start;
}
```

Complete code for the *DarrStk* class is given on disk in the file *darrstk.h*. The test program *tstdastk.cpp* is also provided.

Resizable Stacks

Fixed-size, array-based stacks provide the most efficient form of stack; however, it can be inconvenient to fix the size of the stack. A linked list is the obvious candidate to implement a resizable stack. We provided examples of this in Chapter 3. Unfortunately, when we use a linked list, a new node must be allocated from the heap with every push, and a node must be de-allocated with every pop. For some heap-implementations, this can be a time-consuming process. In Chapter 8, we demonstrated one way around this problem: implement an auxiliary list to cache nodes that would otherwise be freed.

A resizable array, as implemented in Chapter 4, provides another alternative. However, this approach presents a problem: each time the array grows beyond its allocated bounds, it has to be copied into a new location that has more room.

Stacks of Stacks

There is an array-based solution that's better than all of the alternatives just presented. The idea is based on working with multiple stacks. As a stack becomes full, a switch is made to a new stack. As a stack becomes empty, a switch is made back to a previously used stack. This type of resizable stack can be implemented using a *stack-of-stacks*. Initially, the stack-of-stacks is empty. When the first element is to be added, a new substack is allocated and a pointer to it is pushed onto the stack-of-stacks. When the first substack becomes full, another substack is allocated and its pointer is pushed onto the stack-of-stacks. As elements are removed and a substack becomes empty, the substack is popped from the stack-of-stacks.

You can implement a stack-of-stacks using the *DarrStk* template, with the element type being the *DarrStk* type itself. In the following example, we'll declare such a stack, with room to hold *mxstks* substacks:

```
DarrStk< DarrStk<TYPE> > stkostk(mxstks);
```

When *stkostk* is first allocated, the individual substacks remain unconstructed. As a result, the only space initially occupied by *stkostk* is the space for the instance variables of *DarrStk* (*start, finish, nxt,* and *dimlen*) multiplied *mxstks* times. Substacks are constructed only when elements are pushed onto the stack. Here's how an element *x* of type *TYPE* can be pushed onto and popped from the stack:

```
// Push function:

if (!stkostk.IsFull()) {
    if (stkostk.IsEmpty() || stkostk.Top()->IsFull()) {
      stkostk.Push(DarrStk<TYPE>(blksize));
    }
    return stkostk.Top()->Push(x);
}
```

```
else return 0;

// Pop function:

if (!stkostk.IsEmpty()) {
   if (stkostk.Top()->IsEmpty()) {
      stkostk.Rewind(1);
      if (stkostk.IsEmpty()) return 0;
   }
   return stkostk.Top()->Pop(x);
}
else return 0;
```

A working example of a stack-of-stacks is given on disk in the file *stkostk.cpp*.

The RarrStk Class

The nested template, stack-of-stacks approach works fine, but some stack operations—such as *Rewind()* and *History()*—are somewhat difficult to implement under this approach. For this reason, we'll implement a stack-of-stacks more directly, using the following *RarrStk* class:

```
template<class TYPE>
class RarrStk {
protected:
  TYPE **stkostk;            // Stack-of-stacks pointers
  TYPE *nxt, *start, *finish; // Current stack variables
  unsigned maxnelems, stksize, nxtstk, maxstks;
  int Setup(unsigned nb);
  int PushStk();
  void PopStk(unsigned b);
  void Dealloc();
public:
  RarrStk(unsigned stksz, unsigned mxstks=1);
  RarrStk(const RarrStk<TYPE> &s);
  ~RarrStk();
  void operator=(const RarrStk<TYPE> &s);
  int Copy(const RarrStk<TYPE> &s);
  int Push(const TYPE &x);
  int Pop(TYPE &x);
  int Pop();
  TYPE *Top();
  const TYPE *Top() const;
  TYPE *History(unsigned n);
  const TYPE *History(unsigned n) const;
```

```
   void Rewind(unsigned n = 0);
   int IsFull() const;
   int IsEmpty() const;
   unsigned Size() const;
};
```

Complete code for the *RarrStk* class is given in the files *rarrstk.h* and *rarrstk.mth*. A test program is provided in the file *tstrastk.cpp*.

A *RarrStk* object is made up of an array of stack pointers called *stkostk* and one or more substacks. Each substack is allocated and de-allocated separately as needed, and *stkostk* keeps track of their locations. As is true with the *ArrStk* class, *RarrStk* uses the pointers *nxt*, *start*, and *finish*, but this time they point to elements in the current substack. When a switch is made to another substack, these pointers are modified accordingly. Figure 9.7 shows an example of a *RarrStk* object with two substacks allocated (but with room for four stacks).

The *RarrStk* constructor, which calls *Setup()*, creates an empty stack with no substacks allocated, and the *stkostk* array is initialized to hold null pointers.

```
template<class TYPE>
RarrStk<TYPE>::RarrStk(unsigned stksz, unsigned mxstks)
{
  stksize = stksz;
  Setup(mxstks);
}

template<class TYPE>
int RarrStk<TYPE>::Setup(unsigned ns)
{
```

Figure 9.7 A partially filled RarrStk object.

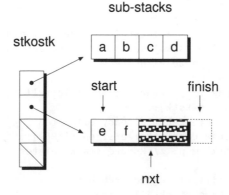

```
    nxtstk = 0; nxt = 0; start = 0; finish = 0;
    stkostk = new TYPE *[ns]; // Up to ns sub-stacks
    if (stkostk) {
      maxstks = ns;
      while(ns) stkostk[-ns] = 0;
    }
    else maxstks = 0;
    maxnelems = stksize * maxstks;
    return maxstks > 0;
}
```

When calling the constructor, you specify the size of each substack and the number of substacks that you wish to allow. Note that a *RarrStk* object does have a maximum size (equal to *stksize * maxstks*), but unlike an *ArrStk* object, this size doesn't affect the initial amount of memory reserved. Initially, *RarrStk* only requires enough room to store the *stkostk* array of pointers.

Elements are pushed on the stack in the same way that we used previously, with one exception: if the current substack is full, a new substack is started. Figure 9.8 illustrates this process. The following *Push()* and *PushStk()* routines show how the pushing is done. You'll notice that in-place construction is used for the new element:

```
template<class TYPE>
int RarrStk<TYPE>::Push(const TYPE &x)
{
  if (nxt == finish) {          // Need another stack
    if (!PushStk()) return 0;   // Couldn't allocate
  }
  new(nxt++) TYPE(x);  // In-place copy construction
  return 1;            // Success
}


template<class TYPE>
int RarrStk<TYPE>::PushStk()
// Ensures room has been allocated for the next highest
// stack (ie: stk # nxtstk.) Returns 1 if successful;
// returns 0 if unable to allocate.
{
  if (nxtstk == maxstks) return 0; // Table full
  TYPE *p = stkostk[nxtstk];
  if (p == 0) { // Block not already allocated
    p = (TYPE *)new char[stksize*sizeof(TYPE)];
    stkostk[nxtstk] = p; // Record stack pointer
  }
  // else stack still allocated from before
  if (p) { // We have stack allocated
```

```
      nxt = start = p;
      finish = p + stksize;
      nxtstk++;
      return 1;
  }
  else { // Allocation error, so leave everything alone
      return 0;
  }
}
```

The *PushStk()* routine—responsible for ensuring that a new substack gets allocated—is somewhat tricky. First, the substack may already be allocated (more on this later), which we determine by checking for a non-null pointer in *stkostk*. Second, since we're using in-place construction, the new substack is allocated as an array of characters to prevent the element constructors from being called prematurely. Note how the variable *nxtstk* keeps track of the next available location in *stkostk*, and how it's possible for *stkostk* to become completely full.

Popping an element from the stack uses the reverse approach. If the current substack becomes empty when an element is popped off the stack, the sub-stack can be de-allocated. However, the substack shouldn't be de-allocated immediately. You should postpone the de-allocation to avoid the "thrashing" that can occur at the boundary of a substack. Consider what would happen if the first element of a substack is popped and a new element is then immediately pushed. If the substack were de-allocated as soon as it became empty, it would have to be immediately re-allocated when a new element is added. To avoid this, the following *Pop()* function de-allocates a substack only when the

Figure 9.8 Pushing onto a RarrStk object.

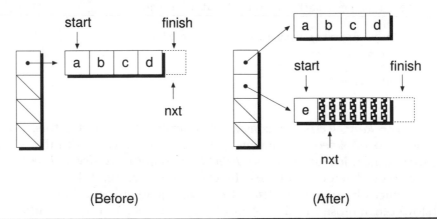

(Before)   (After)

one precedes it becomes empty. When a substack is ready to be freed, the *PopStk()* function is called. Figure 9.9 illustrates the process.

```
template<class TYPE>
int RarrStk<TYPE>::Pop(TYPE &x)
// Pops the top element from the stack, returning
// a copy of it in x. Returns 1 if stack wasn't empty
// before push; otherwise, returns 0. If stack was empty, the
// data in x will be untouched.
{
  if (nxt == start) {
     // Pop next higher stack if this has not already been done
     PopStk(nxtstk);
     // Return if stack is empty, but note that there may
     // still be a stack allocated (when nxtstk = 1)
     if (nxtstk <= 1) return 0;
     // Otherwise, we must move to end of lower stack
     —nxtstk; // nxtstk guaranteed >= 1 after decrement
     start = stkostk[nxtstk-1];
     finish = start + stksize;
     nxt = finish - 1;
  }
  else —nxt;
  x = *nxt;
  nxt->TYPE::~TYPE();
  return 1;
}

template<class TYPE>
void RarrStk<TYPE>::PopStk(unsigned b)
// De-allocates stack b if not already de-allocated,
// destructing elements along the way if INPLACECONST
// isn't true. Sets pointer in stack table
// to null. Does nothing if b is out of range.
{
  if (b >= maxstks) return; // b is out of range
  if (stkostk[b] == 0) return;
  delete[] (char *)(stkostk[b]);
  stkostk[b] = 0;
}
```

The *RarrStk* class contains a full complement of constructors, a destructor, and an overloaded assignment operator. As is the case with the *ArrStk* class, *RarrStk* includes functions like *IsEmpty()*, *IsFull()*, *History()*, *Top()*, *Rewind()*, and so on. The details of these functions are given on disk.

Stacks based on the *RarrStk* class are quite efficient, but they are slightly slower than those based on *ArrStk*—due to the need to allocate and de-allocate

Figure 9.9 Delayed de-allocation of a substack.

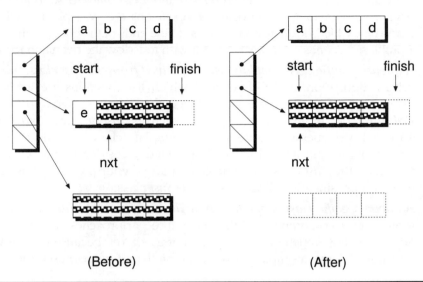

(Before)   (After)

sub-stacks. This problem can be alleviated by increasing the size of the blocks, and thus reducing the frequency of substack allocations. Note that *RarrStk* objects are significantly faster than a linked list approach. The *RarrStk* objects also occupy less space, since each element doesn't need an extra link pointer. The only disadvantage is a slight increase in the code required (which could be magnified if many classes are instantiated from the template).

To allow you to compare *RarrStk* objects with linked-list based stacks, we've provided the following additional files on disk: *liststk.h, liststk.mth, tstlstk.cpp,* and *stktimer.cpp.* The latter program tests the runtime efficiency of the two approaches.

LIST-BASED QUEUES

We'll now focus on the implementations of queues. We'll begin by discussing list-based queues, since they are the easiest to implement. Next, we'll look at compact array-based implementations. Recall that, with a queue, elements are inserted at the rear of the queue and extracted from the front. A singly-linked list with a back pointer can handle these operations quite nicely. There are different methods we could use:

1. *Implement a linked-list queue class from scratch.* This is the most direct method. However, with this approach we must duplicate a lot of list functionality that could be reused for other lists.

2. *Use the Slist class of Chapter 8 as is, without creating a special queue version.* We can use functions like *AddToBack()* and *DelFront()* to support the queue operations. However, all the other list operations are available as well, such as *DelNext(),* which violate restricted access to the ends of the queue. Whether this is a problem depends on how strictly you wish to follow the definition for a queue.

3. *A queue-specific class template can be derived from the Slist class.* We can use private derivation, and thus control which list functions are available. By using inline functions, we can change the names of *AddToBack()* and *DelFront()* to more high-level names such as *Insert()* and *Extract().* This approach gets messy because an extra template class, *Slist,* must be instantiated, plus we run into all sorts of protected-access problems. Of course, if you need the *Slist* class for some other part of your program, this approach may be best since you'll be reusing the *Slist* class.

4. *A queue-specific class template can be derived from the Slistb base class.* This represents a compromise of the other three approaches. By deriving from *Slistb,* we allow much of the code to be reused. Yet, because the derivation is direct, we'll have a simpler implementation than if we had used the *Slist* class.

For this book, we've chosen the fourth method, since it is perhaps the best engineering tradeoff. However, the method that works best for you might depend on a lot of factors; don't hesitate to implement queues using your own methods.

We can derive a *ListQ* class from *Slistb,* whose purpose is to implement list-based queues:

```
template<class TYPE>
class ListQ : public Slistb {
protected:
  virtual Snode<TYPE> *AllocNode(const TYPE &x);
  virtual Snodeb *DupNode(const Snodeb *n);
  virtual void FreeNode(Snodeb *n);
public:
  ListQ();
  ListQ(const ListQ<TYPE> &s);
  ~ListQ();
  void operator=(const ListQ<TYPE> &s);
  int Extract(TYPE &x);
  int Extract();
  int Insert(const TYPE &x);
  TYPE *Head();
  const TYPE *Head() const;
  int IsFull() const;
};
```

Complete code for the *ListQ* class is given on disk in the files *listq.h, listq.mth,* and *snode.h*. A test program is given in *tstlq.cpp*.

The *ListQ* class is very similar to the *Slist* class, but has fewer functions. For instance, we chose not to support queue concatenations, even though this might be useful in some cases. As was true with the *Slist* class, *ListQ* allocates nodes on the heap. We could, of course, use the free-list technique for node caching or use array-based allocation.

The most important functions of *ListQ* are *Insert()* and *Extract()*, which implement the basic queue operations:

```
template<class TYPE>
int ListQ<TYPE>::Insert(const TYPE &x)
// Creates a new node having a copy of x for its data
// and puts in on the back of the queue. Returns 1
// if allocation successful; otherwise, returns 0.
{
  Snode<TYPE> *p = AllocNode(x);
  if (p == 0) return 0;
  AttachToBack(p);
  return 1;
}


template<class TYPE>
int ListQ<TYPE>::Extract(TYPE &x)
// Gets the data from the front node of the queue and
// copies it into x. If queue is empty, x is left
// untouched and a 0 is returned; otherwise, returns a 1.
{
  Snode<TYPE> *p = (Snode<TYPE> *)RmvFront();
  if (p == 0) return 0;
  x = p->info;
  FreeNode(p);
  return 1;
}
```

The *Insert()* and *Extract()* functions use the *AttachToBack()* and *RmvFront()* functions of *Slistb*, as well as the virtual functions *FreeNode()* and *AllocNode()*.

Sometimes it's useful to peek at the front element in the queue without actually removing it. The *Head()* function is used for that purpose:

```
template<class TYPE>
TYPE *ListQ<TYPE>::Head()
// Returns the data contained in the head node of the queue,
// or a null pointer if the queue is empty
```

```
{
  return IsEmpty() ? 0 : &(((Snode<TYPE> *)Front())->info);
}
```

Figure 9.10 illustrates the process of adding and removing elements from a *ListQ* object.

LIST-BASED STAQUES

You can add stack-like operations to the *ListQ* class and derive a combination stack and queue (staque) class. Alternatively, you can derive the staque class from a stack class or, by using multiple inheritance, combine a stack and queue class. In the first case, the *Pop()* function would be identical to *Extract()* and the *Push()* operation could be implemented by making a call to the *AddToFront()* function of *Slistb*. The details for this are given on disk.

Complete code for a list-based staque class, *ListSQ*, is given on disk in the files *listsq.h* and *listsq.mth*. This class is derived from a list-based stack class, *ListStk*, which is given in the files *liststk.h* and *liststk.mth*. A test program is provided in *tstlsq.cpp*.

LIST-BASED DEQUES

Here, a singly-linked list with a back pointer isn't quite up to the job. The problem is that we can't efficiently remove the last node from the list, because we must scan

---

Figure 9.10 Using a ListQ object.

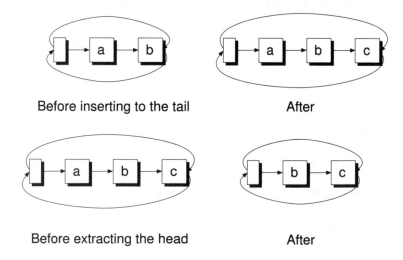

Before inserting to the tail   After

Before extracting the head   After

the list from beginning to end to find the node immediately preceding the last one.

You can either choose to accept this inefficiency or use a doubly-linked list. Of course, a doubly-linked list has its own inefficiency, costing an extra pointer per node. As always, you are faced with the classic speed versus space tradeoff. Here, sacrificing space for speed is probably the better choice. The space required by a queue is rarely an issue. However, the speed to remove an element might be. (If space is an issue, an array-based queue is a better approach, as you'll see later on.)

By using the doubly-linked list approach, we can implement a deque with the following *ListDQ* class, which is derived from *Dlistb*:

```
template<class TYPE>
class ListDQ : public Dlistb {
protected:
  virtual Dnode<TYPE> *AllocNode(const TYPE &x);
  virtual Dnodeb *DupNode(const Dnodeb *n);
  virtual void FreeNode(Dnodeb *n);
public:
  ListDQ();
  ListDQ(const ListDQ<TYPE> &s);
  ~ListDQ();
  void operator=(const ListDQ<TYPE> &s);
  int ExtractHead(TYPE &x);
  int ExtractTail(TYPE &x);
  int InsertHead(const TYPE &x);
  int InsertTail(const TYPE &x);
  TYPE *Head();
  const TYPE *Head() const;
  TYPE *Tail();
  const TYPE *Tail() const;
  int IsFull() const;
};
```

Complete code for the *ListDQ* class is given in the files *listdq.h*, *listdq.mth*, and *dnode.h*. A test program is provided in the file *tstldq.cpp*.

The design of the *ListDQ* class is similar to *ListQ*, but splits the *Insert()* and *Extract()* functions into four functions—*InsertHead()*, *InsertTail()*, *ExtractHead()*, and *ExtractTail()*:

```
template<class TYPE>
int ListDQ<TYPE>::InsertHead(const TYPE &x)
{
  Dnode<TYPE> *p = AllocNode(x);
  if (p == 0) return 0;
  AttachToFront(p);
```

```
    return 1;
}

template<class TYPE>
int ListDQ<TYPE>::InsertTail(const TYPE &x)
{
  Dnode<TYPE> *p = AllocNode(x);
  if (p == 0) return 0;
  AttachToBack(p);
  return 1;
}

template<class TYPE>
int ListDQ<TYPE>::ExtractHead(TYPE &x)
{
  Dnode<TYPE> *p = (Dnode<TYPE> *)RmvFront();
  if (p == 0) return 0;
  x = p->info;
  FreeNode(p);
  return 1;
}

template<class TYPE>
int ListDQ<TYPE>::ExtractTail(TYPE &x)
{
  Dnode<TYPE> *p = (Dnode<TYPE> *)RmvBack();
  if (p == 0) return 0;
  x = p->info;
  FreeNode(p);
  return 1;
}
```

ARRAY-BASED QUEUES

List-based queues are especially useful because you don't have to pre-allocate storage for the maximum size of the queue. However, if the queues you are using tend to be of some fixed size, then arrays offer more compact representations. Such array-based queues will be discussed next.

The simplest way to implement an array-based queue is to have the first element of the array be the head of the queue, and utilize a pointer to the tail of the queue. It's easy to insert an element into this type of queue. We simply increment the tail pointer to the next available slot. However, we run into a problem in extracting from the front of the queue, because doing so means all remaining elements of the array must be shifted up—a time-consuming process. Figure 9.11 illustrates this inefficiency.

Figure 9.11 An inefficient array-based queue.

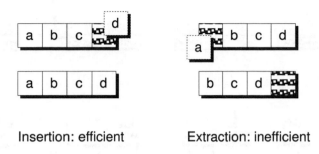

Insertion: efficient   Extraction: inefficient

An alternative is to use a *chasing pointer* technique. The idea is to add another pointer to the head of the queue. The head pointer is initialized to the start of the array. As elements are inserted, the tail pointer is incremented. As elements are extracted, the head pointer is incremented, chasing the tail pointer. With this strategy, both insertion and extraction are efficient, as illustrated in Figure 9.12.

The chasing pointer technique does present some problems. As elements are extracted, the storage space at the beginning of the array is discarded and never reused. Also, the head and tail pointers are always incremented (but never decremented). Thus, even if the number of extractions equals the number of insertions, the array eventually runs out of space.

To solve these problems, we can use a *circular array*, also called a *ring buffer*. In such an array, the end wraps around to the beginning. Circular arrays don't physically exist. Instead, they are simulated by using normal linear arrays, where all pointers or indexes scanning the array are reset to the starting element when the ending element has been passed. Figure 9.13 illustrates this wraparound effect.

The ArrQ Class

Next, we'll develop an array-based queue class, *ArrQ*, that uses the circular array technique. The design for this class is very similar to the *ArrStk* class, in the following ways:

• The *ArrQ* class isn't responsible for allocating memory for the queue. The derived classes *SarrQ* and *DarrQ* determine whether the memory is allocated statically or dynamically. These classes are similar to *SarrStk* and *DarrStk*.

• Pointers are used to represent the head and tail of the queue, and also for the actual bounds of the underlying array. This is more efficient than using indexes, since we can avoid the multiplication needed by subscripting.

Figure 9.12 An array-based queue with chasing pointers.

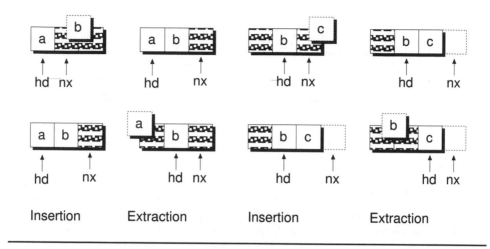

Insertion   Extraction   Insertion   Extraction

- In-place construction is used when elements are added and explicit destruction is used when elements are removed. This approach leads to a more rigorous and robust design.
- The class is a concrete data type implemented as a template, with the appropriate constructors, destructor, and overloaded assignment operator.

Figure 9.13 A circular array with wrapround pointers.

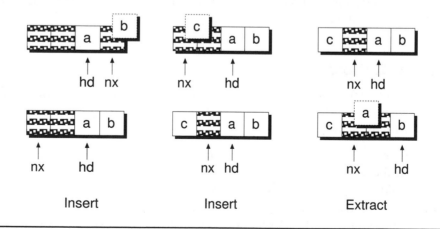

Insert   Insert   Extract

Here is the *ArrQ* class definition:

```
template<class TYPE>
class ArrQ {
protected:
  TYPE *st,    // Pointer to start element
       *fn,    // Pointer to finish element
       *hd,    // Pointer to head element in the queue
       *nx;    // Pointer to next available element
  int isfull; // Flag to indicate a full queue
  unsigned dimlen; // Maximum number of elements
  void Setup(TYPE *m, unsigned n);
  ArrQ(const ArrQ<TYPE> &); // To disallow copy constructing
  TYPE *Inc(TYPE *x) const;
  TYPE *Dec(TYPE *x) const;
public:
  ArrQ(TYPE *m, unsigned n);
  virtual ~ArrQ();
  void operator=(const ArrQ<TYPE> &s);
  int Copy(const ArrQ<TYPE> &s);
  void Clear();
  int Extract(TYPE &x);
  int Extract();
  int Insert(const TYPE &x);
  TYPE *Head();
  const TYPE *Head() const;
  int IsEmpty() const;
  int IsFull() const;
  unsigned Size() const;
};
```

Complete code for the *ArrQ* class is given on disk in the files *arrq.h* and *arrq.mth*. Static and dynamic derived classes are given in the files *sarrq.h* and *darrq.h*. Test programs can be found in the files *tstsaq.cpp* and *tstdaq.cpp*.

Four pointers are used to represent the queue. The variable *st* points to the starting element in the array, *fn* points to the last element in the array, *hd* points to the logical start of the queue, and *nx* points to the next element available for insertions. The tail of the queue can be found at location *nx-1*. The *ArrQ* constructor sets up these pointers by calling *Setup()*.

```
template<class TYPE>
ArrQ<TYPE>::ArrQ(TYPE *m, unsigned n)
// Constructs a new queue with a maximum of n elements
// stored at location m, assumed to be already allocated
{
```

```
    Setup(m, n);
}

template<class TYPE>
void ArrQ<TYPE>::Setup(TYPE *m, unsigned n)
{
  st = m;
  if (st && n) { // Array isn't null
      fn = st+n-1;
      dimlen = n;
      isfull = 0;
  }
  else { // A null array, which is always 'full'
      fn = st;
      dimlen = 0;
      isfull = 1;
  }
  hd = st;
  nx = st;
}
```

Figure 9.14(a) shows the configuration of an empty queue as created by *Setup()*. Note how the *nx* and *hd* pointers are equal at this stage. The condition *nx==hd* is one way to test for an empty queue. However, this condition also occurs when the queue is full, as illustrated by Figure 9.14(b).

We can solve this ambiguity in two ways. Under one approach, we never let the array fill up entirely, holding the last remaining element in reserve. (The location of this element rotates through the array as the queue is accessed.) In this scheme, when *nx ==hd-1,* the queue is said to be full. Unfortunately, the reserved element represents wasted space, which can be costly if the array elements are large. Under the second approach, we maintain a flag (which we call *isfull*) that is set when the queue becomes full during an insertion and reset

Figure 9.14 Ambiguous empty and full conditions.

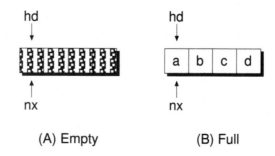

(A) Empty   (B) Full

as elements are extracted. The following *IsEmpty()* and *IsFull()* functions show how the *isfull* flag resolves the empty/full ambiguity:

```
template<class TYPE>
int ArrQ<TYPE>::IsEmpty() const
{
  return hd == nx && !isfull;
}

template<class TYPE>
int ArrQ<TYPE>::IsFull() const
{
  return isfull;
}
```

By maintaining the *isfull* flag, we avoid wasting one of the array elements, but we do create some complications. Here are the *Insert()* and *Extract()* functions, which illustrate how the *hd* and *nx* pointers are updated, and how the *isfull* flag is maintained:

```
template<class TYPE>
int ArrQ<TYPE>::Insert(const TYPE &x)
// Copies x into the next available element at the end
// of the queue. If queue is full, nothing happens.
{
  if (IsFull()) return 0;
  new(nx) TYPE(x);
  nx = Inc(nx);
  if (nx == hd) isfull = 1; // We just went full
  return 1;
}

template<class TYPE>
int ArrQ<TYPE>::Extract(TYPE &x)
// Gets the data from the head element and stores a copy of
// it in x. Removes and possibly destroys the head element.
// If queue is empty, x is left untouched and a
// 0 is returned; otherwise, a 1 is returned.
{
  if (IsEmpty()) return 0;
  x = *hd;
  hd->TYPE::~TYPE();
  hd = Inc(hd); // We have a new head
  isfull = 0;   // And we certainly can't be full anymore
  return 1;
}
```

The functions *Inc()* and *Dec()* are used to conveniently wrap the pointers around when we reach the ends of the array:

```
template<class TYPE>
TYPE *ArrQ<TYPE>::Inc(TYPE *x) const
// Increments a pointer and wraps around to
// the start if necessary
{
  return (x == fn) ? st : x+1;
}

template<class TYPE>
TYPE *ArrQ<TYPE>::Dec(TYPE *x) const
// Decrements a pointer, wrapping around to
// the end if necessary
{
  return (x == st) ? fn : x-1;
}
```

Array-Based Staques

We can now derive a new class that adds stack-like operations to the *ArrQ* class, similar to the way used for list-based stacks. Such a class, *ArrSQ*, is given on disk.

Complete code for an array-based staque class is given on disk in the files *arrsq.h* and *arrsq.mth*. Static and dynamic versions, *SarrSQ* and *DarrSQ*, are provided in the files *sarrsq.h* and *darrsq.h*. Two test programs are provided in *tstsasq.cpp* and *tstdasq.cpp*.

The ArrDQ Class

A double-ended queue class is easy to derive from *ArrQ*, as the following *ArrDQ* class shows:

```
template<class TYPE>
class ArrDQ : public ArrQ<TYPE> {
protected:
  ArrDQ(const ArrDQ<TYPE> &s);
public:
  ArrDQ(TYPE *m, unsigned n);
  void operator=(const ArrQ<TYPE> &s);
  int ExtractHead(TYPE &x);
  int ExtractTail(TYPE &x);
  int InsertHead(const TYPE &x);
```

```
    int InsertTail(const TYPE &x);
    TYPE *Tail();
    const TYPE *Tail() const;
};
```

Complete code for the *ArrDQ* class is given on disk in the files *arrdq.h* and *arrdq.mth*. Static and dynamic classes, *SarrDQ* and *DarrDQ,* are given in the files *sarrdq.h* and *darrdq.h*. Test programs are provided in the files *tstsadq.cpp* and *tstdadq.cpp*.

The *Insert()* and *Extract()* functions of the *ArrQ* class are replaced by *InsertHead()*, *InsertTail()*, *ExtractHead()*, and *ExtractTail()*.

```
template<class TYPE>
int ArrDQ<TYPE>::InsertHead(const TYPE &x)
// Puts a new element at the front of the queue, holding
// a copy of x
{
    if (IsFull()) return 0;
    hd = Dec(hd);
    new(hd) TYPE(x);
    if (nx == hd) isfull = 1;
    return 1;
}

template<class TYPE>
int ArrDQ<TYPE>::InsertTail(const TYPE &x)
// Puts a new element at the end of the queue, holding a
// copy of x
{
    return ArrQ<TYPE>::Insert(x);
}

template<class TYPE>
int ArrDQ<TYPE>::ExtractHead(TYPE &x)
// Copies the data of the front element into x and
// removes the element from the queue
{
    return ArrQ<TYPE>::Extract(x);
}


template<class TYPE>
int ArrDQ<TYPE>::ExtractTail(TYPE &x)
// Copies the data of the rear element into x and
// removes the element from the queue
{
```

```
  if (IsEmpty()) return 0;
  nx = Dec(nx);
  x = *nx;
  nx->TYPE::~TYPE();
  isfull = 0;
  return 1;
}
```

Note that we could have derived the *ArrDQ* class from the *ArrSQ* class, since we would only need to add the function to remove elements from the end of the queue. We chose not to do this because the chain of template-based derivations (*ArrQ* to *ArrSQ* to *ArrDQ* to *SarrDQ* and *DarrDQ*) starts to get a little unwieldy. The derivation of *ArrDQ* directly from *ArrQ* eliminates one class from this chain.

HETEROGENOUS STACKS AND QUEUES

The discussion so far has implicitly assumed that the stacks and queues store only one kind of object, and are thus homogenous. However, you will probably have situations where it is useful to store different types of objects. Any of the techniques given earlier in Chapters 5 and 8 for creating heterogenous arrays and linked-lists could also be used for stacks and queues. As always, you can accomplish this by storing indirect pointers to objects, perhaps using reference-counted smart pointers to provide the safest designs.

SUMMARY

In this chapter, you've seen how to efficiently implement stacks and queues by using two opposing data structures: arrays and linked lists. Both forms offer advantages. Linked lists allow more flexibility for variable stack and queue lengths, while arrays offer more compact representations when a fixed size is acceptable. The *RarrStk* class provides a very efficient implementation of resizable stacks by using a stack-of-stacks. Note that resizable array-based queues could be implemented in a way similar to the *RarrStk* class, using a *queue of queues*. The details are somewhat messy, though, because the deferred allocation and de-allocation of the subqueues must be handled in both directions.

Perhaps the most important design feature presented in this chapter is the use of in-place construction and explicit destruction of elements when they are added and removed from the stacks and queues. Most texts on C++ do not mention this technique, yet in-place construction does lead to a more robust design.

Binary Trees

L inked-lists are examples of linear non-contiguous data structures, where movement takes place in a single dimension (forward and backward). In this chapter, we'll discuss a form of non-linear, non-contiguous data structures known as *trees*, which add a second up/down dimension. In particular, we'll explain special types of trees known as *binary trees*, which are useful in search operations.

WHAT ARE TREES?

A tree is a hierarchical collection of nodes. One of the nodes, known as the *root*, is at the top of the hierarchy. Each node can have at most one link coming into it. The node where the link originates is called the *parent node*. The root node has no parent. The links leaving a node (any number of links are allowed) point to *child* nodes. Trees are recursive structures. Each child node is itself the root of a *subtree*. At the bottom of the tree are *leaf nodes,* which have no children.

There is a directionality to the links of a tree. In the strictest definition of a tree, the links point down the tree, but never up. In addition, a tree cannot contain cycles. That is, no path originating from a node can return to that node. Figure 10.1(a) shows a set of nodes that have the properties of trees. Figure 10.1(b) shows a set of nodes that do not constitute a tree. That's because node *d* has two parents, and two cycles are present (*a-b-d* and *a-c-d*).

Trees represent a special case of more general structures known as *graphs*. In a graph, there are no restrictions on the number of links that can enter or leave a node, and cycles may be present in the graph. See the companion volume [Flamig 93] for a discussion of graphs.

Figure 10.1 A tree and a non-tree.

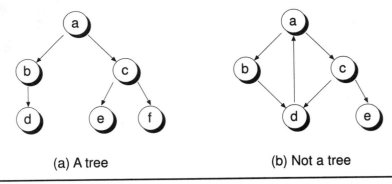

(a) A tree   (b) Not a tree

Every tree has a *height*, which is defined as the maximum number of nodes that must be visited on any path from the root to a leaf. For instance, the tree in Figure 10.1(a) has a height of 3. In turn, the *depth* of a node is the number of nodes along the path from the root to that node. For instance, node *c* in Figure 10.1(a) has a depth of 1.

Trees provide a natural way to represent the hierarchical relationship of data. For example, Figure 10.2 shows a tree representing the hierarchical organization of a company. Figure 10.3 shows an example of a tree representing the expression $a*b+c$. Here, the operators $*$ and $+$ have an order of precedence, where $+$ binds looser than $*$.

Note In many of the figures in this chapter—including Figures 10.2 and 10.3—the direction of the arrows is implied. Unless otherwise shown, the direction is always from the root downward.

Figure 10.2 An organization tree for a typical company.

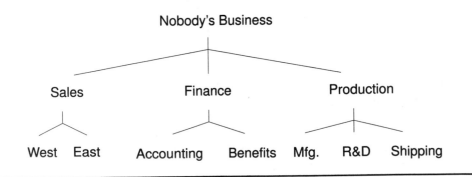

Figure 10.3 An expression tree.

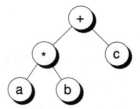

Binary Trees

In general, tree nodes can have any number of children. In a *binary tree*, the nodes have no more than two children. Figures 10.1(a) and 10.3 are examples of binary trees. Figure 10.2 isn't a binary tree because several of its nodes have three children. A node in a binary tree isn't required to have two children. For example, node *b* in Figure 10.1(a) has only one child. Of course, the leaves of a binary tree have no children.

Binary trees are easy to implement because they have a small, fixed number of child links. Because of this characteristic, binary trees are the most common type of trees and form the basis of many important data structures.

Binary Tree Node Classes

As was true for the linked-list nodes described in Chapter 8, it's useful to define an abstract binary tree node class that doesn't store data, and then derive, using templates, a family of node classes holding different types of data. The following *Bnodeb* and *Bnode* classes use this technique:

```
struct Bnodeb {  // An abstract binary tree node
  Bnodeb *left;  // Pointer to left child
  Bnodeb *right; // Pointer to right child
};

template<class TYPE>
struct Bnode : public Bnodeb { // Binary tree node with data
  TYPE info;
  Bnode();
  Bnode(const TYPE &x, Bnode<TYPE> *l=0, Bnode<TYPE> *r=0);
  Bnode<TYPE> *&Left();
  Bnode<TYPE> *&Right();
};

template<class TYPE>
```

```
Bnode<TYPE>::Bnode()
{
  left = 0; right = 0;
}

template<class TYPE>
Bnode<TYPE>::Bnode(const TYPE &x, Bnode<TYPE> *1, Bnode<TYPE> *r)
: info(x)
{
  left = 1; right = r;
}

template<class TYPE>
Bnode<TYPE> *&Bnode<TYPE>::Left()
{
  return (Bnode<TYPE> *)left;
}

template<class TYPE>
Bnode<TYPE> *&Bnode<TYPE>::Right()
{
  return (Bnode<TYPE> *)right;
}
```

The *Bnodeb* and *Bnode* class definitions are given on disk in the files *bnodeb.h* and *bnode.h*.

Many of the binary tree operations are data independent. That's the reason for the *Bnodeb* class. We can write functions that take *Bnodeb* pointers as parameters and share these functions across all binary trees, regardless of the type of data actually stored in the nodes. This tames the source code explosion that might otherwise result from the use of templates.

We do pay a price for allowing data independence. When we need to use nodes with data, typecasting problems occur. For instance, the following code fragment will not compile without the typecast shown:

```
Bnode<int> *t;
...
t = (Bnode<int> *)(t->left); // Base to derived typecast
```

Presumably, all nodes in the tree *t* store integer data. However, *left* is typed as a pointer to *Bnodeb* object, so we need to typecast the expression *t->left* to be a *Bnode<int>* pointer. You've seen a similar problem with the linked list nodes described in Chapter 8. The solution is the same: provide convenient functions that hide the typecasting. That's the purpose of *Left()* and *Right()*. We can rewrite our code fragment as:

```
Bnode<int> *t;
...
t = t->Left();
```

Note carefully that *Left()* and *Right()* actually return references to pointers. This approach allows us to use these functions on the left side of assignments. For instance:

```
Bnode<int> *t, *p;
...
t->Left() = p;
```

Actually, we don't need to use the *Left()* function in this case, due to the one-way assignment compatibility between derived and base types. For instance, we could write

```
Bnode<int> *t, *p;
...
t->left = p; // Implicit derived to base typecast
```

In the code that follows, we use the pointers *left* and *right* directly whenever we can, since the syntax is simpler. We use *Left()* and *Right()* only when necessary. All this typecasting is a bother, but we can't entirely eliminate it and still allow for the use of data-independent code.

The *Bnode<TYPE>* class has two constructors that are convenient for building trees. The constructors set the left and right pointers to null, unless you specify otherwise. In the following example, we'll build the tree shown in Figure 10.3:

```
Bnode<char> a('a'), b('b'), c('c');
Bnode<char> times('*', &a, &b);
Bnode<char> plus('+', &times, &c);
```

You'll notice that *Bnodeb* and *Bnode* are declared to have all public members. With the linked list nodes described in Chapter 8, we used encapsulation to the fullest, being careful to make all members private when possible. For binary tree nodes, the logistics involved in using fully encapsulated objects get very tedious and messy. For instance, we'll write many standalone functions that operate on *Bnodeb* pointers—to provide maximum code sharing. While we could make all of these functions friends, and thus make the members of *Bnodeb* private, it's arguable that little is gained by doing this.

TREE TRAVERSALS

Navigating through trees is at the heart of all tree operations, so it's useful to examine the common issues that arise in tree navigation. The methods we'll show for binary trees can be modified for more general trees.

A *tree traversal* is a method of visiting every node in the tree. By "visit," we mean that some type of operation is performed. For example, you may wish to print the contents of the nodes. Four basic traversals are commonly used:

1. In a *preorder traversal*, first the root is visited, then the left subtree, and then the right subtree, recursively.

2. In an *inorder traversal*, first the left subtree is visited, then the root, and then the right subtree, recursively.

3. In a *postorder traversal*, first the left subtree is visited, then the right subtree, and then the root, recursively.

4. In a *level-order traversal*, the nodes are visited level by level, starting from the root, and going from left to right.

Figure 10.4 shows the expression tree presented in Figure 10.3, and the results of traversing the tree using the four types of traversals (where the "visit" function prints node contents). In the context of expression trees, preorder traversal yields what is known as the *polish notation* for the expression, inorder traversal yields the *infix notation* (with parenthesis removed, though), and postorder traversal yields the *reverse polish notation*.

The traversals all have symmetrical cases. For instance, we've defined the traversals to go from left to right. They could alternatively be defined to go right to left, although that is less common in practice.

We'll now explore the first three traversal algorithms, since they can be coded similarly. Level-order traversal will be discussed later.

Recursive Traversals

The first three traversal algorithms are recursive in nature. They must walk down the tree and then back up. Recall, however, that the links of a tree go downward,

---

Figure 10.4 The four tree traversals.

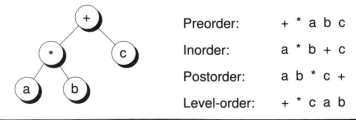

Preorder:	+ * a b c
Inorder:	a * b + c
Postorder:	a b * c +
Level-order:	+ * c a b

---

not upward. Thus, to move back up the tree, each visited parent must be saved for later use. A stack is the natural data structure to use here. As you walk down the tree, parent node pointers can be pushed on the stack. When you go up the tree, these pointers can be popped from the stack. Later, we'll show how to use an explicit stack for this purpose. But first, we'll use the implicit processor stack by writing recursive functions for the traversal algorithms. Here are three such functions, along with a defined type, *VisitFunc*, which points to a function to be used for the visit action:

```
typedef void (*VisitFunc)(Bnodeb *n);

void PreOrder(Bnodeb *t, VisitFunc Visit)
{
  if (t) {
    Visit(t);
    PreOrder(t->left, Visit);
    PreOrder(t->right, Visit);
  }
}


void InOrder(Bnodeb *t, VisitFunc Visit)
{
  if (t) {
    InOrder(t->left, Visit);
    Visit(t);
    InOrder(t->right, Visit);
  }
}

void PostOrder(Bnodeb *t, VisitFunc Visit)
{
  if (t) {
    PostOrder(t->left, Visit);
    PostOrder(t->right, Visit);
    Visit(t);
  }
}
```

The only difference between these functions is the placement of the *Visit()* calls. The placements intuitively suggest the type of traversal that takes place. You'll notice that these functions use generic *Bnodeb* pointers, and thus they will work for all binary trees. The trick lies in defining the *Visit()* function to work with the type of nodes actually being used. For example, here's how we might set up traversals of the tree given earlier in Figure 10.3:

```
void PrtChNode(Bnodeb *b)
{
```

```
     cout << ((Bnode<char> *)b)->info << ' ';
}

Bnode<char> a('a'), b('b'), c('c');
Bnode<char> times('*', &a, &b);
Bnode<char> plus('+', &times, &c);

PreOrder(&plus, PrtChNode);  cout << '\n';
InOrder(&plus, PrtChNode);   cout << '\n';
PostOrder(&plus, PrtChNode); cout << '\n';
```

Note the typecast in *PrtChNode()*. The function must conform to the function pointer type *VisitFunc*, and thus its parameter must be typed as a *Bnodeb* pointer. The function assumes, however, that the node is really a *Bnode<char>* node. All caveats apply for such typecasts.

Eliminating Tail Recursion

Since recursion uses processor stack space, it's desirable to eliminate or reduce the recursion as much as possible. In our tree-traversal algorithms, the amount of stack space consumed depends on the height of the tree. That is, for a tree of height *n*, *n* parent nodes are placed on the stack. So, for our recursive functions, the recursive calls are up to *n* levels deep.

Look carefully at the *PreOrder()* and *InOrder()* functions. In these functions, nothing follows the last recursive calls. This type of recursion is known as *tail recursion*. In a tail-recursive call, the local variables are saved on the processor stack, but they don't really need to be since no action follows the recursive call that needs those variables. Thus, tail recursion can be optimized by eliminating the recursive call and turning it into iteration. For example, here is the *PreOrder()* function written with tail recursion transformed into a *while* loop. The *InOrder()* function can be coded similarly:

```
void PreOrder(Bnodeb *t, VisitFunc Visit)
// Tail recursion eliminated
{
  while(t) {
    Visit(t);
    PreOrder(t->left, Visit);
    t = t->right;
  }
}
```

Instead of a call to *PreOrder(t->right)*, *t* is simply set to *t->right* and the *while* loop cycles until a null pointer is found. Note that the recursive call for *t->left* cannot be eliminated since this call is not tail recursive. Also, no call in *PostOrder()* is tail recursive, so we can't optimize that function any further.

Flattening out Recursion

In the recursive calls, the parent node pointer, the *Visit* function pointer, and the return address are all saved on the processor stack. However, we actually only need to save the parent node pointer. The recursion can thus be optimized by using an explicit stack that saves only node pointers. In doing so, we can also flatten out the recursion and turn it completely into iteration.

The following *PreOrderFlat()* function, modified from the *PreOrder()* function given earlier with tail recursion eliminated, shows the use of an explicit stack:

```
void PreOrderFlat(Bnodeb *t, VisitFunc Visit)
{
  ListStk<Bnodeb *> path;

  while(1) {
    if (t) {
      Visit(t);
      // Simulate call PreOrderFlat(t->left, Visit);
      path.Push(t);
      t = t->left;
    }
    else {
      // Simulate function return
      if (path.Pop(t) == 0) break;
      // Optimize the tail recursion
      t = t->right;
    }
  }
}
```

Here, we've used the *ListStk* class from Chapter 9, holding pointers to *Bnodeb* nodes. This stack represents the current path of parents through the tree. Note how the call to *PreOrder(t->left)* is replaced by a *Push()*, followed by the assignment *t = t->left*. In the original recursive function, the function returns when *t* is null. This is simulated by doing a *Pop()* from the stack. An *InOrderFlat()* function can be similarly defined. Simply move the *Visit()* call so that it immediately precedes the statement *t = t->right*.

It's not as easy to turn postorder traversal into iteration because we have no tail recursion to start with. In the *PostOrder()* function, two recursive calls are placed back to back. To use an explicit stack, we must keep track of which recursive call we are in so that we know how to simulate the function return.

After the first recursive call, we must pop the parent pointer from the stack and then do another recursive call. After the second recursive call, we must pop the parent from the stack and then visit the node.

Figure 10.5 shows the three different movements that take place during a post order traversal:

1. Down to the left
2. Up from the left and down to the right
3. Up from the right and then on up the tree.

We can keep track of these movements with a binary state variable. In one state, we're going down the tree. In the other state, we're going up the tree. However, we must clarify whether we're coming up from the left or right. Note that the stack only stores the parent pointer, not which side of the parent we are on. We *could* store that information as well, but there's a better way. After popping the parent from the stack, we can compare its left or right child pointer to the node we're currently on to determine which side we are coming from. The following *PostOrderFlat()* function utilizes this method:

```
void PostOrderFlat(Bnodeb *t, VisitFunc Visit)
{
  ListStk<Bnodeb *> path;
  int state = 0;

  while(1) {
    if (state == 0) {
      // Ready to go down to the left
      if (t) {
         path.Push(t);
         t = t->left;
      }
      else state = 1;
    }
    else { // State 1: Ready to come up from either direction
```

Figure 10.5 The three movements in a traversal.

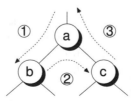

```
      Bnodeb *c = t;
      if (path.IsEmpty()) break;
      t = *path.Top();
      if (c == t->left && t->right) {
         // Coming back up the tree from the left, and
         // since there is a right child, go right.
         // Note that t is still on top of stack.
         t = t->right;
         state = 0;
      }
      else {
         // Coming back up the tree from the right,
         // or there was no right child, so visit
         // the node and continue on up. (State
         // stays at 1.)
         Visit(t);
         path.Pop();
      }
    }
  }
}
```

This function has some further optimizations in it. Notice in state 1 that we inspect the top of the stack (which holds the parent), rather than popping it. With this approach, we don't have to turn around and push the parent back on the stack, in case we need to go down to the right.

The binary tree traversal functions can be found on disk in the file *bnodeb.cpp*.

To Recurse or Not to Recurse

At first glance, it appears you would always want to use the flat traversal functions since they use less stack space. But the flat versions aren't necessarily better. For instance, some overhead is associated with the use of an explicit stack, which may negate the savings we gain from storing only node pointers. Use of the implicit function call stack may actually be faster due to special machine instructions that can be used.

The flat traversal functions are useful when the node processing you need to do doesn't depend on where you are in the traversal. Printing the nodes in sequence is one example of this. However, for some tree operations, you must manage more variables than just the nodes themselves. The states of these variables must also be saved on some type of stack. For these operations, using an explicit stack can become more cumbersome than using straightforward recursion. For example, here is a postorder recursive function to find the height of a tree:

```
int Height(Bnodeb *t)
{
  int h = 0;
  if (t != 0) {
     int lh = Height(t->left);
     int rh = Height(t->right);
     h = ((lh > rh) ? lh : rh) + 1;
  }
  return h;
}
```

The height of a tree is the maximum of the height of its two subtrees. In this case, it's easier to write the function recursively. The flat version is awkward and error prone.

Level-Order Traversal

The level-order traversal of a tree (where you go from top to bottom, left to right, level by level) is different from the other traversals because it is not recursive. A queue is needed instead of a stack. The following *LvlOrder()* function shows how the traversal can be accomplished:

```
void LvlOrder(Bnodeb *t, VisitFunc Visit)
{
  ListQ<Bnodeb *> nodes_left;

  nodes_left.Insert(t);

  while(1) {
    Bnodeb *p;
    if (nodes_left.Extract(p) == 0) break;
    Visit(p);
    if (p->left != 0) nodes_left.Insert(p->left);
    if (p->right != 0) nodes_left.Insert(p->right);
  }
}
```

In this function, we maintain a queue of nodes to be processed. Nodes are pulled off the queue one at a time, visited, and then the children of the nodes are inserted onto the end of the queue. The net effect is a level order traversal, as shown earlier in Figure 10.4.

TREE WALKING ITERATORS

One interesting way of performing tree traversals is to use *iterator objects*. With iterators, it's possible to sequence through a collection of objects at a high level. An iterator is first initialized to point to a particular collection of objects (such as a linked list, array, or tree) and then, using a function such as *Next()*, we can ask the iterator to give us the next object in sequence. The iterator object keeps track of the state of the iteration between calls to *Next()*. When used on trees, an iterator allows us to "flatten" out a tree and abstract what we mean by "next object."

The following *TreeWalkerb* class shows how to define an iterator for traversing a binary tree, using any of the four traversal orderings given earlier. This class is written generically using *Bnodeb* pointers and can thus be shared by all types of binary trees:

```
enum WalkOrder { pre_order, post_order, in_order, lvl_order };

class TreeWalkerb { // Tree-walking base class
protected:
  ListSQ<Bnodeb *> path;
  Bnodeb *root, *curr;
  WalkOrder worder;
  int state;
  Bnodeb *NextPreOrder();
  Bnodeb *NextInOrder();
  Bnodeb *NextPostOrder();
  Bnodeb *NextLvlOrder();
  Bnodeb *(TreeWalkerb::* NextFptr)();
public:
  TreeWalkerb(Bnodeb *r, WalkOrder w);
  virtual ~TreeWalkerb();
  void Reset();
  void Reset(Bnodeb *r, WalkOrder w);
  Bnodeb *Next();
};
```

Complete code for the *TreeWalkerb* class is given on disk in the files *twalk.h* and *twalk.cpp*. In addition, a derived template class, *TreeWalker,* is provided to work with specific *Bnode<TYPE>* trees.

A *TreeWalkerb* iterator is set up in the constructor by specifying the root of the tree you would like to walk and the traversal order, using the enumerated type *WalkOrder*. A *Reset()* function does all the work:

```
TreeWalkerb::TreeWalkerb(Bnodeb *r, WalkOrder w)
{
  Reset(r, w);
}

void TreeWalkerb::Reset(Bnodeb *r, WalkOrder w)
{
  root = r;
  worder = w;
  if (worder == pre_order) NextFptr = &TreeWalkerb::NextPreOrder;
  else if (worder == in_order) NextFptr = &TreeWalkerb::NextInOrder;
  else if (worder == post_order) NextFptr = &TreeWalkerb::NextPostOrder;
  else NextFptr = &TreeWalkerb::NextLvlOrder;
  state = 0; curr = root;
  path.Clear();
  if (root && worder == lvl_order) path.Insert(root);
}
```

An iterator object keeps track of the start of the tree being iterated, in the variable *root*, plus the node currently being traversed, in the variable *curr*, plus which traversal function to use in the function pointer variable *NextFptr*. Note that *NextFptr* is actually a pointer to a member function, which must be handled differently than ordinary function pointers. See [Stroustrup 91] for more details on member function pointers.

For an iterator object to work, it must keep the state of the iteration between calls to *Next()*. Since our traversals our recursive, a stack is needed. For postorder traversals, we also need the binary state variable that indicates whether we're going up or down the tree. In addition, we need a queue for level-order traversals. Rather than use both stack and queue objects, we use a combination *staque* object instead, which we call *path*.

The *Next()* function is used to return a pointer to the next node in sequence. *Next()* makes a call to the traversal function pointed to by *NextFptr*. (Notice the pointer-to-member function call, using the ->* operator.)

```
Bnodeb *TreeWalkerb::Next()
{
  return (this->*NextFptr)();
}
```

Four functions are provided for each type of traversal. These functions are adaptations of the flat-traversal functions given earlier. The difference is that they are member functions and thus have access to the stack stored in the iterator object. Also, instead of making a call to *Visit()*, the functions return a pointer to the node to be visited. Before doing the return, though, they must perform actions to ensure that the iterator can pick up where it left off in later calls to *Next()*. As an example, here is the *NextPreOrder()* function. You'll notice that it's very similar to the *PreOrderFlat()* function given earlier in the chapter. The other traversal functions can be defined in the same way:

```
Bnodeb *TreeWalkerb::NextPreOrder()
{
  while(1) {
    if (curr) {
      path.Push(curr);
      Bnodeb *p = curr;
      curr = curr->left;   // Set up for next visit
      return p;            // So the node can be "visited"
    }
    else {
      if (path.Pop(curr) == 0) {
        return curr = 0;   // Signal no more nodes
      }
      else curr = curr->right;
    }
  }
}
```

Here is an example of a function that will print out the nodes of a tree using a *TreeWalkerb* object with all four traversal orders:

```
void PrintNode(Bnodeb *t)
// Assumes node is actually a Bnode<char> node
{
  cout << ((Bnode<char> *)t)->info << '\n';
}

void PrintTreeOrderings(Bnode<char> *root)
{
  Bnodeb *nxt;

  if (root == 0) { cout << "Tree is empty\n"; return; }

  cout << "PreOrder:    ";
  TreeWalkerb tw(root, pre_order);
  while((nxt = tw.Next()) != 0) PrintNode(nxt);
  cout << '\n';

  cout << "InOrder:     ";
  tw.Reset(root, in_order);
  while((nxt = tw.Next()) != 0) PrintNode(nxt);
  cout << '\n';
```

```
  cout << "PostOrder:    ";
  tw.Reset(root, post_order);
  while((nxt = tw.Next()) != 0) PrintNode(nxt);
  cout << '\n';

  cout << "Level Order: ";
  tw.Reset(root, lvl_order);
  while((nxt = tw.Next()) != 0) PrintNode(nxt);
  cout << '\n';
}
```

A *TreeWalkerb* iterator has the same problems as the flat-traversal functions. It works great when the nodes can be processed out of context—that is, without regard to where the nodes are in the tree—but it isn't so great when that context must be used in the processing. For example, it's difficult to write the *Height()* function we gave earlier using an iterator. In contrast, it's easy (if somewhat inefficient) to write a function that counts the number of nodes in the tree, as shown in the following function:

```
int NumNodes(Bnodeb *t)
// Determine number of nodes in the tree t
{
  Bnodeb *nxt;
  int cnt = 0;
  TreeWalkerb tw(t, in_order); // Any ordering will do
  while((nxt = tw.Next()) != 0) cnt++;
  return cnt;
}
```

Printing Trees

When you debug code that works with binary trees, it's useful to print the trees, with the structure of the tree clearly shown. In this section, we'll provide two types of tree printing functions that help in this regard. These functions use the traversal functions given in the previous sections, and they assume very little about the type of screen or printer output available. All that's needed is the C++ *iostream* object *cout* to print the nodes line by line.

Printing Sideways

The following *PrintSideWays()* function will print a tree sideways, with the root of the tree on the left and the rightmost node on the first line. Figure 10.6 shows an example.

Figure 10.6 A tree printed sideways.

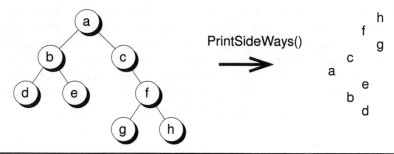

```
typedef void (*PrtFunc)(Bnodeb *n);

void PrintSideWays(Bnodeb *t, PrtFunc PrtNode, int inc, int space)
{
  while(t) {
    PrintSideWays(t->right, PrtNode, inc, space+inc);
    for(int i = 0; i<space; i++) cout << ' ';
    PrtNode(t); cout << '\n';
    t = t->left;
    space += inc;
  }
}
```

This function works by using a recursive inorder traversal of the tree. Note, however, that the traversal takes place from right to left, rather than the usual left to right strategy. This means the first node printed is the rightmost node. At each stage in the recursion, we keep track of the number of spaces to print before the node itself is printed. The *space* variable keeps track of the total (which should start at zero), and *inc* specifies the spacing to allow between nodes. Since the function is written generically using *Bnodeb* pointers, the function pointer *PrtNode* determines the actual function to call in doing the printing. This function is supposed to know the type of data actually stored in the nodes. Here's how *PrintSideWays()* can be called to print the tree given in Figure 10.6:

```
void PrtChNode(Bnodeb *t) { cout << ((Bnode<char> *)t)->info; }

Bnode<char> *t;
... // Set up t to be the tree in Figure 10.6
PrintSideWays(t, PrtChNode, 3, 0);
```

Printing Upright

While printing sideways is straightforward, the output isn't as easy to use as output that's printed upright. However, upright printing is much harder to do, unless your output device supports random-access positioning. Here, we'll develop a routine that prints a tree upright, line by line.

The key to easy upright printing is to make two passes. The first pass determines the position of each node in the tree. Once the positions are determined, a second pass uses a level-order traversal of the tree to print the nodes line by line.

To keep things simple, we'll assume that each node in the tree is given its own column and that nodes at the same level (that is, having the same depth) are printed on the same line. Thus, the line coordinate (which we'll call y) is equal to the depth of the node. The column, or x coordinate, can be found by the following observation: If you examine the tree shown in Figure 10.7, you'll notice that the node having an x position of one will be the first node visited in an inorder traversal, the node having an x position of two will be the second node visited, and so on.

The following *GetNodePosn()* function uses an inorder traversal to determine the (x,y) positions of each node in a tree. Here, *NodeWidth* is a pointer to a function that's supposed to return the printing width of a given node:

```
typedef int (*NodeWidthFunc)(Bnodeb *n);

BnodeXY *GetNodePosn(Bnodeb *t, int &x, int y, NodeWidthFunc NodeWidth)
// Using an inorder traversal, figure out x and y of each node
// in the tree t, assuming that the top left corner of the
// box bounding t is at (x, y). Builds a parallel shadow tree
// of nodes having x and y in them.
{
  if (t == 0) return 0;
  BnodeXY *1 = GetNodePosn(t->left, x, y+1, NodeWidth);
```

Figure.10.7. A row- and column-aligned tree.

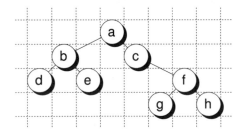

Inorder: d b e a c g f h

```
    BnodeXY *xyt = new BnodeXY;
    xyt->left = 1;
    xyt->x = x;
    x += NodeWidth(t);
    xyt->y = y;
    y++;
    xyt->right = GetNodePosn(t->right, x, y, NodeWidth);
    return xyt;
}
```

One major problem lies in finding a place to store the node position information. You could always include *(x, y)* fields in the nodes themselves. However, that would limit the generality of the function. The *GetNodePosn()* function uses a different technique. It builds an auxilary *shadow tree* that has the same structure of the tree being traversed. The nodes of this shadow tree keep track of node positions. The node type is given by the following *BnodeXY* structure, derived from *Bnodeb*:

```
struct BnodeXY : public Bnodeb {
  int x, y;
  BnodeXY *Left()  { return (BnodeXY *)left; }
  BnodeXY *Right() { return (BnodeXY *)right; }
};
```

After the node positions have been determined, the tree nodes can be printed line by line, using a level-order traversal, with the *x* position of the nodes determining the spacing between the nodes. The following *PrintUp()* function gives the details:

```
void PrintUp(Bnodeb *t, PrtFunc PrtNode, NodeWidthFunc NodeWidth)
{
  int spacing, last_sp, x, oldy;
  Bnodeb *nxt;
  BnodeXY *xynxt;

  if (t == 0) { cout << "Empty tree\n"; return; }

  x = 1;
  BnodeXY *xyt = GetNodePosn(t, x, 0, NodeWidth);

  TreeWalkerb tw(t, lvl_order);
  TreeWalker<BnodeXY> xytw(xyt, lvl_order);

  oldy = 0;
  last_sp = 0;
  while(1) {
    xynxt = xytw.Next();
```

```
      if (xynxt == 0) break;
      if (xynxt->y != oldy) {
         oldy = xynxt->y;
         cout << '\n';
         last_sp = 0;
      }
      spacing = xynxt->x - last_sp - 1;
      if (spacing < 0) spacing = 0;
      while(spacing--) cout << ' ';
      nxt = tw.Next();
      PrtNode(nxt);
      last_sp = xynxt->x + NodeWidth(nxt) - 1;
   }
   cout << "\n\n";

   // Need to delete shadow tree. Easy to do with postorder traversal
   xytw.Reset(xyt, post_order);
   while(1) {
      xynxt = xytw.Next();
      if (xynxt == 0) break;
      delete xynxt;
   }
}
```

Note that two level-order iterators are used in *PrintUp()* (the latter uses the *TreeWalker* template class) to traverse both the main tree and the shadow tree in parallel. You may wonder why we need to store the y position of each node. During a level-order traversal using an iterator, there's no way to tell when we've gone to a new level. Remember that using an iterator loses the shape information of the tree. (In fact, none of the iterative traversals, by themselves, provide enough shape information to reconstruct the tree. See [Lings 86] for more discussion of tree reconstruction.) We detect when a new level has been reached by comparing the y coordinate of the current node with that of the previous node.

Figure 10.8 shows the printed result for the tree shown in Figure 10.7. We used the following code to print the tree:

```
void PrtChNode(Bnodeb *t)
{
   cout << ((Bnode<char> *)t)->info;
}

int ChNodeWidth(Bnodeb *t)
{
   return 1; // This is the printing width
}
```

```
Bnode<char> *t;
// Build tree in Figure 10.7
...
PrintUp(t, PrtChNode, ChNodeWidth);
```

Complete code for printing a tree sideways and upright is given in the files *treeprt.h*, *treeprt.mth*, and *treeprt.cpp*.

BINARY SEARCH TREES

Next, we look at a special class of trees known as *binary search trees*. A binary search tree has binary nodes and the following additional property: Given a node *t*, each node to the left is "smaller" than *t*, and each node to the right is "larger." This definition applies recursively down the left and right subtrees. Figure 10.9 shows a binary search tree where characters are stored in the nodes.

Figure 10.9 also shows what happens if you do an inorder traversal of a binary search tree: you'll get a list of the node contents in sorted order. In fact, that's probably how the name *inorder* originated.

You may wonder what we mean by "smaller" and "larger" in our definition. This depends on the type of data being stored at the nodes. If, for instance, the data is integers, then the meaning of smaller and larger is obvious. More typically, though, the node data is some kind of structure, with one of the fields (called the *key*) used to make comparisons. Next, we'll explain how to search a binary tree and how to set up the comparisons for any type of node.

Binary Tree Searching

An algorithm for searching a binary search tree follows immediately from the binary search tree property. Although the search algorithm can be cast in a recursive fashion, it's just as easy (and more efficient) to write it iteratively. Here is a *Search()* function that shows how this is done:

Figure 10.8 A tree printed upright.

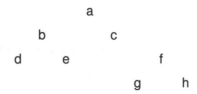

Figure 10.9 A binary search tree.

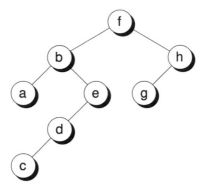

Inorder: a b c d e f g h

```
template<class TYPE>
Bnode<TYPE> *Search(Bnode<TYPE> *t, const TYPE &x)
// Returns pointer to a node matching the data x if
// such a node is in the tree t; otherwise, a 0 is returned
{
  while (t) {
    if (x == t->info) break;
    t = (x < t->info) ? t->Left() : t->Right();
  }
  return t;
}
```

Figure 10.10 shows the path taken when searching for a node in a sample tree. The *Search()* function assumes that *TYPE* has the comparison operators '==' and '<'defined. In the case where *TYPE* is a built-in type—such as integer or character—this is easy because the operators are already defined. But suppose *TYPE* is a structure that holds a customer name and a unique integer id. We could use either field as the search key. Here's how you might define the customer structure using the name as the key:

```
struct Customer {
  char name[80];
  int id;
  Customer(char *n, int i=0); // Notice default argument
};
```

Figure 10.10 Searching a binary tree.

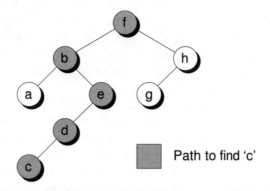

Path to find 'c'

```
Customer::Customer(char *n, int i)
{
  strncpy(name, n, 80);
  name[79] = 0; // Ensure null termination
  Id = i;
}

int operator==(Customer &a, Customer &b)
{
  return !strcmp(a.name, b.name);
}

int operator<(Customer &a, Customer &b)
{
  return strcmp(a.name, b.name) < 0;
}

... // Other operators similarly defined

Bnode<Customer> *custdb;
...// Build the tree, then search it
if (Search(custdb, "Ford Prefect")) cout << "Customer found\n";
```

Note that the search string gets converted by the constructor into a *Customer* object (the Id is given a default value). Obviously, more direct and efficient arrangements are possible. Sometimes, only the key is stored in the nodes, along with a pointer to the actual data. That is also easy to set up. The details are highly application dependent.

Why Use Binary Search Trees?

Binary search trees provide an efficient way to search through an ordered collection of objects. Consider the alternative of searching an ordered list. The search must proceed sequentially from one end of the list to the other. On average, $n/2$ nodes must be compared for an ordered list that contains n nodes. In the worst case, all n nodes might need to be compared. For a large collection of objects, this can get very expensive.

The inefficiency is due to the one-dimensionality of a linked list. We would like to have a way to jump into the middle of the list, in order to speed up the search process. In essence, that's what a binary search tree does. It adds a second dimension that allows us to manuever quickly through the nodes. In fact, the longest path we'll ever have to search is equal to the height of the tree. The efficiency of a binary search tree thus depends on the height of the tree. We would like the height to be as small as possible. For a tree holding n nodes, the smallest possible height is $\log n$, so that's how many comparisons are needed on average to search the tree.

To obtain the smallest height, a tree must be *balanced*, where both the left and right subtrees have approximately the same number of nodes. Also, each node should have as many children as possible, with all levels being full except possibly the last. Searching a well-constructed tree can result in significant savings. For example, it takes an average of 20 comparisons to search through a million nodes! Figure 10.11 shows an example of a well-constructed tree.

Unfortunately, trees can become so unbalanced that they're no better for searching than linked lists. Such trees are called *degenerate trees*. Figure 10.12 shows an example. For a degenerate tree, an average of $n/2$ comparisons are needed, with a worst case of n comparisons—the same as for a linked list.

When nodes are being added and deleted in a binary search tree, it's difficult to maintain the balance of the tree. We'll investigate methods of balancing trees in the next chapter. In this chapter, we'll use simple tree-construction methods. These methods may result in very unbalanced trees, depending on what order we insert nodes in the tree.

Figure 10.11 A well-constructed binary search tree.

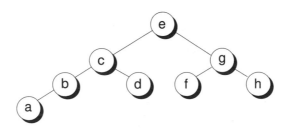

Figure 10.12 A degenerate binary search tree.

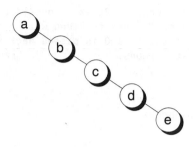

Inserting Nodes into a Binary Search Tree

When adding nodes to a binary search tree, we must be careful to maintain the binary search tree property. This can be done by first searching the tree to see whether the key we're about to add is already in the tree. If the key can't be found, a new node is allocated and added at the same location where it would go if the search had been successful. The following *Add()* function shows this technique:

```
template<class TYPE>
Bnode<TYPE> *Add(Bnode<TYPE> *&root, const TYPE &x, int &exists)
// Returns matching node, new or old. May modify the root pointer.
{
  Bnode<TYPE> *p;
  int side;

  // Look for a place to insert the node
  Bnode<TYPE> *t = SearchP(root, x, p, side);

  if (t == 0) { // No matching node found
    t = new Bnode<TYPE>(x); // left and right should be set to 0
    if (p) {
      if (side) p->right = t; else p->left = t;
    }
    else root = t; // No parent, so we have a new root
    existed = 0;
  }
  else existed = 1;

  return t;
}
```

Note that *Add()* calls a function, *SearchP()*, to determine where the node should be added. The *SearchP()* function is a modification of *Search()* that returns the parent of the matching node, as well as the matching node itself:

```
template<class TYPE>
Bnode<TYPE> *
SearchP(Bnode<TYPE> *t, const TYPE &x, Bnode<TYPE> *&p, int &side)
// Returns matching node in tree t, along with parent. If
// matching node is t itself, a 0 is passed back for the parent.
// Returns 0 if no match found.
{
  p = 0;
  while (t) {
    if (x == t->info) break;
    p = t;
    if (x < t->info) {
        side = 0;
        t = t->Left();
    }
    else {
        side = 1;
        t = t->Right();
    }
  }
  return t;
}
```

The *SearchP()* function keeps track of which side of the parent the matching node occurs on—in the variable called *side*. This isn't strictly necessary because we could do an extra compare in *Add()* to determine the side. The following code fragment, taken from *Add()* and modified, shows how:

```
if (p) {
    // Used to be: if (side) p->right = t; else p->left = t;
    if (p->info < x) p->right = t; else p->left = t;
}
```

If the comparison is an expensive operation, it's best to use the *side* variable instead. Figure 10.13 shows what happens when we use the *Add()* function to add some nodes to a tree.

Figure 10.13 Inserting nodes into a binary search tree.

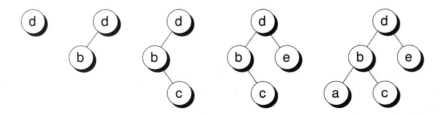

Deleting Nodes from a Binary Search Tree

Deletions from a binary search tree are more involved than insertions. Given a node to delete, we need to consider these three cases:

1. The node is a leaf.
2. The node has only one child.
3. The node has two children.

Case 1 is easy to handle because the node can simply be deleted and the corresponding child pointer of its parent set to null. Figure 10.14 shows an example. Case 2 is almost as easy to manage. Here, the single child can be promoted up the tree to take the place of the deleted node, as shown in Figure 10.15.

Case 3, where the node to be deleted has two children, is more difficult. We must find some node to take the place of the one deleted and still maintain the binary search tree property. There are two obvious candidates: the inorder predecessor and the successor of the node. We can detach one of these nodes from the tree and insert it where the deleted node used to be. A moment's reflection should convince you that using either of these nodes as the replacement will still maintain the binary search tree property.

Figure 10.14 Deleting a leaf node.

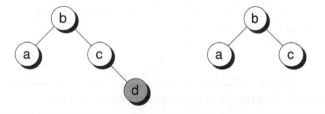

Figure 10.15 Deleting a node that has one child.

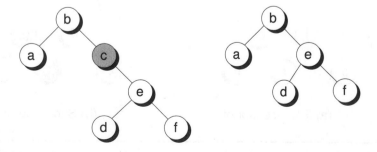

The predecessor of a node can be found by going down to the left once, and then all the way to the right as far as possible. To find the successor, an opposite traversal is used: first to the right, and then down to the left as far as possible. Figure 10.16 shows the path taken to find both the predecessor and successor of a node in a sample tree.

Both the predecessor and successor nodes are guaranteed to have no more than one child, and they may have none. (Think about how the traversals take place: they always end when the corresponding left or right child is null.) Because of this, detaching the predecessor or successor reduces to either Case 1 or 2, both of which are easy to handle. In Figure 10.17, we delete a node from the tree and use its successor as the replacement.

For the replacement, many texts suggest that you copy the data of the replacement node into the node that would have been detached, and then detach the replacement. However, if the node data is large, this involves a lot of data movement. In fact, it defeats one of the reasons for using a non-contiguous data structure! We'll perform the replacement by leaving the node data where it is, and use pointer surgery instead. That's the approach taken by the following *DetachNode()* function. This function is written generically using *Bnodeb* pointers, reinforcing the fact that no data is actually moved:

```
Bnodeb *DetachNode(Bnodeb *&root, Bnodeb *t, Bnodeb *p, int side)
// Detaches node t with parent p from the tree. Node t is
// the left child if side = 0; otherwise, it's the right child.
// If p is 0, then it is the root, and that is handled
// accordingly. Redundantly returns the pointer t. May
// have to update root pointer.
{
```

Figure 10.16 Finding predecessor and successor nodes.

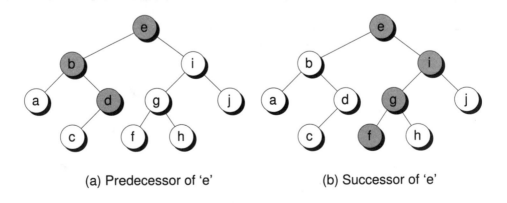

(a) Predecessor of 'e'   (b) Successor of 'e'

Figure 10.17 Deleting a node that has two children.

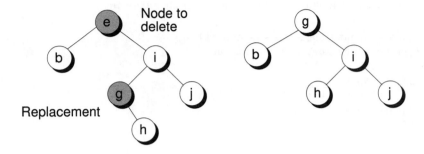

(a) Before deleting 'e'   (b) After deleting 'e'

```
Bnodeb *psucc, *replacement;

if (t) {
    if (t->left == 0 || t->right == 0) {
        // At least one child is null, so use the other
        // as the replacement. (It may be null, too.)
        replacement = (t->left) ? t->left : t->right;
    }
    else { // Neither child is null
        psucc = ParentOfSuccessor(t); // Guaranteed not null
        if (psucc == t) { // Immediate successor
            replacement = psucc->right;
        }
        else {
            // Detach replacement from its current location
            // and relocate it to where t used to be
            replacement = psucc->left;
            psucc->left = psucc->left->right;
            replacement->right = t->right;
        }
        // Finish relocating replacement to go where t used to be
        replacement->left = t->left;
    }
    if (p) { // Fix parent of t to point to replacement
        if (side)
            p->right = replacement; else p->left = replacement;
    }
    else root = replacement; // No parent, so t was the root
}
return t;
}
```

The *DetachNode()* function uses the following *ParentOfSuccessor()* function to find the parent of the successor node. We want the parent so that we can easily detach the successor from its original location:

```
Bnodeb *ParentOfSuccessor(Bnodeb *t)
// If no successor, a 0 is returned
{
  Bnodeb *p = 0;
  // Go right, then all the way left
  Bnodeb *q = t->right;
  if (q) {
    p = t;
    while(q->left) {
      p = q;
      q = q->left;
    }
  }
  return p;
}
```

Both *DetachNode()* and *ParentOfSuccessor()* can be written generically with *Bnodeb* pointers. We don't need to do any key comparisons since the structure of the tree lets us find the nodes we're looking for.

The *DetachNode()* function is called by higher-level functions that determine which node to detach. For example, here's a *Detach()* function that first searches for a node having matching data to *x*, and then proceeds to detach that node:

```
template<class TYPE>
Bnode<TYPE> *Detach(Bnode<TYPE> *&root, const TYPE &x)
// Detaches node matching x from the tree.
// May have to update the root pointer.
{
  int side;
  Bnode<TYPE> *p, *t;

  t = SearchP(root, x, p, side);
  return (Bnode<TYPE> *)DetachNode((Bnodeb *)root, t, p, side);
}
```

Finally, to actually deallocate the node, we use the following *Delete()* function:

```
template<class TYPE>
int Delete(Bnode<TYPE> *&root, const TYPE &x)
// Returns 1 if node actually found; otherwise, returns 0
// May have to update the root pointer
{
```

```
  Bnode<TYPE> *n = Detach(root, x);
  delete n;
  return n != 0;
}
```

Clearing and Copying Binary Trees

Deleting all the nodes from a tree can be done recursively, using a postorder traversal. The following *Clear()* function clears a tree by calling a recursive *DelTree()* function:

```
template<class TYPE>
void Clear(Bnode<TYPE> *&root)
{
  DelTree(root);
  root = 0;
}

template<class TYPE>
void DelTree(Bnode<TYPE> *t)
{
  if (t == 0) return;
  DelTree(t->Left());
  DelTree(t->Right());
  delete t;
}
```

By using postorder traversal, the nodes are deleted from the bottom up. Note that it would be difficult to use any other type of traversal here because we would have to delete nodes before we're through with them. The *DelTree()* function can alternatively be written non-recursively, using a postorder iterator object:

```
template<class TYPE>
void Bstree<TYPE>::DelTree(Bnode<TYPE> *t)
{
  TreeWalker< Bnode<TYPE> > tw(t, postorder);
  Bnode<TYPE> *nxt;
  while((nxt = tw.Next()) != 0) delete nxt;
}
```

To copy a tree, you must first clear the destination tree and then duplicate the nodes of the source tree. The following *Copy()* function calls the *Clear()* function and then calls a recursive *DupTree()* function to do the node duplication. The latter function uses postorder traversal to build the duplicate tree from the bottom up:

```
template<class TYPE>
int Copy(Bnode<TYPE> *&root, const Bstree<TYPE> &t)
{
  Clear(root);
  Bnode<TYPE> *r = DupTree(t.root);
  if (r) {
     root = r;
     return 1;    // Success
  }
  else return 0; // Failure
}

template<class TYPE>
Bnode<TYPE> *DupTree(Bnode<TYPE> *t)
{
  if (t == 0) return 0;
  Bnode<TYPE> *l = DupTree(t->Left());
  Bnode<TYPE> *r = DupTree(t->Right());
  return new Bnode<TYPE>(t->info, l, r);
}
```

Here's an interesting twist to the technique for copying trees: Use an iterator object on the source tree, traverse the tree in some order, and insert duplicated nodes into the destination tree by using the *Add()* function. The following alternative *Copy()* function does this:

```
template<class TYPE>
int Copy(Bnode<TYPE> *&root, const Bstree<TYPE> &t, WalkOrder w)
{
  Clear(root);
  TreeWalker< Bnode<TYPE> > tw(t.root, w);
  Bnode<TYPE> *nxt;
  int dmy;
  while((nxt = tw.Next()) != 0) Add(root, nxt->info, dmy);
  return 1;
}
```

Figure 10.18 shows the results when we use the four different types of traversals on the source tree during copying. Notice that both preorder and level-order traversals produce a destination tree that has the same structure as the source tree. A postorder traversal yields a different structure, but it's still a valid binary search tree.

As you can see, the order that you insert nodes into a binary search tree does make a difference. In fact, if you insert nodes into a tree in sorted order, as exemplified by the inorder traversal copying in Figure 10.18, the result is a degenerate tree. This fact suggests you should avoid inserting nodes into a

Figure 10.18 Copying via source tree traversals.

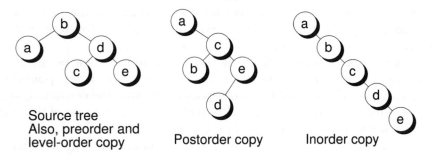

Source tree
Also, preorder and
level-order copy

Postorder copy

Inorder copy

binary search tree in sorted order. In the next chapter, we'll look at ways of circumventing this problem.

THREADED BINARY TREES

You'll notice that operations like *Add()* and *Delete()* are awkward due to the unidirectional capability of the links. We must write the operations in terms of finding the parent of a desired node, rather than find the node directly. This problem is similar to those we had with singly-linked lists in Chapter 8. The clumsiness can be alleviated by adding an extra pointer in each node, which points to the parent of the node. The result is known as a *threaded binary tree*. Figure 10.19 shows an example. A threaded tree is to a normal tree what a doubly-linked list is to a singly-linked list—it allows easy traversal in both directions. Note that, in a strict sense, a threaded binary tree isn't a true tree because it has cycles.

By using a threaded binary tree, it's possible to write the tree-traversal routines without recursion and without a stack. Since a stack isn't needed, tree operations can be faster, due to reduced overhead. However, before you try to reimplement all the algorithms you've seen in this chapter, keep in mind that the price you pay is space overhead in the tree nodes. (This is the same speed

Figure 10.19 A threaded binary tree.

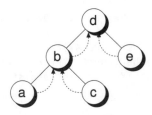

vs. space tradeoff you've seen repeatedly.) You pay for the overhead of parent pointers with every node, regardless of whether you need those pointers. When you use a stack, you pay for the overhead of the stack only when needed, and that overhead grows with the height of the tree, not with the number of nodes in the tree.

We're not recommending that you avoid using parent pointers, only that you be sure to consider the tradeoffs. Code without parent pointers is only slightly more complicated than code with them. After the operations are coded, the fact that they may be a little clumsly becomes a moot point. For maximum speed, however, you may want to use parent pointers.

As a final note, we should tell you that you can implement other forms of threaded trees. For example, one particular type uses extra pointers that allow you to directly find the next and previous nodes assuming an inorder traversal. See [Horosahni 90] for details.

BINARY TREES AS CONCRETE DATA TYPES

We've used standalone functions to implement the basic binary tree operations. However, it might be useful to encapsulate these into a class and to make binary trees look like concrete data types. The following *Bstree* class shows an example:

```
template<class TYPE>
class Bstree { // A binary tree of nodes holding TYPE data
protected:
  Bnode<TYPE> *root;
  Bnode<TYPE> *SearchP(const TYPE &x, Bnode<TYPE> *&p, int &side);
  virtual Bnode<TYPE> *AllocNode
    (const TYPE &x, Bnode<TYPE> *l=0, Bnode<TYPE> *r=0);
  Bnode<TYPE> *DupTree(Bnode<TYPE> *t);
  virtual void FreeNode(Bnode<TYPE> *n);
  void DelTree(Bnode<TYPE> *t);
public:
  Bstree();
  Bstree(const Bstree<TYPE> &t);
  virtual ~Bstree();
  void operator=(const Bstree<TYPE> &t);
  int Copy(const Bstree<TYPE> &t);
  int Copy(const Bstree<TYPE> &t, WalkOrder w);
  void Clear();
  Bnode<TYPE> *Member(const TYPE &x);
  const Bnode<TYPE> *Member(const TYPE &x) const;
  Bnode<TYPE> *Add(const TYPE &x, int &existed);
```

```
  Bnode<TYPE> *Add(const TYPE &x);
  Bnode<TYPE> *Detach(const TYPE &x);
  Bnode<TYPE> *DetachMin();
  Bnode<TYPE> *DetachMax();
  int Delete(const TYPE &x);
  void DeleteMin();
  void DeleteMax();
  Bnode<TYPE> *Root();
  Bnode<TYPE> *Min();
  Bnode<TYPE> *Max();
  int IsEmpty() const;
};
```

Complete code for the *Bstree* class is given on disk in the files *bstree.h*, *bstree.mth*, and *bstreeb.cpp*. A test program is provided in *tstbs.cpp*. This program uses the tree-walking and tree printing functions given earlier in the chapter.

A *Bstree* object serves as a handle to a binary tree. Stored in each *Bstree* object is a pointer, *root*, to the top node of the tree. Many of the functions we gave earlier passed the root of the tree as the first argument. These functions can be adapted for the *Bstree* class by removing the first argument, and relying instead on the implicit *this* pointer that's passed. For example, here's the new *Add( )* function:

```
template<class TYPE>
Bnode<TYPE> *Bstree<TYPE>::Add(const TYPE &x, int &exists)
{
  Bnode<TYPE> *p;
  int side;

  Bnode<TYPE> *t = SearchP(x, p, side);

  if (t == 0) {
    t = AllocNode(x);
    if (p) {
      if (side) p->right = t; else p->left = t;
    }
    else root = t;
    existed = 0;
  }
  else existed = 1;

  return t;
}
```

Summary

The *Bstree* class is set up like most the concrete data type classes in this book—with ample constructors, destructors, overloaded assignment operators, and so on. Whether or not you need all these functions is, of course, up to you. We've added some functions that retrieve and delete the minimum and maximum nodes from the tree. The minimum node can be found by going left as far as possible. The maximum node can be found by going right as far as possible.

Similar to the linked-list classes defined in Chapter 8, we've provided the virtual functions *AllocNode()* and *FreeNode()*, which you can override to change how the tree nodes are allocated. For example, a binary tree can be stored contiguously using an array of nodes, as well as on the heap with non-contiguous nodes.

A few hints for building trees with arrays: You'll want to maintain a singly-linked free list of deleted tree nodes. This can be done by reusing the *left* (or, alternatively, *right*) child pointers to serve as the free list's *next* pointers. Also, nothing prevents you from dispensing with pointers altogether and instead using two parallel arrays of indexes that correspond to the *left* and *right* child links.

If you don't plan on overriding *AllocNode()* and *FreeNode()*, you can declare them as static, along with the recursive functions *DupTree()* and *DelTree()*. This will result in more efficient code, since in the recursive function calls, the implicit *this* pointer won't be passed.

Balanced
Trees

I n Chapter 10, we explained that, for maximum efficiency, a binary search tree should be balanced. However, the tree-construction algorithms we gave can lead to decidedly unbalanced trees. In this chapter, we'll explore some of the techniques you can use to keep trees balanced. In particular, we'll look at *2-3-4 trees* and *red-black trees*.

DEGENERATE TREES

Very unbalanced trees are referred to as *degenerate trees*, so called because their searching performance degenerates to that of linked lists. Figure 11.1 shows two examples of degenerate trees. The first tree was built by inserting the keys *a* through *i* in sorted order into a binary search tree. The second tree was built using the insertion sequence *a-i-b-h-c-g-d-f-e*. This pathological sequence is often used to test the balancing capability of a tree. Figure 11.2 shows what the tree in Figure 11.1(b) would look like if it were balanced.

INTERNAL AND EXTERNAL NODES

At this point, we need to define two terms: *internal node* and *external node*. An internal node is a tree node having at least one key, and possibly some children. So far, all we've shown are internal nodes. It's sometimes convenient to have another type of node, called an external node, and pretend that all null child links point to such a node. An external node doesn't exist, but serves as a conceptual placeholder for nodes to be inserted.

Figure 11.1 Degenerate trees.

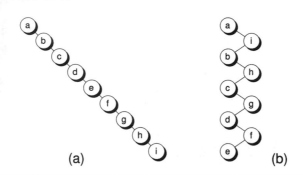

(a)   (b)

In this chapter, we'll draw internal nodes using circles, with letters as labels. External nodes are denoted by drawing links leading nowhere, and perhaps labelled using numbers, or they may not be drawn at all. Figure 11.3 shows a sample tree illustrating both internal and external nodes.

Sometimes we'll draw only a portion of a tree, with the top node of this portion having an implied parent (or no parent at all if it's the root). Subtrees are indicated using the same notation as external nodes, by drawing links leading nowhere and having numbers for labels. In fact, you can consider an external node to be an empty subtree.

There is a reason for treating external nodes and subtrees the same. In the tree transformations to come, we'll strive to maintain certain properties of the trees. In the drawings we'll show, those properties will be maintained regardless of whether labelled links are external nodes or subtrees, assuming the properties held before the transformations, of course.

Figure 11.2 A balanced tree.

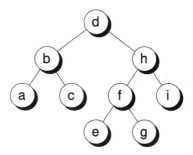

Figure 11.3 Internal and external nodes.

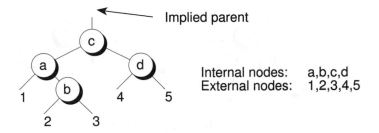

Internal nodes: a,b,c,d
External nodes: 1,2,3,4,5

BALANCING ACTS

There are two basic ways used to keep trees balanced:

1. Use tree rotations.
2. Allow nodes to have more than two children.

Tree Rotations

Certain types of tree-restructurings, known as *rotations*, can aid in balancing trees. Figure 11.4 illustrates the two types of *single rotations*.

The following sample code for single rotations uses generic *Bnodeb* pointers (as defined in Chapter 10), and assumes that all relevant pointers aren't null:

```
Bnodeb *RotateRight(Bnodeb *p, Bnodeb *t)
// Rotate right around p, assuming t is p's left child
// Returns t, which will be the new child of p's parent
{
  p->left = t->right;
  t->right = p;
  return t;
}

Bnodeb *RotateLeft(Bnodeb *p, Bnodeb *t)
// Symmetrical case
{
  p->right = t->left;
  t->left = p;
  return t;
}
```

Figure 11.4 Single rotations.

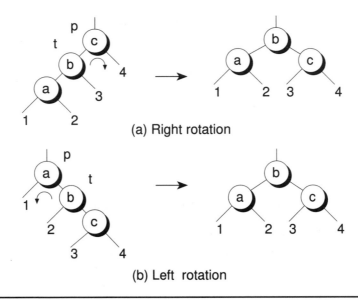

(a) Right rotation

(b) Left rotation

Another type of rotation is known as a *double rotation*. Figure 11.5 shows the two symmetrical cases. Here's the sample code:

```
Bnodeb *RotateLeftRight(Bnodeb *g, Bnodeb *p, Bnodeb *t)
// Rotate first around p, then around g. Assumes p is left
// child of g, and t is the right child of p. Returns new
// child of g's parent.
{
  p->right = t->left;
  t->left = p;
  g->left = t->right;
  t->right = g;
  return t;
}

Bnodeb *RotateRightLeft(Bnodeb *g, Bnodeb *p, Bnodeb *t)
// Symmetrical case
{
  p->left = t->right;
  t->right = p;
  g->right = t->left;
  t->left = g;
  return t;
}
```

Figure 11.5 Double rotations.

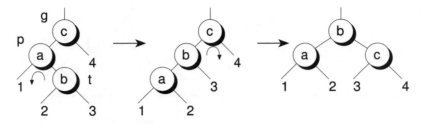

(a) Left-right rotation

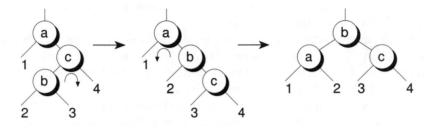

(b) Right-left rotation

Both single and double rotations have one important feature: inorder traversals of the trees before and after the rotations are preserved. Thus, rotations help balance trees, but still maintain the binary search tree property.

Rotations don't guarantee a balanced tree, however. For example, Figure 11.6 shows a right rotation that makes a tree more unbalanced. The trick lies in determining when to do rotations and what kind of rotations to do. The red-black trees discussed later have certain rules used to determine when and how to rotate.

Multi-Way Trees

We can also help keep trees balanced by allowing nodes to have more than two children. Instead of using binary trees, we can have multi-way trees. A multi-way tree node with n children is known as an *n-node*. An *n*-node has *n-1* keys that are used for comparisons. For example, Figure 11.7 shows a 4-node with three keys. Nodes with keys less than a are inserted down subtree 1. Nodes greater than a but less than b are inserted down subtree 2. Nodes greater than b but less than c are inserted down subtree 3. And finally, nodes with keys greater than c are inserted down subtree 4.

Figure 11.6 An unbalancing rotation.

For a given set of keys, a balanced multi-way tree will have a smaller height than a balanced binary tree, because more keys can be stored per node. In our 4-node example, we can collapse what would be two or three levels of a binary tree into one level. This ability to collapse levels makes multi-way trees easier to balance than binary trees.

One special type of multi-way tree is known as a *B-tree*, which we'll study in depth in Chapter 14. A B-tree of order *m* has nodes that can have up to *m* children. In this chapter, we'll look at B-trees of order four. Such trees are often called *2-3-4 trees*. A 2-3-4 tree has three types of nodes: 2-nodes (that is, binary nodes), 3-nodes, and 4-nodes. Figure 11.8 shows a sample 2-3-4 tree.

Insertion into a 2-3-4 tree works as follows: First, search the tree looking for the node to insert the new key into. If the candidate is a 2-node, then insert the key, making the node a 3-node. If the candidate is a 3-node, then insert the key, making the node a 4-node. If the candidate is a 4-node, it is full and must be split. The node is split into two 2-nodes, with the left key going to the left 2-node, the middle key moving up to the parent node, and the right key going to the right 2-node. The key to be inserted is then added to the appropriate 2-node.

Figure 11.9 shows how to split a 4-node, where there is no parent. The middle key is pushed up to a new root. If there is a parent, the parent itself may have to be split. The splitting process then propagates up the tree. Thus, insertion consists of a top-down searching pass, followed by a bottom-up splitting pass. Figure 11.10 shows an example of building a 2-3-4 tree using the same pathological sequence *a-i-b-h-c-g-d-f-e* that we've used before.

One consequence of 4-node splitting is that the tree grows upward, rather than downward as in a binary tree. As a result, the external nodes of a 2-3-4 tree are always on the same level, and the tree is quite balanced. (These same properties hold in general for all B-trees.)

Figure 11.7 A 4-node.

Figure 11.8 A 2-3-4 tree.

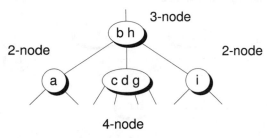

We won't actually implement 2-3-4 trees using the three different types of nodes. You can actually represent 2-3-4 trees using binary nodes, as we'll discuss next.

RED-BLACK TREES

A *red-black tree* is a binary representation of a 2-3-4 tree. (Red-black trees can be used to represent a wide variety of trees. See [GuibSedg 78].) In a red-black tree, the links are given the colors red and black. These colors are used in mapping the 2-node, 3-node, and 4-nodes of a 2-3-4 tree into binary nodes. Figure 11.11 shows the mappings. In this figure and others to follow, red links are shown with thick lines, whereas black links are shown with lines of normal thickness. A node having a black parent link is referred to as a *black node*. A node with a red parent link is a *red node*. In the diagrams, we chose to color the links using thin/thick lines (rather than actually coloring the nodes).

The red-black mappings work as follows: a 2-node is represented using a single binary node with two black children. A 3-node is represented as a pair of binary nodes—one red, one black. Hence there is a red link between the nodes. Note that 3-nodes can be represented with two different orientations. The orientation used depends on the balancing required, as you'll see later. A 4-

Figure 11.9 Splitting a 4-node.

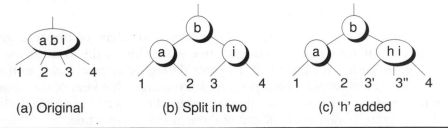

(a) Original   (b) Split in two   (c) 'h' added

Figure 11.10 Building a 2-3-4 tree.

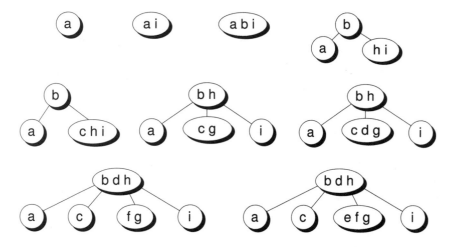

Insertion sequence: a-i-b-h-c-g-d-f-e

node is represented as a set of three binary nodes, with the parent node black and the child nodes red. Hence, two red links are used.

Three basic properties emerge from the way the red-black mappings are defined:

1. *There's no way to have two red links in a row on any path in the tree.* That's because there's no way to map this arrangement back to a 2-3-4 tree. (What kind of node would have both a red parent and a red child?)

2. *The external nodes of a red-black tree have the same black-depth.* The black-depth of a node is the number of black nodes found on the path from the root to that node. Remember that red links correspond to 3-nodes and 4-nodes, and thus don't contribute to the height of the equivalent 2-3-4 tree. This fact, coupled with the fact that external nodes of the 2-3-4 tree are at the same height, means that external nodes of a red-black tree have the same black-depth.

3. *The root node is always black.* Since the root doesn't have a parent, there's no way for it to have a red parent link.

Figure 11.12 shows the red-black tree equivalent of the tree given in Figure 11.10. Note that the red-black tree is structurally the same as the binary tree given earlier in Figure 11.2. The only difference is the coloring of the links. The link colors serve as guideposts in determining what kind of rotations to do when balancing the tree. Note that the external nodes all have a black-depth of 2. This corresponds to the height of the equivalent 2-3-4 tree.

Figure 11.11 Red-black mappings for 2-3-4 nodes.

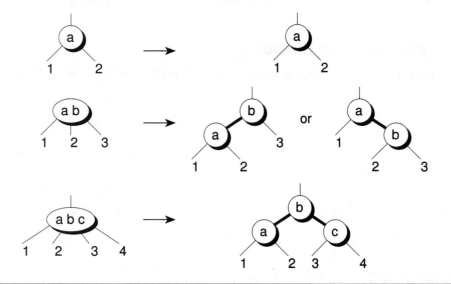

The tree shown in Figure 11.12 is fairly balanced, but isn't as balanced as its 2-3-4 tree counterpart, and is twice as high. Why the difference? The 3-nodes and 4-nodes of the 2-3-4 tree must be simulated using multiple binary nodes, each set consuming two levels of the tree. However, it can be shown that no path in a red-black tree is longer than twice as long as the shortest path in the tree. Thus, although the red-black trees aren't perfectly balanced, their worst case isn't all that bad.

Figure 11.13 illustrates an illegal red-black tree, with two consecutive red links in a row (*d-h* and *h-i*). Also, the external nodes have different black-depths as indicated in the figure. The resulting tree is still a valid binary search tree, but

Figure 11.12 A red-black tree.

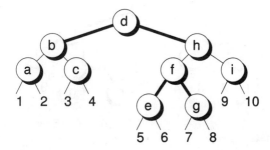

because it doesn't have the strict red-black tree properties, updates to the tree (assuming they could even be done) would tend to produce an unbalanced tree.

Red-Black Tree Classes

We'll represent red-black tree nodes with the following *RBnodeb* and *RBnode* classes:

```
#define RED 0
#define BLACK 1

struct RBnodeb : Bnodeb {
  char color;
  RBnodeb *&Left();
  RBnodeb *&Right();
};

template<class TYPE>
struct RBnode : RBnodeb {
  TYPE info;
  RBnode();
  RBnode(const TYPE &x, char c, RBnode<TYPE> *l=0, RBnode<TYPE> *r=0);
  RBnode<TYPE> *&Left();
  RBnode<TYPE> *&Right();
};
```

As with all designs, it's worthwhile to strive for data independence whenever possible. That's the purpose of the *RBnodeb* class. This class is derived from the *Bnodeb* class of Chapter 10, and adds a *color* field, but no other data. The color field represents the color of the link coming into the node—0 for red, 1 for black. We've represented color as a character, which represents additional

---

Figure 11.13 An illegal red-black tree.

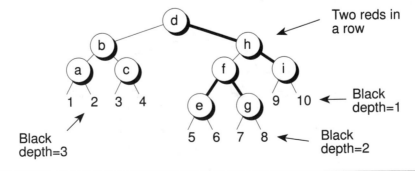

overhead in every red-black node. Actually, only one bit is required. In your own classes, you may be able to arrange this bit to be stored in some unused location in the node's data field. An alternative representation would have colors associated with the child links, rather than the nodes themselves. However, this requires two bits per node, rather than one.

Since *RBnodeb* is derived from *Bnodeb*, it can be used in many generic binary tree functions—such as the tree-traversal functions or the tree-walking iterators. The *RBnode* class is a template derived from *RBnodeb* that adds data to the node. Unfortunately, an *RBnode* object cannot be substituted for a *Bnode* object (a binary node with data), since the *info* field of these two types of nodes is at a different offset in the node structure. As usual, convenience functions *Left()* and *Right()* are supplied to help alleviate type casting problems. The details are given on disk.

The *RBtree* class implements red-black trees as concrete data types, with the appropriate constructors, destructors, assignment functions, and other supporting functions. This class is very similar in design to the *Bstree* class developed in Chapter 10. We'll look only at the main operations of searching, inserting, and deleting. The remaining details are given on disk.

```
template<class TYPE>
class RBtree {
protected:
  RBnode<TYPE> *root;
  // Other protected functions—such as AllocNode(), DupTree(),
  // FreeNode(), and DelTree()…
public:
  RBnode<TYPE> *Member(const TYPE &x);
  RBnode<TYPE> *Add(const TYPE &x, int &existed);
  RBnode<TYPE> *Detach(const TYPE &x);
  int Delete(const TYPE &x);
  // Constructor functions, plus other functions for copying,
  // clearing, and deleting trees, and functions for handling
  // min/max elements, and so forth…
};
```

Complete code for red-black trees is given on disk in the files *RBnode.h*, *RBtree.h*, *RBtreeb.cpp*, and *RBtree.mth*. A test program is given in the files *tstrb.cpp* and *tsttree.cpp*. Many of the files from Chapter 10 are used as support files.

Searching a Red-Black Tree

A red-black tree can be searched in the same way as an ordinary binary search tree, as the following *Member()* function shows. Note that the colors of the nodes are not used in the search. The fact that the tree is balanced in no way impinges on the searching code (other than to make the searches faster due to shorter trees, of course).

```
template<class TYPE>
RBnode<TYPE> *RBtree<TYPE>::Member(const TYPE &x)
// Returns pointer to node containing data x if
// such a node is in the tree t; otherwise, a 0 is returned
// ASSUMES TYPE has '<' and '==' defined.
{
  RBnode<TYPE> *t = root;
  while (t) {
    if (x == t->info) break;
    t = (x < t->info) ? t->Left() : t->Right();
  }
  return t;
}
```

Inserting into a Red-Black Tree

We described an insertion process earlier for 2-3-4 trees that involved two passes: a top-down pass to determine where the new key should go, and a bottom-up pass to handle any full 4-nodes that need to be split. It's possible to do the insertion in a single top-down pass, and that's the method we'll use for red-black trees.

Single-pass top-down insertions can be done by ensuring that the new key won't be added to a full leaf node. We can do this by splitting any 4-node we see on the path to the leaf into two 2-nodes. Splitting a 4-node, as represented with red-black nodes, is particularly easy. As Figure 11.14 illustrates, the process involves three color flips, and that's all. Note how the two child links are turned to black, but the parent link is turned to red. This is done to preserve the black-depths of the external nodes 1, 2, 3, and 4 (which may be subtrees). In all the red-black tree transformations to follow, we always ensure that the relative black-depths of the external nodes or subtrees are preserved. That way, we can guarantee that the new tree will still be a valid red-black tree. A side effect is that the tree will be kept as balanced as possible.

Since the top node of the split 4-node becomes red during a split, a problem occurs if its parent is also red, because we then end up with two reds in a row. This must be fixed by using appropriate rotations. We'll look at all the possible cases now.

Figure 11.15 shows the two orientations of a 4-node connected to a 2-node. In both orientations, we end up with a 3-node having two 2-nodes as children when the 4-node is split. The results are still legal red-black trees, so nothing else has to be done.

Figure 11.14 Splitting a 4-node.

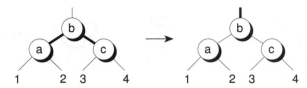

Figure 11.16 illustrates the three cases that occur when a 4-node is connected to a 3-node. Here, the 4-node can be the left child, middle child, or right child of the 3-node. Recall that, in a red-black representation, a 3-node has two orientations. Thus, there are six cases to consider in the red-black tree representations. In Figure 11.17, we show three of these cases. Figures 11.17(a) and 11.17(b) show the two cases that arise when the 4-node is the right child of the 3-node, with the two possible 3-node orientations. Not shown are the two symmetrical cases that occur when the 4-node is the left child. Figure 11.17(c) shows one of the cases that occurs when the 4-node is the middle child. Again, there is a symmetrical case not shown.

In Figure 11.17(a), splitting the 4-node leads to a valid red-black tree, so nothing more needs to be done other than the color flips. However, in Figures 11.17(b) and 11.17(c), splitting the 4-node leads to trees having two reds in a row. Thus, after the color flips, rotations must be performed to restore the red-black property. For the case in Figure 11.17(b), a single rotation is needed. For the case in Figure 11.17(c), a double rotation is required. Note that the colors "follow" the rotations. In all three figures, you should verify for yourself that the black-depths of the external nodes are preserved.

Figure 11.15 Splitting a 4-node connected to a 2-node.

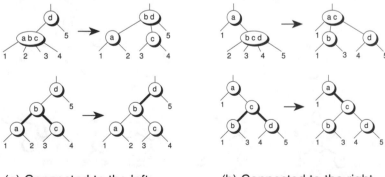

(a) Connected to the left   (b) Connected to the right

Figure 11.16 Splitting 4-nodes connected to 3-nodes.

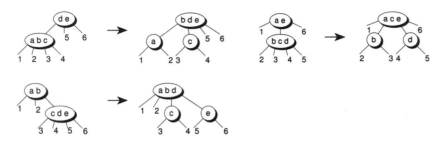

We don't need to be concerned about any 4-node to 4-node cases. That's because the parent 4-node will be split before we get to the child 4-node.

The insertion code is given in the routines *Add()* and *InsBalance()*. The *Add()* function walks down the tree looking for a place to insert the new key, splitting any 4-nodes along the way. After a split, there may be two red nodes in a row. If so, a call is made to *InsBalance()*, which performs the proper rotations. *Add()* keeps track of the current node *t*, its parent *p*, grandparent *g*, and great-grandparent *gg*, all of which are needed to do the rotations. To make the call to *InsBalance()* efficient, the pointers are packaged up into the structure *PtrPak*, and a single parameter is then passed for these pointers. A pointer to the root node is also passed, since the root may change due to a rotation.

Figure 11.17 Splitting 4-nodes connected to 3-nodes, red-black style.

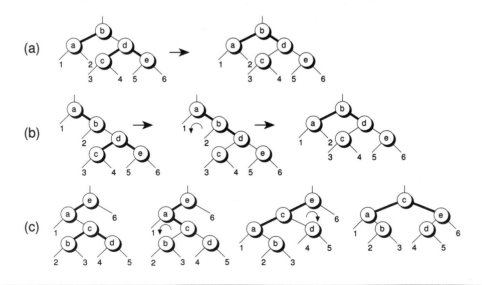

When the bottom of the tree is reached and the key to be inserted isn't found, a new node is added, colored red, and if needed, an adjusting balance is performed. (It's useful to pretend the new node is a black 4-node that is split, with its colors adjusted like any split 4-node.) If the key already exists, a flag is set to indicate that. It's important to realize that *Add()* may cause the tree to be restructured even if the key already exists.

If the root is a 4-node before the insertion, it will be "split" and the root becomes red. The *Add()* function corrects this situation by always setting the root black. During this color change, the black-depths of the external nodes increase by one, but the tree remains valid, since the black-depths are still all identical.

```cpp
struct PtrPack {
  RBnodeb *t, *p, *g, *gg, *s, *rs, *ls, *m, *pm;
};

template<class TYPE>
RBnode<TYPE> *RBtree<TYPE>::Add(const TYPE &x, int &exists)
// Add the key x to the tree if it doesn't already exist.
// Returns a pointer to the node containing the key, and
// sets the exists flag accordingly.
{
  PtrPack pp;
  int side;

  exists = 1;
  pp.t = root; pp.p = 0; pp.g = 0; pp.gg = 0;

  while(pp.t && x != ((RBnode<TYPE> *)(pp.t))->info) {
    // If on a 4-node, we must split it into two 2-nodes
    if ((pp.t->left && pp.t->Left()->color == RED) &&
        (pp.t->right && pp.t->Right()->color == RED)) {
      pp.t->color = RED;
      pp.t->Left()->color = BLACK;
      pp.t->Right()->color = BLACK;
      // Check for two reds in a row, and adjust if so
      if (pp.p && pp.p->color == RED)
        root = (RBnode<TYPE> *)InsBalance(root, pp);
        // else Figure 11.15 or Figure 11.17(a)
    }
    pp.gg = pp.g; pp.g = pp.p; pp.p = pp.t;
    if (x < ((RBnode<TYPE> *)(pp.t))->info) {
      pp.t = pp.t->Left(); side = 0;
    }
    else {
      pp.t = pp.t->Right(); side = 1;
    }
  }
```

```
   // Reached the bottom, with no matching node
   if (pp.t == 0) {
      exists = 0;
      pp.t = AllocNode(x, RED);
      if (pp.t == 0) return 0; // Couldn't add
      if (pp.p) {
         if (side) pp.p->right = pp.t; else pp.p->left = pp.t;
      }
      else root = (RBnode<TYPE> *)(pp.t);
      // Check for two reds in a row, and adjust if so
      if (pp.p && pp.p->color == RED)
         root = (RBnode<TYPE> *)InsBalance(root, pp);
   }

   root->color = BLACK; // Root always made black

   return (RBnode<TYPE> *)(pp.t);
}


// Define some macros for convenience

#define T  (pp.t)
#define P  (pp.p)
#define G  (pp.g)
#define GG (pp.gg)
#define S  (pp.s)
#define RS (pp.rs)
#define LS (pp.ls)
#define M  (pp.m)
#define PM (pp.pm)

RBnodeb *InsBalance(RBnodeb *root, PtrPack &pp)
// Balance adjusting for top-down insertions. Eliminates
// both p and t from being red by doing rotations and
// color changes. g, p, t are assumed not null coming in.
// gg may be null. At the end of this routine, only t
// and p will be valid with respect to each other. g and gg will
// not reflect the proper ordering.
   RBnodeb *cofgg; // New child of great-grandparent
   int side;

   side = GG && GG->right == G;

   if (G->left == P) {
      if (P->right == T) { // Do double rotate. (Figure 11.17(c))
         G->left = T->right;
         T->right = G;
```

```
           P->right = T->left;
           T->left = P;
           P = GG;
           cofgg = T;
        }
        else { // Do single rotate right. (Figure 11.17(b) reversed)
           G->left = P->right;
           P->right = G;
           cofgg = P;
        }
    }
    else { // G->right == p
      if (P->left == T) {   // Do double rotate. (Figure 11.17(c) reversed)
         G->right = T->left;
         T->left = G;
         P->left = T->right;
         T->right = P;
         P = GG;
         cofgg = T;
      }
      else { // Do single rotate left. (Figure 11.17(b))
         G->right = P->left;
         P->left = G;
         cofgg = P;
      }
    }
  }

  cofgg->color = BLACK;
  G->color = RED;

  if (GG) {
     if (side) GG->right = cofgg; else GG->left = cofgg;
  }
  else root = cofgg;

  return root;
}
```

Figure 11.18 shows an example of building a red-black tree using the pathological insertion sequence *a-i-b-h-c-g-d-f-e*. The resulting tree is equivalent to the 2-3-4 tree in Figure 11.10, except that the 4-node root has been split into two 2-nodes. Note that the tree is quite balanced.

Deleting from a Red-Black Tree

Recall from Chapter 10 how deletions work in a regular binary search tree: The basic idea is to swap the key of the node to be deleted with the key of the

---

Figure 11.18 Building a red-black tree.

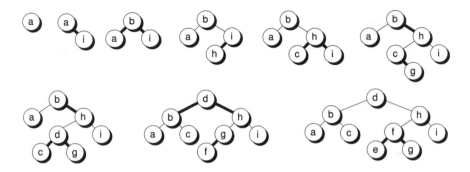

Insertion sequence: a-i-b-h-c-g-d-f-e

---

node's successor. (We used pointer surgery rather than actually swapping keys. Also, the predecessor could be used instead of the successor.) Then, the successor is deleted, which reduces to the case of removing a node with at least one null child. As we showed in Chapter 10, this case is easy to handle.

Deleting from a red-black tree works very much the same way. There's a catch, though: If the successor is black, and we remove it from the tree, then all the nodes under the successor (including any external nodes) will have their black-depths reduced by one, resulting in an illegal red-black tree. When the successor is red, this problem doesn't occur.

Thus, we must somehow handle the case where the successor is black. One approach is to ensure that the successor is always red. This can be done by a single top-down pass, in the following way: an "extra" red can be pushed down the tree as we work our way towards the successor. (We must also keep track of the node to be deleted when it is encountered.) Thus, when the successor is reached, it's guaranteed to be red. The trick is to keep the tree a valid red-black tree. We accomplish this by doing appropriate rotations and color flips, keeping the black-depths of all external nodes identical. Recall that this approach keeps the leaves of the equivalent 2-3-4 tree at the same level, and thus the tree remains fairly balanced.

From the viewpoint of the equivalent 2-3-4 tree, pushing an extra red down the tree involves three types of operations:

1. Merging two 2-nodes into a single 4-node.

2. Flipping the red-black orientations of 3-nodes.

3. Rotating 3-nodes and 4-nodes from one side of the tree to the other. The rotations always take place toward the side containing the current node being traversed.

Figure 11.19 shows examples of the first and third cases. The second case is not shown since it doesn't structurally change the equivalent 2-3-4 tree; it just changes the orientation of the red-black interpretation. Please note that these cases have other orientations not shown in the figure. It's interesting that the act of merging 2-nodes into 4-nodes is exactly the opposite of what we do during insertions, where 4-nodes are split in two. Thus, deletions are the opposite of insertions, with the added step of pushing an extra red down the tree.

Figures 11.20, 11.21, and 11.22 show the orientations and transformations for the three balancing operations, in terms of red-black trees. In all three figures, the node labelled *t* is the current node being traversed, *p* is its parent, *g* is its grandparent, *s* is its sibling, and *ls* and *rs* are the left and right children of *s*. Vertical lines shown for grandparents mean that the parent node can either be on the left or right. Dashed lines indicate links that can be either red or black. You should verify for yourself that the transformations shown preserve the relative black-depths of all external nodes.

The algorithm for deleting a node from a red-black tree is split into four procedures: *Delete()*, *Detach()*, *DelBalance()*, and *DoReplacement()*. The *Delete()* function (not given) calls *Detach()* to detach the node from the tree, and then frees the node. *Detach()* works by walking the tree from the top down, searching for the node to delete, recording its location, and then continuing to walk the tree pretending that the node wasn't found. By doing this, when a null node is reached, the current parent will be the successor node. All the while, rotations and color flips are done by calling *DelBalance()*. At the end, the *DoReplacement()* function is called to "swap" the key of the node to delete with the key of the successor. (Actually, the replacement is done by pointer surgery, rather than actually swapping the keys.)

Figure 11.19 Sample top-down deletion transformations.

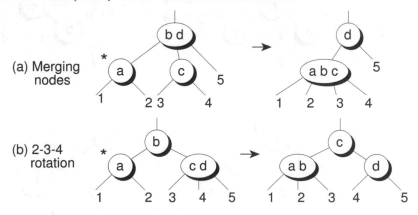

(a) Merging nodes

(b) 2-3-4 rotation

* Current node on traversal path

Figure 11.20 Case 1: Merging 2-nodes into a 4-node.

To save function-calling overhead, the necessary pointers are packaged into a *PtrPak* structure (defined earlier), which is then passed via another pointer. The root is also passed in case it needs to be updated.

Here are the *Detach()*, *DelBalance()*, and *DoReplacement()* functions. Note that *DelBalance()* and *DoReplacement()* are written using generic *RBnodeb* pointers and are thus shared by all red-black trees, regardless of the type of data they hold.

```
template<class TYPE>
RBnode<TYPE> *RBtree<TYPE>::Detach(const TYPE &x)
// Detaches (but does not free) the node having key x from the tree
{
  struct PtrPack pp;
```

Figure 11.21 Case 2: Reorienting a 3-node.

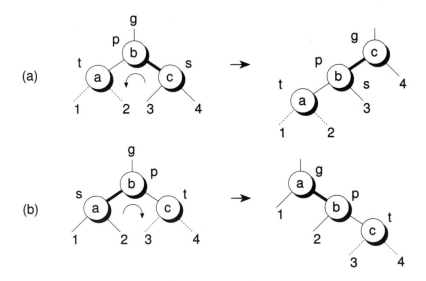

Figure 11.22 Case 3: Rotating 2-3-4 trees in red-black form.

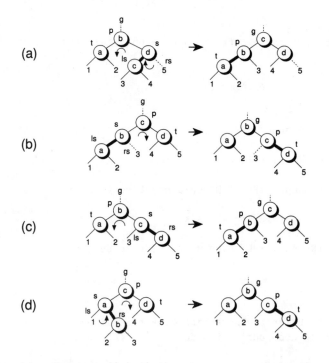

```
if (root == 0) return 0;

pp.t = root; pp.p = 0; pp.g = 0; pp.m = 0; pp.pm = 0;

while (pp.t) {

  // Go down the tree one level, searching for node to delete

  if ( ((RBnode<TYPE> *)(pp.t))->info == x ) {
     pp.m = pp.t;  // Record matching node
     pp.pm = pp.p; // And its parent
  }

  // Update ancestor pointers
  pp.g = pp.p; pp.p = pp.t;

  if (x < ((RBnode<TYPE> *)(pp.t))->info) {
     pp.t = pp.p->Left(); pp.s = pp.p->Right();
  }
  else {
```

```
            pp.t = pp.p->Right(); pp.s = pp.p->Left();
      }

      if (pp.s) {
          pp.ls = pp.s->Left(); pp.rs = pp.s->Right();
      }
      else {
          pp.ls = 0; pp.rs = 0;
      }

      root = (RBnode<TYPE> *)DelBalance(root, pp);

   } // end of while loop

   root = (RBnode<TYPE> *)DoReplacement(root, pp);

   if (root) root->color = BLACK;

   return (RBnode<TYPE> *)pp.m; // Node to delete

}


RBnodeb *DelBalance(RBnodeb *root, PtrPack &pp)
// Balancing code during top-down deletion
{
  if ((T == 0 || T->color == BLACK) && S && S->color == RED) {

      // Case 2: t black, s red. t might be null,
      // but s and p must not be. Flip the orientation
      // of the 3-node that s is a part of.

      // Fix g child to be s. Also s may become p of m
      if (G) {
          if (G->left == P) G->left = S; else G->right = S;
      }
      else root = S;
      if (P == M) PM = S;
      // Finish rotating
      if (P->left == T) { // Figure 11.21(a)
          // RotateLeft(p);
          P->right = LS;
          S->left = P;
          G = S;
          S = LS;
      }
      else { // Figure 11.21(b)
          // RotateRight(p);
```

```
          P->left = RS;
          S->right = P;
          G = S;
          S = RS;
      }
      // Fix children of s
      if (S) { LS = S->Left(); RS = S->Right(); }
      // Fixup colors
      P->color = RED; G->color = BLACK;
  }

  if (T && T->color == BLACK &&
      (T->left == 0 || T->Left()->color == BLACK) &&
      (T->right == 0 || T->Right()->color == BLACK)) {

      if (S && S->color == BLACK &&
          (S->left == 0 || S->Left()->color == BLACK) &&
          (S->right == 0 || S->Right()->color == BLACK)) {

        // Case 1: t and s are black 2-nodes. Merge them
        // into a 4-node. (Figure 11.20.)

        P->color = BLACK; T->color = RED; S->color = RED;

      }
      else if (LS && LS->color == RED) {

        // Case 3: t is a black 2-node, s is 3- or 4-node,
        // LS is red (RS might be). Rotate 3- or 4-node to
        // the side that t is on.

        if (P->left == T) { // Figure 11.22(b)
          // Fix colors
          LS->color = P->color; P->color = BLACK; T->color = RED;
          // Fix g child to be LS. Also LS may become p of m.
          if (G) {
              if (G->left == P) G->left = LS; else G->right = LS;
          }
          else root = LS;
          if (P == M) PM = LS;
          // Finish: DoubleRotateLeft(s, p)
          P->right = LS->left;
          LS->left = P;
          S->left = LS->right;
          LS->right = S;
          G = LS;
          // We won't fix s and children since they get re-assigned
          // at the top of next loop
```

```
      }
      else { // Figure 11.22(b)
         // Fix colors
         S->color = P->color; LS->color = BLACK;
         P->color = BLACK; T->color = RED;
         // Fix g child to be s. Also s may become p of m.
         if (G) {
            if (G->left == P) G->left = S; else G->right = S;
         }
         else root = S;
         if (P == M) PM = S;
         // Finish: RotateRight(p);
         P->left = RS;
         S->right = P;
         G = S;
         // We won't fix s and children since they get re-assigned
         // at the top of next loop
      }

   }
   else if (RS && RS->color == RED) {

      // Case 3: t is a 2-node, s is a 3-node, LS black, RS red
      // Rotate 3-node to the side of t

      if (P->left == T) { // Figure 11.22(b)
         // Fix colors
         RS->color = BLACK; S->color = P->color;
         P->color = BLACK; T->color = RED;
         // Fix g child to be s. Also, s may become p of m.
         if (G) {
            if (G->left == P) G->left = S; else G->right = S;
         }
         else root = S;
         if (P == M) PM = S;
         // Finish: RotateLeft(p);
         P->right = LS;
         S->left = P;
         G = S;
         // We won't fix s and children, since they get reassigned
         // at the top of next loop
      }
      else { // Figure 11.22(d)
         // Fix colors
         RS->color = P->color; P->color = BLACK; T->color = RED;
         // Fix g child to become RS. Also, RS may become p of m.
         if (G) {
            if (G->left == P) G->left = RS; else G->right = RS;
```

```
              }
              else root = RS;
              if (P == M) PM = RS;
              // Finish: DoubleRotateRight(s, p);
              P->left = RS->right;
              RS->right = P;
              S->right = RS->left;
              RS->left = S;
              G = RS;
              // We won't fix s and children, since they get reassigned
              // at the top of next loop
          }

      }
  }

  return root;
}


RBnodeb *DoReplacement(RBnodeb *root, PtrPack &pp)
{
  // At this point, m is the node to delete, pm is its parent,
  // p is the replacement node, g is its parent. If m has no
  // successor, p will = m, and replacement is the non-null
  // child of m.

  if (M) { // Matching node was found
    if (P == M || M->left == 0 || M->right == 0) {
      // No successor, and/or at least one child null
        // Get non-null child, if any; else p will be null
        P = (M->left) ? M->Left() : M->Right();
    }
    else { // m has a successor to use as a replacement
        if (G != M) {
          // Successor isn't immediate child of m, so detach
          // from where it is, attach to where m is
          G->left = P->right;
          P->right = M->right;
        }
        // Finish attaching where m is
        P->left = M->left;
    }
    // p should have same color as m since it's going where m was
    if (P) P->color = M->color;
  }

  // Fix pm child link to be p
```

```
if (M) {
    if (PM) {
        if (PM->left == M) PM->left = P; else PM->right = P;
    }
    else root = P; // New root, possibly null
}

return root;
}
```

Figure 11.23 shows the tree given in Figure 11.18 as it is destroyed by removing nodes in the sequence *e-f-d-g-c-h-b-i-a*.

There's one curious fact about the deletion algorithm. Even if the node to be deleted from the tree isn't found, the tree structure may still be modified, as node merging and tree rotations are performed in anticipation of a node deletion. If the *Detach()* routine is called repeatedly this way, the tree structuring will eventually converge onto a "stable" configuration.

BOUNDARY CONDITIONS

The insertion and deletion routines given in this chapter are complicated by the need to test for boundary conditions, such as non-existent parents, grandparents, children, or siblings. You'll notice explicit tests for null pointers in the code to handle these conditions. The routines can be simplified somewhat by creating a special sentinel node to be used for all otherwise non-existent nodes. This node can be colored black, and all null child links can be modified to point to this sentinel. For more details on using artificial nodes like this, see [GuibSedg 78].

Figure 11.23 Removing nodes from a red-black tree.

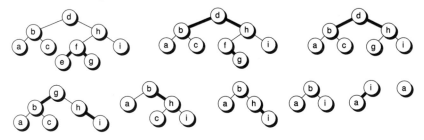

Removal sequence: e-f-d-g-c-h-b-i-a

SUMMARY

If you need to ensure that a binary search tree never degenerates to worst-case scenarios, then a 2-3-4 tree, as implemented using a binary red-black tree, is the data structure of choice. Recall that 2-3-4 trees are B-trees of order 4. It's possible to generalize the technique behind red-black trees to work for B-trees of any order, by having links with more than two color choices. However, it's not really beneficial to do this; it's better instead to implement B-trees directly with multi-way nodes. This is due to the I/O paging characteristics of most disk devices. For example, there will be some page size that corresponds to a B-tree node of a certain order that will be optimal for any given disk. We'll explore B-trees on disk in Chapter 14. Just remember that red-black trees are efficient implementations of B-trees of order 4 that happen to perform well in memory.

Splay
Trees

The balanced trees presented in Chapter 11 are optimal when the keys in the trees are accessed in a uniform way. However, if a few keys are accessed more frequently than others, a balanced tree isn't necessarily the best choice. It's better to have the most frequently used keys close to the top of the tree, so that the searching costs, amortized over the life of the tree, are optimal. We'll now take a look at data structures called *splay trees* that have this goal in mind. Splay trees were invented by D. Sleator and R. Tarjan. See [Sleatar 85] for the definitive paper on splay trees. These intriguing structures have many uses, but we'll examine them in the context of binary search trees and priority queues.

SELF-ORGANIZING TREES

A splay tree is an example of a *self-organizing structure* that adapts itself to changing conditions. The principle behind self organization is simple: When a node is accessed, it is moved to the top of the tree. Then, if the node is accessed again, it is available with only minimal searching. As the tree is used, the most frequently accessed nodes tend to float to the top. When the access patterns change, other keys float to the top.

Rotation is the best way to move a node to the top, since this approach preserves the binary search tree property. Various strategies are possible for choosing the rotations to perform. In one strategy, a single rotation is used to move the desired node one level closer to the root. Another strategy involves moving the node all the way to the top using a series of single rotations. Unfortunately, neither of these strategies performs well in practice. However, a third approach *does* a yield good results: *splaying*.

Bottom-Up Splaying

The splaying algorithm is similar to the previous strategy given in that it moves the desired node all the way to the root, but the movement is performed in a rigorously defined way. Assume that you have a pointer to the node you would like to move to the top. Three rules are involved, which are applied repeatedly from the bottom up until the node is at the root. (These rules assume you have some way to find the parent of a node.)

1. *Zig.* When the desired node is one level below the root, a single rotation is performed (called a *zig* in splaying parlance) to move the node to the root. Figure 12.1(a) shows an example. (There is also a symmetrical orientation, which is not shown.)

2. *Zig-zig.* When the desired node is more than one level deep, and the parent and grandparent are aligned the same way, two single rotations in the same direction (called a *zig-zig*) are performed to move the node closer to the root. Figure 12.1(b) shows an example. (Again, there is a symmetrical orientation not shown.)

3. *Zig-zag.* When the desired node is more than one level deep, and its parent and grandparent are aligned in opposite directions, then a double rotation (called a *zig-zag*) is performed. Figure 12.1(c) shows an example (with the symmetrical case omitted once again).

Figure 12.1 The three splaying cases.

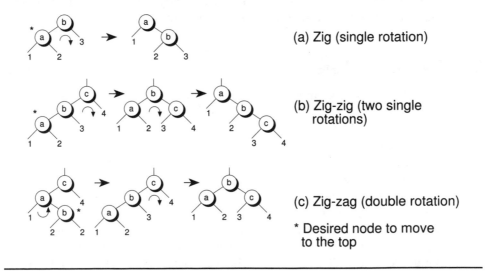

(a) Zig (single rotation)

(b) Zig-zig (two single rotations)

(c) Zig-zag (double rotation)

* Desired node to move to the top

Figure 12.2 shows a complete example of splaying, with all three rules being applied. In this example, node *c* is the desired node to be moved to the root. Note that the tree undergoes a large amount of restructuring. This is typical of splaying. Don't be misled by the fact that the final tree is more balanced than the original. Splaying can greatly unbalance the tree. For example, Figure 12.3 shows how accessing the nodes of a tree in sorted order can lead to a degenerate tree.

The purpose of splaying isn't to balance the tree, but rather to move the most frequently used nodes to the top. Splay trees have been found to have the following behavior: For a tree of *n* nodes, as many as *n* steps may be required to find any given node. This happens when searching for a node at the bottom of a degenerate tree. However, if a sufficiently long series of searches is performed, the searching averages out to just log*n* steps, due to the way splaying restructures the tree. In other words, splay trees have an amortized efficiency of log*n*, the same as for balanced trees. Unfortunately, splay trees have the same worst case that linked lists have.

Figure 12.2 Bottom-up splaying.

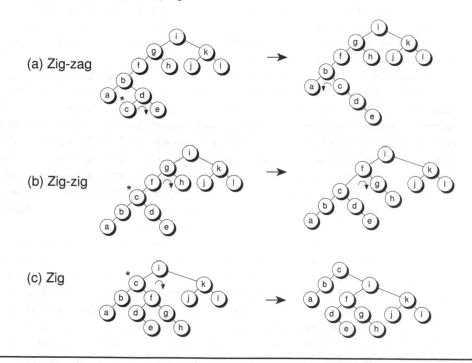

(a) Zig-zag

(b) Zig-zig

(c) Zig

Figure 12.3 Degenerate splaying.

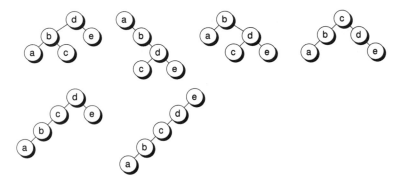

Splay sequence: a-b-c-d-e

Top-Down Splaying

So far, we've described splaying in terms of bottom-up operations. If splaying is used in conjunction with searching, this implies two passes: a top-down pass to find the node, and then the bottom-up splaying pass. The bottom-up pass requires that you either have saved the parent pointers on a stack on the way down or that each node stores a parent pointer.

It's possible to combine splaying and searching into a single top-down pass, eliminating the problem of finding the parents. In top-down splaying, the strategy is to split the tree into middle, left, and right subtrees. The middle subtree contains that portion of the splayed tree not yet visited. The left subtree contains those nodes known to be smaller than any node in the middle subtree, and the right subtree contains those nodes known to be greater than any node in the middle subtree. As we pass down the tree searching for the desired node, we perform the required splaying rotations and then split off chunks of the tree, attaching them to either the left or right subtrees. When the splaying is finished, the trees are combined again to produce the splayed tree.

In the figures to follow, the left subtree is labelled *L* and the right subtree is labelled *R*. The root nodes are actually dummy header nodes holding no data. In the left subtree, nodes are always attached on the right side. In fact, the attachment point, drawn as a black square, is always the right child of the maximum node. The left child link of *L*, which would otherwise be null, is used to point directly to the maximum node. When *L* is empty, we make the left child link point back to *L*. The right subtree has a symmetrical orientation, with the attachment point always the left child of the minimum node, and with the right child of *R* pointing to the minimum node.

As is true with bottom-up splaying, top-down splaying involves three configurations. The zig operation, which corresponds to a single rotation, is accomplished by cutting off part of the tree and attaching it to the appropriate subtree, depending on the direction of the rotation. Figure 12.4 illustrates the process. Note that the splayed node becomes the root of the middle subtree. The following *LinkRight()* and *LinkLeft()* routines show how the attachments can be coded. Here, *p* is the root of the middle subtree, and *l* and *r* point to the roots of the left and right subtrees, respectively. The routines use generic *Bnodeb* pointers, and thus are independent of the data stored in the nodes.

```
Bnodeb *LinkRight(Bnodeb *p, Bnodeb *r)
// p->left becomes the new parent of the tree that p
// used to belong to, so we return p->left
{
  Bnodeb *newp = p->left;
  p->left = 0;
  r->right->left = p; // Set left child of minimum node
  r->right = p;       // Point directly to minimum node
  return newp;
}

Bnodeb *LinkLeft(Bnodeb *p, Bnodeb *l)
// p->right becomes the new parent of the tree that p
// used to belong to, so we return p->right
{
  Bnodeb *newp = p->right;
  p->right = 0;
  l->left->right = p; // Set right child of maximum node
  l->left = p;        // Point directly to maximum node
  return newp;
}
```

Figure 12.4 Top-down zigging.

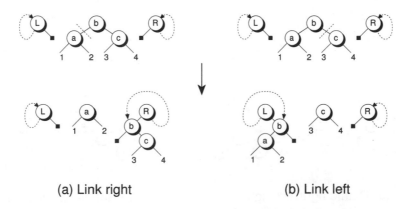

(a) Link right   (b) Link left

Figure 12.5 illustrates the zig-zig operation, in both the left and right orientations. Again, the splayed node becomes the root of the middle subtree. Recall that a zig-zig corresponds to two single rotations in the same direction. In top-down splaying, the last rotation is accomplished by either *LinkRight()* or *LinkLeft()*. The first rotation is handled by one of the following rotation routines: *RotateRight()* or *RotateLeft()*.

```
Bnodeb *RotateRight(Bnodeb *p)
// Rotates right about p. Returns a pointer
// to the node that takes the place of p.
{
  Bnodeb *t = p->left;
  p->left = t->right;
  t->right = p;
  return t;
}

Bnodeb *RotateLeft(Bnodeb *p)
// Rotates left about p. Returns a pointer
// to the node that takes the place of p.
{
  Bnodeb *t = p->right;
  p->right = t->left;
  t->left = p;
  return t;
}
```

Figure 12.5 Top-down zig-zigging.

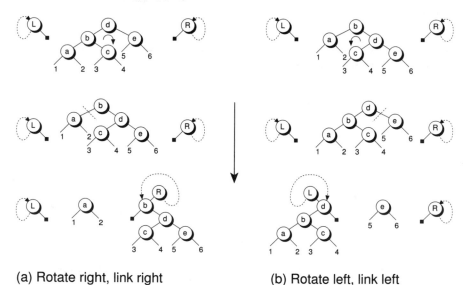

(a) Rotate right, link right　　　　(b) Rotate left, link left

Figure 12.6 illustrates the zig-zag configuration, in which a double rotation is performed. Using *LinkRight()* and *LinkLeft()* in a series has the same effect as doing the two opposite rotations that make up a double rotation. As always, the splayed node becomes the root of the middle subtree.

The operations for zig, zig-zig, and zig-zag are applied repeatedly until the desired node (the one having the matching key) becomes the root of the middle subtree. At this point, the three subtrees are assembled back into a single tree, as illustrated in Figure 12.7. The splayed node becomes the root of the reassembled tree. The following *Assemble()* routine gives the necessary pointer manipulations.

```
void Assemble(Bnodeb *p, Bnodeb *l, Bnodeb *r)
// Assembles p, l, and r into one tree, with p as the root,
// l & r as the left and right subtrees of p, and the old
// left and right subtrees of p as right and left subtrees
// of l & r, respectively
{
  if (l->right) {
    l->left->right = p->left;
    p->left = l->right;
  }
  if (r->left) {
    r->right->left = p->right;
    p->right = r->left;
  }
}
```

Figure 12.6. Top-down zig-zagging.

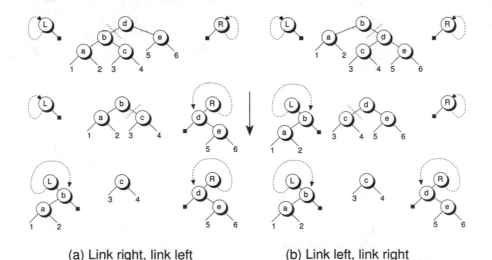

(a) Link right, link left   (b) Link left, link right

Figure 12.7 Reassembling a splayed tree.

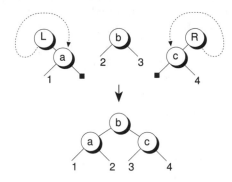

Figure 12.8 shows a complete example of top-down splaying. First a zig-zig is performed, followed by a zig-zag, and finally a zig. We've used the same tree as the one shown earlier in Figure 12.2 (illustrating bottom-up splaying). Note that the resulting splayed trees are different, although the splayed node *c* is at the root in both. The difference in the two cases exists because the rotations are performed in different orders.

Figure 12.8 Top-down splaying.

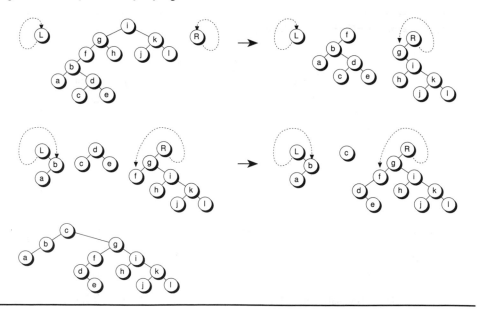

We are now in a position to show how a search routine for a splay tree might be coded. But first, we'll define some classes to be used for splay trees.

SPLAY TREE CLASSES

We'll now implement splay trees using a simple two-class hierarchy. The following *SplayTreeb* class defines a data-independent base class. This class is unusual in that it has all static member functions, which are declared protected. This is done to hide the names of these otherwise ordinary functions, and to make them accessible only to the *SplayTree* class that you are about to see. The functions included in *SplayTreeb* are the *LinkRight()*, *LinkLeft()*, *RotateRight()*, and *RotateLeft()* functions shown earlier. Also included are some functions for manipulating the minimum and maximum nodes in the tree, which we'll discuss later.

```
class SplayTreeb {
protected:
  static Bnodeb *LinkRight(Bnodeb *p, Bnodeb *r);
  static Bnodeb *LinkLeft(Bnodeb *p, Bnodeb *l);
  static void Assemble(Bnodeb *p, Bnodeb *l, Bnodeb *r);
  static Bnodeb *SplayMin(Bnodeb *t);
  static Bnodeb *SplayMax(Bnodeb *t);
  static Bnodeb *DetachMin(Bnodeb *&root);
  static Bnodeb *DetachMax(Bnodeb *&root);
};
```

The following *SplayTree* class is derived from the *SplayTreeb* class:

```
template<class TYPE>
class SplayTree : public SplayTreeb {
protected:
  Bnodeb *root;
  void SearchAndSplay(const TYPE &x);
  Bnode<TYPE> *SearchP(const TYPE &x, Bnode<TYPE> *&p, int &side);
  // Allocation functions. . .
public:
  // Constructors, destructors, copy functions,
  // and other supporting functions. . .
  Bnode<TYPE> *Member(const TYPE &x);
  int Add(const TYPE &x, int &existed);
  Bnode<TYPE> *AddFixed(const TYPE &x, int &existed);
  Bnode<TYPE> *Detach(const TYPE &x);
  Bnode<TYPE> *DetachMin();
  Bnode<TYPE> *DetachMax();
  int Delete(const TYPE &x);
  void DeleteMin();
  void DeleteMax();
```

```
  Bnode<TYPE> *Min();
  Bnode<TYPE> *Max();
  int IsEmpty();
  Bnode<TYPE> *Root() const;
};
```

Complete code for splay trees is given on disk in the files *splay.h*, *splay.cpp*, and *splay.mth*. A test program is given in *tstsplay.cpp*. In addition, many supporting files from Chapter 10 are used.

As usual, the *SplayTree* class is implemented as a concrete data type, with various constructors, destructors, overloaded assignment operators, allocation functions, and so on. These functions are similar to those used in the *Bstree* and *RBtree* classes of earlier chapters, and won't be discussed further. Instead, we'll focus on routines for searching, inserting, and deleting nodes.

Searching in a Splay Tree

The following *SearchAndSplay()* routine shows how to search for a node in a splay tree. The basic idea is to do a standard binary search and perform top-down splaying at the same time. The appropriate splaying operations to perform are determined by comparing the current node *t* with the desired key, as well as testing the children of *t*.

```
template<class TYPE>
void SplayTree<TYPE>::SearchAndSplay(const TYPE &x)
// Search for node containing the key x, moving that
// node to the root using top-down splaying
{
  Bnodeb l, r; // Temp subtrees holding no data

  if (root == 0) return;

  l.left = &l; l.right = 0;
  r.left = 0;  r.right = &r;

  while (x != Root()->info) { // While root doesn't match
    if (x < Root()->info) {   // Search left down the tree
      if (root->left) {
        if (x == Root()->Left()->info) {
          // zig
          root = LinkRight(root, &r);
```

```
         }
         else if (x < Root()->Left()->info) {
            // zig-zig
            root = RotateRight(root);
            if (root->left) root = LinkRight(root, &r);
         }
         else if (x > Root()->Left()->info) {
            // zig-zag
            root = LinkRight(root, &r);
            if (root->right) root = LinkLeft(root, &l);
         }
      } else break;   // Node isn't in the tree
   }
   else {                // x > root->info, so search right down the tree
      if (root->right) {
         if (x == Root()->Right()->info) {
            // zig
            root = LinkLeft(root, &l);
         }
         else if (x > Root()->Right()->info) {
            // zig-zig
            root = RotateLeft(root);
            if (root->right) root = LinkLeft(root, &l);
         }
         else if (x < Root()->Right()->info) {
            // zig-zag
            root = LinkLeft(root, &l);
            if (root->left) root = LinkRight(root, &r);
         }
      } else break; // Node isn't in the tree
   }
 }

 Assemble(root, &l, &r);
}
```

If the matching node is in the tree, it will become the root of the tree after the search. However, if the node isn't in the tree, either the predecessor or successor of the node will become the root. Thus, the root must be tested to see if it is indeed the matching node, as the following *Member()* function illustrates:

```
template<class TYPE>
Bnode<TYPE> *SplayTree<TYPE>::Member(const TYPE &x)
{
  SearchAndSplay(x);
  return (Root() && Root()->info == x) ? Root() : 0;
}
```

Inserting into a Splay Tree

Unlike a normal binary search tree, nodes are added to a splay tree at the root. To make this work, the *SplayAndSearch()* routine is first called. If the node already exists, the insertion is skipped. If the node doesn't exist, a new node is allocated to become the new root. The splaying that takes place during the unsuccessful search restructures the tree so that splicing in the new root is easy. The old root will be the predecessor or successor of the new root. We make the old root the left or right child of the new root. In turn, one of the children of the old root will become the other child of the new root. Figure 12.9 shows an example. The following *Add()* function gives the details.

```
template<class TYPE>
int SplayTree<TYPE>::Add(const TYPE &x, int &existed)
// Search for a node containing key x in the tree. If found,
// set existed to 1 and return. If not found, add a new
// node to the tree containing x. This node will become
// the new root.
// Returns 1 if successful; returns 0 if allocation failed
{
  Bnode<TYPE> *p;

  SearchAndSplay(x); // Moves closest match to the root

  existed = (Root() && Root()->info == x) ? 1 : 0;

  if (!existed) {
    p = AllocNode(x);
    if (p == 0) return 0;
    // p is about to become the new root
    if (Root()) {
      // Determine which side of p the old root should go on
      if (x < Root()->info) {
        p->right = root;
        p->left = root->left;
        root->left = 0;
      }
      else {  // x > root->info at this point
        p->left = root;
        p->right = root->right;
        root->right = 0;
      }
    }
    root = p;
  }
  return 1;
}
```

Figure 12.9 Insertion into a splay tree.

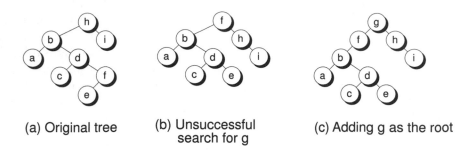

(a) Original tree
(b) Unsuccessful
search for g
(c) Adding g as the root

Deleting from a Splay Tree

In Chapter 10, we detached a node from a binary search tree by swapping the node's key with that of its successor, and then detaching the successor. We can use a similar process with a splay tree, except that we want to perform splaying at the same time, so that the amortized searching cost will remain at $\log n$.

The deletion can be performed by first calling *SearchAndSplay()* to move the node to delete to the root. Then, we splay the successor node to the top of the right subtree by calling a special *SplayMin()* function. (The successor of the root is always the minimum node of the right subtree.) We'll describe the *SplayMin()* function in the next section. Note that the successor node is guaranteed to have a null left child (Can you figure out why?). Thus, we can easily make the successor the new root and make, as its left child, the left child of the old root. Figure 12.10 illustrates this process. If the root doesn't have a successor, the left child of the root can take its place. If there is no left child, the tree is now empty.

We could also use an alternate, symmetrical operation for the detachment: The predecessor node could be used as the replacement by splaying the

Figure 12.10. Detaching a node from a splay tree.

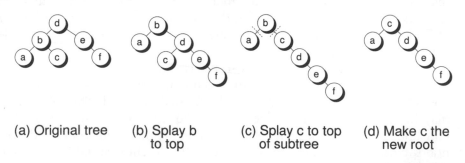

(a) Original tree
(b) Splay b
to top
(c) Splay c to top
of subtree
(d) Make c the
new root

maximum node of the left subtree to the top, making it the new root, and using the right child of the old root as the right child of the new root.

At this point, the node targeted for deletion is detached from the tree. The following *Detach()* function gives the details. The node can then be de-allocated if desired. A *Delete()* routine (not shown) handles this chore. Note that, if the node to be detached isn't found in the tree, the tree may be restructured anyway by *SearchAndSplay()*—in anticipation of the possible detachment.

```
template<class TYPE>
Bnode<TYPE> *SplayTree<TYPE>::Detach(const TYPE &x)
// Searches for a node matching x and detaches it from
// the tree. Returns a pointer to the node detached;
// returns 0 if not found.
{
  if (root == 0) return 0;
  SearchAndSplay(x);
  if (Root()->info == x) { // Matching node found
     Bnode<TYPE> *oldroot = Root();
     if (root->right) {
        root = SplayMin(root->right);
        root->left = oldroot->left;
     }
     else root = root->left;
     return oldroot;
  }
  return 0;
}
```

SPLAY TREES AS PRIORITY QUEUES

In Chapter 9, we briefly mentioned priority queues, in which items are inserted in any order, but extracted in sorted order, based on a priority determined by a key within each item. Because splay trees are highly adaptable, they can be used quite effectively as priority queues. The technique involves inserting items into the splay tree in binary search tree order, and then extracting either the minimum (or maximum) node. The following discussion assumes that we wish to extract the minimum node, but the techniques described can easily be modified to extract the maximum node.

A regular binary search tree can be used as a priority queue, but a splay tree is more effective. Recall that the minimum node of a tree can be found by continuously walking left until a null left child is found. The minimum node may be near the bottom of the tree, so the first extraction may not be very efficient. However, in a splay tree, extracting the minimum node tends to cause nodes close the minimum to migrate to the top. Thus, subsequent extractions can be quite efficient.

However, if intervening insertions take place, the minimum node may fall toward the bottom again. This can be circumvented by modifying the behavior for insertions: Don't do splaying when a node is inserted. Instead, use an ordinary binary search tree insertion. Recall that such insertions don't restructure the tree. Instead, the new node is added somewhere close to the bottom. The minimum node will thus remain close to the top for a subsequent extraction. If the new node *is* the minimum, it will be added below the old minimum (in fact, on the left), and thus will be quite close to the top.

Note   The technique just described is believed to have been invented by the author.

Figure 12.11 illustrates a splay tree used as a priority queue. Note that, once the splaying begins, the minimum node stays close to the top. If the extraction process begins on a degenerate tree with n nodes, with the minimum node at the bottom, the worst-case cost is n steps. However, the amortized cost will probably be closer to $\log n$ steps, and may be much better than this. Because the insertions don't do splaying, it helps if the insertions are intermixed with extractions (which is likely to be the case). If there is a long series of insertions without extractions, an expensive extraction might be forthcoming, but subsequent extractions are likely to be cheap due to the splaying that finally takes place. It is difficult to precisely analyze the costs of the insertions and extractions for the strategy given here. The costs when using normal splaying operations for priority queue insertion have been empirically analyzed [Jones 86].

Figure 12.11 Priority queue splaying.

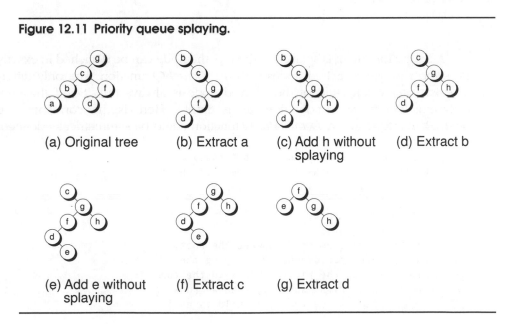

(a) Original tree   (b) Extract a   (c) Add h without splaying   (d) Extract b

(e) Add e without splaying   (f) Extract c   (g) Extract d

The following *SplayMin()* function shows how the minimum node can be splayed to the top. This function is an adaptation of the *SearchAndSplay()* function. But here, we don't need to do any searching, since the minimum node is always to our left. Note that the splaying will be in the form of zig-zagging operations, except for perhaps the final operation, which may be a single zig. A *SplayMax()* function can be symmetrically defined. Here, the maximum is always on the right.

```
Bnodeb *SplayTreeb::SplayMin(Bnodeb *t)
// Move the minimum of t up the tree, replacing t
// as the root. The new root is returned.
{
  Bnodeb l, r;

  if (t == 0) return 0;

  l.left = &l; l.right = 0;
  r.left = 0;  r.right = &r;

  while(t->left) {
    // Go left as far as possible, splaying along the way
    // We have either a zig-zig, or a zig orientation
    if (t->left->left) t = RotateRight(t);
    t = LinkRight(t, &r); // t->left guaranteed not null
  }

  Assemble(t, &l, &r);
  return t;
}
```

After the minimum is splayed to the top, the node can be detached in exactly the same way we detached nodes with the *Detach()* function. The only difference is that the left child of the splayed node is always null. So, if the right subtree is empty, we know the tree is empty. Here is the corresponding *DetachMin()* function. A *DetachMax()* function could be symmetrically defined:

```
Bnodeb *SplayTreeb::DetachMin(Bnodeb *&root)
// Detach the minimum node of the tree, returning
// a pointer to it, or 0 if tree is empty
{
  if (root == 0) return 0;
  root = SplayMin(root);
  // Replace the minimum node, now at the root,
  // with its successor, found by splaying the
  // minimum node of the right subtree to the top.
  // If there is no right subtree, then we know the
  // tree is empty, since the left child is null.
```

```
    Bnodeb *oldroot = root;
    if (root->right) {
        root = SplayMin(root->right);
        root->left = oldroot->left;
    }
    else root = 0;
    return oldroot;
}
```

To insert a node into a splay tree-based priority queue without splaying, we can use functions identical to the *SearchP()* and *Add()* functions of the *Bstree* class described in Chapter 10. (We won't repeat those functions here.) For the code given on disk, we've renamed *Add()* to *AddFixed()* to differentiate it from the *Add()* function that uses splaying.

While splay trees make good non-contiguous priority queues, other data structures, called *heaps* (not to be confused with the heaps used for dynamic memory allocation), work well for contiguous priority queues. Heaps are advantageous because they can be implemented without storing left and right pointers in the nodes. Only the data needs to be stored. For details on heaps, see the companion volume [Flamig 93].

SUMMARY

Splay trees are intriguing structures because they are so adaptable. For example, we can use a splay tree for normal binary searching operations, and then decide to switch gears and use it like a priority queue. In fact, we can switch between extracting the minimum nodes and extracting the maximum nodes, and the splay tree will automatically adjust itself. (However, alternating between minimum and maximum extractions will lead to bad performance. There are better structures for this type of activity, called *min-max* priority queues. See [Atk 86].)

Unfortunately, splay trees do not necessarily make good general-purpose search trees. There are two fundamental problems:

1. *Splay trees have the same worst-case searching performance as linked list.* For a large number of nodes, this may be unacceptable. If you want to guarantee $\log n$ performance for any single operation, a balanced binary search tree is better.

2. *For the most efficient operation, a splay tree must always restructure the tree, even during what would otherwise be read-only searching, and even when the searching is unsuccessful.* Thus, you couldn't use a splay tree to search a database on CD-ROM, for instance. You could implement the searching to forego the splaying, but then the amortized efficiency would suffer. Alternatively, you could "train" the splay tree by using a long series of typical

accesses, using splaying, and then "freeze" the structure. From then on, you could search without the splaying. However, this would only be effective if no new nodes were added, and if the access patterns didn't change.

Splay trees are advantageous when the access patterns favor a few nodes over the rest. A priority queue provides a good example because the nodes being favored are the ones with the smallest keys. These nodes tend to percolate to the top during the minimum node extraction process.

File-Based
Objects

U p to this point in the book, we've implemented data structures that reside in memory. However, it can be just as useful to have data structures that reside in files on disk. In this chapter, you'll see a system of classes that allow you to have such *file-based objects*.

One data structure that's often used in conjunction with files, called a *cache*, is a set of memory buffers that hold copies of file-based objects. Since reading from and writing to files is a relatively slow process, caches are used to enhance performance. Rather than fetching objects from the file every time they are needed, the copies kept in memory are accessed instead.

In this chapter, you'll see a unique cache design invented by the author. By using smart pointers called *cached-object pointers* (or *Coptrs*, pronounced as *cop-ters*), you can work with file-based objects with a pointer syntax that's similar to what you normally use for objects in memory. As you use *Coptrs*, the objects being referenced are stored and fetched to and from a file by way of a cache—almost transparently behind the scenes.

Persistent objects, which can save their state between program invocations, are currently a popular OOP topic. The file-based objects presented here are a weak form of persistent objects. Our file-based objects don't have the full capabilities of normal objects, lacking the ability to have pointers, destructors, and virtual functions. These file-based objects can, however, have constructors. In fact, you can construct file-based objects using an overloaded *new* operator with a syntax very close to that used for normal objects.

Even though our file-based objects aren't full objects, they are still quite useful for database applications. For example, you'll see how to use file-based objects to implement binary search trees that reside on disk. In fact, the material in this chapter lays the groundwork for Chapter 14, where we implement file-based *B-trees*.

A FILE-BASED ALLOCATOR CLASS

At the heart of our file-based object design is the following *Fmgr* class (and associated data structures) that manages objects stored in files:

```
struct FmgrHeader { // Goes at the beginning of every fmgr file
  long fs;           // Address to first block of "heap" free space
  long fe;           // Address of byte after end of file
  long hs;           // Address of the start of the "heap"
  char sg[4];        // Signature used for every fmgr-based file
};

struct FBlkHeader { // For free blocks
  int check_word;    // For file integrity checks (optional)
  unsigned len;      // Length of block not including header
  long next;         // Pointer to next free block
};

const long CURRADDR = -1; // Indicates current location

class Fmgr : public CountedObj {
public:
  enum Io_op      { fetch, store, seek };
  enum AccessMode { read_write, read_only };
  enum CheckWord  { BLKINUSE = 0xFDFD, FREEBLK = 0xFEFE };
protected:
  char name[128];    // Name of the file
  static char sg[4]; // Signature for fmgr style files
  FmgrHeader h;      // File header as stored in memory
  FILE *fp;          // Stream file handle
  Io_op lastop;      // Last I/O operation
  char status;       // Status bits
  // Various internal functions...
public:
  Fmgr();
  virtual ~Fmgr();
  virtual int Create(char *fname, long static_sz = 0);
  virtual int Open(char *fname, AccessMode mode = read_write);
  virtual void Close(int flush=1);
  virtual void Flush();
  long Alloc(unsigned nbytes);
  void Free(unsigned nbytes, long p);
  void Fetch(void *d, unsigned n, long p = CURRADDR);
  void Store(const void *d, unsigned n, long p = CURRADDR);
  void Seek(long ofs, int seek_mode = SEEK_SET);
  int IsOpen() const;
  int ReadOnly() const;
  int ReadyForWriting() const;
  void ClearErr();
```

```
   void Throw(StatusCode c, char *src=0, int lno=0, char *msg=0);
   int OK() const;
   int operator!() const;
   operator const int () const;
};
```

```
typedef SmartPtr<Fmgr> FmgrPtr;
```

Unfortunately, we don't have space to explain all the design details of the *Fmgr* class. Instead, we'll provide a high-level description of how the class works. As always, the class is fully documented on disk. Keep in mind that the *Fmgr* class was painstakingly designed to be as versatile and efficient as possible.

 Complete code for the *Fmgr* class is given on disk in the files *fmgr.h* and *fmgr.cpp*. The sample program about to be shown is given in the file *fmgrtst.cpp*.

Features of the Fmgr Class

The *Fmgr* class is the file-based equivalent of a heap manager. It has two functions, *Alloc()* and *Free()*, which are analogous to the C functions *malloc()* and *free()*. In addition, the *Fmgr* class has *Fetch()* and *Store()* functions that let you read and write objects. This example creates an *Fmgr* file and stores a *Part* object in it:

```
// fmgrtst.cpp: Sample program using an Fmgr object
#include <iostream.h>
#include "fmgr.h"

struct Part {
  int id;
  float price;
  Part(int i=0, float p=0) { id = i; price = p; }
};

main()
{
  Part part(17, 42.0);    // Memory buffer of part to be stored
  FmgrPtr f(new Fmgr);    // Should always create dynamically
  f->Create("test.dat"); // Create and open file

  long addr = f->Alloc(sizeof(Part)); // Allocate room for part
  f->Store(&part, sizeof(Part), addr);

  // Close and reopen file (for testing)
  f->Open("test.dat"); // Open() closes first
```

```
// See if we can get the part back
f->Fetch(&part, sizeof(Part), addr);
cout << "Part: <" << part.id << ", " << part.price << ">\n";

// Now delete the part

f->Free(sizeof(Part), addr);

return 0; // (File automatically closed by destructor)
}
```

Fmgr files are reference counted to help detect synchronization problems when closing files. For instance, you may have several caches connected to the same file. By using smart pointers, we can disconnect the caches in any order. The file can only be closed when the last cache is disconnected. In the class definition, you'll notice that *Fmgr* is derived from the *CountedObj* class we gave in Chapter 5. You access *Fmgr* files through *FmgrPtr* objects, which are smart pointers defined as *SmartPtr<Fmgr>* types. As with all *SmartPtrs*, the reference counted object (in this case an *Fmgr* object) must be allocated dynamically.

The *Fmgr* class is fairly sophisticated, but it's still a low-level design. For example, although *Fmgr* will allocate objects for you, it doesn't keep track of their locations. Note how we kept the address of the *Part* in the *addr* variable. This is akin to allocating an object in memory and then recording its address in a pointer.

Further evidence of the low-level nature of *Fmgr* can be found in functions like *Alloc()*, *Fetch()*, *Store()*, and *Free()*, which must be told the size of the objects being used. Also, *Fetch()* and *Store()* use *void* pointers to pass the object data. We could derive template-based classes from *Fmgr* to serve as high-level type-casting interfaces. In fact, we showed an example of this in the *RecFile* and *FileOf* classes in Chapter 3. In this chapter, we'll show an alternative technique. The type-casting will be encapsulated in pointers, with a different pointer type for each type of object. Before we discuss these pointers, we'll review the layout of *Fmgr*-based files.

Layout of an Fmgr File

All *Fmgr* files have the same layout, being composed of three parts, (as illustrated in Figure 13.1): a header, a static data area, and a dynamic data area. The header is composed of four fields, as shown in Figure 13.2. The first three are used by the allocation routines (which we'll describe shortly). The fourth field is a four-byte signature of *FMGR*. This signature is used by the *Open()* routine to determine whether a file is indeed an *Fmgr*-based file. Note that, while the file is open, the file header is also stored in memory using the *FmgrHeader* object *h*.

Figure 13.1 Fmgr file layout.

0
15
0
Fmgr header
Static data
hs
Dynamic data
(Heap)
fe

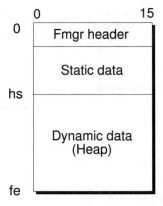

Following the header is a static data area, whose size is specified by the creator of the file. This area is analogous to the static data segment of your program, and can be used to store objects whose locations should be fixed. The static area is a good place to store small indices. For example, we'll store addresses to the roots of trees at known locations in the static area, so that we can easily find the roots.

The Fmgr Heap

The dynamic data area is analogous to a heap residing in memory. It starts out empty and grows when objects are allocated. The end of the heap is always the end of the file. Thus, the file grows as the heap grows.

The header fields *hs*, *fe*, and *fs* are used to maintain the heap. The *hs* field stores the address of the start of the heap. This field is used when the first object is allocated. Initially, *hs* points to the end of the static area, whose location is also stored in *fe*. As the heap grows, *fe* is adjusted to point to the end of the file, and represents the location where the file can be extended again, if necessary. Figure 13.3 shows how an object is added to an empty heap.

Figure 13.2 Fmgr header layout.

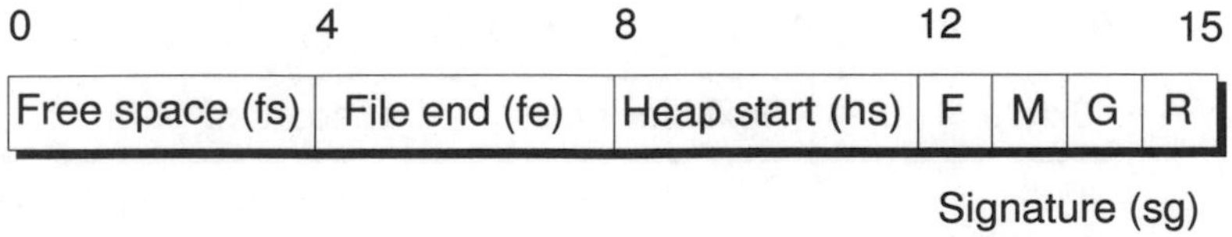

0
4
8
12
15
Free space (fs)
File end (fe)
Heap start (hs)
F
M
G
R
Signature (sg)

Figure 13.3 Allocating a new object.

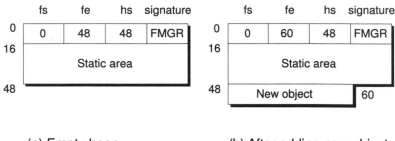

(a) Empty heap   (b) After adding new object

The *fe* field isn't strictly necessary because the end of the file could always be found by asking the operating system for the file size. However, keeping track of the end of the file ourselves is more efficient and can be used to make file integrity checks. For instance, if *fe* is tested and found not to be the size of the file, we know the file has been corrupted.

Objects are de-allocated by placing them on the *free space list*. This list is not unlike the free lists we used with linked lists in Chapter 8. The start of the free space is stored in the *fs* field. This field is initially zero. When an object is freed, its block of data is placed on the free list. The first portion of the block is overwritten with a *free block header*, as illustrated in Figure 13.4. This header holds a check word (given an arbitrary value of 0xfefe), the length of the block (not including the header itself), and a *long* integer giving the address of the next free block. This latter field is null when the block's at the end of the list.

Figure 13.5 shows the layout of a file with two of its four objects (object 1 and object 3) freed and placed on the free list. In this figure, object 1 was freed first, and object 3 freed last. Note that freed objects are always added to the front of the list and that the list is null terminated.

When a new object is to be allocated and the free list isn't empty (that is, *fs* isn't zero), then the list is walked, looking for a block of an appropriate size. The block must either be equal to the size of the object or greater than the size of the object plus the size of the free block header. The block is split in two—

Figure 13.4 Free block header layout.

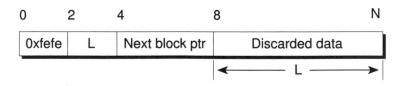

Figure 13.5 Objects on the free list.

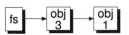

Conceptual view of
the free list

one part for the object and the other part to be placed on the free list again. The address of the first part is returned to become the address of the object. Note that no data is written to the block at this time. As far as the file is concerned, the object stays uninitialized until we write to its location.

The strategy we use for finding an appropriate free block is called the *first-fit* strategy because we scan down the free list until we find the first block the object will fit into. We may have to scan down the entire list, which can be quite long. And even then, there's no guarantee we'll find a good block. If we don't, then the file is extended to accomodate the new object and the *fe* field is adjusted accordingly.

We could use other, more sophisticated strategies. For instance, we could keep the list sorted in some way to shorten the time spent searching for a good block to use. We use the first-fit strategy because it's the simplest. Fortunately, when all the objects tend to be the same size, the first-fit strategy works quite well. This will be the case in later examples where we'll store a single homogenous tree in a file in which the nodes are all the same size. Keep in mind that nothing stops you from storing all types of data in a single file. It's just that the first-fit allocator may not yield optimum performance for these situations. For a discussion about heap allocation strategies, see [Knuth 73].

In the allocation strategy presented here, almost no overhead is required for objects that are allocated. The free block header is used only when objects are deleted, and then the header overwrites a portion of the object. For this strategy to function properly, however, the object must be large enough to hold a free block header. The size of the header as we've defined it is eight bytes, and that's the minimum size of an allocated object. If you try to allocate a smaller object, eight bytes will be allocated anyway and some of the space will be wasted.

Recall that the header contains an integer check word. This field is used for file integrity checks. For instance, if you follow the *next* field of a free block header and land on a block that doesn't start with this check word, you know the file has been corrupted. The check word is optional, and if you remove it, the minimum allocated size will be reduced to six bytes. However, we strongly recommend keeping the check word because it's a great debugging aid.

Exception Handling

A proposed addition to C++, *exception handling,* gives you the ability to elegantly handle errors, or *exceptions,* that arise during program execution. When an invalid condition is detected, an exception is *thrown,* and is *caught* by code that can hopefully make a sane recovery. For the caching design you are about to see, exception handling would be invaluable. Unfortunately, at the time of this writing, exception handling isn't yet available. So, we've implemented the following *ExceptionHandler* class to crudely simulate exception handling:

```
class ExceptionHandler {
protected:
  virtual void Report(char *src, int lno, char *msg, char *dev);
  virtual void TakeAction();
public:
  ExceptionCode status;
  ExceptionHandler();
  void Clear();
  virtual void Throw(ExceptionCode c,
    char *src=0, int lno=0, char *msg=0, char *dev=0);
};

#define THROW(c) Throw(c, __FILE__, __LINE__)
```

Complete code for the *ExceptionHandler* class is given on disk in the files *exchdlr.h* and *exchdlr.cpp.*

Exceptions are thrown by calling the *Throw()* function. An exception code is passed, along with parameters indicating the line number and source file where the *Throw()* function was called. Other auxiliary messages defined by the user can be passed as well. In most cases, *Throw()* prints the messages and then terminates the program. Unlike true exception handling, no attempt is made to recover from an error. The *THROW()* macro, which calls *Throw(),* is provided for convenience. It sets the line number and source file parameters, and defaults the others to zero.

The exception codes are defined in the following enumeration:

```
enum ExceptionCode {
  DANGLINGPTR,
  NULLPTR,
  CACHEFULL,
  STKFULL,
  CLOSERR,
  // Many other codes ...
};
```

The following *Close()* function of *Fmgr* shows how to throw exceptions. A check is made to ensure that no dangling smart pointer references will be made to the file about to be closed. An exception is also thrown if an error unexpectedly occurs when closing the file:

```
void Fmgr::Close(int flush)
// Closes the file if not already closed, flushing the
// basic header if flush = 1. Does nothing if in the
// error state. Checks for dangling references to
// this file.
{
  if (OK()) {
    if (refcnt > 1) THROW(DANGLINGPTR);
    if (flush && !ReadOnly()) WriteHdr();
    if (::fclose(fp) != 0) THROW(CLOSERR);
    strcpy(name, closed_file_name);
  }
  status &= 0xfd; // Reset open bit
}
```

The *Fmgr* class actually has its own *Throw()* function, which traps certain exception codes and modifies them based on the context we're in:

```
void Fmgr::Throw(ExceptionCode c, char *src, int lno, char *msg)
{
  if (c == NOTWRITEABLE && OK()) c = READONLYERR;
  if (c == NOTREADY && (status & 1)) c = NOTOPENERR;
  excp->Throw(c, src, lno, msg, name);
  status &= 0xfe; // Reset good bit
}
```

After fixing the exception code, this function calls the basic *Throw()* function via the global exception handler pointer *excp*, which is declared in the *exchdlr.cpp* file. You can customize the exception handling by deriving a new class from *ExceptionHandler* and then pointing *excp* to a derived handler.

Here is the message that's printed when *Close()* throws a *DANGLINGPTR* exception:

```
EXCEPTION on line 132 of fmgr.cpp
Dangling 'smart pointer'
Error occured with file tree.dat
```

As we've mentioned before, the exception handling described here is a very weak form of what is proposed for C++. For a description of the proposed design, see [Stroustrup 91].

TOWARD A CACHING SYSTEM

In this section, we look at some issues involved in safely using the *Fmgr* class, and how handling those issues leads us logically to the caching design you are about to see.

To use a file-based object, we need two components (besides the file): a buffer for a copy of the object stored in memory and the address of the object in the file. In trivial programs (such as the *fmgrtst.cpp* program given earlier), working with these two components separately isn't a problem. In larger, non-trivial programs, however, four basic issues emerge:

1. When using more than one file-based object, it's easy to associate a file address with the wrong memory buffer. We need a way to keep the addresses and memory buffers paired together. We can do this by defining a structure with both components as members. We'll call such structures *Buckets*. Here's how a *Bucket* structure could be defined:

```
template<class TYPE> struct Bucket { TYPE data; long addr; }
```

2. Nothing stops you from having two addresses that point to the same object in the file, even though each address has its own associated memory buffer. This is a particularly insidious form of aliasing. Which memory buffer has the "official" data that should be written to the file? We would like to guarantee a unique object address for each memory buffer. If we're using buckets, that means no two buckets should have identical *addr* members.

3. Even though each bucket should have a unique file address, we don't necessarily want to make only one reference to any given bucket. For example, assume that buckets store tree nodes and that we use pointers to buckets in implementing tree operations, such as searching and inserting. You've seen from earlier chapters that it is quite common to copy pointers during tree operations, which results in a lot of aliasing. This aliasing is bad enough for objects stored in memory, but it's even worse for file-based objects. We must ensure that bucket pointers work in concert with each other. Using smart pointers to buckets with reference counts is one way to do this.

4. In applications with a large number of file-based objects, such as a file-based tree with many tree nodes, it's not possible or desirable to keep all the objects in memory. Thus, we end up shuffling objects in and out of a fixed number of buckets and onto disk. We must keep track of which buckets can be reused at any given time—a difficult and error-prone task. It would be nice to automate this process.

We can solve all of these problems by using a collection of buckets known as a *cache*. The purpose of a cache is to be the intermediary mechanism between code using a file-based object and the file itself. You make requests to the cache for a particular object (keyed by its file address), and the cache sees to it that the object is fetched from disk and stored in a bucket. If the object is already in a bucket, no fetching need be done. (This, by the way, guarantees a unique file address for each bucket.) When the appropriate bucket is reserved, a pointer to the bucket is returned to be used by the code wishing to access the file-based object.

As requests are made to the cache, more buckets are reserved. Eventually, the cache fills up. When another bucket is needed, the data in one of the occupied buckets must be flushed back to disk so the bucket can be reused for the new request. A special flag can be kept with each bucket, known as the *dirty bit*, which indicates whether the bucket data has been modified since it was last loaded. If the dirty bit is set, the object data in the bucket is written to disk. If the dirty bit isn't set, the bucket can be reused without further action.

Of course, the problem with this scheme lies in determining which buckets can be reused. By adding reference counts to the buckets, this becomes easy: A bucket can be reused if there are no references to it. Since the buckets are reference counted, it makes sense to access them with smart pointers. The *Coptrs* to be presented later allow you to do just that. A *Coptr* is a smart pointer to a cache bucket. When *Coptrs* are assigned to each other, the reference counts of the corresponding buckets are updated. The reference count of the original bucket of the target *Coptr* gets decremented, whereas the reference count of the source bucket gets incremented. In this way, *Coptrs* can share buckets without any confusion.

In using a cache to solve aliasing problems, a fortuitous side effect occurs. Code that uses caching generally runs faster than code without caching. Thus, we get both safer and faster code.

Figure 13.6 illustrates the organization of a caching system that incorporates all of the design features just discussed. Next, we'll look at the design of this system in detail.

CACHE BUCKETS

In this section, we examine the design of cache buckets. As we've done throughout the book, we'll separate the design into two parts. We'll first define buckets independently of the data stored in those buckets, then add the data. This provides the greatest amount of code sharing. Here is the *Bucketb* class, which defines buckets independently of the bucket data:

```
class Bucketb {
protected:
  long addr;      // Location of bucket's data in the file
  int refcnt;     // How many references to this bucket
  char dirty;     // True when data doesn't match what's in file
```

```
    Bucketb *prev;   // Pointers to adjacent buckets in the cache
    Bucketb *next;   // in most-recently reserved order.
    void MakeNull() { addr = 0; refcnt = 0; dirty = 0; }
public:
    Bucketb()               { } // Other classes do the initialization
    void Lock()             { ++refcnt; }
    void Unlock()           { -refcnt; }
    int IsLocked()          { return refcnt; }
    void SetDirty()         { dirty = 1; }
    int IsNull()            { return addr == 0; }
    void Flush(Fmgr &f) { if (addr && dirty) Store(f); }
    virtual void Fetch(Fmgr &f) = 0; // Depends on bucket data
    virtual void Store(Fmgr &f) = 0; // Depends on bucket data
    friend class Cacheb;
    friend class Coptrb;
    friend void Report(Cacheb &c, int full_report=0);
};
```

The *addr*, *refcnt*, and *dirty* members implement the features of buckets described in the previous section. Two other members, *prev* and *next*, are pointers used in organizing the buckets in a doubly-linked list. We'll discuss these pointers when the *Cacheb* class is examined.

The most striking feature about the *Bucketb* class is that it can be completely inlined. This means that very little, if any, overhead is induced by using the *Bucketb* class over more low-level and hard-coded techniques. Only two of the member functions, *Fetch()* and *Store()*, depend on the type of data stored, so we've declared these functions as pure virtual. Three of the functions—*Lock()*, *Unlock()*, and *IsLocked()*—are used to access and manipulate the reference

Figure 13.6 Organization of a caching system

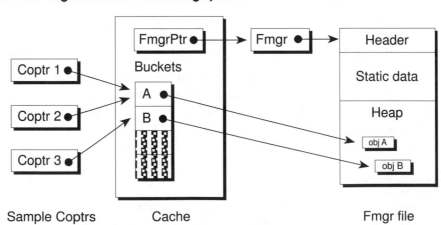

count stored in the bucket. The rationale behind the names of these functions will become apparent when we discuss the *Cacheb* class.

From the *Bucketb* class, we can derive a template class called *Bucket* that defines a family of classes, each specific to a particular type of data we wish to store. There are several ways to derive the *Bucket* class. The first way is the most obvious; include a TYPE object inside the *Bucket*, as in:

```
template<class TYPE>
class Bucket : public Bucketb {
public:
  TYPE info;
  // Other definitions ...
};
```

To access the bucket data, we need to go through the *info* field. For example, suppose we define file-based tree nodes holding integers, and we wish to store these tree nodes in buckets. Here's how we might write code to use these buckets:

```
struct Node {
  char data;        // The node data
  long left, right; // We use long integers, not pointers
  Node();
  Node(const char &x, long left=0. long right=0);
};


...
Bucket<Node> *root;
...
root->info->left = 42L; // Set the left child of root
```

Going through the *info* field is clumsy. We would prefer to write expressions like *root->left*. To do this, the buckets must somehow act like tree nodes, yet we still want them to behave like buckets, too. Multiple inheritance is the perfect tool to accomplish this. Here's a new definition for *Bucket* that uses both *Bucketb* and *TYPE* as base classes:

```
template<class TYPE>
class Bucket : public Bucketb, public TYPE {
public:
  Bucket();
  virtual void Fetch(Fmgr &f);
  virtual void Store(Fmgr &f);
};
```

Note   Some compilers don't allow you to use a template parameter as a base class (even though that's perfectly legal in C++). If this is the case with your compiler, you'll have to remove the template syntax, and code this class directly for the types you have in mind. Fortunately, this class is small enough that it can be replicated by hand easily. But you'll also have to hand-code the upcoming *Cache* and *Coptr* classes.

By using multiple inheritance for the *Bucket* class, we can write code like the following:

```
Bucket<Node> *root;
...
root->left = 42L; // Accessing one of TYPE's members
root->SetDirty(); // Accessing one of Bucketb's members
```

The *Bucket* class is one of those rare classes that is simultaneously simple, elegant, and powerful. Just three functions need to be added to the *Bucketb* class to derive a data-dependent class: a constructor and the virtual functions *Fetch()* and *Store()*.

```
template<class TYPE>
Bucket<TYPE>::Bucket()
// Calls default Bucketb() and TYPE() constructors
{
}

template<class TYPE>
void Bucket<TYPE>::Fetch(Fmgr &f)
// Fetch TYPE object data from the file f
{
  f.Fetch((TYPE *)this, sizeof(TYPE), addr);
  dirty = 0;
}

template<class TYPE>
void Bucket<TYPE>::Store(Fmgr &f)
// Store TYPE object data onto the file f
{
  f.Store((TYPE *)this, sizeof(TYPE), addr);
  dirty = 0;
}
```

The *Fetch()* and *Store()* routines employ a subtle but powerful trick. When it's time to fetch or store the data in the bucket, we only want to use the TYPE portion of the bucket. Members like *addr, refcnt,* and *dirty* shouldn't be stored on disk. But how do we accesss only the *TYPE* portion of the bucket? We can employ a little-known feature of multiple inheritance: Given a pointer *D* to a multiply derived object with base classes *A* and *B*, you can get a pointer to the *A* portion of the object by type casting *D* to an *A* pointer. Similarly, to get the *B* portion of *D*, a *B* pointer type cast can be used. For example:

```
class D : public A, public B { ... };

D *Dptr;  A *Aptr;  B *Bptr;

Aptr = (A *)Dptr; // Grab A portion of D
Bptr = (B *)Dptr; // Grab B portion of D
```

When the compiler sees the last two statements, it calculates the pointers *Aptr* and *Bptr* by adding the appropriate offset to the *this* pointer of the object pointed to by *Dptr*. Figure 13.7 illustrates this process. Note that the precise layout of multiply-derived objects is implementation dependent. Figure 13.7 shows one possible layout. Also, the offsets to add to the *this* pointer are constant and can be calculated at compile time. Thus, multiply derived-to-base-class pointer conversions can be quite fast.

For a *Bucket<TYPE>* pointer, a *TYPE* pointer type cast will give you a pointer to the *TYPE* portion of the bucket. Thus, the *Fetch()* and *Store()* routines type cast the *this* pointer of the *Bucket* to calculate a pointer to the *TYPE* data. This pointer is then passed when calling the *Fetch()* and *Store()* routines of *Fmgr*.

In using the *TYPE* parameter, you need to observe these restrictions:

• *TYPE should not have any embedded pointers.* The values of pointers are transitory, changing from one program invocation to the next. Thus, it's of little use (and probably erroneous) to store pointers on disk. However, you can store file offsets (usually in *long* integers). These offsets can be used to

Figure 13.7 Multiple inheritance and type casting

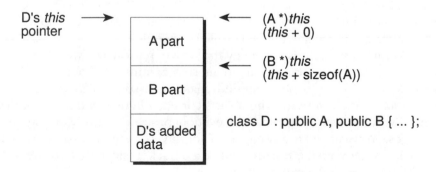

reference other file-based objects, and can take the place of pointers. The tree node example we gave earlier illustrates this.

- *TYPE cannot have any virtual functions.* If *TYPE* has virtual functions, the virtual function table pointer will be stored on disk with the object. Of course, the value of this pointer may not be valid from one program invocation to the next. You could arrange to have the virtual function table pointer updated to the correct value after the object has been loaded, but that is highly implementation dependent. (This approach would be dependent on the way objects are organized, which isn't standardized.)

- *TYPE should not have a destructor.* Although the compiler-generated destructor of *Bucket* will implicitly call the *TYPE* destructor, it is not clear that the *TYPE* destructor can do anything that makes sense. The cache classes to be presented are not set up to call the *TYPE* destructor when a bucket is overwritten, thus *TYPE* shouldn't have a destructor (other than an empty one).

- *TYPE must have a default constructor.* The *Bucket* class constructor requires a default *TYPE* constructor. It's also useful for *TYPE* to have other constructors, as you'll see later.

- *TYPE cannot be a built-in type.* That's because *TYPE* is used as a base class of *Bucket*, and built-in types can't be used as base classes.

Complete code for the *Bucketb* and *Bucket* classes is given on disk in the files *bucketb.h*, *bucket.h*, and *bucket.mth*.

CACHING STRATEGIES

The main task of a cache is to handle requests for file-based objects. The cache must determine whether an object is already loaded and, if not, the cache must reserve a bucket for the object and load it in memory. However, what should the cache do when all the buckets are filled? We must provide a way for the cache to choose which bucket to overwrite with the new object. Caches are differentiated by the strategies they use to determine which buckets to reuse. For optimal performance, those buckets with data not likely to be used again soon should be chosen as candidates. In general, this is difficult to determine.

Fortunately, there is a strategy that works reasonably well. This strategy is based on the observation that, in most programs, the object most recently requested is likely to be requested again very soon. This principle is often called *locality of reference*. The objects currently in use tend to be localized to a small working set. As program execution proceeds, this working set slowly changes. You can take advantage of locality of reference by designing your caches to overwrite the least-recently used bucket, since that bucket is the least likely to be needed again any time soon.

Caches that overwrite least-recently used buckets are often called *LRU caches*. In an LRU cache, the buckets are kept in order based on how "old" the buckets are—that is, how long ago they were last used. There are various ways to "age" buckets. The simplest way is to keep the buckets on a self-organizing linked list. Each time a bucket is used, it is moved to the front of the list. Thus, the most recently used buckets tend to be at the front. Those buckets that haven't been used recently will fall to the back of the list. When a new bucket is needed, it can be chosen from the back of the list. Figure 13.8 illustrates the LRU strategy.

Our cache design uses a slight modification of the LRU strategy. We will use *Coptrs* that reference cache buckets directly, with each *Coptr* being initialized after a bucket is reserved. If we were to use a strict LRU strategy, the buckets would have to be reorganized every time a *Coptr* was *used*. This would be clearly inefficient. Instead, we reorganize the buckets only at the time a bucket is reserved. In effect, we use a *least-recently reserved* (LRR) strategy. Although it's difficult to prove this, the LRR strategy is likely to perform as well as, or better than, the LRU strategy.

The Cache Classes

We use two classes to implement caches. The *Cacheb* class incorporates those functions that are independent of the type of buckets, whereas *Cache* is the type-specific template version:

```
class Cacheb {
protected:
  long hits, misses; // For performance statistics
  int nbuckets;      // Size of cache
  FmgrPtr fptr;      // File cache is connected to
  Bucketb *head;     // Most recently reserved bucket
```

Figure 13.8 A Self-organizing LRU Cache

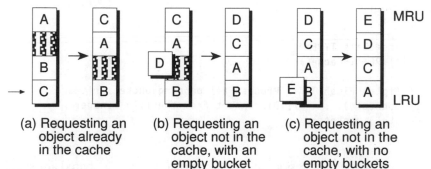

(a) Requesting an object already in the cache

(b) Requesting an object not in the cache, with an empty bucket

(c) Requesting an object not in the cache, with no empty buckets

```
    Bucketb *AcquireBkt();
    Bucketb *FindBkt(long addr);
    void MoveToFront(Bucketb *b);
    Cacheb(Bucketb *b, int n, unsigned bkt_size);
    virtual ~Cacheb();
public:
    friend class Coptrb;
    void Connect(FmgrPtr &fp);
    void Disconnect();
    void Flush(int empty_bkts = 0);
    void Clear();
    virtual Bucketb *ReserveBkt(long addr, int ensure_loaded=1);
    friend void Report(Cacheb &c, int full_report=0);
};

template<class TYPE>
class Cache : public Cacheb {
protected:
    Bucket<TYPE> *buckets;
public:
    Cache(int n);
    virtual ~Cache();
};
```

Complete code for the *Cacheb* and *Cache* classes is given on disk in the files *cacheb.h*, *cacheb.cpp*, and *cache.h*.

The type-specific *Cache* class adds just two functions, which handle the allocation and de-allocation of the cache buckets. The buckets are stored in an array of size *n*, as shown in the following *Cache* constructor and destructor:

```
template<class TYPE>
Cache<TYPE>::Cache(int n)
// Allocate buckets. Send them to Cacheb() for further setup.
: Cacheb(buckets = new Bucket<TYPE>[n], n, sizeof(Bucket<TYPE>))
{
}

template<class TYPE>
Cache<TYPE>::~Cache()
{
    if (fptr) Flush(); // Process all pending bucket writes
    Disconnect();      // Disconnect from the file manager
    delete[] buckets;
}
```

Most of the code resides in the *Cacheb* class, which is shared among all caches. This means you can have many different caches with little source code explosion.

Although the buckets are stored in an array, the *Cacheb* class organizes them as a circular doubly-linked list, as shown in the following *Cacheb()* constructor. Thus, the buckets are actually organized as a hybrid structure. Unlike the circular lists we defined in Chapter 8, we don't use a dummy header node in the bucket list.

```
Cacheb::Cacheb(Bucketb *b, int n, unsigned bkt_size)
// Assumes n buckets of size bkt_size have already been
// allocated. Sets up their prev and next pointers to form
// a circular list.
: fptr(0) // Start with a null file manager
{
  Bucketb *p = b;
  for (int i = 0; i<n; i++) {
     p->MakeNull();
     p->prev = (Bucketb *)((char *)p - bkt_size);
     p->next = (Bucketb *)((char *)p + bkt_size);
     p = p->next;
  }
  // Make the list circular
  Bucketb *tail = (Bucketb *)((char *)b + (n-1)*bkt_size);
  tail->next = b;
  b->prev = tail;
  // Set up other cache variables
  nbuckets = n; head = b; hits = 0; misses = 0;
}
```

The buckets are organized in a doubly-linked list to facilitate the LRR strategy of the cache. When a bucket is reserved, it is moved to the front of the list, using the following *MoveToFront()* function. This in effect makes the bucket the *most-recently reserved* (MRR) bucket:

```
void Cacheb::MoveToFront(Bucketb *b)
// Logically move bucket to front of list so that it is
// treated as the most recently reserved bucket.
// Shortcuts are used when possible.
{
  if (b == head->prev) { // b is tail
    head = head->prev;
  }
  else if (b != head) {
    // Unhook bucket from where it is
    b->prev->next = b->next;
    b->next->prev = b->prev;
    // Put it before head
    b->next = head;
    b->prev = head->prev;
    b->prev->next = b;
```

```
      head->prev = b;
      head = b;
   }
}
```

Often, *MoveToFront()* will need to move the LRR bucket at the back of the list to the front—to make it the MRR bucket. Thus, *MoveToFront()* traps for this case and uses an optimized movement. Because of the circularity of the list, only the *head* pointer needs to be updated.

When an object is requested from the cache, the *ReserveBkt()* function is called:

```
Bucketb *Cacheb::ReserveBkt(long addr, int ensure_loaded)
{
  Bucketb *b;

  if (addr == 0) return 0; // Don't reserve bkt for null object

  b = FindBkt(addr);
  if (b == 0) { // Bkt data not loaded, so acquire a bucket
     misses++;
     b = AcquireBkt();
     if (b) {
        b->addr = addr;
        if (ensure_loaded && addr) b->Fetch(*fptr);
        if (!fptr->OK()) b = 0; else b->Lock();
     }
  }
  else {
    hits++;
    MoveToFront(b);
    b->Lock();
  }

  return b;
}
```

The *ReserveBkt()* function uses the file address of the object requested as a key and searches through the cache for the object by calling *FindBkt()*. This latter function does a sequential search starting from the MRR bucket because, most likely, the object being requested was requested just recently.

```
Bucketb *Cacheb::FindBkt(long addr)
{
  Bucketb *b = head; // Start with the MRR bucket
  do {
    if (b->addr == addr) return b;
    b = b->next;
```

```
  } while(b != head);
  return 0; // No bucket found
}
```

If the requested object is not found, a bucket is acquired by calling the *AcquireBkt()* function:

```
Bucketb *Cacheb::AcquireBkt()
{
  Bucketb *b = head->prev;          // LRR bucket
  while(1) {
    if (!b->IsLocked()) break;
    b = b->prev;
    if (b == head->prev) {
      excp->THROW(CACHEFULL);       // Most likely will exit program
      return 0;                     // Make compiler happy
    }
  }
  b->Flush(*fptr);
  MoveToFront(b);
  return b;
}
```

Because buckets are going to be used directly via *Coptr*s, we can't simply have *AcquireBkt()* return the LRR bucket. That bucket may be referenced by one or more *Coptr*s. A bucket that has a non-zero reference count is called a *locked bucket*. So *AcquireBkt()* starts with the LRR bucket and searches toward the MRR bucket, stopping at the first *unlocked* bucket it finds. When an unlocked bucket is found, we prepare for it to be overwritten by flushing any dirty data it might contain. The bucket is then moved to the front of the list to become the MRR bucket.

It's possible that all buckets in the cache will be locked. When this occurs, the cache is full, and an exception is thrown. Note that we can't simply grab a bucket and use it. That would leave us with one or more dangling *Coptr*s.

After acquiring a bucket, the *ReserveBkt()* function fetches the object data from the file so that the data is loaded and ready to go. However, if the object being requested has yet to be constructed, there's no data in the file to load. The *ensure_loaded* flag is used to indicate this situation so that the bucket data isn't erroneously loaded.

Once a bucket has been either found or acquired, the reference count of the bucket is incremented by calling *Lock()*. The bucket is then moved to become the MRR bucket. A pointer to the bucket is returned, presumably to be assigned to a *Coptr*.

You may want to have more than one cache connected to the same file. Recall that the *Fmgr* class is reference counted to handle this situation. The following *Connect()* and *Disconnect()* functions are used to connect or disconnect a cache from a file:

```
void Cacheb::Connect(FmgrPtr &f)
// Connects cache to file f, assumed already opened
{
  Clear();  // Flush any pending data for the old file
  fptr = f; // Connect to a new one
}

void Cacheb::Disconnect()
// Disconnects cache from the file it was connected to
{
  Clear();   // Flush any pending data
  fptr = 0; // Connect to null object
}
```

Recall that *FmgrPtr* is a smart pointer. The assignment *fptr = f* in *Connect()* decrements the reference count of the old *Fmgr* in use and increments the reference count for *f*. A cache can be disconnected from a file by connecting it to the null *Fmgr* object, using the statement *fptr=0*. Both *Connect()* and *Disconnect()* clear the cache before changing the connection. The following *Clear()* and *Flush()* functions are used:

```
void Cacheb::Clear()
// Flush all buckets in the cache, and then null them out
{
  if (fptr) Flush(1);
  hits = 0; misses = 0;
}

void Cacheb::Flush(int empty_bkts)
// Flushes all buckets in the cache. Makes them empty if
// empty_bkts is true. Checks for dangling Coptrs.
{
  // Flush, starting at the front
  Bucketb *b = head;
  do {
    if (empty_bkts && b->IsLocked()) excp->THROW(DANGLINGPTR);
    if (fptr->ReadyForWriting()) b->Flush(*fptr);
    if (empty_bkts) b->MakeNull();
    b = b->next;
  } while(b != head);
}
```

When *Clear()* calls *Flush()*, it sets the *empty_bkts* flag to true. This causes not only the bucket data to be flushed, but also makes the buckets "null" by setting their *addr, refcnt,* and *dirty* variables to zero. A bucket to be emptied should not have any pointers referencing it. That condition is checked and an exception is thrown if true. Thus, before calling *Clear()*, all *Coptr*s must be unbound from the buckets they are referencing.

CACHED-OBJECT POINTERS (COPTRS)

Since the cache buckets are reference counted, we need smart pointers to work in conjunction with them. We use cached-object pointers (*Coptr*s) for that purpose. *Coptr*s are implemented with two classes: a data independent *Coptrb* class and the type-specific *Coptr* class template:

```
class Coptrb { // Data independent base class for Coptrs
protected:
  long addr;                      // File address of bucket data
  Bucketb *bkt;                   // Pointer to bucket in the cache
  Cacheb *cache;                  // Pointer to the cache being used
  char bound;                     // True if pointer is bound to a bucket
  void Copy(const Coptrb &c);
  Bucketb *Alloc(unsigned n, long p=0);
  void Delete(unsigned n);
  void Bind();
  Coptrb(Cacheb &c, long p);
  Coptrb(const Coptrb &c);
  void operator=(const Coptrb &c) { } // Disallowed
public:
  ~Coptrb();
  void Grab();
  void Release();
  void NotifyUseOf();
  operator long() const;
};

template<class TYPE>
class Coptr : public Coptrb {
public:
  friend void *operator new(size_t n, Coptr<TYPE> &cp, long p);
  void Delete();
  Coptr(Cache<TYPE> &c, long p = 0);
  Coptr(const Coptr<TYPE> &c);
  void operator=(const Coptr<TYPE> &c);
  void operator=(long p);
```

```
    Bucket<TYPE> &operator*();
    Bucket<TYPE> *operator->();
};
```

Complete code for the *Coptrb* and *Coptr* classes is given on disk in the files *coptrb.h*, *coptrb.cpp*, and *coptr.h*.

Each *Coptr* stores the file address *addr* of the object being pointed to, a pointer *bkt* to the bucket containing the memory buffer of the object, and a pointer *cache* to the *Cache* the *Coptr* is connected to. Another important variable is the *bound* flag. This flag indicates whether the *Coptr* is currently bound to a bucket.

Before a *Coptr* can be used, it must be connected to a cache. The *Coptr()* constructor, which calls the following base class *Coptrb()* constructor, is used for this purpose:

```
Coptrb::Coptrb(Cacheb &c, long p)
// General Coptr constructor. Note that a cache
// is required. The Coptr stays unbound until needed.
{
    cache = &c; addr = p; bound = 0; bkt = 0;
}
```

*Coptr*s can optionally be given the address *p* of the object being referenced. Note that *p* defaults to zero. A *Coptr* with an address of zero is treated as a null pointer. Thus, by default, *Coptr*s are initialized as null pointers.

The main function of a *Coptr* is to take a file address and make it appear to be a pointer to a *TYPE* object. This magic is accomplished by the clever combination of smart-pointer-style reference counting and multiply-derived buckets. The two most important functions of a *Coptr* are the following -> and * operator functions:

```
template<class TYPE>
Bucket<TYPE> &Coptr<TYPE>::operator*()
{
    if (!bound) Bind();
    return *(Bucket<TYPE> *)bkt;
}

template<class TYPE>
Bucket<TYPE> *Coptr<TYPE>::operator->()
{
    if (!bound) Bind();
    return (Bucket<TYPE> *)bkt;
}
```

Auto-Loading of Cached Objects

An important *Coptr* feature is the automatic loading of object data into the cache. Whenever a *Coptr* is accessed through the overloaded operators -> and *, the *bound* flag is checked to see whether the *Coptr* is currently bound to a bucket. If not, the *Bind()* function (described later) is called to reserve a bucket for the *Coptr*. In the *operator*()* function, a reference to this bucket is returned. The *operator->()* function returns a pointer to the bucket. (The type casts are needed because *bkt* is typed as a generic *Bucketb* pointer.)

Due to multiple inheritance, we can use the return values of our operator functions to access both the members of *Bucketb* and the members of *TYPE*. The following example constructs a *Coptr* to a tree node (which we defined earlier) and uses the *Coptr* to access the *SetDirty()* member of *Bucketb* and the *left* member of *Node*:

```
#include "coptr.h"

main()
{
  FmgrPtr f(new Fmgr); // Set up a file
  f->Open("test.dat"); // Open it

  Cache<Node> c(12);   // Set up a cache of 12 buckets
  c.Connect(f);        // Connect it to the file

  // Construct a Coptr pointing to a Node at file address 42
  Coptr<Node> p(c, 42L);

  p->left = 17L; // 'left' member of Node accessed
  p->SetDirty(); // Call Bucketb's SetDirty() function

  p.Release();    // Must release Coptr before clearing cache
  c.Disconnect(); // Disconnect the cache; all buckets flushed
  f->Close();     // Close the file; all buffers flushed
}
```

Coptrs are designed to follow one principle: A bucket isn't loaded until needed. When *Coptr p* is initialized to point to a *Node* at the file address 42 (presumably the *Node* has already been allocated), that *Node* isn't loaded into a bucket until the *left* member of *Node* is accessed.

Detecting Modifications to Cached Objects

Even though *Coptrs* cause file-based objects to be fetched automatically, we must tell a *Coptr* specifically when the objects need to be written back to disk.

After the statement *p->left = 17* is executed, the in-memory copy of the *Node* is different from what's stored on disk. We inform the cache of this fact by calling *SetDirty()*. If the corresponding bucket is to be overwritten later (or the cache cleared), the cache knows to flush the bucket data to disk.

If the delay in writing the bucket data to disk is unacceptable, you can call *Store()* instead of *SetDirty()*. This causes the bucket data to be written immediately. In fact, you could add a flag to the *Bucketb* class, which, when true, causes *SetDirty()* to store the object data to disk, rather than simply set the dirty bit. By doing this, you have in effect created what is known as a *write-through cache*. A write-through cache is safer than a regular cache. There's less danger of losing data that should be on disk but is still in memory when a hardware failure (such as power loss) occurs. We chose not to implement our caches this way. It's better to choose by hand whether to call *SetDirty()* or *Store()*. That way, you have more flexibility in trading speed over safety.

You may wonder why we even need *SetDirty()*. Couldn't the caching system automatically detect when the bucket data has been modified? The answer is yes in principle, but no in practice. You can detect when an object is modified by overloading its assignment operator, and setting the bucket's dirty bit when an assignment is detected. There are two problems, however.

First, you have to overload the assignment operator for each member of the object, and this must be done recursively if the members themselves are nested objects. The second problem is worse. Even if each member can detect assignments, how do those members set the bucket's dirty bit? Remember, nested objects don't have access to the objects that enclose them. A pointer to the dirty bit could be stored in each member, but this would waste a lot of space, and that space would be taken up in the file as well. Also, just adding the dirty bit pointers to each member would be difficult. How would you go about using predefined objects?

There are alternatives, but they are all less than satisfactory. One alternative is to keep two copies of each object in memory. The first copy represents the state of the object as it was loaded from disk. The second copy is used during all in-memory accesses. When it's time to flush the bucket, these two copies are compared to see if the second copy, containing any changes, should be written to disk. This technique would be simple to implement, but it wastes time in making the extra copies, and it also wastes storage.

You might wonder why you couldn't just set the dirty bit each time the overloaded -> and * operators are called for a *Coptr*. The problem is that the dirty bit would be set even if we're just reading the values of the members, rather than modifying them. The result is that the bucket data might be written back to disk during a flushing operation when it didn't need to be. You might as well forget about the dirty bits and always write cached objects back to disk, since that would have the same effect.

Binding Objects

*Coptr*s are bound to buckets by calling the following *Bind()* function. This binding is usually done for you automatically, but you can do the binding yourself by calling *Grab()*:

```
void Coptrb::Bind()
// Binds the Coptr to a bucket containing data stored at
// file location addr. Note that we may already be pointing
// to the correct bucket, so check for that.
// Assumes the Coptr not already bound. For internal use only.
{
  if (bkt && bkt->addr == addr) { // Fast binding
     if (addr) {
        bkt->Lock();
        bound = 1;
     }
     else excp->THROW(NULLPTR);
  }
  else {
     bkt = cache->ReserveBkt(addr, 1);
     if (bkt) bound = 1; else excp->THROW(NULLPTR);
  }
}


void Coptrb::Grab()
// Like Bind(), but makes no assumptions about the Coptr
// being unbound coming in. For public use.
{
  if (!bound) Bind();
}
```

The *Bind()* function has both safety and speed considerations built in. *Bind()* assumes you are trying to bind a non-null pointer (with *addr* being non-zero). If that's not the case, a *NULLPTR* exception is thrown. This is how *Coptr*s check for null pointers. Note that this test only occurs when binding to a bucket, and not on every access to a *Coptr*. This dramatically speeds up the use of *Coptr*s, yet it doesn't sacrifice safety. You can pass around null *Coptr*s all you want, and no error occurs until you try to access the associated non-existent objects.

Bind() is also built for speed in another way. If the *bkt* pointer isn't null, a test is made to see if *bkt* is already pointing to the right bucket. If it is, the bucket is simply locked. This saves the searching that would otherwise be required. If *bkt* is null or doesn't point to the right bucket, a relatively expensive call to *ReserveBkt()* is made, which searches the cache looking for a bucket. Note that *ReserveBkt()* handles the locking of the bucket in this case. For certain applications, fast binding can take place more often than you might think. You'll see this later when we discuss recursive traversals of trees on disk.

Assigning Coptrs

*Coptr*s can be assigned by using the overloaded assignment operator, which in turn calls the *Copy()* function:

```
template<class TYPE>
void Coptr<TYPE>::operator=(const Coptr<TYPE> &c) {copy(e); }

void Coptrb::Copy(const Coptrb &c)
{
  Release();
  addr = c.addr; bkt = c.bkt; bound = 0; cache = c.cache;
}
```

The *Copy()* function releases any bucket the destination *Coptr* might be referencing by calling *Release()* (described later), and then assigns the members of the source *Coptr*. The *Coptr()* copy constructor is similar to *Copy()* except the call to *Release()* isn't needed.

```
template<class TYPE>
Coptr<TYPE>::Coptr<TYPE>(const Coptrb &c)
{
  addr = c.addr; bkt = c.bkt; cache = c.cache; bound = 0;
}
```

As is true with ordinary pointers, when *Coptr*s are copied, the data being referenced isn't copied. In fact, for *Coptr*s, the destination is left unbound, even though the source *Coptr* might be bound. This practice is in keeping with the principle that *Coptr*s aren't bound until needed. Using this principle has important performance ramifications. Consider operations on file-based trees. During the tree operations, many pointers are assigned, often with very transitory values. By deferring the pointer binding until it's absolutely necessary, we can ensure data isn't loaded during otherwise transitory pointer assignments.

Even though the destination is unbound, it has the source *Coptr*'s *bkt* pointer. When it's time to bind the destination, it can probably be done quickly by using fast binding. The only time this wouldn't occur is if, in the interim, the referenced bucket became unlocked and overwritten.

*Coptr*s can also be used as though they are *long* file addresses. The following two operator functions help facilitate this:

```
Coptrb::operator long() const
// We let a Coptr look like a file address, since in a way
// it's just a smart version of a file address
{
  return addr;
}
```

```
template<class TYPE>
void Coptr<TYPE>::operator=(long p)
// Redirects the Coptr to a new address. Releases the old
// bucket (if any) and does not bind to a new one.
{
  Release();
  addr = p;
}
```

These two functions allow us to work easily with file-based tree nodes, which have *long* integers instead of pointers for links to child nodes. For example, we can write functions such as the following *GetMin()* function:

```
// File-based example

struct Node {
  char info;
  long left, right;
  Node();
  Node(const char &x, long l=0, long r=0);
}

Coptr<Node> GetMin(Coptr<Node> t)
// Get the minimum node of tree t
{
  while(t) t = t->left;
  return t;
}
```

We'll now work through this small example to see what actually occurs behind the scenes. First, the parameter *t* is passed by value, which causes the *Coptr()* copy constructor to be called. After the copying, *t* has an address, a cache pointer, and even a bucket pointer (which may point to the right bucket if we're lucky). However, *t* is unbound at this time.

When the **while** loop is entered, *t* is tested for null. This is accomplished by converting *t* to a long integer whose value is the address of the object that *t* points to. If that value is non-zero, we know we're pointing to a real object. Then, *t* is assigned to the address of its *left* child. The assignment operator taking a *long* integer is called here, since *t->left* is a *long* integer. Note that the expression *t->left* causes *t* to be bound (with the *Node* loaded from disk if necessary) so that the value of *left* is defined. However, *t* is immediately unbound by the assignment statement, since it takes on a new address. Upon return from the function, we make and return an unbound copy of the final version of *t*.

The striking observation here is that *GetMin()* looks almost identical to the function we would write if the tree resided in memory. To make a memory-based version of *GetMin()*, all we need to change is how the pointers are typed.

```
// Memory-based example

struct Node {
  char info;
  Node *left, *right;
  Node();
  Node(const char &x, node * l=0, node * r=0);
}

Node *GetMin(Node *t)
// Get the minimum node of tree t
{
  while(t) t = t->left;
  return t;
}
```

The ability to write code for file-based objects so that it appears almost identical to code written for memory-based objects has important ramifications. If you've ever tried to write code for file-based trees, you know what we mean. For example, try writing code for red-black trees using low-level functions such as *Fetch()* and *Store()*. It's a virtual nightmare due to the aliasing that occurs when pointers are being frequently assigned and modified. It's difficult to tell when something needs to be written to disk and which memory buffer has the right values. It's easy to be wrong.

By using *Coptrs*, it's relatively painless to write code for file-based trees. As a very fortunate side effect, the use of caching makes the code run much faster as well. In fact, using a cache for a file-based tree can make a huge difference in performance. You'll get at least double the performance, and sometimes much better than that.

Unfortunately, using *Coptrs* isn't always quite as transparent as we would like. In the next section, you'll see that, in some cases, we must coax the *Coptrs* along by manually intervening with the binding process. Also, don't forget that we must manually set dirty bits for any objects we modify. Failure to do this can wreak havoc on the data structures being stored to disk.

Releasing Coptrs

Coptrs are unbound from the buckets they reference by using a call to the *Release()* function:

```
void Coptrb::Release()
{
  if (bound) {
    bkt->Unlock();
```

```
      bound = 0;
   }
}
```

Unlike binding, releasing *Coptr*s is only done semi-automatically. It's not possible to tell, in general, when a *Coptr* needs to be released. There are some obvious situations when we can tell, however. For instance, you saw automatic releasing during *Coptr* assignments. Another situation occurs when the *Coptr* gets destroyed. Here is the *Coptr* destructor:

```
Coptrb::~Coptrb() {Release(); }
```

When we use *Coptr*s in code involving straight iteration, the two automatic release points of assignment and destruction work just fine. However, consider the following recursive inorder traversal of a file-based tree:

```
void InOrder(Coptr<Node> t)
{
  while(t) {
    InOrder(Coptr<Node>(t, t->left));
    Visit(t);
    t = t->right; // Automatic releasing takes place here
  }
}
```

Consider what happens during this function. The copy constructor for *t* is called during the pass-by-value parameter passing. At this point, *t* is unbound. In the recursive call, a temporary *Coptr* is created by using the copy constructor with a second argument, which indicates the address for the *Coptr*. The address given is to *t*'s left child, and the expression *t->left* causes *t* to become bound. The temporary *Coptr* is unbound. As a side effect of the copy, the temporary *Coptr* gets *t*'s cache pointer, which is important because all *Coptr*s are required to reference a cache. We must use the same cache that *t* has, or things would quickly go haywire.

When the recursive function call is made, another unbound copy of the temporary *Coptr* is made. This copy becomes bound during the next recursive call, and so on. When we return from a recursive call, the temporary copy gets released and destroyed automatically.

At each level of recursion, a new version of *t* is bound. Recall that the buckets for these bound *Coptr*s are locked and can't be reused. Essentially, the cache must have as many buckets as the depth of the tree, plus a few extra buckets for other *Coptr*s that might be in use. Otherwise, the cache would overflow. If you don't want to calculate ahead of time how big the cache needs to be (which would tend be difficult anyway), the alternative is to ensure that *t* is unbound during the recursion. This can be done by manually releasing *t* before the recursive call. We may also want to release the temporary *Coptr* before calling *Visit()*. For example:

```
void InOrder(Coptr<Node> t)
{
  while(t) {
    Coptr<Node> temp(t, t->left);
    t.Release();     // Must do this or cache becomes full
    InOrder(temp);
    temp.Release(); // May want to do this
    Visit(t);        // t probably gets rebound during this call
    t = t->right;    // t will be rebound here if not already bound
  }
}
```

Note that *t* probably gets rebound during the *Visit()* function. If we're lucky, the rebinding will be fast, since *t*'s bucket pointer may still be pointing to the right bucket. Remember that releasing a *Coptr* doesn't cause the bucket to go away. The bucket is merely made available for reuse, and then only if there are no other *Coptr*s referencing the bucket. If you're lucky, the bucket will still be intact when you need it again.

The conclusion from this discussion is that, as long as you're using iteration, *Coptr*s can be manipulated virtually the same as ordinary pointers. (You still must set dirty bits, though.) However, with recursion, the fact that *Coptr*s are really more than ordinary pointers becomes apparent, and we must carefully consider the bind and release points.

Allocating Objects Referenced by Coptrs

Since *Coptr*s look a lot like ordinary pointers, it would be nice if we could allocate and construct file-based objects with them using the *new* operator. In fact, we can, as you'll now see. The workhorse function is the following *Alloc()* function:

```
Bucketb *Coptrb::Alloc(size_t n, long p)
{
  Release(); // Let go of any currently bound data
  if (p == 0) p = cache->fptr->Alloc(n);
  bkt = cache->ReserveBkt(p, 0);
  if (bkt) {
    bkt->SetDirty(); // Data to be modified by the constructor
    addr = p;
    bound = 1;
  }
  else {
```

```
        addr = 0; // bound will = 0 here as well
  }
  return bkt;
}
```

This function allocates *n* bytes (presumably *sizeof(TYPE)*) at address *p* in the cache's file, and sets up a cache bucket to support it. If *p* isn't zero coming in, it means the *TYPE* object has already been allocated. (This can be used when creating a new object in the static area of the file.) Note that *ReserveBkt()* sets up the file address, cache pointer, and reference count, but it doesn't load any data. A pointer to the bucket is returned.

The *Alloc()* function is used by the following overloaded *new* operator:

```
template<class TYPE>
void *operator new(size_t n, Coptr<TYPE> &cp, long p)
{
  return (TYPE *)((Bucket<TYPE> *)(cp.Alloc(n, p)));
}
```

This function has only one statement, but there's a lot of subtlety and power packed into that statement. First, *Alloc()* is called using size *n* and address *p* (which defaults to zero), and a pointer to a reserved bucket is returned. Since the pointer is typed as a generic *Bucketb* pointer, it is type cast to a more specific *Bucket<TYPE>* pointer. Then, some magic happens. We type cast the pointer to be a *TYPE* pointer. Recall that *Bucket<TYPE>* is multiply derived. Thus, the type cast to a *TYPE* pointer causes a pointer to the *TYPE* portion of the bucket to be computed. This *TYPE* pointer is then returned from *new*, and is passed to the constructor as the *this* pointer of the *TYPE* object to be constructed. (We had to pass the pointer back as a *void* pointer to satisfy the syntax for the *new* operator.)

Here is an example of the overloaded *new* operator in action:

```
Coptr<Node> t(cache);   // Set up a null Coptr
new(t) Node('a', 0, 0); // Allocate and construct a Node
```

The single call to *new* causes a *Node* to be allocated in the file used by the cache, a bucket to be reserved in the cache, and the *Node* portion of that bucket to be constructed. Note that, in effect, we're partially constructing a multiply-derived object (think about that for a while). This is a nice trick to have in your arsenal.

If you want to construct an object at a pre-allocated address (perhaps in the static area of the file), you can pass an extra parameter to *new*:

```
new(t, 42L) Node('a', 0, 0); // Construct object at address 42
```

This form of *new* is the file-based analogue to in-place construction.

You can also free a file-based object by way of a *Coptr*. The following *Delete()* function is used. It calls a lower-level *Delete()* function of the *Coptrb* class.

```
template<class TYPE>
void Coptr<TYPE>::Delete()
// Frees the data associated with the Coptr c. The Coptr is
// then set to null.
{
  Coptrb::Delete(sizeof(TYPE));
}


void Coptrb::Delete(unsigned n)
// De-allocates the file object pointed to by this Coptr, supposedly
// of size n. De-allocation only takes place if this Coptr is
// pointing to a bucket bound by nothing else. The Coptr is unbound
// afterward and both the bucket and the Coptr are made null.
{
  if (bound && bkt->IsLocked() == 1 ||
      !bound && (!bkt || !bkt->IsLocked())) {
    cache->fptr->Free(n, addr);
    Release();
    bkt->MakeNull();
    addr = 0;
  }
  else excp->THROW(DANGLINGPTR);
}
```

Note that you can only call *Delete()* for *Coptr*s that have unique buckets or aren't bound. Otherwise, you have dangling pointers and an exception is thrown. Here is an example that uses *Delete()*:

```
Coptr<Node> t(cache);     // Set up a null coptr
new(t) Node('a', 0, 0);   // Allocate and construct a Node
....
t.Delete();               // Free the Node from the file
```

You might wonder why we can't use the *delete* operator. Here's one attempt at defining an overloaded version of *delete*:

```
template<class TYPE>
void Coptr<TYPE>::operator delete(void *p)
{
  ((Coptrb *)p)->Delete(sizeof(TYPE));
}
```

Due to the rules of C++, we must pass a *void* pointer to *delete*. While it's easy to do a type cast to a *Coptrb* pointer in calling the low-level *Delete()*

function, the call to *delete* becomes awkward since we must take the address of the *Coptr* during the call. For instance:

```
Coptr<Node> t(cache);    // Set up a null coptr
new(t) Node('a', 0, 0);  // Allocate and construct a Node
....
delete &t;               // Must take the address of t
```

This was deemed to be too confusing and error prone, so we decided to use a *Delete()* function call instead.

CREATING FILE-BASED BINARY SEARCH TREES

On disk, you'll find complete code for building file-based binary search trees. This code uses all the techniques we've described in this chapter, and is a direct "port" of the memory-based binary search tree code given in Chapter 10. When you examine the file-based code, notice how similar the code is to the memory-based version.

Complete code for file-based binary search trees is given on disk in *ftree.cpp* and *ftree2.cpp*. The latter illustrates how easy it is to have more than one tree stored in the same file, each tree having its own cache.

PERFORMANCE TUNING

You may wonder just how fast *Coptr*s are. Since they use caching implicitly, they will be reasonably fast. However, even disregarding slow file access, *Coptr*s won't be as fast as memory-based objects. That's because on every access to a *Coptr*, a test is made to see if it's bound. This test, while simple, still takes time. You can fine-tune the performance of your file-based objects by carefully analyzing the bind and release points, and handling the binding and unbinding yourself.

For example, you can use a *Coptr* initially to get access to a bucket, and then use an ordinary pointer to the bucket from that point on. Here's some code that illustrates this:

```
Coptr<Node> t(cache);
new(t) Node('a', 0, 0);
...
Bucket<Node> *p = &(*t); // Get direct bucket pointer
...
p->left = 42;            // Access bucket directly
p->SetDirty();
...
t.Release();            // p no longer valid
```

Of course, using code like this leads to a lot of unsafe aliasing, so you must be extremely careful.

You can also optimize performance by manually intervening in the LRR caching strategy. Recall that, when using the caches designed here, a bucket moves to the front to become the MRR bucket only when that bucket has just been reserved for a *Coptr*. During the course of using the *Coptr*, the bucket may actually fall to the back of the list if it hasn't been reserved by other *Coptr*s in the interim. You can notify the cache that the bucket is being used frequently by calling the *NotifyUseOf()* function:

```
void Coptrb::NotifyUseOf()
// Moves the referenced bucket to the front of the
// cache queue. For cache performance tuning.
{
   if (bound) cache->MoveToFront(bkt);
}
```

For example:

```
Coptr<Node> t;
...
t.NotifyUseOf();
```

You don't have to use *NotifyUseOf()*. Even if a bucket is at the back of the list, it won't be reused as long as there are references to it.

SUMMARY

In this chapter, you've seen a versatile and powerful way to manage objects stored on files. While the code is template-based to make it type-safe, there's a minimal amount of source code explosion. The classes were carefully designed so that most of the work is done with data-independent code that is shared by all types of objects stored.

To make using *Coptr*s simple and elegant, we've employed several multiple inheritance and type-casting tracks. Unfortunately, some current compilers can't handle the statements that use these tricks, even though legal C++ is used. However, the code as given compiles and runs fine with Borland C++ 3.1, currently the only widely used native-code compiler that supports templates.

14

B-trees

In this, the final chapter of the book, we'll discuss *B-trees*, which are balanced multi-way trees. B-trees have become commonplace in database applications because they offer fast disk-based searching. B-trees were invented by Bayer and McCreight (see [BayeMc 72]) and are a natural evolution of earlier database designs. The basic premise behind these designs is that, to access a disk efficiently, it's best to load chunks of data, called *pages*, rather than small individual items.

In a B-tree, one tree node can be made to correspond to a page. Because binary nodes aren't usually large enough to take up one page, a B-tree node stores multiple keys and branches. A beneficial side effect of such *multi-way* nodes is that the height of the tree can be smaller than that of a binary tree. Using multi-way nodes also makes it easier to balance the tree. Both of these properties lead to even faster searching than can be obtained by using disk paging alone.

This chapter first shows the data structures used to implement B-trees, followed by the operations on B-trees in order of complexity—from searching to inserting and deleting. Since B-trees were designed with files in mind, we'll make our B-trees file-based, using the classes developed in Chapter 13 for this purpose.

PROPERTIES OF B-TREES

B-trees are classified by their *order*, which refers to the maximum number of branches in a node. For example, in a B-tree of order 4, each node can have up to 4 branches. Corresponding to these branches are 3 keys that help determine which branch to take during a search. In general, a B-tree of order m has nodes with up to *m* branches and *m-1* keys. Note that the order specifies the *maximum* number of branches. A node may have fewer branches than the maximum. Figure 14.1 shows a B-tree of order 4, with all nodes full. You've seen B-trees of order 4 before. They are the 2-3-4 trees we introduced in Chapter 11. (We've drawn them differently in this chapter, however.)

Not all multi-way trees are B-trees. A multi-way tree is considered to be a B-tree only if it is balanced. In the classical definition of a B-tree of order *m*, the balance is achieved by maintaining the following properties:

- Except for the root node, all nodes must have at least *(m-1)/2* keys and *(m-1)/2* + 1 branches. This means all nodes except the root are roughly half full. For example, in an order 5 B-tree, all non-root nodes must have at least two keys. For an order 4 B-tree, the nodes must have at least one key.

- The leaves of the tree are always on the same level.

Note Some texts define the order of a B-tree differently than we have here. In the alternative definition, a B-tree of order *d* has nodes with a maximum of *2d* keys and *2d+1* branches. Implied in this definition is that the maximum number of keys is always even, and the minimum number of keys in a non-root node is *d*. In our definition, the maximum number of keys can be odd.

As was the case with 2-3-4 trees, the key to efficient B-trees lies in maintaining the two properties just mentioned. Doing so will yield balanced trees that are reasonably compact.

Multi-Way Nodes

At the heart of B-trees are the multi-way nodes that make up the trees. Multi-way nodes are essentially generalizations of binary nodes. Rather than show generic template-based nodes in this chapter, we'll show a direct design that's typical of what might be used in practice. (You're probably tired of seeing templates, anyway.)

For keys, we'll use a character string of some maximum size. Stored with each key is a *long* integer that represents the associated data. While in some

Figure 14.1 A B-tree of order 4.

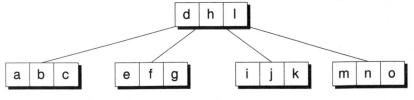

applications you might be able to fit all of your data in the *long* integer, the intent is for this variable to be the file address of the data—as stored elsewhere. For example, you might store the B-tree in one file that serves as an index to another file holding the actual data.

Node Entries

Since there is always one more branch than keys in a multi-way node, defining such nodes is somewhat awkward. We'll use the following strategy: Each node will have a *left* branch that leads to all nodes with keys smaller than the smallest key in the given node. The other *right* branches will be paired with a key, each branch leading to all nodes with keys greater than the given key, but less than the key to the right of the given key. We'll call a key, along with its associated data and branch fields, an *entry*. The following structure defines an entry:

```
const int MAXKEYSIZE = 16; // Maximum size of a key

struct Entry {
  char key[MAXKEYSIZE];
  long data;  // Data, or "pointer" to the data record
  long right; // Points to right child
  Entry();
  Entry(const char *s);
  Entry(const char *s, long d);
  Entry(const Entry &src);
  void operator=(const Entry &src);
  void operator=(const char *s);
  friend int Compare(const Entry &a, const Entry &b);
  friend int FullCompare(const Entry &a, const Entry &b);
};
```

Complete code for the *Entry* class, along with the upcoming *Mnode* class, is given on disk in the files *mnode.h* and *mnode.cpp*.

We define the maximum size of a key (including the null byte) in the global constant *MAXKEYSIZE*. Alternatively, we could define *Entry* to be a template, with the size as the template parameter. The key type could also be a template parameter. The functions for the *Entry* class are straightforward. However, two of the functions, *Compare()* and *FullCompare()*, need some explanation:

```
int Compare(const Entry &a, const Entry &b)
{
    return strcmp(a.key, b.key);
}
```

```
int FullCompare(const Entry &a, const Entry &b)
{
  int rv = strcmp(a.key, b.key);
  if (rv > 0) return 1;
  if (rv < 0) return -1;
  if (a.data > b.data) return 1;
  if (a.data < b.data) return -1;
  return 0;
}
```

The *Compare()* function is used when searching for data based on a key. The idea here is that, once an entry is found, the *data* field can be used to retrieve the data for the entry. However, when deleting an entry, the *data* field should already be known, so the *FullCompare()* function, which treats the *data* field as a secondary key, is used to find the specific entry to delete. Thus, duplicate keys are supported, but each key and data pair must be unique. Both compare functions use the *strcmp()* convention of returning a value less than 0 for *a < b*, 0 for *a == b*, and a value greater than 0 for *a > b*.

The Mnode Class

An array of entries can be packaged into a multi-way node, as defined by the following *Mnode* class:

```
const int NBR = 4; // Order of the tree

struct Mnode {
  int cnt;    // Must come before left
  long left; // Points to leftmost child. Must come before entry[].
  Entry entry[NBR-1];
  Mnode();
  int Search(const Entry &e, int &posn);
  int FullSearch(const Entry &e, int &posn);
  void Split(Mnode &b, int split_posn);
  void InsEntry(Entry &e, int posn);
  void Concatenate(Entry &e);
  void Concatenate(Mnode &n);
  void DelEntry(int posn);
  long &Branch(int posn);
  int LastPosn();
  int IsEmpty();
  int IsFull();
  int IsPoor();
```

```
   int IsPlentiful();
};
```

In this class, *NBR* is the order of the tree and is the maximum number of branches possible for the node. Since there is one less key than branch, *NBR-1* entries are reserved. The *cnt* field indicates how may entries are actually in use. The extra branch, *left*, is placed immediately before the entries, as illustrated in Figure 14.2. This arrangement allows us to index the branches from -1 to *NBR-2*, where the -1th branch represents the *left* branch, the 0th branch is the *right* branch of the first entry, and so on. The *Branch()* function takes advantage of this special layout. For this function to work, there must be no gaps between the *left* and *entry* fields of *Mnode*. This rule could be relaxed by testing explicitly for -1 and returning the *left* branch in that case.

```
long &Mnode::Branch(int posn)
// Returns the branch for the given position. Due to the layout
// of the node, we'll get the left branch if posn = -1.
{
   return entry[posn].right;
}
```

The *Mnode* class has functions to support searching for keys in a node, and for inserting entries into and deleting entries from a node. Next, we'll present a few of the functions to give you an idea how *Mnodes* operate. The functions of *Mnode* are fairly straightforward, and are fully described on disk. Note that the *Search()* function sequentially scans the entries of the node, looking for a match. If you are using B-trees with large node sizes, a binary search through the array of entries would be faster. (See [Flamig 93] for an example that implements an algorithm for binary searching an array.) The *FullSearch()* function can be defined by simply replacing the call to *Compare()* with a call to *FullCompare()*.

Figure 14.2 Layout of an Mnode of order 4.

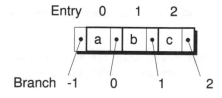

* The cnt and data fields are not shown

```
Mnode::Mnode()
// Set up an empty node
{
  cnt = 0; left = 0;
}

int Mnode::Search(const Entry &e, int &posn)
// Tries to match e's key with the keys in the entries
// of this node. Returns -1 if e's key is less than all
// keys in the node, returns 0 if there was a match, or
// returns 1 if e's key is greater than all keys in the
// node. Passes back posn of matching entry if any, or
// the posn of the entry containing the appropriate branch
// to keep searching down.
{
  posn = cnt-1;

  while(posn >= 0) {
    int rv = Compare(e, entry[posn]);
    if (rv > 0) return 1;
    if (rv == 0) return 0;
    posn--;
  }
  return -1;
}

void Mnode::InsEntry(Entry &e, int posn)
// Inserts entry e into node at position posn
{
  memmove(entry+posn+1, entry+posn, (cnt-posn)*sizeof(Entry));
  entry[posn] = e;
  cnt++;
}

void Mnode::DelEntry(int posn)
// Deletes the entry at position posn
{
  cnt--;
  memmove(entry+posn, entry+posn+1, (cnt-posn)*sizeof(Entry));
}

// Returns 1 if node has fewer than the minimum number of entries
int Mnode::IsPoor() { return cnt < (NBR-1)/2; }

// Returns 1 if node has more than the minimum number of entries
int Mnode::IsPlentiful() { return cnt > (NBR-1)/2; }
```

THE B-TREE CLASS

The following *B-tree* class, and its associated data structures, can be used to set up a B-tree:

```
// Function return status codes

const int NODE_OVERFLOW =  2;
const int SUCCESS       =  1;
const int FAIL          =  0;
const int DUPLKEY       = -1;
const int ALLOCERR      = -2;

struct BtreeHeader {  // Stored with every tree
  long root_addr;
  unsigned order;
  unsigned num_entries;
  unsigned num_nodes;
  int height;
};

class Btree {          // Btree file class
protected:

  FmgrPtr f;           // File the Btree is connected to
  long bh_addr;        // Address of the Btree header
  BtreeHeader bh;      // Btree header
  Cache<Mnode> cache;  // Node cache
  Coptr<Mnode> root;   // Pointer to the root node

  void ReadHdr();
  void WriteHdr();

  int Insert(Entry &e, Coptr<Mnode> t);
  int Delete(Entry &e, Coptr<Mnode> t);
  void RestoreBalance(Coptr<Mnode> p, int posn);
  void RotateRight(Coptr<Mnode> p, int posn);
  void RotateLeft(Coptr<Mnode> p, int posn);
  void Merge(Coptr<Mnode> p, int posn);

  static void PrintNode(Coptr<Mnode> &n);
  static void PrintTree(Coptr<Mnode> t, int sp);

public:

  Btree(int cs = 8);
  ~Btree();
```

```
// File-management routines

int Connect(FmgrPtr &fptr, int create,
   long bh_addr=sizeof(FmgrHeader));
void Disconnect();
int Create(char *fname, long bh_addr=sizeof(FmgrHeader));
int Open(char *fname, Fmgr::AccessMode mode,
   long bh_addr=sizeof(FmgrHeader));
void Flush(int clear=0);
void Close();

int Search(Entry &e);
int FullSearch(const Entry &e);
int Add(char *k, long d=0);
int Remove(char *k, long d = 0);

int IsEmpty() const;

int IsOpen() const;
int OK() const;
int operator!() const;
operator int() const;
void ClearErr();

void Statistics(int full);
void PrintTree();

};
```

Complete code for the *B-tree* class is given on disk in the files *btree.h* and *btree.cpp* test program is provided in the file *btreet1.cpp*.

Since the *B-tree* class is file based, it has numerous file-management functions, such as *Connect()*, *Disconnect()*, *Create()*, *Open()*, *Close()*, and *Flush()*, among others. These functions allow multiple B-trees to be stored in a single file. Each B-tree has a header, defined in *B-treeHeader*, which points to the root node of the tree, and stores some other pertinent data used mostly for testing. The headers are meant to be stored in the static data area of the file, although their exact locations are user defined. Unfortunately, we don't have sufficient space to describe the file-management functions in detail. Refer to the disk for more information.

Each B-tree has its own cache of buckets that store *Mnodes*. Also, a *Coptr* to the root of the tree is kept for easy access. The constructor is used to initialize these members, as well as to set the file manager pointer to null at the outset:

```
Btree::Btree(int cs)
// Create a Btree with a null file manager, and with a
```

```
// cache size of cs
: f(0), cache(cs), root(cache)
{
}
```

SEARCHING A B-TREE

The following *Search()* routine can be used to search a B-tree. The searching algorithm is very similar to that used for a binary tree, except now there are more keys and branches to choose from. The *Mnode Search()* function is at the heart of the search. Since the tree is file based, note how *Coptrs* are used instead of *Mnode* pointers:

```
int Btree::Search(Entry &e)
// Search the tree for the first node having a matching
// entry (i.e., keys must match). If found, the data
// field of e is filled in. Returns SUCCESS or FAIL.
{
  Coptr<Mnode> t(root);
  int rv, posn;

  while(t) {
    rv = t->Search(e, posn); // Search node t, get back posn
    if (rv == 0) {           // Found a match
      e = t->entry[posn];    // Causes the data to be filled in
      return SUCCESS;
    }
    t = t->Branch(posn);     // No match, keep walking
  }

  return FAIL;
}
```

The *Search()* function assumes you've set up an entry with the *key* field defined. When a match is found, the data field is filled in with the appropriate value. This example calls *Search()*:

```
Entry e("look for me");

if (mytree.Search(e) == SUCCESS) {
   cout << "Entry found, with data: " << e.data << '\n';
}
```

A companion function, *FullSearch()*, compares both the key and data fields of the entry. This function is similar to search, except the call to *Mnode's* *Search()* function is replaced by a call to *Mnode's* *FullSearch()* function.

INSERTION INTO A B-TREE

In Chapter 11, we described how to insert nodes into a 2-3-4 tree. The method involves inserting a new entry into a leaf and, if the appropriate leaf is full, it is split in two, with node splits propagating up the tree as necessary. Not surprisingly, a similar method is used for general B-trees. The only drawback is that it isn't possible to define an efficient, single-pass, top-down algorithm for general B-trees. (At least, nobody has come up with such a method.) Instead, we'll use a two-pass recursive algorithm.

First, we walk down the tree until we either find a matching key and data pair (which means we have a duplicate entry—not allowed) or we hit a leaf node. At this point, we attempt to insert the new entry into the leaf. If the leaf isn't already full, we can simply do the insertion. Otherwise, the node is split in half. For this technique to work, we must send one of the entries up the tree to be inserted into the parent. We always use the median entry (as defined in sorted order) for this purpose. Note that the median may actually be the entry we tried to insert in the first place.

If the parent is full and can't handle the median entry, the parent must be split as well, with the parent's median entry (which may be different from the original median entry) sent further up the tree. Eventually, the root node might have to be split in half, and a new root created to contain the median entry. Due to the bottom-up node splitting, B-trees always grow at the root. This keeps the leaves all at the same level, and results in a well-balanced tree.

Figure 14.3 shows some insertions when the corresponding leaf nodes aren't full. Figure 14.4 shows a node being split to accommodate a new key. Figure 14.5 shows an example of two splits occurring, one which involves growing a new root.

Figure 14.3 Inserting into a B-tree without splits.

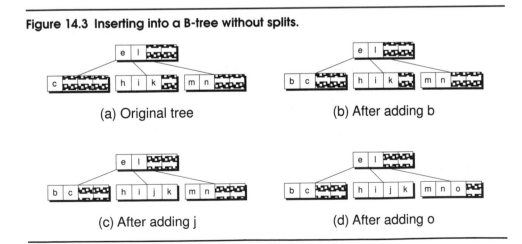

(a) Original tree

(b) After adding b

(c) After adding j

(d) After adding o

Figure 14.4 Inserting into a B-tree with a split.

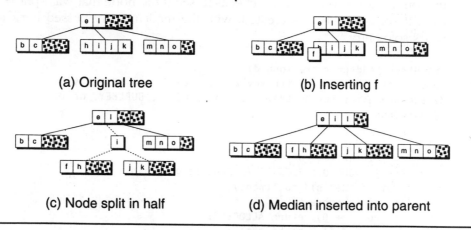

(a) Original tree   (b) Inserting f

(c) Node split in half   (d) Median inserted into parent

The insertion algorithm is partitioned into two functions. The *Add()* function is the top-level "driver" function. It constructs an entry to be searched, and then calls the recursive *Insert()* function. This latter function walks down to a leaf node, inserts the entry there, and then propagates any splits up the tree as the recursion unwinds. Function return status codes are used to control the recursion.

When *Insert()* returns a *NODE_OVERFLOW* code, this means the node below was split, and the median entry is passed back for further processing.

Figure 14.5 Propagating splits and growing a new root.

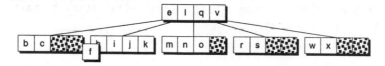

(a) Before inserting f and causing splits

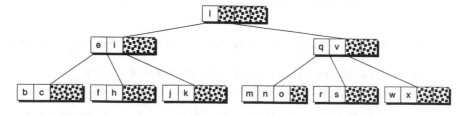

(b) After two splits, including the root

Eventually, the top of the tree is reached, and the last call to *Insert()* is unwound. At this point, *Add()* checks to see if the node that was split was the root. If so, a new root is created, with the median entry passed back as the root's sole entry.

```
int Btree::Add(char *k, long d)
// Creates a new entry with key k and data d, and attempts to
// add the entry to the tree. Returns SUCCESS, DUPLKEY, or
// ALLOCERR.
{
  Entry e(k, d);
  int rv = Insert(e, root);
  if (rv == NODE_OVERFLOW) { // Need to grow a new root
      Coptr<Mnode> old_root(root);
      new(root) Mnode;
      if (root == 0) return ALLOCERR;
      bh.num_nodes++; bh.height++;
      bh.root_addr = root;
      root->left = old_root;
      root->InsEntry(e, 0);
      rv = SUCCESS;
  }
  if (rv == SUCCESS) bh.num_entries++;
  return rv;
}

int Btree::Insert(Entry &e, Coptr<Mnode> t)
// Recursive function that tries to insert entry e into subtree t.
// Returns SUCCESS, DUPLKEY, ALLOCERR, or NODE_OVERFLOW.
// If NODE_OVERFLOW, then e becomes the median_entry to pass
// back to t's parent.
{
  int rv, posn;

  if (t == 0) {
     // We went beyond the leaves. Pretend that we've overflowed.
     e.right = 0;
     return NODE_OVERFLOW;
  }

  // Search the node t. If entry found, send back duplicate key error.

  rv = t->FullSearch(e, posn); // Use both key and data
  if (rv == 0) return DUPLKEY;

  // Entry not found; go down to the appropriate leaf to store entry

  Coptr<Mnode> child(t);
```

```
child = t->Branch(posn);
t.Release();          // Prevents cache from filling up during recursion
rv = Insert(e, child); // Recursive call

// Back from recursion; see if we have an overflow

child.Release();          // Prevents cache from filling up
if (rv != NODE_OVERFLOW) return rv;

// We have overflowed the node below us. See if we can
// insert the entry e (now the median) into node t.

posn++; // Move to the appropriate entry for insertion

if (!t->IsFull()) {      // Simply add entry to node t
   t->InsEntry(e, posn);
   t->SetDirty();
   return SUCCESS;
}
else { // Need to split node t.

   // Create new node to be the right node. t will be the left node.

   Coptr<Mnode> r(t);
   new(r) Mnode;
   if (r == 0) return ALLOCERR;
   bh.num_nodes++;

   // Move roughly half the nodes to the right node. If inserting
   // entry into left node, we need to move the split position back
   // one, so that when the median is taken, the split node will have
   // enough entries.

   int split_posn = NBR/2;
   if (posn < split_posn) split_posn-;
   t->Split(*r, split_posn);
   t->SetDirty();

   // Determine where entry e should go

   if (posn > split_posn) {  // e goes to the right node
      // First entry of right node is the median
      Entry median_entry = r->entry[0];
      r->DelEntry(0);
      // Insert e into its correct spot
      r->InsEntry(e, posn-split_posn-1);
      e = median_entry;      // For passing up the tree
   }
   else if (posn < split_posn) { // e goes to the left node
```

```
        t->InsEntry(e, posn);   t->SetDirty();
        e = r->entry[0]; // Get median from the right
        r->DelEntry(0);
    }

    // At this point, e is median entry to add to parent.
    // Record what e's right pointer is·going to be.
    r->left = e.right;
    e.right = r;

    return NODE_OVERFLOW;
    }
}
```

As you examine the *Add()* and *Insert()* routines, note how *Coptr*s allow us to write the routines almost as though we were working with trees in memory. The process isn't quite automatic, as we've explained in Chapter 13. For example, before a recursive call, we must release any *Coptr*s that might be bound—to prevent the cache from becoming full.

We must also remember to set the dirty bits for any nodes that might be modified. We've made it a convention to set dirty bits each time we modify a node, even though the dirty bits might already have been set due to prior modifications. With careful analysis, it's possible to optimize the setting of the dirty bits. But when you first write the code, the redundancy is well worth it. If you forget to set a dirty bit, the code will eventually fail, but the problem may remain undetected for a long time and may be difficult to locate.

DELETING ENTRIES FROM A B-TREE

As you might expect, deleting from a B-tree is much more involved than insertion. We use the same technique that's used for all search trees. When the entry to be deleted isn't in a leaf node, we replace the entry with its successor, and then delete the successor entry from its original home, which will always be a leaf node. Recall that, with red-black trees (and their 2-3-4 tree equivalents), even deleting from a leaf isn't always so simple. We must maintain the balance of the tree. The same applies to B-trees.

B-tree Rotations

For B-trees, maintaining balance translates into ensuring that each non-root node is at least half full. (Notice that the splitting process just described for insertions does just that.) After deleting an entry from a leaf, we check to see whether the node still has the minimum required number of entries. If not, we must borrow an entry from some other node. The appropriate nodes to borrow entries from are the left and right siblings. We can't just simply move an entry from a sibling, however. We must maintain the order of the entries so that the tree can be searched properly. We can do this by first moving the sibling entry into the parent node, then moving the original parent entry into the node needing the entry.

This borrowing process is interesting because, in effect, we end up performing tree rotations that are the generalized versions of what we used for binary trees. Figure 14.6 illustrates both left and right rotations. When doing a left rotation, we always borrow the leftmost entry of the right sibling. In a right rotation, the rightmost entry of the left sibling is used.

When both the left and right siblings have entries to spare, it's arbitrary which sibling you borrow from. In the code we'll present later, we always choose the left sibling. In some cases, neither sibling has any extra entries. When this happens, we can combine the given node with one of the siblings. (Again, the choice is arbitrary.) This merging process involves an entry from the parent node as well.

Merging Nodes

Figure 14.7 illustrates two examples that merge a node with its left and right siblings. In this figure, we've assumed the nodes shown are in the middle of a B-tree. As we did with the red-black trees defined in Chapter 11, we've represented external nodes (which are subtrees that may be null) using links that go nowhere and that are labeled with numbers. These numbers help you to easily see how the links are re-arranged. Note that, in the case of a left merge, the original parent entry has its right link set to the left link of the right node. Thus, we don't lose

Figure 14.6 B-tree rotations.

(a) Left rotation (borrowing from the right)

(b) Right rotation (borrowing from the left)

Figure 14.7 Merging B-tree nodes.

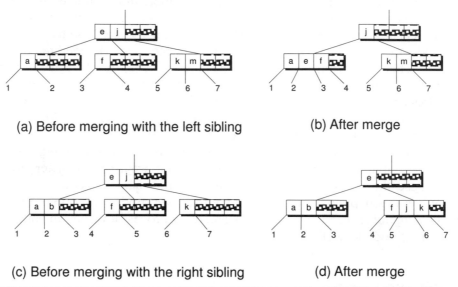

(a) Before merging with the left sibling   (b) After merge

(c) Before merging with the right sibling   (d) After merge

track of any nodes below ones involved in the merge. Right-hand merges have a similar linking process.

When nodes are merged, we end up with one less entry in the parent node. It's possible for the parent to end up with too few entries, so it must borrow entries or merge with one of its siblings. This borrowing and merging may thus propagate up the tree. Note that it's legal for the root to have fewer than the minimum number of entries. But what if the root becomes empty due to a merge? In this case, the tree shrinks one level, with the new root being the node to the left of the old empty root. Figure 14.8 illustrates this process.

The Deletion Functions

It's relatively easy to describe how deletions work in a B-tree, but it's another matter entirely to write code for deletions. We've split the task into six functions: *Remove()*, *Delete()*, *RestoreBalance()*, *RotateLeft()*, *RotateRight()*, and *Merge()*. The *Remove()* function is the "driver," which sets up the entry to delete and calls the recursive *Delete()* function. This latter function searches the tree for the entry to delete, using recursive calls to itself. When the entry is found, the tree is further traversed in search of the successor entry to use as the replacement. When the entry has been replaced, the function is recursively called again to delete the successor entry in its original leaf node.

Figure 14.8 Shrinking a B-tree.

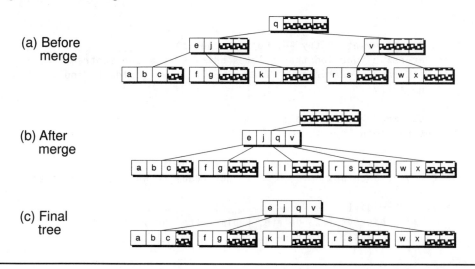

(a) Before merge

(b) After merge

(c) Final tree

The recursion bottoms out when an entry is to be deleted from a leaf node. At this point, the entry is removed from the node. Then, *RestoreBalance()* is called to do whatever rotation or merging is necessary to ensure that the node with the deleted entry has at least the minimum number of entries. As the recursion in *Delete()* unwinds, the merging is propagated up the tree as needed. Eventually, the program execution returns to the *Remove()* function. A test is made to see if the root node has become empty due to a merge that took place below it. If so, the root is removed from the tree and the node to the root's left becomes the new root. If the old empty root is the only node in the tree, it is left empty. Thus, we also have at least one node in the tree, even if it's empty.

Here are the six functions used for deletions:

```
int Btree::Remove(char *k, long d)
// Deletes entry having key k and data d from the tree.
// Returns SUCCESS, or FAIL if we couldn't find the entry.
{
  Entry e(k, d);
  int rv = Delete(e, root);
  if (rv == SUCCESS && root->IsEmpty() && bh.height > 1) {
    // We need to shrink the tree
    Coptr<Mnode> p = root;
    root = root->Branch(-1);
    bh.root_addr = root;
    bh.num_nodes-; bh.height-;
    p.Delete();
```

```
    }
    return rv;
}

int Btree::Delete(Entry &e, Coptr<Mnode> p)
// Recursive function that deletes entry e from the subtree
// with root p. Returns SUCCESS, or FAIL if we couldn't find
// the entry.
{
  Coptr<Mnode> t(p), s(p);
  int rv, posn, sr;

  sr = p->FullSearch(e, posn); // Search node p
  t = p->Branch(posn);         // Get ready to walk down the tree

  if (sr == 0) {
     // p has entry to delete. Replace the entry with its
     // successor, if there is one.
     if (t) {
        s = t;
        while(s->Branch(-1)) s = s->Branch(-1);
        p->entry[posn] = s->entry[0];
        p->Branch(posn) = t; // Remember to restore the branch
        p->SetDirty();       // Don't forget
        // Now, using recursion, delete the successor entry.
        // Release the coptrs in use, to keep cache from.
        // filling up during the recursion, and to prevent
        // dangling pointer exceptions
        p.Release();
        Entry &se = s->entry[0];
        s.Release();
        if (Delete(se, t) != SUCCESS)
           excp->THROW(ASSERTERR); // We should have found the entry
     }
     else { // At a leaf, so the deletion is easy
        p->DelEntry(posn);
        p->SetDirty(); // Don't forget
        bh.num_entries-;
     }
     rv = SUCCESS;
  }
  else {
     if (t) {
                        // Walk down the tree, looking for entry
        p.Release();    // Keep cache from filling up on recursive call
        rv = Delete(e, t);
     }
     else return FAIL; // Couldn't find said entry
  }
```

```
    if (rv == SUCCESS && t && t->IsPoor()) {
       // The node below p doesn't have enough entries. We need to
       // move some entries to it and thereby restore the balance.
       t.Release(); // To prevent dangling ptrs
       RestoreBalance(p, posn);
    }

    return rv;
}


void Btree::RestoreBalance(Coptr<Mnode> p, int posn)
// Node down branch at position posn in node p has one too
// few entries. Give it an entry from either its left or right
// sibling, or perhaps just merge the node with a sibling.
{
    Coptr<Mnode> t(p);

    if (posn == -1) {
       // We have no left sibling, so try the right sibling
       t = p->Branch(0);
       if (t->IsPlentiful()) { // Can we borrow from the right?
          RotateLeft(p, 0);    // Do so
       }
       else {            // Right sibling has no spare entries
          t.Release(); // To prevent dangling ptr errors
          Merge(p, 0); // Merge with right node and parent entry
       }
    }
    else if (posn == p->LastPosn()) {
       // We have no right sibling, so try the left sibling
       t = p->Branch(posn-1);
       if (t->IsPlentiful()) {  // Can we borrow from the left?
          RotateRight(p, posn); // Do so
       }
       else { // Left sibling has no spare entries.
          t.Release();      // To prevent dangling ptr errors
          Merge(p, posn); // Merge with left node and parent entry
       }
    }
    else {
       // We have both left and right siblings
       t = p->Branch(posn-1);
       if (t->IsPlentiful()) {  // Can we borrow from the left?
          RotateRight(p, posn); // Do so
       }
       else {
          t = p->Branch(posn+1);
          if (t->IsPlentiful()) {    // Can we borrow from the right?
```

```
            RotateLeft(p, posn+1); // Do so
      }
      else {
         // Neither the left or right sibling has spare entries.
         // Merge arbitrarily with the left node.
         t.Release();    // To prevent dangling ptr errors
         Merge(p, posn); // Merging with the left
      }
   }
  }
}


void Btree::RotateRight(Coptr<Mnode> p, int posn)
// Performs a "right rotation" using the entry at node p,
// position posn as the pivot point. Assumes p is not
// a leaf and that a left and right child exist.
// Also assumes right child isn't full, and that p and
// left child aren't empty.
{
  Coptr<Mnode> l(p), r(p);

  r = p->Branch(posn);   // Right child of p
  l = p->Branch(posn-1); // Left child of p

  // Move entry from parent p into rightmost entry of right node.
  // This entry will have the old left branch of right node. (The
  // left branch will be updated later.)

  p->Branch(posn) = r->left;        p->SetDirty();
  r->InsEntry(p->entry[posn], 0);   r->SetDirty();

  // Now, move rightmost entry of the left node into p. This
  // entry's branch becomes the right node's left pointer.
  // Be sure to point entry to right node.

  int last_posn = l->LastPosn();
  r->left = l->Branch(last_posn);        r->SetDirty();
  l->Branch(last_posn) = r;              l->SetDirty();
  p->entry[posn] = l->entry[last_posn];  p->SetDirty();
  l->DelEntry(last_posn);                l->SetDirty();

}

void Btree::RotateLeft(Coptr<Mnode> p, int posn)
// Does a "left rotation" using the entry at node p,
// position posn as the pivot point. Assumes p is not
// a leaf and that a left and right child exist.
```

```
    // Also assumes left child isn't full, and that p and
    // right child aren't empty
    {
      Coptr<Mnode> l(p), r(p);

      r = p->Branch(posn);    // Right child of p
      l = p->Branch(posn-1);  // Left child of p

      // Move entry from parent p into leftmost entry of left node.
      // This entry gets the left pointer of the right node.

      p->Branch(posn) = r->left;        p->SetDirty();
      l->Concatenate(p->entry[posn]);  l->SetDirty();

      // Now, move rightmost entry of the right node into p. Make
      // sure this entry points to the right node. Also, we have
      // a new left branch of the right node.

      r->left = r->Branch(0);
      r->Branch(0) = r;                 r->SetDirty();
      p->entry[posn] = r->entry[0];     p->SetDirty();
      r->DelEntry(0);                   r->SetDirty();

    }

    void Btree::Merge(Coptr<Mnode> p, int posn)
    // Merges the node on the branch left of the entry at position
    // posn of node p with the entry of p, and the node on the
    // branch to the right of the entry of p. Assumes posn in range.
    {
      Coptr<Mnode> l(p), r(p); // Ptrs to left and right children

      r = p->Branch(posn);     // Right child of p
      l = p->Branch(posn-1);   // Left child of p

      // (1) Fix entry of p to point to left branch of r
      // (2) Insert this into leftmost entry of l
      // (3) Add all of r's entries
      // (4) Delete entry from p, then delete r

      p->Branch(posn) = r->left;        p->SetDirty();
      l->Concatenate(p->entry[posn]);  l->SetDirty();
      l->Concatenate(*r);               l->SetDirty();
      p->DelEntry(posn);                p->SetDirty();
      r.Delete();
      bh.num_nodes--;
    }
```

BEYOND BASIC B-TREES

The design we've just presented for B-trees is simple and basic. We "hard coded" the type of keys stored in the B-tree nodes as character strings. We also used global constants such as *MAXKEYSIZE* and *NBR* to size the nodes. These could obviously be made into template parameters, and it is possible to write a generic *B-tree* class that allows you to share the code for B-trees across all types of nodes.

For instance, you could build an abstract node class that doesn't know the order of the node, or the key types stored within it. Then, more type-specific template classes could be derived. However, it gets a little tricky to use the abstract nodes, since *Coptr*s are being used. Because the node types are parameters to *Coptr*s, the fact that one node type is derived from another does not mean that the corresponding *Coptr*s have any special base-to-derived relationship. The different *Coptr* classes remain siblings of the *Coptrb* class, and are otherwise not related. Thus, where you can use implicit derived-to-base type equivalence with ordinary node pointers, with *Coptr*s, you must do explicit type casting.

One problem with the B-tree design presented here: Fixed-length keys are used, which aren't desirable when the keys are character strings. A lot of wasted space results in the nodes when the keys aren't the maximum size. It's possible to design B-tree nodes that allow for variable-length keys, where each key occupies only as much room as needed in a node. As many keys as possible can be packed into each node. This means the nodes can have a variable number of keys and branches. The result is a *variable order B-tree*. In such a tree, we use half the size of the node as the criteria for minimum node size, rather than using half the number of keys.

Searching and inserting into a variable-order B-tree is about as simple as it is for trees with fixed orders. However, deletion is more complicated (as if it weren't complicated enough). With fixed-length keys, the rotation and merge operations are fairly straightforward. We can always guarantee that one key can take the place of another, because they all have the same size. With variable-length keys, such replacements can't be guaranteed. For example, if we attempt to do a rotation when the sibling key is larger than the parent key, there's no guarantee that the sibling key will fit in the parent node.

We designed the insertion and deletion routines using recursive functions. It's possible to use an explicit stack instead, and thus convert the recursion into iteration. Each stack element must have both a node pointer and an index representing which entry in the node we are on. If you use *Coptr*s for the node pointers, they must be released before putting them on the stack. Because the bucket pointers for released *Coptr*s will still be intact, there's a good chance that when you pop the *Coptr*s off the stack, you can quickly rebind them to their respective buckets.

There's an important advantage that results from using an explicit stack. You can have a built-in iterator, which allows you to move back and forth through the entries in the tree in sorted order. This feature is particularly handy in such applications as a customer contact list. For example, you can search for a customer record using the customer name, and then quickly scan back and forth through other customer records in sorted order.

 For information about obtaining source code for a variable-order B-tree class with a built-in iterator, see the *README* file on disk.

In our B-tree design, we included "data" with each key. (Usually, this data is simply the file address of the real data record.) In some variations of B-trees, only the leaf nodes have data. The internal nodes only contain the keys to be used in the search process. These types of trees are sometimes called *B+-trees*. You can go one step further and, instead of storing the full keys in each node, you store only prefixes of each key, enough to guide the search process to the correct leaf node. Trees with these types of keys are often called prefix *B-trees*. For a discussion about some of these B-tree variants, see [Aoe 91].

SUMMARY

B-trees, or variations of them, have become the data structures of choice for database applications. B-trees allow fast database searching, due to the ability to optimally size the nodes to the paging requirements of a file system, and due to the relative flatness that results by using multi-way nodes. By using a cache in conjunction with the B-tree nodes themselves, you can speed up the searching even more.

While B-trees were designed with files in mind, it's possible to use memory-based B-trees. However, you're probably better off using red-black trees for trees that totally reside in memory. That's because the larger nodes of a B-tree don't provide an advantage for memory-based designs. You must search sequentially through the entries of a node, looking for the appropriate branch to take. For nodes with many entries, this can become time-consuming. (With file-based trees, searching within a node is often masked by the relatively slower file access needed to retrieve the node.) Of course, you could use a binary search to find the appropriate location in the array of entries. However, you're not much better off than if you had simply used a binary tree.

References

BALANCED TREES

[Aoe 91] *Computer Algorithms: Key Search Strategies*, (IEEE Computer Society Press), Edited by J. Aoe, 1991. ISBN 0-8186-2123-0.

[BayeMc 72] "Organization and maintenance of large ordered indexes," R. Bayer and C. McCreight, *Acta Informatica*, Vol. 1, No. 3, 1972, pp. 173-189.

[GuibaSedge 78] "A Dichromatic Framework for Balanced Trees," L. Guibas and R. Sedgewick, *Proceedings of the 19th Annual Symposium on Foundations of Computer Science*, IEEE, 1978.

[SleatorTar 85] Self-Adjusting Binary Search Trees, D. Sleator and R. Tarjan, *Journal of the ACM*, Vol. 32, No. 3, July, 1985, pp. 652-686.

C++ PROGRAMMING

[Coplien 92] *Advanced C++ Programming Styles and Idioms*, (Addison Wesley), J. Coplien, 1992. ISBN 0-201-54855-0.

[Stroustrup 91] *The C++ Programming Language, 2nd Edition*, (Addison Wesley), B. Stroustrup, 1991. ISBN 0-201-53992-6.

GENERAL ALGORITHMS AND DATA STRUCTURES

[Flamig 93] *Practical Algorithms in C++*, (John Wiley & Sons), B. Flamig, Fall, 1993.

[HoroSahni 90] *Fundamentals of Data Structures in Pascal, 3rd Edition*, (Computer Science Press), E. Horowitz and Sartaj Sahni, 1990. ISBN 0-7167-8217-0.

[Knuth 73] *The Art of Computer Programming: Fundamental Algorithms, Vol. 1*, (Addison Wesley), D. Knuth, 1973.

[Knuth 73b] *The Art of Computer Programming: Sorting and Searching, Vol. 3*, (Addison Wesley), D. Knuth, 1973. ISBN 0-201-03803-X.

[Lings 86] *Information Structures: A uniform approach using Pascal*, (Chapman and Hall Computing), B. Lings, 1986. ISBN 0-412-26500-1.

[Mohle 92] Private communications with M. Mohle about general design principles for data structures and algorithms, 1992.

OBJECT-ORIENTED DESIGN

[Booch 91] *Object Oriented Design with Applications*, (The Benjamin/Cummings Publishing Company), G. Booch, 1991.

[RumBla 91] *Object-Oriented Modeling and Design*, (Prentice Hall), J. Rumbaugh, M. Blaha, W. Premerlani, F. Eddy, and W. Lorenson, 1991.

PRIORITY QUEUES

[Atk 86] "Min-Max Heaps and Generalized Priority Queues," M. Atkinson, J. Sack, N. Santoro, and T. Strothotte, *Communications of the ACM*, Vol. 29, No. 10, October, 1986, pp. 996-1000.

[Jones 86] "An Empirical Comparison Of Priority-Queue and Event-Set Implementations," D. Jones, *Communications of the ACM*, Vol. 29, No. 4, April 1986, pp. 300-311.

Index

S